S ZONES
and CANADA

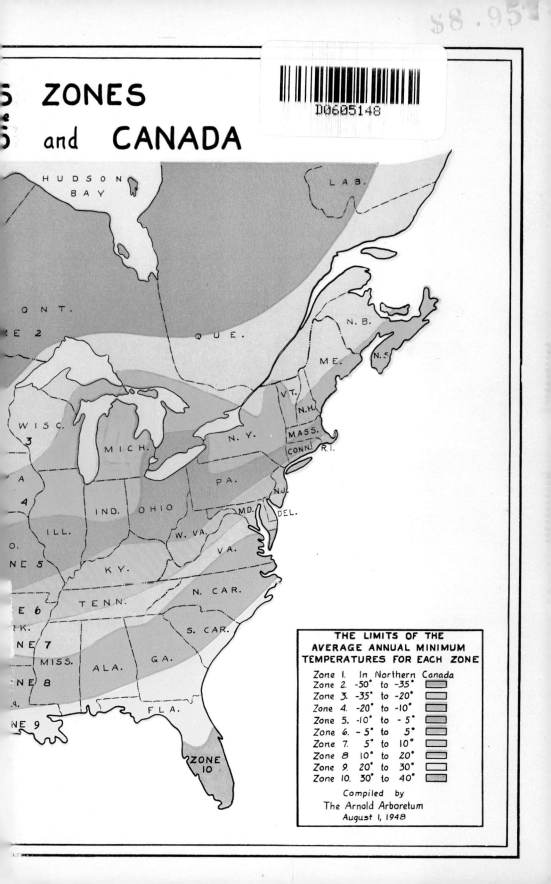

HUDSON
BAY

LAB.

ONT.

E 2

QUE.

N.B.

ME.

N.S

WISC.

3

MICH.

N.Y.

VT.

N.H.

MASS.

CONN. R.I.

A

PA.

4

IND.

OHIO

MD.

NJ.

DEL.

O.

ILL.

W. VA.

VA.

NE 5

KY.

N. CAR.

E 6

TENN.

RK.

S. CAR.

NE 7

MISS.

ALA.

GA.

NE 8

A.

FLA.

NE 9

ZONE
10

THE LIMITS OF THE AVERAGE ANNUAL MINIMUM TEMPERATURES FOR EACH ZONE	
Zone 1.	In Northern Canada
Zone 2.	-50° to -35°
Zone 3.	-35° to -20°
Zone 4.	-20° to -10°
Zone 5.	-10° to -5°
Zone 6.	-5° to 5°
Zone 7.	5° to 10°
Zone 8.	10° to 20°
Zone 9.	20° to 30°
Zone 10.	30° to 40°

Compiled by
The Arnold Arboretum
August 1, 1948

TREES FOR AMERICAN GARDENS

THE MACMILLAN COMPANY
NEW YORK · CHICAGO
DALLAS · ATLANTA · SAN FRANCISCO
LONDON · MANILA

IN CANADA
BRETT-MACMILLAN LTD.
GALT, ONTARIO

DONALD WYMAN

TREES
FOR
AMERICAN GARDENS

NEW YORK

THE MACMILLAN COMPANY

Sixth Printing 1965

PRINTED IN THE UNITED STATES OF AMERICA

FOREWORD

This is the companion volume to "Shrubs and Vines for American Gardens" published in 1949. It is written with the same objectives in mind. Some of the information in that book has necessarily been transferred to this book, especially the Hardiness Map and some of the information on Blooming, Fruiting and Foliage Colors, so that all information pertaining to the growing of ornamental trees will be included in this one volume. A very few plants appear in both volumes merely because they can be grown either as trees or as shrubs. The methods used in describing and evaluating the plants are identical in both volumes.

In the following pages, nearly 750 species and varieties of trees now being grown in America are recommended for continued landscape planting. Approximately 1600 additional species and varieties are relegated to a secondary list in which the plants are either inferior to or certainly no better than those in the recommended list. As with the book on shrubs, it is admitted that not everyone will agree with such an arbitrary division, but with the tremendous amount of plant material being grown in this country at present, it is time that some one indicated which plants were superior to others. The present work is an attempt to do just this with the trees. Although such lists may evoke criticism, the time and effort necessary for their preparation will have been well spent if it starts the plant-using public thinking in discriminating terms as far as ornamental plants are concerned.

It is of interest to note that half of the recommended trees are of Asiatic origin, less than half are native to North America, and about one-sixth of the total number are native of Europe.

Most of the pictures have been taken by the author and Mr. Heman A. Howard of the Arnold Arboretum staff or from the extensive photograph files at the Arnold Arboretum. Numerous correspondents all over the country have contributed greatly with valuable information. Special credit is due to Professor Alfred Rehder who spent a lifetime on the staff of the Arnold Arboretum, and his many publications concerning the ornamental woody plants grown in North America. His published information and criticisms of the information in this manuscript have been drawn on heavily. This present book, as well as its immediate predecessor, is the result of an attempt to bring together some of the information accumulated by the

Arnold Arboretum and place it before the gardening public in a usable form. Special credit is also given Dr. C. E. Kobuski of the Arnold Arboretum and Mrs. Florence D. Wyman for their valuable assistance in proof reading.

No acknowledgement would be complete without full credit being given the Arnold Arboretum of Harvard University and its staff. The continued support and assistance the author has received from this world-famous institution during the past fifteen years has made the present work possible.

Donald Wyman

Arnold Arboretum
Jamaica Plain, Mass.

TABLE OF CONTENTS

INTRODUCTION

THE trees of any country are the most important plants that can be grown. It is the trees that give the shade and beauty to the land, prevent the soil from washing into the sea, and give shelter to the thousands of different birds and animals. Far too few books have been written concerning the trees of value for ornamental planting in this country.

We should try to know the trees native in our own land better and learn to use them more in landscape planting. They are among the most majestically beautiful plants with which we can possibly work. However, in the following pages of this book it will be noticed that less than one half of the trees recommended for landscape use are native to North America. Just about as many are imports from China, Japan and Korea and about one sixth of the total are natives of Europe. Consequently, it becomes important that we not only know our own trees, but also those of other temperate regions of the world as well if we are to make the most of the landscape opportunities available to us now.

When the first European settlers came to these shores, they brought with them small seedlings or seeds of trees from their homes in Europe. In Williamsburg, Virginia, for instance, there are records of such trees as the English Yew being planted before 1700. Some of the economically valued trees like the Peach were brought over by the Spaniards a century earlier. It is easy to understand how the early settlers would want some of the plants from their native land in the new. Then, as time went on and they began to realize the tremendous demand in the old country for some of the plants in America, they, too, began to use native plants, especially as the frontier was gradually pushed westward and new plants were discovered.

It was not until about 1850 that the adaptability of the tremendous wealth of material in China and Japan became evident. It was only then that Occidentals had free access to Japan, although many had weathered the trials and tribulations of the rugged travel in China. The climate of Japan and certain parts of China is very similar to that of North America, and as time went on, the ability of Asiatic plants to thrive in North America became an accepted fact. The Tree of Heaven (*Ailanthus altissima*) is now a weed tree in almost every city on our eastern seaboard. The Ginkgo, many of the magnolias, oriental cherries and crab apples have now become familiar garden plants to millions of home owners in America.

Exotic trees are not necessarily "better" than our native trees. Nothing can be more beautiful, from a general landscape viewpoint, than our own Flowering Dogwood (*Cornus florida*) or the White Fir (*Abies concolor*) from the Rocky Mountains, or the graceful Douglas-fir (*Pseudotsuga taxifolia*) of the Pacific Coast.

However, it must be admitted that oriental (and European) trees have added a very great deal to the general beauty of our landscape plantings, and cannot be overlooked in any type of planting in America today. These exotic trees should be accepted on the same basis as our own natives, judged by the same standards and planted in the same gardens and along the same highways. The intelligent horticulturist will learn about these plants and use them. It is for this purpose that this book is written.

The evaluation of trees, that is, the determining of their monetary value, is a controversial subject. It becomes important after a fire, hurricane or severe storm in which the tree has been damaged or blown over and the property owner has to replace it and figure the amount of depreciation to his property for income tax purposes. Professional arborists throughout the country have at least nine methods of figuring these depreciation values.

It is evident that the real value of a tree must vary with the species— a Red Oak would be more valuable than a Silver Maple; with the location— a 25-inch White Oak shading the front part of a house would be worth more than the same White Oak hidden in the woods; with condition of the tree and with land value. A 13-inch Red Maple has been judged by each one of the nine systems used at one time or another, and the value of the tree comes out anywhere from $75.00 to $389.83—a variation which is much too great to prove any one method reliable.

It is impossible here to discuss all these methods and their merits. Suffice it to say that most trees in landscape plantings, especially the larger trees, are worth more than a simple replacement cost, merely because in many cases it is impossible to replace a tree the size and shape of the one destroyed. Estimates are made by reliable arborists after damage has been done and many of these are sufficiently accurate to be accepted by the Bureau of Internal Revenue. The knowledge, experience and fairness of the one doing the evaluating determines usually the accuracy of the resulting estimate.

With the publication of "Shrubs and Vines for American Gardens" in 1949, I started a precedent in publishing the names of a long list of shrubs and vines which might be considered to be only of secondary ornamental importance, probably no better than—and many inferior to—those plants recommended in the main part of the book. The same procedure is followed in this companion book on trees.

In order to have all the material for the study of trees between two covers, the hardiness map published in the book on shrubs, together with much of the discussion on hardiness and order of bloom is reproduced here, otherwise the material on the following pages deals only with trees.

A tree is usually considered to be a tall woody plant which normally grows with one main trunk. However, it is difficult to define precisely the difference between a tall shrub and a small tree. For the purposes of this book, and to reduce to a minimum the number of plants concerned, a tree is considered to be a plant which can be grown with a single trunk and is over twenty feet in height. There are some plants which normally are considered as shrubs, but which can be grown with a single trunk as *Viburnum prunifolium, V. sieboldi, Chionanthus virginica* and *Magnolia stellata.* Some of these plants are included in this discussion on trees.

Any list of "the best" plants is always open to criticism and will never be complete, especially when it is made by one individual. However, such a list is offered here in the hope that it will considerably aid those who use trees for landscape purposes. It should be pointed out that most of the hardy trees (although not all) have been grown side by side in the Arnold Arboretum where there has been an excellent opportunity to compare them. This does not mean that such a trial proves satisfactory for all the diversified growing conditions throughout the country. Far from it! There are other arboretums and botanical gardens situated at many other places where such trials are continually going on, and the experiences of these institutions have been drawn on heavily in order to make this list of recommended trees.

As an example, the double-flowered oriental cherries is a group with hundreds of trees, many of them highly exploited in this country. Some have flowers that are very fragrant, some do not. Other things being equal (i.e. size and color of flowers, height of tree, hardiness, etc.) why grow the trees with flowers that are not fragrant? The selection of twelve oriental cherries was chosen from over fifty that have been grown at one time or another in this country as representing the best available.

The same is true of the ornamental crab apples. Over 250 are available from commercial sources in America, yet there is a great similarity among them. Even now there are some forty-four recommended flowering crab apples in the lists following, representing plants of all heights, varying degrees of double flowers, sizes and colors of flowers and fruits, habits and leaf color. New crab apples are appearing almost every year, but it is highly important that they have some quality superior to those of varieties already available (or discarded) in order to be kept as worth-while additions to the group.

So often when discussing a plant, it is difficult to know whether it actually exists. Taxonomic botanists have a disconcerting habit of describing something that is long-since dead and represented only by a dried specimen in an herbarium. All plants mentioned in the following recommended list are actually growing in the United States, and locations for them are known.

Scientific names have been simplified in agreement with an increasing demand by the non-Latin student to have simplified names. All specific names are written without capital letters, and no "ii" endings have been used. A slight degree of accuracy has been sacrificed in order to simplify the scientific or true names of plants as much as possible. Clonal or English varietal names are given in quotation marks. Thus *Malus* "Dorothea" is very definitely a clon, and must be propagated asexually. Botanical varietal names (*Malus baccata mandshurica*) indicates a group of plants which, if they have the same characteristics, all are given the same name, regardless of whether they are propagated sexually by seed, or asexually by cuttings or grafts.

Pruning, spraying and general maintenance of trees is not dealt with in this book, since there are several available which cover the subject thoroughly.

The plants discussed are for all parts of Canada and the United States except the subtropical areas. There are parts of southern California, the Gulf States and Florida, where the climate is such that hundreds of subtropical and even tropical trees can be grown. This very definitely is a special subject in itself, of interest to people living in a very small portion of this great country. Only a very few subtropical trees are considered here, but many of the plants that are listed can be grown very well in these areas. Consequently, although not covered thoroughly, some planting information can be gleaned from the following lists for these areas.

Something should be said here about plant patents. At the present time there is no minute check on the plants coming up for patenting to insure that they are "different" from something that has gone before. Many specific instances should be cited of patented plants which are almost identical with older established varieties. The patent does protect the commercial grower who has something different, and for that reason has merit. The point in mentioning this here is to caution the plant-buying public that merely because a plant is patented does not mean that it is "superior," "different" or even "better" ornamentally than something that has been previously grown. Since there is no authoritative check on this, patented plants should merely be considered at their face value until thoroughly tried out. Some day it is hoped that sufficient checks will be adopted so that when a patented plant bears that label it will be decidedly different from everything else. Until that time comes, the general public should not give more attention to a patented plant than any other; it may well be no better than an old established variety whose qualities are well known.

Extensive plant disease and insect scourges have swept this country in the past half century. The chestnut blight, the Gypsy Moth and Japanese beetle, the Dutch elm disease and Phloem necrosis of elms have done serious damage, and as this is being written, the Oak wilt is beginning to threaten certain areas. There are many ornamental trees available for all kinds of purposes, and merely because one tree is seriously infested (the American Elm as one example) is no reason why we should throw up our hands in despair. Other trees, although they may not have the majestic habit of growth of the American Elm, may have ornamental qualities that are superior—interesting flowers and fruit—and be less susceptible to insect troubles at the same time!

The planting of street trees is becoming increasingly important in light of the elm troubles. It used to be that the American Elm was the only street tree. After a century of growth, it is true that it reaches majestic heights, but at the same time the removal of a large number of diseased trees can quickly drain the budget of any city forestry department. Might there not be food for thought in the idea of using smaller trees for planting city streets, which admittedly would not live to the great age of the elm or reach its great height, but which would not cost a fortune to remove?

Park executives, town foresters, landscape architects, nurserymen and just plain gardeners can do well to learn more about the 745 native and exotic trees in the following recommended lists. It is these which should be first considered in making landscape plantings, for they include the best trees growing in North America today.

HARDINESS

THE ability of a plant or tree to grow in a certain area is usually closely associated with its hardiness. Palm trees do not live outdoors in New England, although the native flowering dogwood (*Cornus florida*) will thrive in the southeastern United States where palms grow. The park superintendent or town forester is familiar with trees that are suitable for highway planting in his area, but the proverbial question about a new plant is always "Is it hardy in our area?" It would be convenient for everyone if a complete list of plants could be given with minute hardiness data, so that one would merely have to glance at the list to know whether or not any one plant would be hardy in any particular location. Such a list is not available, for hardiness is a highly complex matter. It is essential to understand a few things about it in order to be able to make the decision as to whether or not a new plant might grow in a given location.

Hardiness is closely associated with three things—temperature, rainfall and soil—probably of importance in that order. When three variable factors such as these are combined to give one result, it can become most confusing to keep track of simple fundamentals. The United States Department of Agriculture has studied this problem for some time and has issued maps of the United States on which are superimposed twenty-three "climatic provinces," thirty-two "plant growth regions" and fifty "important soil regions." Such information is most valuable for those who can assimilate it, but it can be most confusing to the layman. It would seem, after years of thorough study of this topic, that a hardiness map based entirely on simple temperature fluctuations would be sufficiently indicative for most horticulturists, provided, of course, that its limitations were thoroughly understood. Alfred Rehder adopted this principle in his first volume "Manual of Cultivated Trees and Shrubs," Macmillan, 1927. For further details see page 9. Consequently, the hardiness map in this book is based on this principle and is identical with the one used in "Shrubs and Vines for American Gardens," Macmillan, 1949.

A tree can grow in one situation for centuries, hence the type of soil in which it does best is an important point in planting. In small areas or on highly priced land, the soil can be modified by excavation and the introduction of completely new soil. Continual modification is sometimes possible with the use of mulches and fertilizers. However, the modification of soil in this way can become very expensive, especially in the growing of trees. It is far better to select at the start the kind of tree which will do well in the soil already on the site, rather than to plant a tree of known soil preferences other than those available, and then plan to modify the soil throughout the life of the tree.

The same thing can be said about rainfall. If the rainfall is low in a certain area, and moisture loving plants are used, they can be watered as long as there is water and the willingness to do the extra work. Usually, in dry areas, the plants that must be continually watered are so burdensome that they are eventually discarded. There is little that can be done about an overabundance of moisture or rain. Consequently, as far as this phase of hardiness is concerned, it is best to select trees at the start which are known to survive in the area concerned, especially in areas with long summer (or winter) droughts. Recently I saw a chart of the average rainfall worked out on a state-wide basis. It meant little, for in each state the rainfall can vary widely—sufficiently to make such a chart of little help in planting. However, it was of interest to know that the rainfall in the United States varies from an annual average of under 10 inches in most of Nevada to 60 inches on the Pacific coast of Oregon and Washington, three hundred miles away. It goes without saying that many of the trees perfectly "hardy" on the Pacific coast would have a very difficult time in most parts of Nevada, due to lack of sufficient moisture alone.

A study of the rainfall over North America will show that, by and large, the greatest centers of population (i.e., where gardening and tree planting are greatest) are in areas considered to have "normal" amounts of rainfall, where most plants will live and thrive without too much additional watering. There are always populated centers in the midst of areas suspectible to prolonged droughts, such as the Great Plains, but when the extent of the horticultural activity in areas like northern Illinois or Ohio or the eastern seaboard is compared with the little-populated, drought areas of the Southwest, it will be admitted that the greatest horticultural areas have sufficient rainfall. Hence, a simplified hardiness map, of use to the greatest number of plantsmen, need not include data on rainfall.

Temperature, usually minimum temperature, is the most important single factor governing hardiness in the heavily populated areas of North America. These are the records which anyone can obtain merely by noting the daily minimum temperature on a thermometer placed out of doors.

Injury may occur in several ways when caused by fluctuations in temperature. It may occur with a sudden, out-of-season "freeze," a sudden drop in temperature or a long period of very low temperatures. Considerable investigation has shown that very low temperature is the chief factor in killing plant tissue. Pomologists have been very much interested in the "sun scald" of fruit tree trunks, a killing of the living tissue usually on the southwest side (in northern orchards). A sudden drop in temperature may do this killing in one night. If a sunny, slightly warm afternoon is immediately followed by a sudden drop in temperature after sunset—possibly to 10° Farenheit—this may kill the living tissues of some fruit tree varieties. The temperature gradient will be steepest on the side exposed to the warm afternoon sun, hence the "sun scald" of trunks on the southwest side. On the other hand, a gradual drop in temperature to this same point over a period of several hours might have no harmful effects whatsoever.

Temperature records in the Arnold Arboretum at Boston have yielded valuable data. There was severe winter injury during the winters of 1933–34, 1935, 1942–43, during which periods there were no more than eight days when the minimum temperature went to zero or below. It is of interest to note that it was only in these three winters that plants suffered severe winter injury and in no winters from 1943 to the time of this writing have minimum temperatures reached zero. This does not mean that all plants suffer with a minimum temperature of zero. Far from it! There are, however, so many tender varieties of plants growing in the Arnold Arboretum that, from the evidence, when zero temperatures are reached rather widespread damage on some of them can be expected. This, then, is a killing of tissue done mostly at low temperature.

There is evidence to prove that the tissues of some plants may not be injured by low temperatures, if the drop to those temperatures is gradual and not sudden. Just what these temperatures are and how long they can be withstood by certain plants can only be ascertained by careful experimentation.

Soil moisture enters the hardiness picture to this extent—evergreens, particularly, are giving off a certain amount of water from their leaves throughout the entire winter. Deciduous plants give off some from their twigs but not nearly as much as the evergreens. When winter winds are high, this causes the plants to give off a larger amount of water than they normally would. If the ground is frozen, as it usually is in the winter, the plant roots are unable to absorb additional soil moisture, so there comes a time, if high winds continue, when the evergreen needles or leaves give off too much water and the living tissue is injured, resulting in the characteristic browning or "burning" of the evergreens so common in late February and March.

This same injury can be caused when unseasonably warm days in late winter occur with high air temperatures but do not last sufficiently long to thaw out the ground and allow the roots to take up additional moisture. Because of this, it is important that the soil about all evergreens have plenty of water prior to the time the ground freezes in the fall. Mulching with all kinds of materials—snow included—proves helpful in keeping the ground unfrozen for the longest possible time. Burlap screens and protection with evergreen boughs also prove helpful in reducing water loss due to high winds or unseasonable, warm sunshine while the ground is still frozen. The same principles hold for all areas of the country where the ground freezes in the winter or where winter droughts are pronounced.

Lack of winter hardiness is, of course, evident only after the damage has been done. The plant may die completely. A few of the more vigorous branches may be killed, indicating that those branches may have made a late active growth and not had sufficient time in the fall to harden or mature properly. Then there are the many cases of flower buds being killed. Flowering dogwood, magnolias and many of the fruit trees all suffer in this respect. Flower buds are more susceptible to cold than leaf buds and frequently there is a varietal difference of considerable economic importance. Some peach tree varieties ("Veteran" and "Marigold" are two examples) are notably more flower-bud resistant to cold than others, hence are better adapted for planting in the colder parts of the country.

In recent years, the Flowering Dogwood has suffered injury frequently in the North. Sometimes the cold is of sufficient intensity to kill the flower buds completely, at other times only the two outside flower bracts are injured and the so-called "flower" appears as a peculiar freak with only two white bracts developed and sometimes even these are deformed.

The hardiness map on the inside covers of this book is based solely on average annual minimum temperatures. Most of the data was taken and summarized by the United States Weather Bureau over a forty-year period, hence the map is based on sound fact. Data for Canada was supplied by the Meteorological Division, Department of Transport of the Canadian Government. The United States and Canada are arbitrarily divided into ten zones, nine of which are in the United States. (Alfred Rehder adopted this principle in his first volume "Manual of Cultivated Trees and Shrubs," Macmillan, 1927, but at that time the United States Department of Agriculture Weather Bureau data were not available.) These zones are based on five-, ten- or fifteen-degree differences in the average annual minimum temperatures. Slight variations were made in the map as taken from the Weather Bureau records, in accord with known variations in plant performance on the Eastern Seaboard. Incidentally, part of this map was first published in my book "Hedges Screens and Windbreaks," McGraw Hill, 1938, and later used and augmented by Alfred Rehder in the second edition of his "Manual" (1940).

On a small scale map such as this, it is impossible to show all the minute climatic variations within the limits of each zone. Taking the Grand Canyon as one example, it appears in the Hardiness Map in one zone; yet, due to variations in altitude alone, there are at least four climatic zones, each with a different flora, in this one canyon. Plants grow in the bottom of the Canyon that also thrive on the Mexican deserts, yet on the North Rim (5700 feet above the Canyon floor) plants are found which are native in southern Canada.

Local hardiness studies are being undertaken by certain of the state agricultural experiment stations—New York, for example. Information has been collected and assessed over a period of many years, and a hardiness map has been issued showing considerably more detail than is possible

The tall Pacific Dogwood (Cornus nuttalli) is just as valued on the Pacific
Coast as is Cornus florida in the East.

on the small-scale map in this book. Such studies are decidedly worth while,
for altitude and nearness to large bodies of water do make marked changes
in hardiness for certain plants, and it is valued information for the planting
public to have available.

Consequently, many local variations in the small map submitted are
to be expected. In the list following (pages 103–355) a plant is usually
listed in the coldest zone where it will grow normally, while at the same
time it can be expected to grow in many of the warmer zones. Maximum

temperatures and drought conditions would prove to be the major limiting factors. The following trees, common in many gardens, are listed in the coldest zones where they will normally grow. These should prove reliable indicators for the type of plant material which it is possible to grow in each zone.

ZONE 2
Acer ginnala negundo
Alnus incana
Betula papyrifera
Elaeagnus angustifolia
Juniperus virginiana

ZONE 3
Acer pensylvanicum
Aesculus hippocastanum
Chamaecyparis obtusa
Fagus grandifolia
Pinus strobus

ZONE 4
Abies concolor
Amelanchier laevis
Cornus florida
Liriodendron tulipifera
Tsuga canadensis

ZONE 5
Betula alba
Chamaecyparis lawsoniana
Ilex opaca
Magnolia soulangeana
Picea asperata

ZONE 6
Acer macrophyllum
Broussonetia papyrifera

Davidia involucrata
Salix babylonica
Sequoiadendron giganteum

ZONE 7
Cedrus deodara
Cornus nuttalli
Ilex cassine
Magnolia grandiflora
Magnolia veitchi

ZONE 8
Arbutus unedo
Cornus capitata
Euonymus japonica
Pinus canariensis
Prosopis glandulosa

ZONE 9
Acer floridanum
Callistemon lanceolatus
Cinnamomum camphora
Eucalyptus species
Quercus agrifolia

ZONE 10
Acacia longifolia floribunda
Araucaria excelsa
Ceiba pentandra
Delonix regia
Jacaranda acutifolia

ORDER OF BLOOM

INDISCRIMINATE planting of trees and shrubs without a knowledge of when they flower is certainly not the best way to create a beautiful landscape picture. Best results are naturally obtained when one has a knowledge of the time trees bloom, which ones bloom together, and which ones can be depended upon to bloom in sequence. The actual day on which a certain plant first opens its flowers may vary from year to year according to the vagaries of the weather, but certain species and varieties can always be depended upon to bloom together.

After a careful study of the blooming dates of woody plants over wide areas of the United States, compared with carefully kept notes for long periods in the Arnold Arboretum at Boston, Massachusetts, where nearly six thousand different kinds of woody plants are growing together in the same soil and climate, certain facts concerning the sequence of bloom have become evident. It will be of interest to most horticulturists to note some of the following facts about this phenomenon of nature.

The sequence of bloom proves a most interesting study, for it can include the bloom of wild flowers and perennials as well as trees and shrubs. The blooming period of annuals is on a somewhat different basis, since the time they flower can be modified by the time they are "set out" or by the size to which they are grown in the greenhouse before they are planted outdoors. Trees, shrubs, vines, perennials and wild flowers, growing in one locality fairly unprotected from the weather, all work themselves into a definite sequence of bloom, which sequence does not vary to any appreciable extent from one year to the next. The sequence of bloom in Boston, Massachusetts, will be the same as the sequence in Augusta, Georgia, provided the same plants are normally grown out of doors in those localities.

The length of bloom or the amount of time the plants remain ornamentally effective while in flower does vary. It varies with the kind of plant and with the season. A double-flowering cherry like the variety "Kwanzan" may remain in flower for a full three weeks, and so it can be used effectively with other blooming trees and shrubs. It is reasonable to expect all double-flowered trees to make a longer show while in flower than will varieties with single flowers. Take as another example the Shadblow or *Amelanchier*. These have single flowers and may remain in flower a week, if the weather is cold, or may drop their flower petals only three days after they open, if the weather is unusually warm. In 1944, *Magnolia denudata* first opened its flowers in the Arnold Arboretum on May 2. Unseasonably warm weather occurred during the next few days so that most of the petals of this tree had fallen by May 5. Normally the petals would have remained on the plant at least a week. This same year *Magnolia stellata* remained colorful five days longer than *M. denudata* merely because it had many more petals.

Hence, the amount of time the flowers of trees and shrubs remain in good condition varies a great deal. Length of bloom is not considered here because it is highly unpredictable, but individual gardeners who are interested in this subject could keep notes of their own observations from year to year to show just how much these periods vary in their own localities.

The specific day of the year on which a certain plant first opens its flowers varies with two things. These are important. The first is the location in which the particular plant is growing. The second is the variation of temperature in the particular year (and often in the particular location in question.

BLOOMING DATES VARY WITH LOCATION

All plants bloom on an earlier date when grown in the South than they do when grown in the North. Magnolias, dogwoods, crab apples, and lindens all can be seen blooming in northern Florida at least eight weeks before they start to bloom in New England. Hence, there is a very marked difference in blooming dates due to differences in latitude.

There are also marked differences due to altitude. Shadblow or *Amelanchier* species, as an example, will bloom at the higher altitudes in the Great Smokies of Tennessee nearly at the same time as they will in Maine. Certainly the differences are marked in many, many places throughout the land where flowers high up on the mountains bloom considerably later than they do in the lowlands close by.

Differences in blooming dates due to latitude alone can be graphically shown on maps in a general way so that they can be easily understood. However, variations due to differences in altitude are extremely difficult to portray except on highly complicated maps. For the purposes of this discussion, suffice it to say that differences in blooming dates due to variations in altitude do exist. In many cases they are very marked and are usually of such a local nature that they can be easily worked out and depended upon from one year to the next.

It must be admitted that even in the same locality there may be differences in time of bloom not due to altitude. Forsythia grown next to the foundation of a warm building will bloom days earlier than a plant of the same variety grown a hundred feet away but in an exposed situation. In New England, for instance, a very early blooming shrub such as *Rhododendron mucronulatum*, if grown in a warm, sunny location, blooms sufficiently early so that its flower buds may be badly nipped by late frosts, whereas, if it is grown in a shaded situation with a northern exposure, the opening of the flowers is often retarded for a sufficient number of days to escape such frost injury.

Variations in blooming dates due to latitude are easily portrayed. The march of spring from South to North can be clearly depicted by a map. In adapting this map to show the advance of blooming dates and of spring in general, it is not implied that all plants are anxiously awaiting the time of the last killing frost in order to burst into bloom! However, a study of this map would show that the last killing frost in northern Florida is usually expected about the first of March, while in the vicinity of Boston, about the first of May. The difference between these two is eight weeks, the exact difference in the time of bloom of certain plants like *Cornus florida* or *Kalmia latifolia* or *Philadelphus coronarius* when grown in these two areas.

The actual blooming dates of many trees have been noted in widely separated areas in the United States. In general, the differences in actual bloom of specific plants in any area when compared with Boston is the same as the differences between the date of the last killing frost of that particular place and Boston. Once the sequence of bloom has been established (see page 17) and approximate blooming dates for a specific area listed (in this case Boston), then one can easily obtain an approximate estimate of when the same species will bloom in any other area of the country where they are located.

Like the Hardiness Map, a map depicting the "advance of spring" is fallible and should be used under the same consideration as the Hardiness Map (inside cover). It does, however, give an unmistakable picture of the gradual advance of spring from South to North—and it is sufficiently accurate to bear real study. Actual blooming dates of *Cornus florida* for different areas are given below merely to show how this collected information definitely shows an advance of blooming dates.

Glen St. Mary, Florida	Mid-February
Augusta, Georgia	Late March
St. Louis, Missouri	Early April
Ashville, North Carolina	Mid-April
Washington, D.C.	Late April
Lexington, Kentucky	Late April
Columbus, Ohio	Early May
Philadelphia, Pennsylvania	Early May
London, England	Early May
Chicago, Illinois	Mid-May
Detroit, Michigan	Mid-May
Rochester, New York	Mid-May
Boston, Massachusetts	Mid-May
Seattle, Washington	Mid-May
Portland, Maine	Late May
Southern Ontario, Canada	Late May

BLOOMING DATES VARY WITH ANNUAL WEATHER FLUCTUATIONS

The other factor causing a variance in the specific blooming dates of a particular plant is really a series of factors which might be termed "the vagaries of the weather" or the "earliness" or "lateness" of the season. We speak of spring being "early" this year, or "late," meaning the forsythias or lilacs or azaleas or violets or narcisi are not blooming at the "normal" time. They are blooming earlier if the weather has been unseasonably mild, or later if the weather has been unseasonably cold. Every locality in the country has its own peculiarities in this respect. Take as an example the blooming date of the oriental cherries planted around the Tidal Basin in Washington, D.C. Hundreds of thousands of people flock to Washington to see this beautiful sight annually. The accompanying table shows how the dates change from year to year, merely because of weather variations. (Blooming dates of the cherries at Washington, D.C.—data kept by Paul Russell of the Bureau of Plant Industry, U.S.D.A.)

	Yoshino Cherry (SINGLE)	Kwanzan Cherry (DOUBLE)
1930	April 1	April 22
1931	April 11	April 20
1932	April 15	April 29
1933	April 8	April 22
1934	April 15	April 29
1935	March 31	April 26
1936	April 3	April 17
1937	April 14	April 24
1938	March 23	April 14
1939	March 29	April 20
1940	April 13	April 30
1941	April 12	April 19
1942	April 6	April 19
1943	April 2	April 24
1944	April 9	April 24
1945	March 20	April 1
1946	March 22	April 7
1947	April 13	April 27
1948	March 27	April 12
1949	March 29	April 16
1950	April 9	April 29
1951	April 6	April 22

A very interesting series of figures has been kept by the Arnold Arboretum over a period of years, showing how these annual weather variations affect widely different species of plants. One year may be "early" from start to finish, another (1945) may be unusually "early" at the beginning only to be brought back to "normal" by a prolonged cold spell. It should be emphasized in this respect that in some localities in the United

States, especially in Montana and parts of the South, this "catching up" process can even be depended upon annually.

Such figures merely prove what everyone knows—that actual blooming dates in one locality do vary from year to year. An unusual cold spell in the early spring followed by a warm spell may bring forsythias and lilacs into bloom at the same time. This happened in many places in 1945. Normally, forsythias have finished blooming when lilacs begin. Other variations may hold other groups in flower longer causing a telescoping of an otherwise protracted bloom-period.

Sometimes a very cold spell in the spring will greatly retard all the earlier blooming shrubs. Such was the case during the spring of 1944. Until April 28 there were no plants showing any green leaves at all, and very few plants in bloom. Then April 29, 30 and May 1 were unseasonably warm in New England with temperatures in the upper sixties and seventies. This seemed to be the spark needed for all the retarded flowers and the following ten plants are examples of many which came into full bloom suddenly for the first time that year on May 2.

	NORMAL BLOOMING PERIOD
Acer saccharum	early May
Prunus sargenti	late April
Prunus subhirtella autumnalis	late April
Forsythia species	mid-April
Prunus tomentosa	late April
Prunus armeniaca	late April
Lindera benzoin	mid-April
Magnolia denudata	late April
Magnolia stellata	late April
Rhododendron mucronulatum	mid-April

It is interesting to keep a few notes on the advent of spring each year. I have noticed a particular weeping willow tree from my office window for a number of years. It has the unique habit of turning green overnight when weather conditions are just right. A few days prior to this time the buds are undoubtedly swelling, but as soon as they burst and the tiny leaf blades first appear—then the tree seems suddenly to turn green when viewed from a distance. The dates for this during the last few years are:

1940	May 1st
1941	April 15
1942	April 6
1943	April 28
1944	May 1
1945	March 27
1946	March 27
1947	April 14
1948	April 5
1949	April 4
1950	April 28
1951	April 8

The beautiful Yoshino Cherry is the tree that is planted in large numbers around the Tidal Basin in Washington, D. C.

SOME TREES LISTED IN THEIR ORDER OF BLOOM
IN THE ARNOLD ARBORETUM, BOSTON, MASSACHUSETTS

In this listing, some common perennials are included as well, since they are useful in orienting the time other plants bloom. The list is made up from a long series of notes kept by the author during the past fifteen years as well as notes kept by Professor J. G. Jack of the Arboretum staff between the years 1887 and 1893. Since 1936, additional records have been kept annually in the Arboretum so that the sequence has been checked and rechecked many times. A tree is listed only for the particular date when its bloom is first of value from a landscape point of view, although its flower buds may be conspicuous for several days prior to full bloom. Some trees are included, merely for the record, with flowers which are of little ornamental significance.

It should be stressed that some of the trees will remain in bloom longer than others and hence can be used effectively in gardens with plants that bloom later. Still others are effective in flower bud and might be planted with varieties blooming earlier. Local studies along this line should prove of great interest to individual gardeners.

The following order of bloom is applicable in localities other than New England. If local blooming dates of a few key plants are noted and the differences checked with those given in the following sequence then all the dates can be correspondingly shifted and the sequence can be thus adapted to local climatic conditions.

Order of Bloom

(All trees in the following lists are growing in the Arnold Arboretum under practically the same soil and climatic conditions and have bloomed together in the following sequence.)

MARCH

Acer saccharinum
Corylus species
Salix species

EARLY APRIL

Acer rubrum
Alnus incana
A. rugosa
Cornus mas
C. officinalis
Populus species
Prunus davidiana
Ulmus americana

MID-APRIL

Acer negundo
Betula species
Cercidiphyllum japonicum

LATE APRIL

Acer circinatum
A. diabolicum purpurascens
A. diecki
A. leucoderme
A. platanoides
Amelanchier canadensis
A. laevis
A. spicata
Buxus microphylla
B. sempervirens
Carpinus species
Magnolia denudata
M. kobus
M. kobus borealis
M. loebneri
M. proctoriana
M. salicifolia
M. stellata
Malus baccata mandshurica
Ostrya species
Poncirus trifoliata

Prunus armeniaca
P. apetala
P. canescens
P. cerasifera
P. concinna
P. cyclamina
P. dasycarpa
P. domestica
P. fenzliana
P. incisa and varieties
P. juddi
P. mandshurica
P. nipponica
P. persica and varieties
P. sargenti
P. simoni
P. subhirtella and varieties
P. yedoensis

EARLY MAY

Acer campestre
A. circinatum
A. japonicum
A. mandshuricum
A. mono
A. nigrum
A. pseudo-sieboldianum
A. pseudoplatanus
A. saccharum
A. shirasawanum
A. triflorum
Amelanchier grandiflora
A. florida
A. intermedia
A. oblongifolia
A. sanguinea
A. sera
Carpinus species
Crataegus arnoldiana
Exochorda giraldi
Magnolia soulangeana and varieties
Malus adstringens and varieties
M. arnoldiana

M. *astracanica*
M. *baccata*
M. *berlini*
M. *brevipes*
M. *floribunda*
M. *halliana* and varieties
M. *hartwigi*
M. *hupehensis*
M. *kansuensis*
M. *magdeburgensis*
M. *micromalus*
M. *prunifolia* and varieties
M. *pumila*
M. *pumila niedzwetzkyana*
M. *purpurea* and varieties
M. *robusta* and varieties
M. *scheideckeri*
M. *soulardi*
M. *spectabilis* and varieties
M. *sublobata*
M. *sylvestris*
M. *zumi* and varieties
M. horticultural varieties

    "Arrow"
    "Des Moines"
    "Dolgo"
    "Exzellenz Thiel"
    "Flame"
    "Hopa"
    "Makamik"
    "Morden Rosybloom"
    "Okanagan"
    "Simcoe"
    "Snowflake"
    "Timiskaming"
    "Wabiskaw"
    "Young America"

Nemopanthus mucronatus
Ostrya species
Prunus allegheniensis
P. *americana*
P. *avium*
P. *avium plena*
P. *blireiana* and varieties
P. *domestica*
P. *dunbari*
P. *gigantea*
P. *glandulosa* and varieties

P. "Hally Jolivette"
P. *hortulana*
P. *incana*
P. *instititia*
P. *japonica nakai*
P. *kansuensis*
P. *munsoniana*
P. *padus* and varieties
P. *pensylvanica*
P. *pumila susquehanae*
P. *salicina*
P. *schmitti*
P. *serrulata* varieties

    (Many double-flowered forms starting to bloom and continuing for two weeks at least, depending on the variety, some being slightly earlier than others)

P. *sieboldi*
P. *spinosa*
Pyrus betulaefolia
P. *calleryana*
P. *communis* and varieties
P. *pyrifolia*
P. *serrulata*
P. *ussuriensis*
Sorbopyrus auriculiformis
Syringa oblata dilatata
Zanthoxylum americanum

MID-MAY

Abies species
Acer palmatum
A. *pensylvanicum*
A. *rufinerve*
Aesculus carnea
A. *glabra*
A. *hippocastanum*
Amelanchier amabilis
Amelasorbus jacki
Caragana arborescens
Cercis canadensis
Cornus florida
Cydonia oblonga
Davidia involucrata
Enkianthus campanulatus
Euonymus latifolia
Exochorda korolkowi

E. macrantha
E. racemosa
Fagus species
Halesia carolina
H. monticola
Magnolia fraseri
Malus atrosanguinea
M. bracteata
M. dawsoniana
M. glaucescens
M. ioensis
M. sargenti
M. sieboldi and varieties
Malus horticultural varieties

  "Dorothea"
  "Katherine"
  "Peachblow"

Paulownia tomentosa
Prunus cerasus
P. maacki
P. maritima
P. virginiana
Quercus species

LATE MAY

Acer ginnala
A. heldreichi
A. miyabei
A. trautvetteri
A. zoeschense
Asimina triloba
Cornus alternifolia
C. controversa
Crataegus crus-galli
C. monogyna and varieties
C. nitida
C. oxyacantha
C. oxyacantha pauli
C. pinnatifida
C. pruinosa
C. punctata
C. sorbifolia
C. succulenta
Juglans sieboldiana
Laburnum species
Magnolia acuminata
M. cordata
M. soulangeana lennei

M. tripetala
M. virginiana
M. watsoni
Malus angustifolia
M. coronaria
M. coronaria charlottae
M. honanensis
M. ioensis plena
M. "Prince Georges"
M. toringoides
Photinia villosa
Prunus laucheana
P. maximowicziana
Rhamnus cathartica
Robinia slavini
Sorbaronia jacki
Sorbus species
Symplocos paniculata
Viburnum lentago
V. prunifolium
V. rufidulum
V. sieboldi
Xanthoceras sorbifolium

EARLY JUNE

Chionanthus retusus
C. virginicus
Cladrastis lutea
Cornus kousa
Cotinus coggygria
Decaisnea fargesi
Elaeagnus angustifolia
Euonymus bungeana
Idesia polycarpa
Ilex opaca
Magnolia sieboldi
M. obovata
Malus lancifolia
M. transitoria
Phellodendron species
Rhamnus davurica
R. frangula
Robinia hartwigi
R. kelseyi
R. pseudoacacia
Sassafras albidum
Sophora viciifolia
Styrax japonica
S. obassia

MID-JUNE

Cornus coreana
C. macrophylla
Cotinus americanus
Crataegus calpodendron
C. phaenopyrum
Diospyros virginiana
Euonymus bungeana
E. europaea
Gymnocladus dioicus
Ilex laevigata
I. montana
Ligustrum ibolium
L. ovalifolium
L. vulgare
Liriodendron tulipifera
Syringa amurensis
S. amurensis japonica
S. pekinensis

LATE JUNE

Ailanthus altissima
Catalpa speciosa
Ehretia thyrsiflora
Ilex crenata
Rhododendron maximum
Rhus glabra
R. typhina
Tilia americana
T. amurensis
T. platyphyllos

EARLY JULY

Castanea species
Catalpa bignonioides
C. hybrida
Cornus dunbari
Ilex pedunculosa
Maackia amurensis
Stewartia koreana
S. monadelpha
S. pseudo-camellia
Tilia cordata
T. dasystyla
T. euchlora

T. flavescens
T. mandshurica
T. maximowicziana
T. moltkei
T. monticola
T. neglecta

MID-JULY

Albizzia julibrissin rosea
Hydrangea paniculata praecox
Koelreuteria paniculata
Oxydendrum arboreum
Stewartia ovata
Tilia floridana
T. heterophylla
T. insularis
T. japonica
T. nuda
T. oliveri
T. petiolaris
T. tomentosa
T. venulosa

LATE JULY

Aralia spinosa
Clethra acuminata
C. barbinervis
Kalopanax pictus
Sorbaria arborea

AUGUST

Aralia chinensis
A. elata
Bumelia lanuginosa
Clerodendron trichotomum
Evodia danielli
Hydrangea paniculata grandiflora
Lagerstroemia indica
Sophora japonica

SEPTEMBER

Franklinia alatamaha

OCTOBER

Hamamelis virginiana

ORNAMENTAL FRUITS

THE fruits of trees are not nearly as important ornamentally as are the fruits of shrubs. In the first place, trees are taller, hence their fruits are usually borne above the level of the eye; often so high up in the tree that sometimes one hardly knows they are present. Because of this, they must be borne in great profusion to be effective. There are perhaps less than a dozen genera with large numbers of species bearing bright colored fruits, including such effective landscape plants as the hollies, crab apples, dogwoods, junipers and hawthorns.

Then there is a large group of plants bearing cone fruits that are interesting, when they are borne, but this unfortunately occurs only at irregular intervals. Some years are "poor" cone years, when evergreens over wide areas bear few, if any, fruits. Other years they are borne in great profusion and are of considerable interest on the trees for months at a time. The important point to remember is that profuse cone production is not an annual occurrence, hence such trees should not be planted for their fruits alone.

A third, and very large group of trees bears uninteresting fruits. The elms, oaks and lindens are examples. Even though these fruits may appear in large numbers every year, they are not particularly colorful or of much ornamental value on the trees. These trees we do not consider of value for ornamental fruits. Certainly they have many other meritorious attributes, but if color or effectiveness of fruit is desired, such trees can be overlooked.

There is a sequence in fruiting, just as there is a sequence in blooming. This is of interest and some of it is recorded in the following pages. It is of value to know for instance, that the fruits of some of the crab apples color in late August and then quickly drop, while the fruits of others may not color until late September, but will remain on the tree for weeks and even months. The length of time that the fruit remains colorful is important, for in most cases it is considerably longer than the period of time that the flowers are conspicuous. It varies, of course, with the season, the amount of rainfall, and the type of soil. In the lists given on pages 27–30 the sequence has been plotted for the fruiting of many trees as it has been observed in the Arnold Arboretum.

It is important, however, to understand some of the factors affecting the amount of fruit produced on a certain tree. Good rainfall at the proper time, and good soil, may result in excellent fruits, while on the other hand, little rainfall and poor soil, may result in poorly colored, dried-up fruits.

✳ "Alternate bearing" is a physiological phenomenon resulting in excellent fruit production one year and little the next. Some trees are notoriously "alternate bearing." The crab apple "Katherine" is one example, for it is

The Sargent Crab Apple has excellent small red fruits.

literally covered with fruits one year and has practically none the next. On the other hand, the crab apple "Dorothea" is apparently annual bearing. having splendid crops of fruits annually, provided the weather conditions are just right. Commercial orchardists the country over have to put up with this natural phenomenon, more evident in some varieties of fruit trees than it is in others. There is little that can be done with ornamentals to vary this alternation if it is a hereditary trait.

INCLEMENT WEATHER

The fertilization necessary for the production of fruits is carried out in several different ways. For instance, there are the perfect flowers of the crab apples; the pollen borne on the stamens of one flower can fertilize the pistil of the same flower. Then there are plants like the apricots, the pistils of the flowers on one plant apparently needing pollen produced by the stamens of another plant of different parentage in order to "set" proper fruit. There are many plants like the hollies with sexes separate, that is, with the staminate flowers being borne on one plant and the pistillate flowers on another so that both of these plants must be present to insure fruiting.

Then the means by which the pollen is spread from one plant to the flowers of another plant varies. With some plants, such as hollies, this may be the wind, but with many plants multitudinous insects feed on the pollen and nectar of the flowers and do the greater part of the fertilization. Bees are outstanding in this respect, but there are other insects which are also important pollen carriers.

Weather plays a most important part in the pollination of most plants, and we notice the result of favorable (or unfavorable) weather conditions months after that fertilization period has come and gone. Take, as an example, the peculiar conditions necessary for holly which has its sexes separate. Both wind or air circulation and the presence of many insects are necessary. If the weather is rainy during the time the pollen is ripe, there may be little opportunity for either wind pollinization or insect flight. On the other hand, if the weather is very cold during the time the pollen of a certain plant is ripe, then insect activity is at a low ebb and a plant like the viburnum, for instance, would have to depend primarily on wind pollinization. If the weather is very cold and rainy with little wind during the time of ripe pollen formation, then all these conditions combine to make fertilization of many kinds of shrubs extremely difficult.

The commercial orchardist knows these things because he has studied them in relation to his fruit production for years. He finds it necessary to interplant certain varieties of fruits producing just the right type of pollen for his main crop. He puts hives of bees in his orchards to aid in the general pollen carrying, and he manipulates the hives so that they will be at maximum activity when the flowers are mature.

There is little we can do about modifying the weather on a large scale, but if we have a few plants in our garden on which we want good fruits each year, we could study their optimum needs during the time when pollen is ripe, and endeavor to aid pollen carriers in every way.

SEXES SEPARATE

As has been mentioned, some groups of plants are dioecious, that is, they bear staminate flowers on one plant and pistillate flowers on the other. Of course, the staminate plants will never bear fruits, but neither will the pistillate plants (there are a few exceptions to this) unless the right pollen-bearing plant is within a reasonable distance. Just what the "reasonable distance" is we do not know, for many things enter into an understanding of this problem, and few studies have been made concerning the type of pollen carriers required. Certainly, the closer the sexes are together, the more reasonable it is to expect the pistillate plant to produce a good supply of fruit.

Tree Genera with Flowers Dioecious

(with female or pistillate flowers on one plant and male or pollen bearing flowers on another plant)

Acer—many species	Araucaria	Cercidiphyllum	Cotinus
Ailanthus	Broussonetia	Cephalotaxus	Chionanthus

Diospyros	Juniperus	Phellodendron	Salix
Eucommia	Maclura	Pistacia	Taxus
Ginkgo	Morus	Podocarpus	Torreya
Gleditsia	Myrica	Populus	Zanthoxylum
Ilex			

The hollies (*Ilex*) and yews (*Taxus*) are perhaps the most important plants in this group—at least from the viewpoint of landscaping for which they are highly valued. They should be propagated commercially by cuttings, budding or grafting, so that there is no question at all about their sex. It is particularly difficult to determine one sex from the other in the hollies unless they are in flower or fruit. Nurserymen who propagate the hollies asexually and keep the sexes clearly marked are the ones to patronize for only then can plants of known sex be obtained.

In planting any of the trees in this group especially for fruit production, it is advisable to have a pollen bearing plant in close proximity to the fruiting plant. The exact distance is not known, but certainly the closer the two are together the better are the chances for profuse annual fruit production. These trees are even more dependent on the weather for good fruiting than are some of the others. Since their pollen must be either wind or insect borne, weather conditions must be at an optimum for the very short period the flowers are open. If the weather is too cold for bees and other insects to fly at that time, and is damp and rainy without wind, the chances are that very little fruit will be produced that season.

There is another large group of trees, including all the conifers, which have two kinds of flowers (male and female) but both these appear on the same tree. The birches and alders and even the walnuts and oaks are common examples, only one type of flower, the long pollen-bearing catkins, is really conspicuous in the spring of the year and these cannot be considered very ornamental. Close examination of fir trees in the spring sometimes will show the truly beautiful, reddish, young pistillate flowers that eventually mature into the cones later. The following genera are some in this class:

Male and Female Flowers Separate But on Same Tree

Abies	Cryptomeria	Libocedrus	Quercus
Alnus	Cunninghamia	Ostrya	Sciadopitys
Betula	Cupressus	Picea	Sequoia
Carpinus	Fagus	Pinus	Sequoiadendron
Castanea	Ficus	Platanus	Taxodium
Carya	Juglans	Pseudolarix	Thuja
Cedrus	Keteleeria	Pseudotsuga	Thujopsis
Chamaecyparis	Larix	Pterocarya	Tsuga
Corylus			

There are still two more reasons why trees will not fruit. One of these is age. It takes a Ginkgo tree twenty years before it will bear its first fruits, that is, if all other members of this species perform in the same way that they have in the Arnold Arboretum. Some of the magnolias, also, will not bear flowers or fruit until they are nearly the same age. It is unfortunate that we do not have the approximate ages that all trees first bear their fruits, for here is certainly an excellent field for research. We do know, for instance, that some trees bear flowers and fruits very early in life. *Malus* "Dorothea" for instance, or *Prunus* "Hally Jolivette" will bear flowers the second year and sometimes even the first after grafting. Other trees will take considerably longer, and usually the length of this period necessary for the first production of flowers and fruits is specific for the species and hereditary.

Then there are a very few plants like the plums and the chestnuts which will bear only a very few fruits if a single tree is grown alone. But if several seedlings or clons of the same species are growing adjacent to each other, fruit production will be very much better. With the great advertising that the Chinese Chestnut (*Castanea mollissima*) is receiving at the moment, it is well to keep this fact in mind if fruit production is the main objective.

These are a few of the reasons why trees will not bear fruits or will not fruit well annually. An understanding of these factors may help in solving individual problems relating to poor fruit production as they arise.

LENGTH OF TIME FRUITS REMAIN EFFECTIVE

	Jan.	Feb.	March	April	May	June	July	Aug.	Sept.	Oct.	Nov.	Dec.
Abies species	.	.	.	.	.	.	—	—	—	.	.	.
Acer ginnala	.	.	.	.	.	.	—	—	—	—		
A. griseum	.	.	.	.	.	.	—	—	—			
A. negundo	.	.	.	.	.	—	—					
A. palmatum	.	.	.	.	.	.	.	—	—			
A. pseudoplatanus	.	.	.	.	.	—	—	—				
A. rubrum	.	.	.	—	—							
A. saccharum	.	.	.	—	—	—						
A. tataricum	.	.	.	.	.	—	—	—	—	○		
Aesculus species	.	.	.	.	.	.	—	—				
Ailanthus altissima	.	.	.	.	.	.	—	—	—	—		
Amelanchier canadensis	.	.	.	.	.	—	—					
A. grandiflora	.	.	.	○	.	—	—					
A. laevis	.	.	.	.	.	—	—					
Aralia elata	.	.	.	.	.	.	—	—	.			
Asimina triloba	.	.	.	.	.	.	—	.	—			
Carpinus species	.	.	.	.	—	—	—	—				
Castanea mollissima	.	.	.	.	.	.	—	.	—	.		
Cedrus libani	—	—	—	—	—	—	—	—	—	—	—	—
Chamaecyparis species	—	—	.	.	.	.	—	—	—	—		
Cladrastis lutea	.	.	.	.	.	.	.	—	.	—		
Cornus controversa	.	.	.	.	.	.	.	—	.	—		
C. florida	.	.	.	.	.	.	.	.	—	—		
C. kousa	.	.	.	.	.	.	—	—	.	.		
C. kousa chinensis	.	.	.	.	.	.	.	—	—	.		
C. macrophylla	.	.	.	.	.	.	.	—	—	.		
C. mas	.	.	.	.	.	.	—	—	.	.		
C. mas flava	⊹	⊹	.	.	.	.	—	—	.	⊹		
Crataegus arnoldiana	.	.	.	.	.	—	—					
C. coccinioides	.	.	.	.	.	.	—	—	—	.		
C. crus-galli	—	.	.	.	.	—	—	—				
C. lavallei	.	.	.	.	'	.	.	—	—			
C. mollis	.	.	.	.	.	—	—	.	.			
C. monogyna	.	.	.	.	.	—	—	—				
C. nitida	—	.	.	.	.	—	—	—				
C. oxyacantha	.	.	.	.	.	—	—	—	.			
C. phaenopyrum	—	—	.	.	.	.	—					
C. pinnatifida	.	.	.	.	.	.	—	—	.			
C. prunifolia	.	.	.	.	.	.	—	—				
C. punctata	.	.	.	.	.	.	—	—	.			
C. succulenta	.	.	.	.	.	—	—	—				
C. viridis	—	.	.	.	.	—	—	—				
Diospyros virginiana	.	.	.	.	.	.	.	—	—	○		

27

	Jan.	Feb.	March	April	May	July	July	Aug.	Sept.	Oct.	Nov.	Dec.
Euonymus species								•	———			
Evodia danielli								•	———			
Gleditsia triacanthos									———			•
Gymnocladus dioica									———			•
Halesia monticola									———			•
Hippophae rhamnoides									———		•	
Ilex aquifolium	———											
I. montana									———			
I. opaca	———								•			
I. pedunculosa									———			
Juniperus chinensis	———							———				
J. scopulorum	———								•	———		
J. virginiana	———							———				
Kalopanax pictus									———			
Koelreuteria paniculata									———			
Larix decidua	———————————————————											
Liquidambar styraciflua								———				
Magnolia species								• ———				
Malus arnoldiana									———		•	
M. atrosanguinea									———		•	
M. baccata									———		•	
M. baccata gracilis									———		•	
M. baccata mandshurica									———	•		
M. "Bob White"	———								———			
M. brevipes									———			
M. dawsoniana									———			
M. "Dolgo"								———		•		
M. "Dorothea"									———			
M. "Exzellenz Thiel"									———			
M. "Flame"									———			•
M. floribunda									———	•		
M. halliana parkmani									———		•	
M. halliana spontanea									———		•	
M. "Hopa"									———	•		
M. hupehensis									———	•		
M. "Katherine"									———			•
M. magdeburgensis									———			•
M. "Makamik"									———			
M. micromalus								———	•			
M. "Montreal Beauty"									———			•
M. prunifolia rinki								—	•			
M. purpurea aldenhamensis									———			•
M. purpurea lemoinei									———		•	
M. "Redflesh"								———		•		
M. robusta									———		•	°

28

	Jan.	Feb.	March	April	May	June	July	Aug.	Sept.	Oct.	Nov.	Dec.
M. robusta persicifolia	.	.	.	.	.	.	.	.	—	—		
M. sargenti	.	.	.	.	.	.	.	.	—	—		
M. sieboldi arborescens	.	.	.	.	.	.	.	.	.	—	.	.
M. spectabilis riversi	.	.	.	.	.	.	.	—	—			
M. toringoides	.	.	.	.	.	.	.	—	—	-		
M. zumi calocarpa	—	.	.	.	.	.	.	—	—			
Morus species	.	.	.	.	.	.	.	.	—	—		
Ostrya virginiana	.	.	.	.	.	.	—	—	.	.	.	
Oxydendrum arboreum	.	.	.	.	.	.	.	.	—	—		
Phellodendron species	.	.	.	.	.	.	—	—	—			
Picea abies	—	.	.	.	.	.	—	—	—			
P. engelmanni	—	.	.	.	.	.	—	—	—			
P. glauca	—	.	.	.	.	.	—	—	—			
P. omorika	—	.	.	.	.	.	—	—	—	—		
P. orientalis	—	.	.	.	.	—	—	—	—			
P. polita	—	.	.	.	.	.	—	—	—			
P. pungens	—	.	.	.	.	.	—	—	—			
Pinus banksiana	—	—	—	—	—	—	—	—	—			
P. bungeana	.	.	.	.	.	.	—	—	—	—		
P. densiflora	—	—	—	—	—	—	—	—	—			
P. monticola	—	.	.	.	.	—	—	—	—			
P. nigra	.	.	.	.	.	.	—	—	—			
P. parviflora	—	—	—	—	—	—	—	—	—			
P. pungens	—	—	—	—	—	—	—	—	—			
P. resinosa	—	—	—	—	—	—	—	—	—			
P. rigida	—	—	—	—	—	—	—	—	—	-		
P. strobus	.	.	.	.	.	.	—	—	—	.	.	
P. sylvestris	—	—	—	—	—	—	—	—	—			
P. thunbergi	—	—	—	—	—	—	—	—	—			
P. virginiana	—	—	—	—	—	—	—	—	—			
Platanus species	.	.	.	.	.	.	.	—	—	.		
Prunus avium	.	.	.	.	.	—	.	.	.	.		
P. cerasus	.	.	.	.	.	—	.	.	.	.		
P. padus	.	.	.	.	—	.	.	.	.	.		
P. pensylvanica	.	.	.	.	.	—	.	.	.	.		
P. sargenti	.	.	.	.	.	—	.	.	.	.		
P. serotina	.	.	.	.	.	.	—	.	.	.		
P. subhirtella	.	.	.	.	.	—	.	.	.	.		
P. yedoensis	.	.	.	.	.	—	.	.	.	.		
Pseudolarix amabilis	.	.	.	.	.	.	.	—	—	.		
Pseudotsuga taxifolia	.	.	.	.	.	—	—	—				
Pterocarya fraxinifolia	.	.	.	.	—	.	.	.	.	.		
Rhamnus davurica	.	.	.	.	.	.	.	.	—	.	.	
Sorbus alnifolia	.	.	.	.	.	.	.	—	—	.		
S. aria	.	.	.	.	.	.	.	.	—	.	.	o

29

	Jan.	Feb.	March	April	May	June	July	Aug.	Sept.	Oct.	Nov.	Dec.
S. *aucuparia*	.	.	.	.	.	.	.	———————				.
S. *discolor*	.	.	.	.	.	.	.	———————				.
S. *decora*	.	.	.	.	.	.	.	———		.	.	.
Styrax japonica	.	.	.	.	.	.	———————		.		.	.
Symplocos paniculata	.	.	.	.	.	.	.	.	—	.	.	.
Taxus species	.	.	.	.	.	.	.	.	———————			.
Thuja occidentalis	———————		.	.	.	———————————						
T. orientalis	——	.	.	.	.	———————————						
T. plicata	——	.	.	.	.	———————————						
T. standishi	——	.	.	.	.	—·——————————						
Tsuga species	—	.	.	.	.	———————						
Viburnum lentago	.	.	.	.	.	.	.	———————————			.	.
V. prunifolium	.	.	.	.	.	.	.	———————————			.	o
V. sieboldi	o	o	)	o	o	o	•	———————	o	o	o	ɢ

FOLIAGE COLORS

ALTHOUGH the leaves of most woody plants are green, at least during the growing season, some plants have leaves which are differently colored. Such plants would be those with variegated foliage; those with permanently red or yellow foliage; or those with colored foliage for a short time in spring or fall. These groups of plants with more or less pronounced variations in foliage color are the materials from which the knowing gardener can fashion colorfully-interesting gardens to be enjoyed every season of the year.

Leaves are green because they contain a complex material called chlorophyll. This is essential to the growth of all plants, except the saprophytes and a few parasites, for it is through the action of the chlorophyll that the plant can manufacture the food it requires from crude chemicals in the presence of light and heat. Chlorophyll is a highly complex chemical material being continually manufactured in the leaf and at the same time being continually destroyed. Ordinarily the rate of its breakdown about equals the rate of its manufacture.

There are two general groups of coloring pigments in the leaf with the chlorophyll. These are the carotins (yellow-coloring pigments) and anthocyanin or the red-coloring pigment, both usually omnipresent but masked by chlorophyll. In some plants this delicate balance is upset and the yellows appear in various so-called "yellow-leaved" varieties. The red leaves of some of the Japanese maples afford an example of red-colored foliage. As the season progresses and more and more chlorophyll is manufactured, some of the plants that have colored foliage earlier in spring are capable of manufacturing sufficient chlorophyll to mask completely what was a good colored leaf. Schwedler's variety of the Norway Maple is an example of this. In the very early spring it is most conspicuous for its brilliantly red leaves, but as summer comes, the color gradually fades into a dull, reddish green which lasts until the advent of autumn coloration.

It is probable that variations in soil have some effect on leaf color. For instance, a heavy application of a nitrogenous fertilizer will make the leaves of many plants a good dark green. Plenty of moisture will also help. Soil acidity is another factor for, with a low pH, the leaves of some plants, like those of the Pin Oak, will become deficient in iron and become yellowish, a condition quickly eliminated by feeding the tree soluble ferrous sulphate salts. Consequently, there may be several reasons—physiological, physical and genetic—why the leaves of certain plants are not green at all times. Let us consider the interesting groups of plants with colored foliage and, possibly, become acquainted with some new ones among them so that we can make our gardens more attractive by using them properly.

I. Deciduous Trees Showing the First Foliage Colors in the Spring

The changing color of spring foliage can be almost as beautiful as autumn coloration, but usually it is not quite as pronounced and does not last as long. So many other things are of interest in the early spring that few people pay much attention to this interesting phenomenon, but it is there for all to see if they want to look for it. The following trees are some which are among the first to show their new foliage in the vicinity of Boston, Massachusetts, usually during April. About four weeks after these trees first show their leaves, the majority of the rest will have their foliage open also (except the Bald Cypress which is one of the last to send out its leaves). The colors of all may change from yellow-green to bronze to dark green in varying shades, until June when most will have taken on their normal green color.

Acer campestre—yellow-green
A. griseum—bronze to reddish
A. negundo—yellow-green
A. platanoides "Crimson King"—red
A. platanoides schwedleri—bronze to reddish
A. rubrum—bronze to reddish
Amelanchier canadensis—gray-green
A. laevis—bronze to reddish

Cercidiphyllum japonicum—bronze to reddish
Euonymus europaeus—green
E. sanguinea—green
Malus robusta—yellow-green
M. robusta persicifolia—green
Prunus padus—green
Pyrus ussuriensis—green
Salix alba vitellina—yellow-green
Tilia platyphyllos—yellow-green

II. Some Deciduous Trees with Leaves Colored throughout the Greater Part of the Growing Season

There are some trees with variegated foliage, but few of these are recommended here, for usually they are a sickly looking group. A few do have interest. Much better are some of the trees with gray or bronze or reddish foliage. Some trees do not have foliage of a prominently different color, but just slightly colored—enough to make them of value. A few crab apples, for instance, have foliage that is just slightly reddish, enough to make these trees of interest when planted in front of a normally green foliage background. Many trees have foliage that first appears one color in the early spring but gradually turns normal green by early summer, but the following trees can be used for their colored foliage throughout the entire spring and summer:

GRAY TO GRAY-GREEN

Elaeagnus angustifolia
Hippophae rhamnoides
Populus alba

Salix elaeagnos
Tilia petiolaris (silvery green)
Tilia tomentosa (silvery green)

The Russian Olive (Elaeagnus angustifolia) is valued above all other trees for its excellent gray foliage, which predominates in any landscape, throughout the entire growing season.

YELLOW TO YELLOW-GREEN

Acer negundo auratum
Populus alba richardi

Quercus robur concordia

RED TO REDDISH PURPLE

Acer palmatum atropurpureum
A. palmatum "Oshiu-beni"
A. palmatum sanguineum
A. platanoides "Crimson King"
A. pseudoplatanus purpureum

Prunus blireiana
P. cerasifera atropurpurea
P. cerasifera nigra
P. cerasifera woodi

REDDISH GREEN

Malus "Oekonomierat Echtermeyer"
M. purpurea
M. purpurea aldenhamensis
M. purpurea lemoinei

M. "Redflesh"
M. "Redfield"
M. "Red Silver"
Prunus persica atropurpurea

BRONZE

Acer palmatum dissectum

A. palmatum ornatum

PURPLE

Fagus sylvatica atropunicea
F. sylvatica purpureo-pendula
Quercus robur atropurpurea

Ulmus glabra atropurpurea
U. procera purpurascens

The Colorado Spruce of the Rocky Mountains makes a fine pyramidal tree. There are several forms varying in the color of their foliage.

GREEN WITH YELLOW MARGIN

Acer negundo aureo-marginatum
A. negundo aureo-variegatum

Cornus mas elegantissima (pink in yellow margin)

GREEN WITH WHITE MARGIN

Acer negundo variegatum

III. A Few Evergreen Trees with Foliage Other than Normal Green

Abies concolor—bluish green
Acacia pendula—bluish gray
Cedrus atlantica glauca—bluish
Chamaecyparis lawsoniana argentea—silvery white
C. lawsoniana glauca—steel blue
C. lawsoniana allumi—steel blue
C. nootkatensis—blue-green
C. pisifera aurea—golden yellow
C. pisifera squarrosa—gray-green to blue-green
Cupressus arizonica bonita—gray to bluish green
Ilex aquifolium argenteo-marginata—leaves with a white margin
I. aquifolium aureo-marginata—leaves with a yellow margin
Fagus sylvatica tricolor—white, green and pink

Juniperus scopulorum—green to light blue
J. scopulorum—"Chandler Blue"—blue
J. scopulorum—"Hill Silver" bluish
J. virginiana burki—steel blue
J. virginiana glauca—silvery blue
Myrica californica—bronze green
Olea europaea—gray-green
Picea engelmanni—bluish green
Picea glauca densata—bluish green
P. pungens—blue-green
P. pungens argentea—silvery green
P. pungens coerulea—bluish green
P. pungens glauca—bluish green
P. pungens kosteriana—bluish green
P. pungens moerheimi—blue
Pinus densiflora oculis-draconis—yellowish green
P. parviflora—bluish green

P. *strobus glauca*—bluish green

P. *sylvestris*—blue-green

Pittosporum eugenioides — yellowish green

Pseudotsuga taxifolia—varies from green to blue-green

Thuja orientalis "texana glauca"—blue-green

T. *plicata atrovirens*—very dark green

Tsuga canadensis atrovirens—very dark green

AUTUMN COLOR

The eastern United States is fortunately located in one of the few regions of the world where brilliant autumn coloration of foliage prevails. There is only one small region of autumn coloration in the southern hemisphere, and that is in South America. In the northern hemisphere, there is a large section of eastern Asia, including central and northern Japan and a small part of southwestern Europe where brilliant fall coloration can be observed. In North America, the region characterized by brilliant autumn foliage extends from the Gulf of St. Lawrence to Florida and westward to the Great Plains, areas which have extensive deciduous forests and considerable rainfall. Here the general climatic conditions are often just what is needed to produce that lovely phenomenon of nature—the autumn coloration of deciduous foliage.

In North America the most brilliant displays of autumn color are, of course, in southeastern Canada, the northeastern United States and in certain other areas at higher altitudes. The farther south one goes, the less brilliant is the display, particularly in low areas along the seacoast. In the higher altitudes of the South, such as the Blue Ridge Mountains, the color is usually just as brilliant as in northeastern United States. Many places in western North America are likewise fortunate, with vivid autumn color, especially in the higher altitudes. Autumn color is excellent in the vicinity of Seattle, Portland and San Francisco.

It is chiefly in areas of predominantly deciduous forests that autumn color displays are best, and these areas occur chiefly in two general regions in the world. Plants growing in deciduous forests in tropical regions usually drop their leaves towards the end of the dry season. Since these leaves usually dry up before they fall (because of lack of water), they do not develop brilliant colors but usually turn brown and then fall off. In the case of plants growing in deciduous forests in temperate regions—especially in areas with ample rainfall equally distributed throughout the year—the leaves fall at the approach of cold weather, and because the plants have been well supplied with water, leaves of many trees change color before they fall. This gorgeous phenomenon in the woods and forests is what attracts our attention at this particular time each year.

In some years, the autumn color is much more pronounced than in others. There are always plants, the foliage of which turns yellow in the fall, but it is the brilliant reds and gorgeous scarlets which, in combination with the yellows, make autumn color of outstanding beauty. It is chiefly the reds and scarlets which are intensified by the right climatic conditions.

Why Leaves Are Yellow

A certain stage is reached where there is little if any chlorophyll manufactured. Most of the chlorophyll already made eventually is destroyed. This is the reason that leaves are yellow, for the two yellow pigments usually present, carotin and xanthophyll, are continually masked by the chlorophyll. When most of the chlorophyll is destroyed, these pigments become apparent. These same coloring materials are present in large quantities in egg yolk, carrots, and in some yellow flowers.

When green plants are taken into dark places, such as a cellar, the leaves often turn yellow. Also, young shoots grown in the cellar are usually yellow. This is because chlorophyll is manufactured only in the presence of light. When light is absent, plants are unable to manufacture new chlorophyll and the yellow pigments become predominent as soon as the previously manufactured chlorophyll has been utilized.

The gradual cessation of chlorophyll manufacture and the final breakdown of that previously made completes the first stage in autumn coloration, and so certain plants become yellow. There are other plants, some magnolias for instance, the leaves of which do not turn yellow, but change from green directly to brown. For some reason, the breakdown of chlorophyll does not start soon enough or is not complete enough to result in the appearance of the yellow pigments. The yellow color appears in the foliage of many other plants regardless of the weather conditions. There is an interesting high degree of individuality in certain species. Red Maple, for instance, usually turns a good red in fall, but certain individuals may color yellow. The same can be said of sugar maples and several other plants. This is an interesting physiological problem worthy of considerable investigation.

Why Leaves Are Red

The Sassafras, some of the maples, oaks, sumacs, Sourwood, Tupelo and other plants are particularly outstanding for their brilliant red autumn color, and the brilliance of their color apparently varies from year to year. The red in their leaves is caused by a third pigment called anthocyanin, which results from the accumulation of sugars and tannins in the leaf. In some of the maples valued for their sugar production, it is probably the sugars which cause this red color. The oaks, however, probably owe their high autumn coloration to the presence of tannins.

Two factors are necessary in the production of red autumn color. The first is light. There must be warm, bright sunny days in the fall, during which time the leaves naturally manufacture a great deal of sugar. Secondly, such days must be followed by cool nights, during which the temperature is below 45°F. Plant physiologists have shown definitely that, under such

The Sargent Cherry is the tallest growing and hardiest of all the oriental cherries. It is a standard tree and is graced with red autumn color—something few cherries can boast.

conditions, there is little or no translocation of sugars and other materials from the leaf to other parts of the plant. In other words, when cool nights occur, following warm, bright, sunny days, sugars and other materials are "trapped" in the leaves. The accumulation of these products results in the manufacture of the red anthocyanin pigment.

The combination of these factors is well understood when one observes a certain tree that may be red only on that side exposed to the sun. Other leaves not directly in the sun's rays may be green or yellow. Leaves exposed to the sun have been able to manufacture more sugars which, when accumulated and "trapped" in the leaves by cold night temperatures, may result in the red color. It is interesting to note that trees and shrubs growing in swamps and other low places are often among the first to color in the fall, simply because it is in such places that cold air first settles on still nights.

With these points in mind, it can be seen easily why there is so much divergence of opinion about autumn color. When plants are located where they receive full sunlight, especially in late afternoons during early fall, they should be expected to show pronounced color if weather conditions have been favorable. On the other hand, if a plant grows in shade where it receives no direct sunlight, it cannot be expected to have marked red autumn color.

One species in the Arnold Arboretum annually demonstrates this point. There is a splendid plant of *Fothergilla monticola* exposed to full sunlight in the lowest spot in the Arboretum. In years when the climatic conditions have favored the formation of autumn color, this particular plant of *Fothergilla monticola* is a gorgeous red and yellow—on the western side. On the eastern side, where the foliage is shaded from the late afternoon sun, it is merely yellowish. Fortunately all plants do not show such great variation in autumn color when one side is compared with another, but it is a fact that the western side usually has the deepest colored foliage when there has been plenty of sunshine. This point should be kept in mind in planting. Locations and plants should be selected that will show the best advantage during the period of autumn color.

Dull Autumn Coloration

A warm, cloudy fall, sometimes with much rain, will restrict the formation of bright colors. With insufficient sunlight the sugar production is greatly reduced, and with warm nights what little sugar has been manufactured in the leaves can be readily transported to the trunk and roots where it has no effect on the color of the foliage.

Some leaves of many evergreens change color in autumn. Some pine needles may turn yellow, but usually such color last only for a short time, the needles quickly turning brown. This is particularly true of those evergreen leaves which are normally shed each year, and although the autumn color may not be conspicuous in many evergreen plants, nevertheless it is evident on close examination.

All leaves eventually turn brown. This is not an autumn color, but merely the result of the death or decay of plant tissue. Sometimes leaves turn brown while remaining on the tree, as in the American Beech and some oaks. In other cases, like the Sugar Maple and Spicebush, leaves drop while still brightly colored and turn brown afterwards.

Autumn color is, then, a physiological phenomenon which is very complex. There are plants the leaves of which will always turn yellow regardless of current climatic conditions, but many plants with red fall foliage will be striking in appearance only when warm, sunshiny days prevail, followed by nights with temperatures below 45°F. The sugar formation in the leaf, the amount of sunshine received by the plants, and the temperature of the air are three variable factors which, to a large degree, control autumn coloration.

Trees with Vivid Autumn Color

The following trees are listed according to their most conspicuous autumn color. As has been explained above, these may change from year to year, depending on climatic conditions. For instance, some years *Cladrastis lutea* will be yellow, other years the same trees will be purplish. The degree of color may also depend on soil conditions, it being a well-

The native White Oak can grow into a magnificent well-rounded specimen
worthy of conspicuous display anywhere.

known fact that pin oaks, for instance, which have received heavy applications of nitrogenous fertilizers, will have a much deeper red color than
those grown in poor soils without such fertilizers.

RED

Acer circinatum (red to orange)
A. ginnala
A. mandshuricum
A. nikoense
A. palmatum
A. rubrum
A. saccharum (and yellow)
A. spicatum (orange and scarlet)
A. tataricum (red to yellow)
Amelanchier canadensis (yellow to red)
A. laevis (yellow to red)

Carpinus caroliniana (orange to red)
C. japonica
Cercidiphyllum japonicum (yellow to
   scarlet)
Cornus florida
C. mas
C. nuttalli (red to yellow)
C. officinalis
Cotinus americanus (scarlet to orange)
Crataegus lavallei (bronze-red)
C. nitida (orange to red)

C. phaenopyrum
Franklinia alamaha (orange to red)
Liquidambar styraciflua
Malus dawsoniana (red and yellow)
Nyssa sylvatica
Oxydendrum arboreum
Parrotia persica (red to yellow)
Pistacia chinensis (red to orange)
Prunus maximowiczi
P. nipponica (yellow to red)
P. pensylvanica
P. sargenti

Pyrus calleryana
P. ussuriensis
Quercus borealis
Q. coccinea
Q. palustris
Q. velutina
Sassafras albidum (orange to scarlet)
Sorbus aucuparia
S. discolor
S. folgneri
Stewartia koreana (orange to red)
Viburnum species

YELLOW

Acer macrophyllum
A. pensylvanicum
A. platanoides
Aesculus glabra (orange)
Amelanchier grandiflora (yellow to orange)
A. laevis
Asimina triloba
Betula species
Carya species
Castanea mollissima (yellow to bronze)
Cercis species

Chionanthus virginicus
Cladrastis lutea (orange to yellow)
Fagus grandifolia (golden bronze)
F. sylvatica (golden bronze)
Fraxinus americana (purple to yellow)
Ginkgo biloba
Magnolia stellata (bronze)
Pseudolarix amabilis
Quercus alba (purplish)
Quercus imbricaria (russet)
Sorbus alnifolia (orange to yellow)

NO AUTUMN COLOR

Acer campestre
A. negundo
A. pseudoplatanus
Aesculus hippocastanum
Ailanthus altissima
Albizzia julibrissin
Alnus glutinosa
Carpinus betulus
Cedrela sinensis
Corylus colurna
Crataegus monogyna
C. oxyacantha
Elaeagnus angustifolia

Eucommia ulmoides
Fraxinus excelsior
Juglans species
Laburnum species
Magnolia species
Malus, many species
Quercus robur
Robinia species
Sophora japonica
Syringa amurensis japonica
Tilia cordata
T. euchlora
T. europaea

TREES FOR VARIOUS PURPOSES

PARK superintendents, landscape gardeners and amateur horticulturists frequently are at a loss to think of more than two or three trees for a particular situation. One of the common questions we receive these days concerns substitutes for the American Elm. What are these substitutes and how might they be used? How many of them are there? What are the "low maintenance" trees? Which trees have merit in seashore gardens or in difficult growing conditions? The more difficult the growing conditions, or the more specific the requirements for the trees to fill the situation, the more difficult it becomes to make the proper selection. This should not be done haphazardly by the simple means of trial and error; it should be done intelligently from lists in which a major number of the possibilities are listed so that trees can be considered without omitting any.

Lists prove helpful to the experienced park superintendent as well as the amateur, for it is much easier to make a proper selection from a complete list of trees known to meet certain specific growing requirements than to select more or less unknown plants at random, without detailed information concerning their individual qualifications.

The following trees are grouped in various suggested lists. The experienced plantsman realizes that there are situations sufficiently difficult so that it is almost impossible to force any trees to grow in them, and that the first step is to try to overcome such situations rather than to select the trees and hope that they may just possibly succeed. After considering the trees suggested in the following lists, the plantsman will be much better prepared to make his proper selections and to gauge the possibilities for success of other plants he may wish to add to these lists as the result of his own experiences. These are not offered as being "complete" by any means, but they are offered as worthy suggestions which the individual can well augment in considering his own growing conditions and experiences.

Small Trees Withstanding Shade

Very few trees require shaded conditions in which to grow. Some will withstand such conditions, but the deeper the shade the more difficult for any tree to grow properly. Certainly trees will not flower and fruit as well as in full sunlight and usually there is considerable root competition from other trees also.

Acer circinatum
A. pensylvanicum
A. spicatum
Amelanchier species
Cercis canadensis
Cornus florida

Ilex species
Prunus pensylvanica
Rhododendron maximum
Thuja occidentalis
Tsuga species

Trees for Moist Soil

It is usually advisable to drain wet spots, particularly those where water stands for any length of time. The following trees can withstand wet soil conditions better than most:

Acer rubrum
Alnus species
Casuarina species
Ilex species
Larix laricina
Libocedrus decurrens
Liquidambar styraciflua
Magnolia virginiana

Melaleuca leucadendron
Myrica cerifera
Nyssa sylvatica
Quercus bicolor
Salix species
Taxodium distichum
Thuja occidentalis

Trees Withstanding Dry or Poor Sterile Soils

It is always risky to recommend any trees for growing in poor dry soils without knowing just what this means. In a region with 45 inches of annual rainfall, it might mean merely a sandy soil, through which an adequate amount of rain filters always leaving the soil fairly dry. This condition could (and should) be corrected by mixing organic matter with the soil where the tree is to be planted and mulching the soil about the roots of the tree with some good material. Both these methods should aid in assisting to make more of the rainfall available to the tree by holding it until it is used.

On the other hand, dry soils are consistent throughout the Midwest where rainfall is very low (20 inches in some places or less). In such areas very few trees will grow.

Then there are the unusually alkaline soils which are mostly dry also, especially in the western part of North America, where growing trees is particularly difficult. The following trees will not all grow in any one of these situations, but a few may. There are undoubtedly others, especially those in the list of trees growing at the seashore, which might also be included.

Acacia longifolia floribunda
Acer negundo
Ailanthus altissima
Albizzia julibrissin
Aralia elata
Bauhinia species
Brachychiton species
Betula populifolia

Betula davurica
Broussonetia papyrifera
Casuarina species
Celtis australis
Ceratonia siliqua
Cupressus macrocarpa
Eucalyptus species
Ficus species

Fraxinus velutina
Grevillea robusta
Juniperus species
Keteleeria fortunei
Koelreuteria paniculata
Leptospermum laevigatum
Maclura pomifera
Melia azedarach
Melaleuca species
Olea europaea
Parkinsonia aculeata
Pinus banksiana
P. canariensis
P. rigida

P. torreyana
P. virginiana
Populus alba
P. fremonti
Prosopis glandulosa
Quercus kelloggi
Q. marilandica
Q. montana
Robinia species
Sassafras albidum
Schinus molle
Sophora japonica
Ulmus pumila

Trees for Seashore Planting

Many trees can be grown in gardens near the seashore, especially if the soil is good. As the soil becomes more sandy and exposure more pronounced,

Blue Spruce (Picea pungens) on the left and the native Pitch Pine (Pinus rigida) growing together on the New England Seacoast.

fewer and fewer trees are able to withstand such conditions, year in and year out, without some injury. The following trees are well adapted for use in seashore gardens, in fact, some withstand salt water spray. For really trying seashore conditions, this list of trees should be considered first before any other selections are made:

Acer platanoides
A. pseudoplatanus
Aesculus hippocastanum
Ailanthus altissima
Amelanchier canadensis
Araucaria species
Casuarina equisitifolia
C. stricta
Crataegus crus-galli
Cryptomeria japonica
Cupressus macrocarpa
Elaeagnus angustifolia
Eucalyptus species
Fraxinus velutina
Hippophae rhamnoides
Ilex opaca
Juniperus excelsa stricta
J. lucayana
J. virginiana
Lagunaria patersoni
Magnolia grandiflora
Maytenus boaria
Melaleuca leucadendron
Nyssa sylvatica
Olea europaea
Picea asperata
P. pungens glauca
Pinus halepensis

P. nigra
P. pinaster
P. radiata
P. rigida
P. sylvestris
P. thunbergi
Pittosporum undulatum
Populus alba
Prunus serotina
Quercus agrifolia
Q. alba
Q. ilex
Q. marilandica
Q. virginiana
Robinia pseudoacacia
Roystonea regia
Sabal palmetto
Schinus molle
S. terebinthifolius
Thuja occidentalis
T. orientalis
Tilia cordata
T. euchlora
Ulmus parvifolia
Ulmus pumila
Umbellularia californica
Washingtonia robusta

The Hardiest Trees

A most interesting study which has been carried on for many years by Mr. F. L. Skinner of Dropmore, Manitoba, Canada, is the variation in hardiness of different geographical clons of the same species. With winter temperatures of —50°F. he is well situated to study this type of variation. He has found that plants of many species grown from seed collected near the center of their known habitats are not hardy, whereas plants grown from seed collected from the northernmost limits of their habitats often prove hardy in his very severe climate. A specific example was a row of *Ulmus pumila* seedlings in his nursery, some of which were grown from seed collected in Harbin, Manchuria, and some from a tree producing seed in southern Manitoba. In September 1942, the temperature went down to zero and later that winter to —55°F. In the spring of 1943, the seedlings from Manchuria were alive out to the tips of the branches, the remainder of the seedlings were killed completely, roots and all.

Several examples of this type of injury have occurred in the Arnold Arboretum to lend proof to this fact that geographical forms are very important when an attempt is being made to establish seedlings in very cold

The Scotch Pine doing well on the seacoast in New England.

places. Seed collected from plants growing near the northernmost limits of their habitats is likely to give rise to seedlings that will prove hardier than will seedlings grown from seed collected in the milder parts of those habitats.

The following ornamental trees are among those hardy in the coldest parts of settled areas in the United States and Canada:

zone 1	zone 2
Larix laricina	*Acer ginnala*
Populus tremuloides	*A. negundo*

A. spicatum
Alnus incana
Betula papyrifera
B. pendula
Carpinus caroliniana
Elaeagnus angustifolia
Fraxinus pennsylvanica lanceolata
Juniperus virginiana
Larix decidua
Malus baccata
M. "Flame"
M. ioensis plena
Picea abies
P. engelmanni
P. glauca densata
P. pungens
Pinus banksiana
P. cembra
P. flexilis
P. resinosa
P. sylvestris
Populus berolinensis
P. deltoides
P. nigra italica
P. simoni
P. tacamahaca
Prunus maacki
P. pensylvanica
Pyrus ussuriensis
Rhamnus davurica
Salix alba
Sorbus aucuparia
S. decora
Syringa amurensis japonica
Thuja occidentalis
Tilia cordata
Ulmus americana
Viburnum lentago

ZONE 3
Abies veitchi
Acer pensylvanicum
A. platanoides
A. rubrum
A. saccharum
Aesculus carnea brioti
A. glabra
A. hippocastanum baumanni
A. octandra
Alnus glutinosa
Aralia elata
Betula lenta
Chamaecyparis obtusa
C. pisifera
Cladrastis lutea
Crataegus succulenta
Euonymus europaea
Fagus grandifolia
Fraxinus americana
F. excelsior
Hippophae rhamnoides
Malus "Dolgo"
M. prunifolia rinki
M. robusta
Pinus koraiensis
P. strobus
Populus alba
Prunus avium
P. cerasifera
P. cerasus
P. padus
P. serotina
Quercus bicolor
Rhododendron maximum
Robinia pseudoacacia
R. viscosa
Tilia europaea
T. platyphyllos
Viburnum prunifolium

Trees Withstanding City Conditions

Vegetation in the city has a very difficult time fighting for an existence. Poor soil, insufficient light, insufficient water, excessive smoke and gas fumes in the air are only a few of the disadvantages. The more intense these become, the fewer the plants and trees which can be grown. Evergreens, in particular, are difficult subjects for growing in the city, especially evergreen trees. Shrubs can be replaced now and then when they become very

A native tree distributed over a wide area, the White Ash can be a good specimen, although sometimes it reseeds itself so persistently that it may often be considered a weed tree.

weakened by adverse conditions, but the trees have to be in one situation for such a considerable length of time in order to look well, that they are also exposed to a lengthy ordeal of trying growing conditions. Dust and soot quickly encrust the leaves and restrict the normal entrance of oxygen into them. Serious damage can be expected from the carbon monoxide gas given off by a stream of automobile traffic. The following trees might well be considered first for planting in the city, for these are among the best suited for withstanding these trying conditions:

Abies concolor	*F. pennsylvanica lanceolata*
Acer campestre	*Ginkgo biloba*
A. negundo	*Gleditsia triacanthos*
A. platanoides	*Koelreuteria paniculata*
A. pseudoplatanus	*Magnolia grandiflora*
Aesculus species	*M. soulangeana*
Ailanthus altissima	*M. stellata*
Albizzia julibrissin rosea	*Malus* species
Aralia elata	*Melia azedarach*
Catalpa species	*Phellodendron amurense*
Cedrela sinensis	*Picea pungens*
Celtis species	*Platanus* species
Crataegus phaenopyrum	*Populus alba*
C. monogyna	*P. canadensis eugenei*
C. oxyacantha	*P. nigra italica*
Elaeagnus angustifolia	*Quercus borealis*
Euonymus europaea	*Rhamnus davurica*
Fraxinus americana	*Robinia pseudoacacia*
F. excelsior	*Sophora japonica*

Taxus cuspidata	*Ulmus americana*
Tilia species	*U. procera*
Tsuga caroliniana	*U. pumila*

Trees Frequently Not Allowed in New Street Plantings

Some trees may have such a bad record in certain locations that there may be local ordinances prohibiting their use as street trees. This may be caused by the fact that such trees split easily; their wood is brittle and breaks easily; their roots clog drains and sewers; they are unusually susceptible to disease or insect pests or they have vicious thorns. Regardless of the exact reason for such bans, the following trees have been prohibited as street trees in some localities:

Acer negundo	*Juglans nigra*
A. rubrum	*Morus* species
A. saccharinum	*Populus* species
Aesculus hippocastanum	*Prunus* species
Carya species	*Robinia* species
Catalpa species	*Salix* species
Crataegus species	*Ulmus fulva*
Fraxinus species	*U. pumila*
Gleditsia triacanthos (with thorns)	

Trees with Thorny Twigs

(Making Barrier Plants When Restrained to Many Stems)

Aralia elata	*Parkinsonia aculeata*
Crataegus species	*Poncirus trifoliata*
Gleditsia triacanthos	*Prunus cerasifera*
Hemiptelea davidi	*Rhamnus davurica*
Hippophae rhamnoides	*Robinia* species
Kalopanax pictus	*Xanthoceras* species
Maclura pomifera	*Ziziphus* species
Pyrus species	

WINDBREAKS AND SHELTERBELTS

Windbreaks can be very essential parts of home and highway plantings, especially in the colder parts of the country where protection is needed against prevailing winter winds and heavy snows. On the Great Plains of the Midwest where many a farm home has no planting of trees whatsoever, shelterbelts are frequently essential. Climatic conditions vary considerably so that the selection of the right trees for the windbreak or shelterbelt is very important.

It has been found that trees moderate the effect of the wind on their leeward side for a distance on the ground equal to approximately twenty times their height. This means that the wind is less, soil evaporation is decreased, severely cold temperatures brought by winds in winter are re-

Juniperus chinensis mas is here used as a splendid screen.

duced, snow accumulation, and hence soil water, is increased—reasons
enough for planting trees as a shelterbelt on windy plains.

A windbreak can be a single row of deciduous or evergreen trees, but
a shelterbelt, to be truly effective, consists of several rows of trees, usually
the rows being six to eight feet apart and the trees about six feet apart in
the row. Sometimes the shelterbelt consists of as many as fifteen rows of
trees, bordered on the outside with hardy shrubs like *Caragana arborescens*
and *Elaeagnus angustifolia,* or evergreens like Red Cedar, Blue Spruce or
Black Hills Spruce and Ponderosa Pine. Several species are used in the
shelterbelt, since soil and climatic conditions vary considerably, and where
one species may not do so well, another will. The tallest trees are, of course,
planted in the middle rows. Windbreaks in certain parts of South Dakota,
for instance, must grow in soil receiving an annual rainfall of only 17 inches,
not sufficient for good growth based on the 48-inch rainfall of the northeastern states.

Where rainfall is more plentiful, windbreaks become important only
for protecting houses and gardens against prevailing winds, often merely
winter winds, and usually one, or at the most two, rows of dense-growing
trees is sufficient.

Trees for Windbreaks

These trees make good windbreaks in areas other than the Great
Plains. The best windbreaks are of course the evergreens, but since they
grow slowly and it takes some time for them to be effective, fast-growing

deciduous windbreaks are frequently planted in front of the evergreens and then eventually cut out when the evergreens become large enough to prove effective.

Acer ginnala	*P. resinosa*
A. platanoides	*P. strobus*
A. pseudoplatanus	*Populus alba*
A. rubrum	*P. berolinensis*
A. saccharum	*P. nigra italica*
Carpinus betulus	*P. simoni*
Cornus mas	*P. tremuloides*
Crataegus phaenopyrum	*Pseudotsuga taxifolia*
Eucalyptus species	*Quercus* many species
Fagus species	*Q. imbricaria* (one of best)
Fraxinus americana	*Q. phellos* (one of best)
Fraxinus pennsylvanica lanceolata	*Rhamnus davurica*
Juniperus species	*Syringa amurensis japonica*
Ligustrum lucidum	*Thuja* species
Maclura pomifera	*Tilia* species
Malus baccata	*Tsuga caroliniana*
Picea abies	*Ulmus americana*
P. glauca	*U. pumila*
P. omorika	*Viburnum prunifolium*
Pinus nigra	

Trees for Shelterbelts in Great Plains

These are recommended for the Great Plains area of the Midwest, since they grow and have very tenacious roots even with comparatively little rainfall. Trees like the Hackberry, Honeylocust and *Pinus ponderosa* have roots known to go ten to twenty feet deep in the soil.

Acer negundo	*P. pungens*
A. saccharinum	*Pinus ponderosa*
Caragana arborescens	*Populus* species
Celtis occidentalis	*Prunus americana*
Elaeagnus angustifolia	*P. virginiana*
Fraxinus pennsylvanica lanceolata	*Pseudotsuga taxifolia*
Gleditsia triacanthos	*Quercus macrocarpa*
Juglans nigra	*Salix alba*
Juniperus scopulorum	*S. pentandra*
J. virginiana	*Ulmus americana*
Maclura pomifera	*U. pumila*
Picea glauca albertiana	

Trees of Different Heights

LOW TREES (20–35 FEET TALL)	
Acacia baileyana	*Acer argutum*
A. longifolia floribunda	*A. campestre*
A. pendula	*A. carpinifolium*
	A. circinatum

A Western Red-cedar (Juniperus scopulorum) shelterbelt planting in Kansas, (courtesy of the United States Forest Service).

A. ginnala
A. griseum
A. mandshuricum
A. palmatum
A. spicatum
A. tataricum
Aesculus glabra
Amelanchier grandiflora
Arbutus unedo
Bauhinia variegata
Betula populifolia
Bumelia lanuginosa
Callistemon lanceolatus
Carpinus betulus globosa
Carya tomentosa
Cassia fistula
Casuarina stricta
Cercis siliquastrum racemosa
Chionanthus virginicus
Clethra barbinervis
Cornus kousa
C. mas
C. officinalis
Cotinus americanus
Crataegus species

Cupressus bakeri
Elaeagnus angustifolia
Eribotrya japonica
Erythea armata
Euonymus species
Evodia danielli
Franklinia alatamaha
Ficus carica
Fraxinus ornus
Halesia carolina
Hemiptelea davidi
Hippophae rhamnoides
Hovenia dulcis
Ilex cassine
I. decidua
I. pedunculosa
I. pernyi
I. vomitoria
Juniperus rigida
Koelreuteria paniculata
Laburnum species
Lagerstroemia indica
Laurus nobilis
Leptospermum laevigatum
Leucadendron argenteum

Ligustrum lucidum
Macadamia ternifolia
Magnolia cordata
M. salicifolia
M. sieboldi
M. soulangeana
M. stellata
M. watsoni
M. wilsoni
Malus many species
Maytenus boaria
Olea europaea
Parkinsonia aculeata
Phoenix reclinata
Prunus many speices
Quercus marilandica
Ravenala madagascariensis
Rhamnus davurica
Rhododendron maximum
Salix amygdalina
S. babylonica
S. caprea
Sorbus decora
S. discolor
S. folgneri
Stenolobium stans
Styrax species
Symplocos paniculata
Syringa amurensis japonica
Ulmus carpinifolia sarniensis
U. carpinifolia umbraculifera
Vaccinium arboreum
Viburnum species
Xanthoceras sorbifolium
Zizyphus jujuba

(TREES 35–75 FEET TALL)
Abies koreana
Acacia decurrens dealbata
A. decurrens mollis
Acer floridanum
A. negundo
A. nikoense
A. pennsylvanicum
Ailanthus altissima erythrocarpa
Albizzia julibrissin
Alnus cordata
A. incana

A. rubra
Amelanchier canadensis
A. laevis
Aralia elata
Asimina triloba
Betula davurica
B. mandshurica szechuanica
B. pendula
Brachychiton acerifolium
Broussonetia papyrifera
Camellia japonica
Carpinus betulus
C. caroliniana
C. japonica
Castanea mollissima
Castanospermum australe
Causuarina equisetifolia
Catalpa bignonioides
Cedrela sinensis
Celtis bungeana
C. jessoensis
Cercidiphyllum japonicum
Cercis canadensis
C. chinensis
Ceratonia siliqua
Cinnamomum camphora
Cladrastis lutea
Clethra delavayi
Cornus capitata
C. controversa
C. florida
C. macrophylla
Corylus colurna
Crataegus crus-galli
C. viridis
Cunninghamia lanceolata
Cupressus arizonica bonita
C. macrocarpa
C. sempervirens
Davidia involucrata
Delonix regia
Diospyros kaki
D. virginiana
Eucommia ulmoides
Eugenia paniculata
Ficus macrophylla
Firmiana simplex
Fraxinus ornus

F. pennsylvanica lanceolata
F. velutina
Gordonia lasianthus
Hymenosporum flavum
Ilex aquifolium
I. cassine
I. latifolia
I. montana
I. opaca
I. purpurea
Jacaranda acutifolia
Juglans hindsi
J. sieboldiana cordiformis
Juniperus chinensis
J. drupacea
J. excelsa
J. lucayana
J. pachyphloea
J. scopulorum
Lagunaria patersoni
Larix laricina
Livistona australis
Maclura pomifera
Magnolia denudata
M. fraseri
M. kobus borealis
M. loebneri
M. macrophylla
M. veitchi
M. virginiana
Malus baccata
M. "Cowichan"
M. "Dolgo"
M. "Makamik"
M. robusta
M. "Rosseau"
M. "Sissipuk"
Melaleuca leucadendron
Melia azedarach
Morus alba
Myrica cerifera
Oxydendrum arboreum
Parrotia persica
Paulownia tomentosa
Phellodendron amurense
Picea asperata
P. glauca densata
Pinus banksiana

P. bungeana
P. cembra
P. coulteri
P. flexilis
P. halepensis
P. radiata
P. resinosa
P. rigida
P. sylvestris
P. torreyana
P. virginiana
Pistacia chinensis
Pittosporum eugenioides
Podocarpus elongatus
P. macrophyllus
Poncirus trifoliata
Populus lasiocarpa
P. simoni
Prosopis glandulosa
Prunus avium plena
P. lusitanica
P. maacki
P. maximowiczi
P. padus
P. pensylvanica
P. sargenti
P. yedoensis
Pterostyrax hispida
Pyrus ussuriensis
Quillaja saponaria
Quercus acutissima
Q. bicolor
Q. borealis
Q. chrysolepis
Q. coccinea
Q. falcata
Q. ilex
Q. imbricaria
Q. laurifolia
Q. nigra
Q. palustris
Q. phellos
Q. suber
Q. variabilis
Q. virginiana
Rhododendron maximum
Robinia viscosa
Roystonea regia

Salix alba
S. blanda
S. elaeagnos
S. elegantissima
S. pentandra
Sambucus coerulea
Sassafras albidum (*officinale*)
Sapium sebiferum
Schinus molle
S. terebinthifolius
Sorbus alnifolia
S. aria
S. aucuparia
Spathodea campanulata
Stewartia koreana
S. pseudo-camellia
Symplocos paniculata
Taxus baccata
T. cuspidata
T. media
Thuja occidentalis
T. orientalis
T. standishi
Thujopsis dolabrata
Tilia euchlora
Torreya nucifera
Tsuga caroliniana
Ulmus alata
U. parvifolia
U. pumila
Umbellularia californica

TALL TREES—75 FEET OR OVER
Abies species
Acer macrophyllum
A. platanoides
A. pseudoplatanus
A. rubrum
A. saccharum
Aesculus hippocastanum
A. octandra
Alnus glutinosa
Araucaria araucana
A. excelsa
Betula albo-sinensis
B. lenta
B. nigra
B. payrifera
Carya—most species

Castanopsis chrysophylla
Catalpa speciosa
Cedrus species
Cercidiphyllum japonicum
Ceiba pentandra
Celtis australis
C. laevigata
Chamaecyparis species
Cocos nucifera
Cornus nuttalli
Cryptomeria japonica
Eucalyptus species
Fagus species
Fraxinus americana
F. excelsior
F. oregona
Ginkgo biloba
Gleditsia triacanthos
Gymnocladus dioicus
Grevillea robusta
Halesia monticola
Juglans nigra
J. regia
Juniperus virginiana
Kalopanax pictus
Keteleeria fortunei
Larix decidua
L. leptolepis
Libocedrus decurrens
Liriodendron tulipifera
Liquidambar styraciflua
Magnolia acuminata
M. campbelli
M. grandiflora
M. obovata
Metasequoia glyptostroboides
Nyssa sylvatica
Ostrya virginiana
Picea abies
P. breweriana
P. engelmanni
P. omorika
P. polita
P. pungens
P. smithiana
Pinus coulteri
P. densiflora
P. griffithi
P. jeffreyi

P. koraiensis
P. nigra
P. parviflora
P. pinaster
P. pinea
P. strobus
P. thunbergi
Pittosporum rhombifolium
Platanus species
Populus most species
Prunus sargenti
P. serotina
Pseudolarix amabilis
Pseudotsuga taxifolia
Pterocarya fraxinifolia
Quercus agrifolia
Q. alba
Q. cerris
Q. garryana
Q. kelloggi
Q. montana
Q. robur

Q. velutina
Sabal palmetto
Sciadopitys verticillata
Sequoia sempervirens
Sequoiadendron giganteum
Taxodium distichum
Thuja plicata
Tilia cordata
T. europaea
T. platyphyllos
T. tomentosa
Tsuga canadensis
T. diversifolia
T. heterophylla
Ulmus americana
U. carpinifolia
U. glabra
U. hollandica major
U. procera
Washingtonia robusta
Zelkova serrata

Trees with Fragrant Flowers

Acacia decurrens dealbata
A. pendula
Albizzia julibrissin
A. julibrissin rosea
Arbutus menziesi
Buxus sempervirens
Chionanthus virginicus
Citrus species
Cladrastis lutea—slightly
Crataegus oxyacantha
Elaeagnus angustifolia
Eriobotrya japonica
Franklinia alatamaha
Fraxinus ornus
Hymenosporum flavum
Laburnum alpinum
Laurus nobilis
Liriodendron tulipifera
Magnolia acuminata—slightly
M. campbelli
M. denudata
M. grandiflora
M. kobus
M. macrophylla
M. obovata

M. sieboldi
M. stellata
M. virginiana
M. watsoni
M. wilsoni
Malus species
Melia azedarach
Oxydendrum arboreum
Paulownia tomentosa
Poncirus trifoliata
Prunus conradinae semiplena
P. mume
P. padus
P. serrulata "Amanogawa"
P. serrulata "Botan-zakura"
P. serrulata "Jo-nioi"
P. serrulata "Shirotae"
P. serrulata "Taki-nioi"
P. serrulata "Washino-o"
P. sieboldi
P. yedoensis
Pyrus species
Robinia pseudoacacia
Salix alba vitellina
Sophora japonica

Sorbus species
Styrax japonica
S. obassia
Symplocos paniculata

Tilia species
Umbellularia californica
Viburnum lentago
V. sieboldi

Trees with Fragrant Leaves

Abies balsamea
Cedrus species
Cercidiphyllum japonicum
Cinnamomum camphora—scented wood
Davidia involucrata
Eucalyptus species

Ficus species
Myrica species
Pinus species
Thuja species
Tsuga canadensis

There is nothing like the gray bark of the Beech for beauty.

Trees with Interesting-Colored Bark

The bark of many trees is most interesting, especially on deciduous trees in the winter. Certain characteristics come with mature age. The bark of a young and vigorous oak sapling is quite different from that of a venerable century-old monarch. Many people appreciate the varying colors of the bark of trees, and like to have the lower limbs removed primarily to show this to best advantage. Whether this is good practice or not depends on individual preference, but the bark of all trees can be interesting, regardless of whether it is smooth or deeply furrowed or exfoliating in strips.

The native Gray Birch (Betula populifolia) is not a long lived tree. It is best grown in clumps.

Some trees are superior to others in respect to ornamental bark characteristics. The birches, many of the cherries and the beeches are all greatly valued primarily for their bark. They are planted in conspicuous places where their trunks can always be seen.

There are some trees that are not used to any great extent yet which have vari-colored bark. Mature bark of these trees may be a deep gray (as in the case of Stewartias, *Pinus bungeana* and *Ulmus parvifolia*) and when it peels or flakes off in irregular plates (somewhat like that of sycamores) it leaves lighter colored bark beneath. This most interesting habit gives the bark of these trees a unique appearance the entire year, and makes them excellent subjects for planting in conspicuous places. Usually, the more vigorous the tree, the more colorful the bark.

The following trees are a few with interesting bark of various kinds:

GRAY

Acer rubrum
Amelanchier species
Carpinus species
Celtis species (on upper trunk)
Ceiba pentandra
Cladrastis lutea
Crataegus—many species
Fagus species
Ilex opaca
Juglans regia

Magnolia acuminata
M. soulangeana
Quercus borealis (on young trunk and branches)
Q. velutina (on young trunk and branches)
Sorbus species
Ulmus carpinifolia
U. hollandica superba (on young trunk and branches)

WHITE

Acer floridanum (pale gray)
Betula papyrifera
B. pendula
B. populifolia

Populus alba (sometimes greenish white)
P. tremuloides (sometimes greenish white)

RED

Pinus densiflora
P. resinosa

P. sylvestris

RED TO BROWN, CHERRYLIKE

Betula albo-sinensis—almost orange colored
Prunus—several species

P. sargenti—one of best
P. serrula—one of best
Syringa amurensis japonica

Prunus serrula, a rare species in America but frequently seen in England, has the most glossy red bark of any cherry.

COLORED TWIGS

Acer palmatum (red)

A. *pensylvanicum* (green and white stripes)

A. *pensylvanicum erythrocladum* (winter twigs red)

Poncirus trifoliata (green)

Salix alba chermesina (red)

S. *alba tristis* (yellow)

S. *alba vitellina* (yellow)

S. *blanda* (green)

Sophora japonica (green)

MATURE BARK CORKY

Phellodendron amurense

Quercus suber

Q. variabilis

The Lace-bark Pine from China, Pinus bungeana, has been in America 100 years, yet is too little grown, and almost unknown in some places.

EXFOLIATING OR FLAKING OFF IN IRREGULAR PLATES

Acer griseum—one of best, light brown; peeling off like birch bark

Arbutus unedo—inner bark, bright red; outer bark flaking off irregularly

Betula—several species, white, yellow or reddish; peeling off laterally

Carya ovata—stiff older bark breaks off in longitudinal strips

Cornus officinalis—shreds off like birch bark

Elaeagnus angustifolia—shreds off longitudinally

Eucalyptus species—flakes off irregularly

Juniperus scopulorum—shreds off longitudinally

J. virginiana—shreds off longitudinally

Lagerstroemia indica—flakes off in irregular patches, under bark lighter in color

Parrotia persica—flakes off in irregular patches, older bark red-brown

Platanus species—flakes off in irregular patches, under bark lighter colored

Pinus bungeana—flakes off in irregular patches, under bark lighter colored

Stewartia species—flakes off in irregular patches, under bark lighter colored
Thuja species—shreds off longitudinally
Ulmus parvifolia—flakes off in irregular patches, under bark yellowish (apparently
   not all members of this species have this interesting bark characteristic)

**All the Stewartias have beautiful exfoliat-
ing bark.**

Trees with Different Habits

Some trees, like the Douglas Fir or the American Elm, have very
definite outlines at maturity; many others are more or less indefinite. The
shapes do vary considerably and can be slightly modified by corrective
pruning. However, if a rounded specimen is wanted in the middle of a
huge expanse of field or lawn, it is well to know that the White Oak has
just that form and would serve the purpose admirably. The following short
lists are not complete by any means but will serve the purpose to illustrate
these groups of trees and can easily be augmented by the individual ob-
server who takes an interest in tree forms.

COLUMNAR TREES
Acer platanoides ascendens
A. platanoides columnare
A. platanoides erectum
A. rubrum columnare
A. saccharum monumentale
Betula pendula fastigiata
Chamaecyparis lawsoniana allumi
C. lawsoniana erecta
C. obtusa erecta

Carpinus betulus fastigiata
Crataegus monogyna stricta
C. phaenopyrum fastigiata
Cupressus sempervirens stricta
Fagus sylvatica fastigiata
Ginkgo biloba fastigiata
Juniperus chinensis columnaris
J. chinensis mas
J. virginiana pyramidalis
J. virginiana schotti

The Sentry Maple (Acer saccharum monumentale) fifty years old (left) is comparatively slow growing, but the upright form of the Red Maple (rear) grows much faster, although it does not grow into quite as narrow a tree.

Pinus cembra
P. strobus fastigiata
P. sylvestris fastigiata
Populus alba pyramidalis
P. simoni fastigiata
Prunus sargenti columnare
P. serrulata "Amanogawa"
Quercus robur fastigiata
Robinia pseudoacacia rectissima
Sorbus aucuparia fastigiata
Taxodium distichum
Taxus baccata stricta
Thuja occidentalis "douglasi pyramidalis"
T. occidentalis fastigiata
T. plicata fastigiata
Tilia platyphyllos fastigiata
Ulmus americana ascendens
U. americana "Augustine"
U. americana columnaris
U. americana "Lake City"
U. americana "Moline"
U. americana "Princeton"
U. carpinifolia dampieri
U. carpinifolia sarniensis
U. carpinifolia umbraculifera
U. glabra exoniensis
U. procera viminalis

TREES WITH WEEPING HABIT
Acacia pendula
Betula pendula tristis
B. pendula youngi
Carpinus betulus pendula
Cedrus deodara
Chamaecyparis lawsoniana pendula
Euonymus bungeana pendula
Fagus sylvatica pendula
F. sylvatica purpureo-pendula
Fraxinus excelsior pendula
Juniperus virginiana pendula
Larix decidua pendula
Malus "Exzellenz Thiel"
M. "Oekonomierat Echtermeyer"
Morus alba pendula
Picea breweriana
P. pungens kosteriana
Pinus strobus pendula
Prunus mume pendula
P. mume "Weeping Red"
P. serotina pendula
P. subhirtella pendula
P. subhirtella "pendula flore plena"
P. yedoensis perpendens
Peudotsuga taxifolia pendula
Salix alba tristis
S. blanda

Two forms of the Smooth-leaf Elm (Ulmus carpinifolia) each of which has possibilities for planting where space is limited. Left variety umbraculifera; right, variety koopmanni as they grow in the Arnold Arboretum.

S. *babylonica*
S. *elegantissima*
Sophora japonica pendula
Sorbus aucuparia pendula
S. *folgneri pendula*
Tilia petiolaris
Tsuga canadensis pendula
Ulmus americana pendula
U. *glabra camperdowni*
U. *glabra pendula*

TREES PYRAMIDAL IN OUTLINE
Abies species
Alnus rubra
Betula species
Cedrus species
Chamaecyparis species
Cornus nuttalli
Corylus colurna
Cryptomeria japonica
Cupressus arizonica
C. *sempervirens*
Fagus species
Ilex aquifolium

I. *opaca*
I. *pedunculosa*
Juniperus species
Lagunaria patersoni
Larix species
Liquidambar styraciflua
Magnolia acuminata
M. *grandiflora*
M. *kobus*
M. *loebneri*
M. *obovata*
M. *salicifolia*
Metasequoia glyptostroboides
Nyssa sylvatica
Ostrya virginiana
Oxydendrum arboreum
Picea species
Pinus cembra
P. *koraiensis*
P. *nigra pyramidalis*
P. *parviflora*
P. *resinosa*
Populus berolinensis
Pseudolarix amabilis

The Thurlow-weeping Willow (Salix elegantissima) growing in Boston's
Public Garden in the very heart of the city.

Pseudotsuga taxifolia
Quercus cerris
Q. palustris
Sequoia sempervirens
Sciadopitys verticillata
Sequoiadendron giganteum
Stewartia koreana
Taxodium distichum
Taxus cuspidata
Thuja species
Thujopsis dolabrata
Tilia cordata
T. platyphyllos
T. tomentosa
Tsuga canadensis—some varieties
T. diversifolia

T. heterophylla
Ulmus carpinifolia cornubiensis
U. carpinifolia dampieri
U. carpinifolia sarniensis
U. hollandica superba

TREES WITH HORIZONTAL BRANCHING

Abies species
Albizzia julibrissin
Araucaria excelsa
Cedrus species
Cercis canadensis
Cornus controversa
C. florida
C. kousa
Crataegus species

Ulmus carpinifolia sarniensis, the Jersey Elm, originating on the Isle of Jersey, has a desirable habit.

The gracefully beautiful Deodar Cedar is a popular choice as a specimen tree in many a southern garden.

Metasequoia glyptostroboides
Nyssa sylvatica
Picea species
Pinus densiflora
P. sylvestris
Podocarpus macrophyllus
Pseudolarix amabilis
Quercus alba
Q. palustris
Q. virginiana
Styrax japonica
Taxodium distichum

TREES THAT ARE ROUNDED AND SOME-
TIMES GLOBE SHAPED

Acer palmatum
A. platanoides globosum
Carpinus betulus globosa
Catalpa bignonioides nana
Celtis bungeana
Cornus mas
C. officinalis
Crataegus monogyna inermis
Magnolia soulangeana

Malus arnoldiana
M. brevipes
M. floribunda
M. sargenti
Quercus alba
Robinia pseudoacacia umbraculifera
Tsuga canadensis sargenti
T. diversifolia
Ulmus carpinifolia koopmanni
U. carpinifolia umbraculifera
U. glabra camperdowni
U. glabra pendula

EVERGREEN TREES FOR DEEP SOUTH

Acacia species
Araucaria araucana
A. excelsa
Arbutus menziesi
A. unedo
Callistemon lanceolatus
Camellia species
Castanospermum australe
Castanopsis chrysophylla

The Sargent Weeping Hemlock, a dwarf variety of the Canada Hemlock, growing in the Arnold Arboretum.

Casuarina equisetifolia
C. stricta
Cedrus deodara
Ceratonia siliqua
Cinnamomum camphora
Cornus capitata
Cunninghamia lanceolata
Cupressus arizonica bonita
C. macrocarpa
C. sempervirens
Eriobotyra japonica
Eugenia paniculata
Ficus macrophylla
Gordonia lasianthus
Grevillea robusta
Hymenosporum flavum
Ilex cassine
I. latifolia
I. purpurea
I. vomitoria
Juniperus drupacea
J. excelsa
J. lucayana
J. pachyphloea

Keteleeria fortunei
Lagunaria patersoni
Leptospermum laevigatum
Leucadendron argenteum
Ligustrum lucidum
Macadamia ternifolia
Magnolia grandiflora
Maytenus boaria
Melaleuca leucadendron
Myrica californica
Olea europaea
P. coulteri
P. halepensis
P. pinaster
P. pinea
P. radiata
P. torreyana
Photinia serrulata
Pittosporum eugenioides
P. rhombifolium
Prunus lusitanica
Quillaja saponaria
Quercus agrifolia
Q. chrysolepis

Q. ilex   *Sequoia sempervirens*
Q. suber   *Spathodea campanulata*
Q. virginiana   *Umbellularia californica*
Schinus terebinthifolius   *Vaccinium arboreum*

State Trees

The following trees have been selected by acts of the state legislatures as the various "official" trees of each state, unless noted as "unofficial." In this case, a popular vote has been taken by some interested state-wide organization, but no official act of the legislature has yet been passed. In Iowa, Missouri and Nebraska, no official or unofficial action has been taken in respect to a state tree up to this time. It is interesting to note that the Sugar Maple has been popular enough to be selected by five different states, the Tulip Tree by four, and the Cottonwood (*Populus deltoides*) by three states. This list easily represents a cross section of the native trees valued across the continent.

Alabama—Southern Pine—a compromise bill was passed to include under this general heading three native and valued pines—namely, Slash Pine (*P. caribaea*), Longleaf Pine (*P. palustris*), and Loblolly Pine (*P. taeda*)
Arizona—Arizona Cypress (*Cupressus arizonica*)
Arkansas—"Pine"
California—Redwood (*Sequoia sempervirens*)
Colorado—Colorado Blue Spruce (*Picea pungens glauca*)
Connecticut—White Oak (*Quercus alba*)
Delaware—American Holly (*Ilex opaca*)
Florida—Cabbage Palmetto (*Sabal palmetta*)—unofficial
Georgia—Live Oak (*Quercus virginiana*)
Idaho—Western White Pine (*Pinus monticola*)
Illinois—"Native Oak"
Indiana—Tulip Tree, Tulip or Yellow Poplar (*Liriodendron tulipifera*)
Iowa—
Kansas—Cottonwood (*Populus deltoides* or *balsamifera*)
Kentucky—Tulip Tree, Tulip or Yellow Poplar (*Liriodendron tulipifera*)—unofficial
Louisiana—Southern Magnolia (*Magnolia grandiflora*)
Maine—White Pine (*Pinus strobus*)
Maryland—White Oak (*Quercus alba*)
Massachusetts—American Elm (*Ulmus americana*)
Michigan—"Apple"
Minnesota—White Pine (*Pinus strobus*)
Mississippi—Southern Magnolia (*Magnolia grandiflora*)
Missouri—
Montana—Western Yellow Pine (*Pinus ponderosa*)
Nebraska—
Nevada—Trembling Aspen (*Populus tremuloides*)
New Hampshire—Canoe Birch (*Betula papyrifera*)

New Jersey—Red Oak (*Quercus borealis*)
New Mexico—Pinon or Nut Pine (*Pinus edulis*)
New York—Sugar Maple (*Acer saccharum*)—unofficial
North Carolina—Tulip Tree, Tulip or Yellow Poplar (*Liriodendron tulifera*)—unofficial
North Dakota—Green Ash (*Fraxinus pennsylvanica lanceolata*)
Ohio—Ohio Buckeye (*Aesculus glabra*)—unofficial
Oklahoma—Redbud (*Cercis canadensis*)
Oregon—Douglas-fir (*Pseudotsuga taxifolia*)
Pennsylvania—Canada Hemlock (*Tsuga canadensis*)
Rhode Island—Sugar Maple (*Acer saccharum*)
South Carolina—Cabbage Palmetto (*Sabal palmetto*)
South Dakota—Cottonwood (*Populus deltoides* or *balsamifera*)
Tennessee—Tulip Tree or Tulip Poplar (*Liriodendron tulipifera*)
Texas—Pecan (*Carya pecan*)
Utah—Colorado Blue Spruce (*Picea pungens glauca*)
Vermont—Sugar Maple (*Acer saccharum*)—unofficial
Virginia—Flowering Dogwood (*Cornus florida*)
Washington—Western Hemlock (*Tsuga heterophylla*)—unofficial
West Virginia—Sugar Maple (*Acer saccharum*)
Wisconsin—Sugar Maple (*Acer saccharum*)—unofficial
Wyoming—Cottonwood (*Populus deltoides* or *balsamifera*)

British Columbia—Western or Pacific Dogwood (*Cornus nuttalli*)—unofficial

Specimen Trees with Ornamental Flowers

Acacia species
Acer platanoides
A. rubrum
Aesculus carnea brioti
Albizzia julibrissin
Amelanchier species
Aralia elata
Arbutus menziesi
A. unedo
Bauhinia variegata
Brachychiton acerifolium
Callistemon lanceolatus
Camellia japonica
Cassia fistula
Castanopsis chrysophylla
Castanospermum australe
Catalpa bignonioides
C. speciosa
Cedrela sinensis
Cercis species
Ceratonia siliqua
Chionanthus virginicus
Cladrastis lutea
Clethra delavayi
Cornus species
Crataegus species
Davidia involucrata
Delonix regia
Eriobotrya japonica
Eugenia paniculata
Evodia danielli
Franklinia alatamaha
Gordonia lasianthus
Grevillea robusta
Halesia species
Jacaranda acutifolia
Kalopanax pictus
Koelreuteria paniculata
Laburnum species
Lagerstroemia indica
Lagunaria patersoni
Leptospermum laevigatum

The Japanese Dogwood blooms a month after the native Eastern Dogwood
and is just as beautiful in flower.

Liriodendron tulipifera
Magnolia species
Malus species
Melaleuca leucadendron
Melia azedarach
Oxydendrum arboreum
Parkinsonia aculeata
Paulownia tomentosa
Poncirus trifoliata
Prunus species
Pterostyrax hispida
Pyrus species

Rhododendron maximum
Robinia species
Sambucus coerulea
Sophora japonica
Sorbus species
Spathodea campanulata
Stenolobium stans
Stewartia species
Styrax species
Symplocos paniculata
Syringa amurensis japonica
Viburnum species

The Japanese Flowering Crab Apple, Malus floribunda, is perhaps the most widely used of the oriental crab apples in America today. Hardy wherever apples can be grown it is beautiful in flower in the spring and most colorful in the fall in fruit.

Specimen Trees with Ornamental Fruit

Acer ginnala
A. rubrum
A. spicatum
A. tataricum
Ailanthus altissima erythrocarpa
Arbutus species
Broussonetia papyrifera
Cedrus species
Cornus species
Crataegus species
Eriobotrya japonica
Eugenia paniculata
Euonymus species
Evodia danielli
Hippophae rhamnoides
Ilex species
Juniperus species
Kalopanax pictus

Larix decidua
Liquidambar styraciflua
Magnolia species
Malus species
Melia azedarach
Myrica species
Oxydendrum arboreum
Phellodendron amurense
Photinia species
Prunus pensylvanica
P. serotina
Pseudolarix amabilis
Pseudotsuga taxifolia
Pterocarya fraxinifolia
Rhamnus davurica
Sambucus coerulea
Sapium sebiferum
Schinus molle

S. terebinthifolius
Sorbus species
Symplocos paniculata

Taxus species
Viburnum species

Trees Unusually Susceptible to Pests

Some groups of trees are unusually susceptible to certain insect pests and diseases which frequently mar their beauty unless checked. These trees should never be planted where it is known in advance that they will receive no annual care. Usually (although not always) a single spraying at the proper time will suffice to control the pest and keep the foliage in good condition throughout the growing season, but this is frequently an annual necessity. These facts should be kept in mind especially in highway planting where maintenance is always reduced to a minimum. The trees in this list are not the only ones troubled with insect or disease pests but they are the groups in which destructive pests are most commonly encountered. Many individual tree species are seriously pest ridden and when such is the case notes have been made to this effect in the various discussions pertaining to each tree, pages 103 to 355.

Aesculus species	(*leaf rust*)
Amelanchier species	(*red spider, scale*)
Betula species	(*birch leaf miner*)
Castanea—some species	(*chestnut blight—no cure*)
Crataegus species	(*fire blight, borers, scale, lace bug, leaf miner*)
Euonymus species	(*scale*)
Fraxinus species	(*scale, leaf eating insects*)
Ilex aquifolium and *I. opaca*	(*leaf disease and leaf miner*)
Larix species	(*larch case bearer*)
Malus species	(*borer, scale, leaf eating insects*)
Prunus species	(*borer, scale, leaf eating insects*)
Salix species	(*several diseases and leaf eating insects*)
Sorbus species	(*fire blight, borers, scale, red spider*)
Syringa species	(*borers, scale, mildew*)
Tilia species	(*leaf eating insects, borers*)
Ulmus species	(*Phloem necrosis, Dutch elm disease, many kinds of leaf eating insects*)

Trees Usually Pest-Free

In our experience these trees have usually been free of insect or disease pests. Occasionally they may be sprayed as a precautionary measure, but they can go several years without it. However, it must be admitted that in certain areas where vicious pests like the gypsy moth or the Japanese beetle are prevalent, hardly anything is immune to injury. The magnolias listed here are another example also, for if scale is prevalent on trees of *M. soulangeana* close by, and this is not controlled, undoubtedly the magnolias listed here will eventually be infested. There are not many trees in the class with the Ginkgo which seldom is attacked by any pest, but if trees are being sought which are likely to be pest free under reasonably good growing conditions, the following might be considered:

Ailanthus altissima
Brachychiton acerfolium
Carpinus species
Cedrus species
Celtis australis
Cercidiphyllum japonicum
Chamaecyparis species
Corylus colurna
Cornus officinalis
C. mas
Cotinus americanus
Eucommia ulmoides
Elaeagnus angustifolia
Ficus species
Franklinia alatamaha
Ginkgo biloba

Grevillea robusta
Gleditsia triacanthos
Gymnocladus dioicus
Juniperus species
Kalopanax pictus
Koelreuteria paniculata
Laburnum species
Libocedrus decurrens
Ligustrum lucidum
Liquidambar styraciflua
Magnolia acuminata
M. kobus borealis
M. salicifolia
M. stellata
Myrica species
Ostrya species

The Amur Cork Tree, (Phellodendron amurense) is just as interesting in winter as it is in summer, and is practically pest-free.

Parrotia persica
Phellodendron species
Pistacia chenensis
Podocarpus species
Populus alba
Rhamnus davurica

Sciadopitys verticillata
Sophora japonica
Stewartia species
Styrax species
Taxus species
Viburnum species

Trees Difficult to Transplant

Generally speaking, the smaller the tree the easier it is to transplant. Fortunately, the professional arborists of this country have learned a very great deal about transplanting trees during the past two decades. With the power equipment now available, almost any tree that can be transported can be transplanted, but of course, the bigger the tree the more difficult the operation and the larger (and heavier) the ball of earth required about the roots. Transplanting can be done now by the professional arborist at almost any time of year, but it is naturally easiest when the tree is dormant and not in full leaf.

The experienced arborist is a reliable authority. He has the equipment and the knowledge required for the successful transplanting of large trees. From his varied experience he knows in advance the chances of tree survival—the reason why he can guarantee a certain tree to live if properly cared for after the transplanting operation. The moving of large trees is very definitely a job for such experts.

There are some trees which have proved more difficult to move than others. This does not mean that large trees of these species cannot be moved by the expert. They can, especially if they have been satisfactorily root-pruned sufficiently far in advance. When purchased in smaller sizes from the nurserymen, such trees often come with a ball of earth around their roots, and should be moved just before the time they commence to grow in the spring. Transplanting trees and shrubs is done at different times throughout North America, but because the following trees are known to be difficult to move, this should be done only when conditions are optimum, as they would be in most areas just prior to spring growth.

Arbutus menziesi
Carpinus species
Carya species
Crataegus species
Cupressus arizonica bonita
Gymnocladus dioicus
Ilex vomitoria
Juglans species
Kalopanax pictus
Lagerstroemia indica

Liquidambar styraciflua
Magnolia species
Nyssa sylvatica
Ostrya species
Pyrus species
Quercus alba
Q. coccinea
Xanthoceras sorbifolium
Ziziphus jujuba

Substitutes for the American Elm

No tree has the same wide arching habit as the American Elm, but here are some than can be offered as excellent large shade trees which might be used as substitutes where it is inadvisable to plant large numbers of elms.

Acer platanoides
A. pseudoplatanus
A. saccharum
Celtis laevigata
C. jessoensis
Cercidiphyllum japonicum
Cladrastis lutea
Eucommia ulmoides
Fagus grandifolia
F. sylvatica
Fraxinus americana
F. excelsior
Ginkgo biloba
Gleditsia triacanthos inermis "Moraine"
Kalopanax pictus
Liquidambar styraciflua
Magnolia acuminata
M. cordata
Phellodendron amurense
Platanus acerifolia

P. orientalis
Populus alba
Prunus sargenti
Quercus acutissima
Q. agrifolia
Q. bicolor
Q. borealis
Q. macrocarpa
Q. palustris
Q. phellos
Q. virginiana
Sophora japonica
Tilia cordata
T. euchlora
T. europaea
T. petiolaris
T. platyphyllos
T. tomentosa
Ulmus carpinifolia "Christine Buisman"
Zelkova serrata

A Suggested List of Trees Which Have Color-Interest at Least Two Seasons of the Year

All evergreen trees certainly would be in this group as well as the following deciduous trees:

Acer circinatum
A. ginnala
A. nikoense
A. palmatum
A. pensylvanicum
A. platanoides
A. rubrum
A. spicatum
A. tataricum
Amelanchier species
Betula species
Broussonetia papyrifera
Carpinus species
Carya glabra

C. ovata
Celtis bungeana
Cercidiphyllum japonicum
Cercis species
Chionanthus virginicus
Cladrastis lutea
Cornus species
Crataegus species
Elaeagnus angustifolia
Euonymus latifolia
Evodia danielli
Fagus species
Franklinia alatamaha
Ginkgo biloba

A beautiful white under surface of the leaves and a clean cut shape are
the chief characteristics of the Silver Linden, Tilia tomentosa.

Ilex species
Jacaranda acutifolia
Kalopanax pictus
Lagerstroemia indica
Larix decidua
Liquidambar styraciflua
Liriodendron tulipifera
Magnolia denudata
M. kobus borealis
M. loebneri
M. macrophylla
M. obovata
M. salicifolia
M. stellata
Malus species
Melia azedarach
Myrica species
Nyssa sylvatica
Oxydendrum arboreum
Parrotia persica
Phellodendron amurense
Photinia serrulata
Populus alba
P. tremuloides

Prunus blireiana
P. campanulata
P. lusitanica
P. maximowiczi
P. nipponica
P. pensylvanica
P. sargenti
P. serotina
P. subhirtella
P. yedoensis
Pseudolarix amabilis
Quercus alba
Q. borealis
Q. coccinea
Q. imbricaria
Q. palustris
Q. phellos
Q. velutina
Rhamnus davurica
Salix species
Sambucus coerulea
Sassafras albidun
Sorbus species
Spathodea campanulata

Stewartia species
Syringa amurensis japonica
Tilia species

Ulmus parvifolia
Viburnum species

This Japanese Tree Lilac is the tallest growing of all the lilacs and has large flowers appearing after all other lilacs are past bloom.

Some of the Best Small Shade Trees for Small Properties

Most of the following trees listed are comparatively small at their mature height, but the hemlocks and pines can be easily restrained by correct pruning and certainly should be included in this valued group of ornamentals.

Acer campestre
A. carpinifolium
A. ginnala
A. mandshuricum
A. palmatum atropurpureum
Albizzia julibrissin rosea
Carpinus betulus globosa
C. carolinianum
C. japonica
Cercis canadensis
Cornus florida
C. kousa
Crataegus crusgalli

C. oxyacantha pauli
C. phaenopyrum
Elaeagnus angustifolia
Euonymus latifolia
Franklinia alatamaha
Halesia carolina
Ilex aquifolium
I. opaca
Koelreuteria paniculata
Magnolia salicifolia
M. sieboldi
M. soulangeana
M. stellata

M. watsoni
Malus arnoldiana
M. atrosanguinea
M. "Dorothea"
M. "Flame"
M. floribunda
M. halliana parkmani
M. "Hopa"
M. purpurea aldenhamensis
M. "Sissipuk"
M. zumi calocarpa
Oxydendrum arboreum
Pinus bungeana
P. strobus
Pistacia chinensis

Prunus armeniaca
P. "Hally Jolivette"
P. nipponica
P. padus spaethi
P. serrulata "Fugenzo"
P. serrulata "Kwanzan"
P. subhirtella autumnalis
Styrax japonica
S. obassia
Syringa amurensis japonica
Tsuga canadensis
T. caroliniana
Viburnum prunifolium
V. rufidulum
V. sieboldi

STREET AND HIGHWAY PLANTING

THE planting of our streets and highways has become a highly specialized science. There are certain general principles relating to the use of trees that it might be well for everyone to understand, particularly those who drive the highways of the country, so that they can better appreciate the problems involved. Many things must be taken into consideration in planting trees

An intelligent use of Flowering Dogwood, Pin Oak and Mountain-laurel, have made this section of the Merritt Parkway in Connecticut a most interesting and beautiful one for the motoring public—interesting at every time of year.

along any highway, and the better the landscape engineer understands these and properly evaluates them, the more permanent will be the planting he creates. It has been justly said that some of the splendid old trees in the South, like the Live Oak, when properly planted, will outlast anything along or in the highway that man can build, including the road beds and the bridges. Hence, it is most important to select the right trees and place them properly for permanent growth.

Generally speaking, it is advisable to use mostly trees that are native in the same vicinity in order that the highway as a whole will merge with the surrounding open country. Because of this, definitely shaped trees like Blue Spruce and Fir, especially when the color of the foliage is conspicuous, should not be used along highways where high speeds are common, since they can easily divert the attention of the driver. Also, highly "ornamental" flowering or fruiting trees have been found to be a hazard because they are too conspicuous and also distract the driver. Vandals also stop their cars at inapproprate and even dangerous places on the highway in order to break off flowering or fruiting branches. This

White Pines have been used in this highway planting in suburban Philadelphia.

also creates serious damage to the trees, often permanently marring their beauty.

In the open country, trees should not be regularly spaced, but rather should be planted irregularly 75 to 300 feet apart, so that if one tree dies or must be removed, it does not spoil the continuity of the planting. Regularly-spaced highway trees are the most costly to maintain. Such planting is often done along slower driven parkways, but a few missing trees can easily spoil the regular symmetry of any such planting. Hence, except on carefully policed parkways, the use of conspicuous ornamentals on high speed highways in the open country is not advisable.

Trees might well be informally grouped, placed well back of the right of way so that a future widening of the highway would not necessitate their removal. They should be used to frame pictures in the landscape, to augment what nature already has provided, and in some cases, to hide objectionable views or objects. They are used to define the highways, for they are often planted on the outside of the curves in the road to warn the motorist of an approaching turn. They can be so placed as to give the impression of "funnel" planting—converging lines on either side of the road to give the psychological impression of approaching narrowness, especially when the road narrows or speed should be reduced for some permanent obstruction or hazard.

Trees should certainly not be planted under existing utility wires, or where they will create hazards for the regular plowing of snow. They can be used to soften the harsh lines of bridges or other construction objects. A single variety of tree should not be planted along mile after mile of highway, for this lends monotony to the landscape and especially to the driver who is looking at it.

Selection of the varieties of trees used should be done carefully and with a complete knowledge of what is native in the area to be planted. Trees selected need not necessarily be native of that area but certainly should blend in well with native trees in the area. High headed deciduous trees have been the most favored in the past, evergreen trees being too prominent in the landscape of most areas. However, sturdy-wooded, long-lived trees which have a low maintenance cost should be selected. Disease-resistant and insect-free trees particularly should be chosen to reduce the ever-present maintenance costs. It is mere folly to plant a highway with disease-susceptible trees, knowing in advance that funds are not available for their annual care. Most of the *Prunus* species, for instance, should be omitted, chiefly because they are so susceptible to attacks from the tent caterpillar and other leaf-eating insects that they can be most unsightly unless properly cared for annually.

Flowering and fruiting trees like the oriental crab apples should be avoided, for they do not blend well with the landscape in many areas and are too prominent on high speed highways. Along parkways in urban areas, where driving speeds are slower, they are used as is the Flowering Dogwood, but such planting borders more on park planting than it does on highway planting. Nut trees should not be used for the obvious driving hazards their fruits might create.

STREET PLANTING

While the planting of our major highways is done chiefly by highly trained state and federal experts and is out of the hands of the average citizen, tree planting along the streets of the towns and cities is much closer to him. Frequently it has to do with planting on his own property. There are a few generalities about this type of planting that might also be kept in mind.

Attempting to grow trees in the heart of our largest cities, is one thing, and growing them in the suburban areas of such cities or in the

The picturesque Ginkgo used in a narrow street, where smaller trees might
well have have been planted.

thousands of towns and villages across the country is another. Very
few trees will thrive under the exceedingly tough growing conditions of the
city (see list on page 46) while more might be tried in areas where more
soil-space is available, and where traffic hazards, soot and smoke are not
as severe.

In the case of some of the major office buildings recently erected in our
large northen cities, trees are very much wanted as an ornamental feature,
but they must resist terrific odds in order to survive. The paved walk is all

about them and in some places heating pipes are put near their roots to be turned on in the winter to keep the snow melted on the sidewalks above! About all that can be said of such planting is that only the most resistant varieties should be selected and the amount of open ground about their roots should be as much as will be allowed by the architects. (See list on page 46.)

The minimum amount of open ground for a tree to grow in is a square 8 feet on a side, the larger the better. Often a space 12 x 12 feet is provided. In many European cities and in this country as well, widely woven iron grating is placed over this soil to allow for water to seep through to the roots while at the same time providing for foot traffic over it without pounding it down to such an extent that it bakes almost as hard as concrete when it is dried out. Such a condition is not conducive to the free passage of air or rain water to the roots, without which the tree will frequently sicken and die.

Much attention should be given the matter of tree planting before the street is finally laid out by the town engineers. In the horse and buggy days, trees were planted along the street with tree trunks often abutting the curb. This may have been all right then. Today with automotive transportation what it is, much more room must be given drivers on these streets. If this is not done, accidents (often caused by skidding) are serious, not only to the traffic but to the trees themselves. Many trees will fail to recover from a serious trunk injury in which the bark has been stripped from the trunk for a longitudinal distance of 6 feet and half way around the trunk.

The best method of planting along suburban streets is to allow a strip of ground between the sidewalk and the property line on which trees are planted. This strip should be a minimum of 7 to 8 feet and better still 12 feet if some of the larger-growing types of trees are to be used. This arrangement is ideal, for it does not encroach on private property, yet affords plenty of space for the future development of the trees. It places the tree away from service lines, pipes and sewers that are frequently placed at the edge of the street paving, a decided advantage, for when these are opened up and tree roots are in the way, they are usually mercilessly cut. This system is working remarkably well in the newer suburban developments of many large cities, especially in Denver, Colorado, and some areas about Cleveland, Ohio. The property owner can take care of the grass in this strip, and the town will be responsible for the care of the trees. This type of cooperation between the town and the private property owner is obviously an arrangement only feasible when the street and abutting properties have been laid out with this in mind, and certain town ordinances have been approved for the arrangement to work successfully.

In older suburban areas, where such space is not available but where the houses are set back considerably from the property line along the street, there has been a move on to plant the trees on the edge of the private property. In other words, the sidewalk may or may not abutt the street but even if it does not and there is a small grass strip between the sidewalk and street, no trees would be planted in it. They would instead be planted on private property, particularly if the property line abutted the side walk. This method of tree planting obviously creates several complications. It would require special town ordinances governing the care and removal of such trees. It would also require the major cooperation and enthusiasm of the original property owners along a certain street. Once the system is agreed on and approved, it is seldom that purchasers of such property already planted with street trees would seriously object.

This plan has many good points, especially from the standpoint of the health of the trees. They would be away from the street and its destructive traffic; their major roots would be away from the destructive ditch digging operations frequently encountered, and property owners as a rule would take pride in their general good health. This plan is working in some areas, but it is obvious that it takes considerable cooperation between property owners and town officials. It can result in more beautiful trees and more permanent trees, which both groups should obviously desire.

In many cities and towns neither one of these methods of tree planting is possible and the trees must be planted between the sidewalk and the curb. No tree should ever be planted closer than 3½ feet to the curb, and the farther away it is, the better for the tree and the passing traffic. The ideal width for this strip of grass between curb and sidewalk would be 12 feet and the tree would not be centered in it but planted closer to the sidewalk than the street.

Street trees should not be planted opposite each other but should alternate, allowing for a greater development of the tops. Spacing should be at least 75 feet apart. Planting closer than this (except in the use of very small tree species) only creates more costly maintenance, and sometimes may necessitate the removal of some trees which are crowding others. It is far better to plant fewer trees and take care of them properly, allowing them plenty of room for development, than to crowd them close together in order to make a "show" while they are young, at the same time greatly increasing their maintenance cost later.

One other point should be mentioned in this connection, namely the size of the tree planted. It is being found by many whose responsibility it is to plant trees along our town and city streets that smaller trees are much better to use in general street planting—smaller in size at the start and smaller in permanent stature. It takes quite an expenditure of money, labor and equipment to remove a 100-foot American Elm, as many tree superintendents are finding out. Trees with a mature height of under 40 feet can be far less costly to remove. The landscape effects of the tall tree and the smaller tree may not be the same, but there is a nation-wide trend now to consider using smaller trees along the streets of our cities and town. Some are recommended on page 84.

Admittedly the need for medium or tall trees will vary with circumstances and specific situations.

Also, it is far easier to plant several trees one inch in diameter, than one 4 inches in diameter. The smaller trees are more easily acclimated to the new situation, and if properly root-pruned and top-pruned in the nursery will grow even better the first two years than the larger tree. Water can be added to better advantage, more of the right soil can be given at the start, so the smaller tree usually starts a more vigorous growing condition than does the larger tree. This bears some thought. Smaller trees are more easily broken and admittedly there are always places where larger trees must be planted.

The arborists of the country have the information and the equipment to move trees at every time of year. There will always be a demand for big-tree moving by these experts. However, in the cramped, tough situations in which most street trees are required to start growth, trees of an inch caliper or slightly more usually will get off to a better start than trees of larger caliper. The cost in transplanting is also considerably less. Consequently, the tree superintendent can concentrate on a comparatively deeper hole, on comparatively more good soil, and better attention can be given to the water requirements of the new smaller tree. With mounting labor and transportation costs, these two points are going to prove very important in every street tree planting program in the immediate future.

The question of whether all trees on one street should be of the same species is a troublesome one and best not discussed here. It should be repeated, however, that formal tree planting (i.e. all one species) can prove to be the most costly type along streets where some may be killed or removed for one reason or other, since replacement costs of larger and larger trees mount annually. The method, of course, depends on the situation and possible future use to which the street may be put. Many New England towns that have planted only elm trees in the past now wish that they had used several types of shade trees, for a fast-working disease can take its toll and destroy a "one type" planting quickly.

Some towns, like Brookline, Massachusetts, have a policy whereby small streets are planted with one type of tree only. The governing shade tree commissioners see to it that many different types are used throughout the city. It is not without reason to expect that the majority of property owners on one street might decide on the Sargent Cherry, for instance, whereas on another street another majority would request the Littleleaf European Linden. An intelligent shade tree commission, with certain standard policies, and always ready with helpful suggestions in such cases, could easily mold a most interesting over-all tree planting program that would go a long way to make the town beautiful and interesting and to make the citizens of that town proud of their trees for that reason.

Pin Oaks (Quercus palustris) right and Scarlet Oaks (Q. coccinea) left have been well combined in this highway planting outside Boston (U.S. 1)

Small Street Trees

Here are a few suggestions of small trees that might be used along suburban streets—a glance at the list of Low Trees on page 50 will undoubtedly bring to mind many others. Trees for narrow streets could be selected from the list of Columnar Trees on page 60 where one will find many suggestions. The approximate mature heights of the trees below are given for convenience:

	FEET		FEET
Acer argutum	35	C. kousa	20
A. campestre	25	C. mas	24
A. circinatum	25	C. officinalis	30
A. ginnala	20	Crataegus arnoldiana	30
A. griseum	25	C. coccinioides	20
A. platanoides globosum	30	C. crus-galli	35
A. spicatum	25	C. lavallei	20
A. tataricum	30	C. mollis	30
Carpinus japonica	45	C. monogyna	30
C. caroliniana	35	C. monogyna inermis	20
C. betulus fastigiata	30	C. monogyna stricta	20
C. betulus globosa	20	C. nitida	30
Chionanthus virginicus	30	C. oxyacantha	15
Cornus florida	40	C. phaenopyrum	30

C. phaenopyrum fastigiata	30	Styrax japonica	30
C. pinnatifida major	20	S. obassia	30
C. pruinosa	20	Symplocos paniculata	35
C. punctata	30	Syringa amurensis	30
C. succulenta	15	Tilia platyphyllos fastigiata	20
C. viridis	35	Ulmus carpinifolia dampieri	30
Evodia danielli	25	U. carpinifolia koopmanni	30
Halesia carolina	30	U. carpinifolia sarniensis	30
Koelreuteria paniculata	30	U. carpinifolia umbraculifera	30
Ligustrum lucidum	30	U. procera viminalis	35
Maytenus boaria	35	Viburnum prunifolium	15
Prunus serrulata varieties	20	V. rufidulum	30
P. sargenti columnare	35	V. sieboldi	30

Street Trees for Medium-Width Streets

Acer platanoides	Melia azedarach
Crataegus crus-galli viridis	Ostrya virginiana
Fraxinus velutina	Oxydendrum arboreum
Halesia monticola	Populus simoni
Ligustrum lucidum	Pittosporum undulatum
Liquidiambar styraciflua	Prunus caroliniana
Maytenus boaria	Quercus phellos

Globe Smooth-leaved Elm as it is planted in Moline, Illinois. (Courtesy of Moline Park Department.)

Q. coccinea
Q. laurifolia
Q. suber
Robinia pseudoacacia
Sassafras albidum
Schinus molle
Sophora japonica

Tilia cordata
T. euchlora
T. europaea
T. platyphyllos
T. tomentosa
Ulmus alata
Washingtonia robusta

Street Trees for Wide Streets

Acer saccharum
A. pseudoplatanus
Brachychiton acerifolium

Casuarina equisetifolia
Cedrus species
Celtis laevigata

Sugar Maples line many a country road in New England.

Cercidiphyllum japonicum
Cinnamomum camphora
Cupressus macrocarpa
Eucalyptus species
Fraxinus americana
F. pennsylvanica lanceolata
F. velutina
Ginkgo biloba
Gleditsia triacanthos
G. triacanthos inermis "Moraine"
Grevillea robusta
Kalopanax pictus
Lagunaria patersoni
Liriodendron tulipifera
Magnolia grandiflora
Phellodendron amurense
Pinus strobus

Pittosporum rhombifolium
Platanus acerifolia
P. orientalis
P. racemosa
Populus alba
Prunus sargenti
Quercus agrifolia
Q. borealis
Q. macrocarpa
Q. palustris
Q. phellos
Q. virginiana
Roystonea regia
Ulmus americana
U. carpinifolia "Christine Buisman"
U. procera
Zelkova serrata

Note:—Samuel Baxter who was Horticulturist of the Park System in Philadelphia, Pennsylvania, (1938) kept a card index of some 159,176 individual trees along the Philadelphia streets. If trees grown in greatest quantity means anything, they were most popular in this order:

Platanus acerifolia
Acer platanoides
Quercus palustris
Ginkgo biloba
Quercus rubra
Ulmus americana

Fraxinus americana
Acer saccharum
Cornus florida
Malus species
Broussonetia papyrifera
Miscellaneous

ONE HUNDRED TREE CHAMPIONS

THE American Forestry Association has been keeping a file of the largest recorded specimens of American tree species, a most interesting file now with 400 Big Tree Champions recorded with the trunk circumference (breast high), spread of the branches, height and location of each tree.

This Giant Sequoia has been growing here for many centuries.

One hundred of these are listed below. These recorded "giants" can be expected to be superseded as new and larger trees are recorded, but a glance through the list might prove of interest.

	TRUNK CIRCUMFERENCE AT 4½ FEET	CROWN SPREAD	TOTAL HEIGHT
Abies concolor (White Fir)	25'5"		189'
Acer macrophyllum (Bigleaf Maple)	28'	66'	
Acer negundo (Boxelder)	19'11"	102'	75'
Acer rubrum (Red Maple)	18'7"	60'	60'
Acer saccharum (Sugar Maple)	17'6"	75'	110'

	TRUNK CIRCUMFERENCE AT 4½ FEET	CROWN SPREAD	TOTAL HEIGHT
Ailanthus altissima (Tree of Heaven)	17'10"	64'	82'
Alnus rubra (Red or Oregon Alder)	15'7"		
Amelanchier canadensis (Shadblow)	7'	43'	50'
Arbutus menziesi (Pacific Madrone)	27'8"		
Asimina triloba (Common Paw Paw)	14'3" (at 4')	32'	25'
Betula lenta (Sweet or Black Birch)	10'10"	60'	60'
Betula lutea (Yellow Birch)	14'1"	64'	90'
Betula nigra (River or Red Birch)	12'4" (at 2½')		
Betula papyrifera (Paper or White Birch)	18'		
Carpinus caroliniana (American Hornbeam or Blue Beech)	5'6"	60'	42'
Carya glabra (Pignut Hickory)	14'9"		
Carya pecan (Pecan)	21'4"	145'	135'
Carya laciniosa (Shellbark Hickory)	12'9"	74'	118'
Carya ovata (Shagbark Hickory)	10'6"	60'	68'
Catalpa speciosa (Northern Catalpa)	17'10"	73'	58'
Celtis laevigata (Sugar Hackberry)	15'3"	90'	60'
Cercis canadensis (Eastern Redbud)	8'	40'	
Chamaecyparis lawsoniana (Lawson) Falsecypress or Port Orford Cedar)	27'2"		200'
Cladrastis lutea (American Yellow-wood)	12'2" (at 3')		
Cornus florida (Flowering Dogwood)	5'8"		
Cornus nuttalli (Pacific or Western Dogwood)	6'11"	45'	100'
Crataegus crusgalli (Cockspur Hawthorn)	2'	16'	19'
Crataegus mollis (Downy Hawthorn)	6'3"	46'	35'
Crataegus phaenopyrum (Washington Hawthorn)	2'9"	23'	25'
Crataegus punctata aurea (Yellow Dotted Hawthorn)	4'11"	39'	29'
Cupressus arizonica (Arizona Cypress)	17'3"		91'
Diospyros virginiana (Common Persimmon)	8'1"	49'	59'
Fagus grandifolia (American Beech)	16'7"	80'	75'
Fraxinus americana (White Ash)	21'	90'	98'
Gleditsia triacanthos (Common Honeylocust)	18'9"	112'	92'
Gymnocladus dioicus (Kentucky Coffeetree)	12'6"	75'	75'
Halesia monticola (Mountain Silverbell)	11'9"		
Ilex opaca (American Holly)	11'1"	45'	72'
Juglans cinerea (Butternut or White Walnut)	9'	70'	110'
Juglans nigra (Eastern Black Walnut)	24'4"	70'	65'
Juniperus scopulorum (Rocky Mountain Juniper)	26'8" (base)		44'6"

This ten-year graphic illustration was drawn at the Morton Arboretum, Lisle,
represents 5' of growth and the entire chart represents the average completed

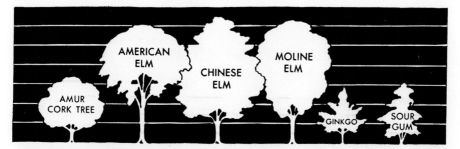

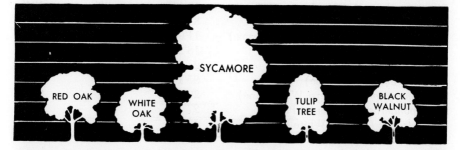

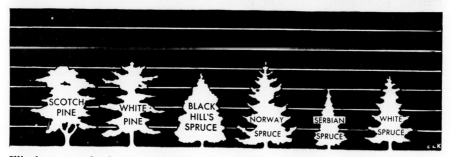

Illinois, as a result of many records kept there on tree growth. Each horizontal line growth of each species at the end of ten years. Compiled by E. L. Kammerer.

	TRUNK CIRCUMFERENCE AT 4½ FEET	CROWN SPREAD	TOTAL HEIGHT
Juniperus virginiana (Eastern Red Cedar)	13'4"	42'	62'
Larix laricina (Eastern Larch or Tamarack)	9'8"	75'	90'
Larix occidentalis (Western Larch)	24'		120'
Libocedrus decurrens (California Incense Cedar)	36'		
Liquidambar styraciflua (American or Red Sweetgum)	14'7"	101'	71'
Liriodendron tulipifera (Tuliptree or Yellow Poplar)	26'6"	98'	83'
Maclura pomifera (Osage-orange)	18'10"	82'	66'
Magnolia acuminata (Cucumbertree Magnolia)	18'4"	60'	125'
Magnolia grandiflora (Southern Magnolia)	14'4"		110'
Morus alba (White Mulberry)	23'		
Nyssa sylvatica (Tupelo)	13'		85'
Oxydendrum arboreum (Sourwood)	6'4"	30'	85'
Picea breweriana (Brewer Spruce)	12'2"		
Picea engelmanni (Engelmann Spruce)	19'11"	30'	104'
Picea glauca (White Spruce)	8'9"		
Picea pungens (Colorado or Blue Spruce)	11'9"		123'
Pinus albicaulis (Whitebark Pine)	18'2"	60'	85'
Pinus flexilis (Limber Pine)	24'5"	50'	44'
Pinus jeffreyi (Jeffrey Pine)	25'1"		130'
Pinus monticola (Western White Pine)	26'5"		207'
Pinus ponderosa (Ponderosa Pine)	27'1"		162'
Pinus strobus (Eastern White Pine)	17'10"		
Pinus taeda (Loblolly Pine)	16'11"	98'	92'
Platanus occidentalis (American Plane-tree; Sycamore)	42'3" (at 5')	100'	150'
Populus alba (White Poplar)	13'7"	65'	75'
Populus deltoides (Eastern Poplar or Cottonwood)	30'		90'
Populus tremuloides (Quaking Aspen)	9'10"		75'
Prunus serotina (Black Cherry)	18'4"	77'	64'
Pseudotsuga taxifolia (Common Douglas Fir)	53'4"		221'
Quercus alba (White Oak)	27'8"	165'	95'
Quercus agrifolia (California Live Oak)	38'	123'	88'
Quercus bicolor (Swamp White Oak)	16'11"	112'	90'
Quercus borealis maxima (Eastern Red Oak)	23'3"	100'	80'
Quercus chrysolepis (Canyon Live Oak)	36'3"	130'	60'
Quercus imbricaria (Shingle Oak)	9'7"	72'	61'
Quercus laurifolia (Laurel Oak)	24'		

This famous specimen of the southern Live Oak (Quercus virginiana) is the famous Middleton Oak, of Middleton Gardens, Charleston, South Carolina. It is estimated to be 900 years old, has a trunk diameter of 12′ with a branch spread of 144′.

	TRUNK CIRCUMFERENCE AT 4½ FEET	CROWN SPREAD	TOTAL HEIGHT
Quercus palustris (Pin Oak)	18′2″		
Quercus macrocarpa (Bur Oak)	21′4″	114′	143′
Quercus montana (Chestnut Oak)	19′1″	111′	82′
Quercus phellos (Willow Oak)	20′	106′	118′
Quercus prinus (Swamp Chestnut or Basket Oak)	30′3″		110′
Quercus velutina (Black Oak)	19′6″	136′	90′
Quercus virginiana (Live Oak)	35′	168′	78′
Robinia pseudoacacia (Black Locust)	15′8″	40′	60′
Salix alba (White Willow)	23′6″	75′	85′
Sussafras varlfolium (Sassafras)	15′8″	52′	65′
Sequoia sempervirens (Redwood)	62′8″		308′
Sequoia gigantea (Giant Sequoia)	101′6″ (Base)		
Sorbus americana (American Mountain-ash)	5′6″		272′
Taxodium distichum (Common Bald-cypress)	34′7″		126′
Taxus brevifolia (Pacific Yew)	12′7″		
Thuja occidentalis (Eastern Arborvitae or Northern White-cedar)	15′6″	50′ (Est. 1600 yrs. old)	125′
Thuja plicata (Giant Arborvitae or Western Redcedar)	62′8″		100′
Tilia americana (American Linden or Basswood)	16′3″	75′	105′

Tsuga canadensis (Canada or Eastern Hemlock)	19'9"	69'	98'
Tsuga heterophylla (Pacific or Western Hemlock)	27'2"		125'
Tsuga mertensiana (Mountain Hemlock)	20'10"		94'
Ulmus americana (American Elm)	28'7"	140'	99'
Umbellularia californica (California Laurel or Oregon-Myrtle)	36'9"		

DWARF TREES

LITTLE will be said here about dwarf trees for this book includes only trees of 20 feet or more in height. There are many dwarf or slow growing trees (with a single trunk) under this height available from commercial sources today, trees which may never grow more than 10 to 15 feet in height. Normal trees have been dwarfed for centuries by oriental gardeners who have an art of their own called "Bon-sai." There is still a

This wind shaped Jeffrey Pine in Yosemite National Park is estimated to be 600 years old. It is forced to grow in this picturesque habit because of extreme exposure and very little available soil on the top of this solid rock.

third group of dwarf trees brought about by the use of slow growing or dwarfing" understocks, especially popularized at the moment in the production of dwarf fruit trees. This interest will most certainly soon carry over into ornamentals for the whole emphasis on planting now is on smaller trees for smaller gardens and smaller streets.

There is a long list of so-called dwarf varieties of standard trees being grown today, and anyone interested in these could have a fascinating time studying them and finding sources for them. Such plants usually arise as "sports" and must be asexually propagated in order to retain their dwarf character. Seedlings grown from them usually revert to the species with their more vigorous characteristics. The Norway Spruce (*Picea abies*) and the Hinoki Cypress (*Chamaecyparis obtusa*) are both known for the large number of slow growing "sports" which have originated from them, usually at first in the form of one branch or "witches Broom" that is obviously slow growing and has been reproduced by cuttings or by grafting. Space does not permit a study of these many plants here for they are outside the realm of this present volume. It might be acceptable to mention briefly three of the means by which gardeners in this country are dwarfing trees.

DWARF FRUIT TREES

In Europe, especially in England, much emphasis has been placed on growing smaller fruit trees merely because gardens are being crowded into smaller areas. The objective is to have a regular type of fruit, even a variety of fruit such as the "McIntosh" Apple for instance, borne on a tree of much smaller habit than the standard "McIntosh" tree. This is done by using some special understock which has a retarding effect on the vegetative growth of the "McIntosh" Apple. Much work with dwarfing understocks was originally done at the East Malling Research Station, East Malling, Kent, England, which is why we hear so much about the "Malling" understocks today. A series of such understocks were selected for apples and given numbers I to XVIII, some better than others, some more dwarfing than others. "Malling No. IX" is used a great deal now for some varieties of apples, resulting in very early bearing—often only two years after grafting, and also resulting in very low trees. Some are under ten feet tall, easily pruned and sprayed by a man on the ground. Such plants are desirable on small properties especially.

These are not the only dwarfing understocks for apples by any means. Much experimenting is being done at the Arnold Arboretum and its companion institution, the Bussey Institute, as well as many of the state and federal experiment stations, to find new and better dwarfing understocks for other fruits as well as apples. A clonal understock is best, i.e., one that is asexually propagated so that all the understocks have the same genetical constitution and will not vary. A tree grafted on such an understock will produce results that can be predicted in advance. Prof. Karl Sax of the Arnold Arboretum has found that some Crab Apple species are interesting as dwarf understocks, especially *Malus sikkimensis*.

Sometimes, as in the case of some pear varieties, "double working" is necessary, that is, one variety is grafted or budded on a certain understock and, after a year's growth another variety is budded or grafted on the first. The second variety may form a poor union with the understock itself, but the intermediate piece makes a strong union and the second variety makes a correspondingly strong union on the intermediate piece. The resulting tree is a strong, well-knit unit, dwarfed by the understock.

It is readily seen that this work with dwarfing understocks is a long arduous one, taking years before final success or failure of the operation can be properly judged. It also takes an advanced technique in the art of propagation. Certain types of dwarf fruit trees are already available, but experimentation on dwarfing has by no means stopped. In fact, quite the reverse is true. It will not be long before dwarfing understocks will be sought for some of our over-vigorous standard trees. Many is the time when a small, slow growing tree is desired in cramped surroundings or on the small place, and such trees are frequently hard to find commercially.

Espaliers

The patient, time consuming work necessary in growing espaliers against wall or trellis is not as yet very popular in America. There are some who are growing fruit trees in this fashion, chiefly pears, apples and peaches. One must have a thorough knowledge of pruning, when it is best done, and how to train and bend young stems so that they can finally be maintained in geometrical patterns against the wall or on a wired support. Since this is an artificial way of coaxing growth, one must keep at it each year in order to keep the tree restrained and also in order that it may produce flowers and bear the proper number of fruits.

Pruning small trees in espalier fashion is an art. No mere words can be substituted for experience in this respect, but a few general principles can be briefly mentioned. In the first place, the original side branches should come from well down on the trunk, possibly a foot from the ground level. The manner in which these are carefully selected and trained so that the tree will be well balanced is most important. These are actually the main shoots; side shoots originating from these leaders must be continually cut or pinched back practically to the fruit spurs, during the months of July, August and September, a painstaking process that must be undertaken at least once a month to keep the plant well restrained.

The leaders must be cut back also, preferably during the winter, the amount depending on the additional training needed. If the tree is a young one and has more area of trellis to cover, this leader pruning would not be as severe as it would be if the tree had reached its desired size. In this case, the leaders would be cut back to a single bud. Usually espaliers are not over 8 feet high.

There are several geometrical patterns into which espaliers can be fashioned, such as the V, the U and the double and triple U, and many others. Branches must be loosely tied to some trellis support so that the weight of the fruits will not break them. Fan espaliers also are popular, but in all types, it is essential that the lateral branches coming from the sides of

An espaliered apple tree. Many plants are carefully grown this way in
England, but in America most gardeners do not wish to take the time
necessary to train them.

the main leaders be continually pruned or pinched back during the growing season.

When it is desired to force a horizontal branch into a vertical position,
the horizontal is tied solidly at the point where the turn is wanted. Then, in
order to get the branch to make a right angle turn without breaking, it
may be necessary to tie it up first only a third of the way, let it grow for
several weeks or even months, then pull it a little more towards the vertical,
and finally the last gap can be closed after a period of time. The fruit spurs
are carefully chosen, some of them removed so that no one branch will be
overloaded. The manner in which the fruit spurs are selected, and others
are removed, develops into the intricate technique that makes for success
or failure with espaliers.

The discouraging part to me has always been the realization that, after
all, these plants are fruit trees and in order to obtain maximum fruit production from them they must be sprayed properly and on schedule, a time
consuming task for all except the most ardent enthusiasts. It does make an
interesting hobby for the one who has the time and patience to pursue it
nevertheless.

Growing dwarf fruit trees either as dwarfs or as espaliers, is a fruit
growing problem, and one on which considerable information has been
published. Space will not permit discussing it further here. Suffice it to say,
considerable interest will be given dwarfing understocks in the immediate

future, particularly for certain ornamental plants. It is a fascinating study, chiefly for the expert plant propagator, and one who has the time and patience to wait years for proper results to become apparent.

"BON-SAI," THE ART OF TRAINING DWARF TREES

Ancient customs have been handed down by the Japanese regarding the training of the interesting dwarf trees so characteristic of the gardens and homes of that country. There are several reasons for their existence. In the first place, Japanese and Chinese gardens are usually small, for space is at a premium. This is particularly true in Japan where the art of making gardens on a very small scale is centuries old. Then, too, the Oriental's well known appreciation of the aesthetic value of living plants has been a prime factor in their cultivation. It often takes fifty to one hundred years to grow a worthy specimen dwarf tree, yet it is possible by twisting the trunk and restraining the growth of tops and roots to give a comparatively young plant the appearance of great age. This treatment requires a thorough knowledge of horticulture as well as painstaking patience, but many Japanese are fascinated with "Bon-sai" and practice it as a pastime.

Training

Most woody plants can be dwarfed if given the proper training. If the branches and roots of growing plants are vigorously restrained from developing rapidly, the individuals soon become dwarfed and this is the principle underlying all training. Then, too, great care is given to the training of the trunk, the spread of the branches and their shape, and the spread of the roots, since each can be so trained as to give the impression of great age. Many methods have been devised through the centuries for attaining these ends. Maples, bamboos, cherries, pines, hollies, oaks, azaleas, junipers, and many other plants have been used. They are grown in comparatively small containers, kept pot-bound throughout their existence, and carefully and judiciously pruned to maintain the desired type of growth.

Whenever possible, the Japanese start with plants that have already been dwarfed by nature. These are searched for in the high mountains, in regions often unfamiliar to the ordinary traveller. Such plants are frequently found growing in high rocky crevices, just barely existing for lack of sufficient nourishment. If these are dug immediately and removed, they might succumb at once, for the delicate balance between the amount of root system and bare existence is easily upset. The plant hunter may locate such plants several years before he will venture to remove them from their rocky dwelling. At first he will root-prune a small portion of the plant and leave it in place for a year; then he will return and root-prune another small portion, repeating this process until it is safe to move the plant. In this way splendid speciments are obtained that have already been trained with the assistance of Mother Nature herself.

If dwarf plants are to be trained from the seedling stage, the smallest and weakest seedlings are selected. Conifers are considerably easier to train, for they do not form adventitious buds as readily as do the broad leaved plants. The seedling is placed in a very small pot. If there is a tap root, it is pruned considerably, and if a central leader is present, it too is cut back. In order to obtain the desired effect, only certain branches are allowed to develop. As an example, *Chamaecyparis obtusa* is ordinarily a very bushy plant, yet the illustration below shows only a few picturesque branches. These few branches have been carefully selected and trained, while the others have been entirely removed. If one of these branches should die, eventually a new bud would be allowed to develop a branch to sufficient size to take the place of the deceased one.

To give the correct appearance of wind-contorted shape, the main stem is often twisted around an upright, and after a formative period the upright is removed. This twisting in itself is a dwarfing process, since frequently it breaks a large number of the conducting vessels in the stem. Branches are twisted in like manner. They may all be trained on one side of the plant, or arranged to droop on one side of the pot, or trained in any one of a dozen different ways. The Japanese gardener usually has a model in mind when he trains his plant, some wind-twisted tree which he is trying

A dwarfed Chamaecyparis obtusa over 200 years old, in the Japanese Dwarf Collection at the Arnold Arboretum.

to reproduce in miniature form, and it is surprising for the uninitiated to observe how accurate these reproductions can be.

Often in nature one observes old gnarled trees the larger roots of which are exposed, especially when growing in rocky places where there is still soil. This effect is reproduced by the "Bon-sai" artist by growing his seedling in charcoal and moss for a period sufficiently long to induce long roots. When the plant is removed to its permanent container, a part of these roots are left to develop above the soil level, eventually aiding materially in giving the plant the appearance of great age.

Pruning, Repotting and Watering

Not all branches are entirely removed. Some of these century-old plants have numerous picturesque stubs, certain gardeners believing that these add to the beauty of the plant. Any diseased tissue on such stubs is carefully scraped, disinfected and painted. Sometimes in order to gain the appearance of stubby old age rapidly, taller plants that have been growing normally are used. The basal branches are cut back to give the stubby appearance. The top is entirely cut off. The plant is dug and after many of the roots have been removed it is placed in a small pot. Then certain of the adventitious buds are allowed to develop, or else scions are grafted at the desired places.

Grafting is also resorted to when certain shoots die. If a very important branch has died, it may take many years for a new one to grow to a sufficient size from an adventitious bud, so that grafting is often resorted to. The Japanese are particularly adept at this and take great pains in training an individual branch by pinching the buds back here, or twisting the branch there, and so forcing the latter to grow in the desired fashion. The pruning and pinching operations are done during the active growing period, since the development of branches from adventitious buds is then more frequent.

Dwarf trees are repotted every four or five years for two reasons. In the first place it is necessary to remove some of the newly developed fibrous roots so that the tree will remain dwarfed. Secondly, it is necessary to mix a small amount of fertilizer with the soil, since as these trees are forced to grow in very small containers, there is not sufficient room for enough soil to allow new root development unless the plant be artificially stimulated with nutrients.

It is also advisable to keep a fresh layer of green moss on the surface of the soil. This not only adds the impression of age, but keeps the soil from drying out. The containers are usually provided with a hole in the base for proper drainage. In the hot summer days there is some danger of the soil becoming too dry, and at such times the plants need special attention. Spraying the foliage with water once or twice a day during the hottest spells of summer is advisable in order to keep the plant in good condition.

Dwarf trees cannot be considered primarily as indoor plants. They may be used indoors for short periods, but must be grown in the open a greater part of the time. Because of their small root system, and the small containers in which they are grown, these dwarf trees cannot lose much water through transpiration and still survive. Consequently they must be grown in a shaded location. The shade house in which this collection is being maintained at the Arnold Arboretum was designed and erected especially for this purpose. Constructed of cypress wood, the top and sides of the house are covered with strips 1½ inches wide with similar spaces left between each strip. This supplies plenty of shade and at the same time keeps the atmosphere considerably cooler and reasonably moist.

Winter Protection

Although many of these trees are hardy, they cannot survive our northern winters because of their shallow root system, unless given some winter protection. A Japanese maple, for instance, growing normally in the ground may survive a winter during which the temperature goes to 20 degrees below zero although the top of the plant may be killed to the ground. However, in these small pots the roots of the dwarf trees would be subjected to temperatures almost as low as those of the surrounding atmosphere, and consequently the whole plant would be killed. During the winter in the North, they are best put in cold frames or pits which are well protected with glass and over which boards and mats are placed during the most severe weather. In our pit where these plants were stored last winter the temperature did not go below freezing, although the temperatures outside the pit dropped to zero on several occasions. Another danger from freezing temperatures is that with the expansion of freezing soil the containers may break. Although these are seldom ornate, since the Japanese believe that the plant itself should be the point of interest, nevertheless their simplicity alone is beautiful and makes them important adjuncts to any such collection and thus worthy of full protection.

Thus, with an exacting knowledge of the numerous rigid requirements of the art of "Bon-sai," the painstaking Japanese gardener is able to reproduce dwarf trees that are exact replicas in everything but size of century-old specimens as they occur in nature. The Japanese have developed other forms of dish gardening, but to the American horticulturist perhaps none is so interesting as "Bon-sai."

GENERAL LIST OF RECOMMENDED TREES

THE following trees have been selected because of their superior landscape qualities. It is not intended that this be a record of botanical descriptions. Far from it! Rather it is a grouping of the chief characters of these trees with special reference to their landscape usefulness. Both Latin and common names are given, height, zone of hardiness referring to the map on the inside covers, origin or habitat and the approximate time of introduction. Information also is given concerning flowers, fruits, foliage, autumn color and winter-twig characters, but only when these are ornamentally significant. If no information is given in any one of these categories, it means that the tree in question is not valued for that particular reason in the garden.

The trees have necessarily been chosen somewhat arbitrarily, but only after careful consideration has been given to those in the secondary list. The hardiest are mostly growing in the Arnold Arboretum where they have been under observation for years. The more tender types are among the best for the warmer areas of the United States. Both amateur and professional gardeners might do well to confine their interest to the trees in the recommended list especially when time and space are limiting factors. All are actually growing in the United States and Canada, most of them being available from commercial sources on record in the Arnold Arboretum. When time, money and space are not limiting factors trees might be selected from the secondary list for further trial.

Occasionally reference is made to the Horticultural Colour Chart of the Royal Horticultural Society. At the time of writing, this is the best color chart for comparing the colors of plants.

If an "x" appears in front of the specific name, i.e. x **Amelanchier grandiflora** it designates this tree as a hybrid, and seed sown from it may not yield seedlings like the parent tree. All offspring propagated from it by seed are clons and to obtain young trees like the parent, propagation must be by asexual means.

An asterisk (*) in front of the flowers, fruit, foliage, autumn color or twigs means that the tree is grown particularly for this outstanding landscape characteristic. If no asterisk appears, these characters may still be good but not meritorious.

ABIES

Firs of one species or another are native over a wide part of North America, especially in the higher altitudes. Some like the Balsam Fir (*Abies balsamea*) and its southern counterpart, the Fraser Fir (*A. fraseri*), do not make good ornamentals because they require the cool moist atmosphere of the mountains. The White Fir (*A. concolor*) grows well in many places other than its native Rocky Mountains, and is frequently seen to do well under city conditions but where soot and gases are not too prevalent.

All firs are generally stiff in habit, pyramidal in shape and have regular whorls of rigid horizontal branches. Because of this, they stand out markedly in any landscape, and as a consequence, should be used

The native firs of the Olympic Mountains (Abies lasiocarpa) in Washington, like most other firs near timberline, grow very narrow.

with discretion. Their needles usually remain on the trees four to five years before falling off. The cones of all firs are borne in an erect position and at maturity are 2 to 5 inches long but quickly fall apart. They are ornamental, but do not appear every year and even then are not conspicuous for a very long time. Firs are seldom troubled with serious insect or disease pests. Their biggest fault is that if their lower branches die or are removed, no new ones will grow back in the same place. Consequently, to be kept symmetrical all the branches must be kept in a vigorous growing conditions. They differ from spruce and hemlock as well as Douglas Fir (Pseudotsuga), which have all their cones in a pendant position, and they do not fall apart at maturity.

One marked characteristic is that the needles, when they fall from the twig, leave it smooth to the touch, leaving no rough leaf bases as in the case of hemlock and spruce. When other means of differentiating between the genera fail, this is certainly bound to work.

It is the firs that are most popular as Christmas trees and which are often grown commercially for this very purpose. It used to be that they could be stuck in a bucket of gravel filled with water and so persuaded to hold their needles much longer than normal. Now various sprays are used to accomplish the same purpose.

At one time or another, over twenty-five species of firs (as well as sixteen varieties) have been growing in the Arnold Arboretum together. Only eight species and two varieties have been sufficiently outstanding to warrant mention here, although some of the others have been used in landscape work in various parts of the country. No fir can be "held" in size or "reduced" by pruning without seriously affecting its usefulness. Hemlocks and many spruces and even pine can be so controlled.

Simple Foliage Key to the Firs

The firs are perhaps the most difficult of the narrow leaved evergreens to tell apart because their needles vary little in size and shape, as well as the color of the twigs and the amount of pubescence.

There are ten fir species native to this country in addition to fifteen exotic species and six varieties, all of which are either native or being grown commercially at some place in the United States and included in the following key. As with the pines and spruces, many more firs are being grown in botanical gardens and arboretums in this country, but their cultivation is limited to such an extent that they are not available at this time to the plant buying public in sufficient quantity to warrant their inclusion in this key.

The habitats are given for all species appearing in the key, for such information is often helpful in identifying these plants in the field.

The simple foliage keys to the evergreens (*Abies, Picea, Pinus Tsuga*) (see each genus) should materially aid the gardening enthusiast or woodsman in his associations with this valued group of plants. The keys cover practically all the pines, hemlocks, spruces and firs native in large areas in this country or grown in quantity in our commercial nurseries. Actually, 104 evergreen trees are included in these keys of which 41 species are native to this country. This is the majority of the evergreen conifers in these groups which one would normally find in the woods, parks, and gardens of the United States and Canada. In using the key merely go to the first number. If the statement there applies to the specimen go to the next **higher** number until the tree is identified. If the statement there does not apply, proceed to the following group headed by the same number and proceed as above. It is hoped that these keys may stimulate an interest in the names and relationships of these conifers. They were planned to be used with living plants. Use them and learn to know your evergreens!

Leaves single, leaving a circular scar when falling; without persistent prominent leaf bases on the twigs. . . . .*Abies, Pseudotsuga*

   1. End bud sharply pointed, long and narrow, with many scales, not resinous; fruit a pendulous cone, needles spreading radially on all sides of twig. Douglas-fir. . . . .*Pseudotsuga taxifolia*
   (British Columbia to Western Texas) Zone 6

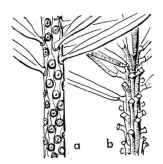

Figure 1. a. Twig of fir showing the smooth twig surface when the leaves have fallen.
      b. Twig of spruce, showing the small leaf bases (making a rough twig surface) which remain after the leaves have fallen.

   1. End bud not long and narrow and sharply pointed, mostly resinous; fruit upright; needles of most species (except *A. pinsapo* and *A. koreana*) not spreading radially on all sides of twig (See Figs. 1, 2) . . . .*Abies* species

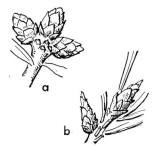

Figure 2. a. Terminal bud of fir.
      b. Terminal bud of Pseudotsuga taxifolia showing its many scales and long pointed character distinctly different from the buds of any fir.

alba—Silver Fir	*lasiocarpa*—Rocky Mountain Fir
amabilis—Cascades Fir	*lasiocarpa arizonica*
balsamea—Balsam Fir	*magnifica*—Red Fur
cephalonica—Greek Fir	*mariesi*—Maries Fir
chensiensis—Shensi Fir	*nordmanniana*—Nordmann Fir
cilicica—Cilician Fir	*pinsapo*—Spanish Fir
concolor—Colorado Fir	*procera* (formerly *A. nobilis*) Noble Fir
concolor violacea	*religiosa*—Sacred Fir
firma—Momi Fir	*sachalinensis*—Saghalin Fir
fraseri—Southern Balsam Fir	*sibirica*—Siberian Fir
grandis—Giant Fir	*spectabilis*—Himalayan Fir
holophylla—Needle Fir	*veitchi*—Veitch Fir
homolepis—Nikko Fir	*venusta*—Bristle-cone Fir
koreana—Korean Fir	

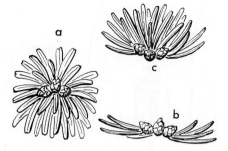

Figure 3. a. Abies koreana showing needles spreading radially.
  b. Abies alba showing needles distinctly 2-ranked.
  c. Abies nordmanniana showing needles appearing on sides and from upper surface of twig.

2. Needles mostly ¾ inch or less in length
   3. Needles spreading radially on all sides of twig
      4. Needles intensely white beneath, usually blunt and rounded at the tip.....................................A. koreana (Korea) Zone 5
      4. Needles greenish to greenish white beneath usually pointed at the tip.....................................A. pinsapo (Spain) Zone 6
   3. Needles not radially distributed; apparently more or less two-ranked, that is, with needles appearing on the two sides of the twig and frequently on the upper surface as well (see Fig. 3)
      4. Needles lustrous green above, white or whitish beneath; stomate lines present on under surface only
         5. Needles, especially on two-year old twigs, directed toward tip of branch (see Fig. 5).........A. mariesi (Japan) Zone 5
         5. Needles, especially on two-year old twigs, more or less at right angles to the twigs (see Fig. 5) (Labrador to W. Virginia and Iowa) Zone 3....A. balsamea (Allegheny Mts., W. Virginia and Tennessee) Zone 4.......................................A fraseri
            (These two are closely related and difficult to tell apart without cones or without a lens. The under surface of the needles of A. fraseri has 8 to 12 lines of stomates in each white band, while that of A. balsamea has only 4 to 8 lines in each white band)
      4. Needles gray-green above and below, due to the fact that stomate lines (seen with a lens) are on both upper and lower needle surfaces
         5. One year twigs ash gray
            6. Bark on trunk gray...............A. lasiocarpa (Alaska to New Mexico) Zone 3
            6. Bark of trunk creamy white and corky
               A. lasiocarpa arizonica
         5. One year twigs rusty brown—foliage bluish green
               A. procera (A. nobilis)
            (Washington to California) Zone 5

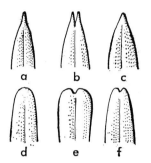

Figure 4. a. Tip of needle of A. holophylla.
b. Tip of needle of young A. firma.
c. Tip of needle of A. cephalonica.
d, e, f. Rounded and slightly notched needles
commonly found on most firs. When any
of these types makes up a majority of the
needles of a specimen, the needles are considered to be blunt as far as this key is
concerned.

2. Needles more than ¾ inch in length
    3. Needles green and lustrous above; no lines of stomates on upper
       surface of needles (when observed with a lens)
        4. Needles definitely pointed at tip
           5. Majority of needles especially on two-year old twigs
              at right angles to the twigs (see Fig. 5)
                6. Branchlets glabrous; vigorous shoots have needles
                   with only one point
                     7. Twigs deeply grooved (see Fig. 5a)
                                                 A. homolepis
                     (Japan) Zone 4
                     7. Twigs not deeply grooved
                        8. White lines clearly visible on the lower
                           surface of the needles; needles fre-
                         quently produced on all sides of twig
                                     A. cephalonica
                        (Greece) Zone 5
                        8. White lines only faintly visible on the
                         lower surface of the needles; needles
                         often curved and pointing directly up-
                         ward, not appearing radially arranged
                                        A. holophylla
                        (Manchuria, Korea) Zone 5
                6. Branchlets slightly pubescent; vigorous young
                   shoots may have needles with two sharp points
                   (see Fig. 4b) ....*A. firma*
                   (Japan) Zone 6
           5. Majority of needles not at right angles to twig (see
            Fig. 5)
               6. Needles less than 1½ inches long
                   7. One-year twigs glabrous.....*A. holophylla*
                     (Manchuria, Korea) Zone 5
                   7. One-year twigs pubescent......*A. religiosa*
                     (Mexico) Zone 9–10
               6. Needles 1½ to 2¼ inches long......*A. venusta*
                 (California) Zone 8
         4. Majority of needles blunt and rounded at tip or slightly
           notched at the tip (see Fig. 4d, e, f)

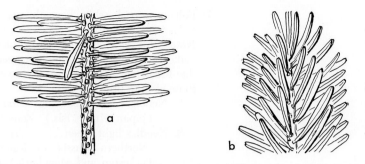

Figure 5. Needles mostly at right angles to twigs as in A. homolepsis, also showing longitudinal lines or grooves in twig.
b. Needles mostly directed towards the tip of twigs as in A. nordmanniana.

5. Needles, especially on two-year old twigs, mostly at right angles to the twigs
  6. Branchlets glabrous
    7. Foliage intensely white beneath; twigs deeply grooved (see Fig. 5a)

A. homolepis

      (Japan) Zone 4
    7. Foliage green beneath; twigs not deeply grooved

      (Central China) Zone 6 . .*A. chensiensis*
  6. Branchlets pubescent
    7. Branchlets slightly pubescent, one-year twigs often have faint grooves; needles on vigorous shoots frequently pointed needles up to 1½ inches long.............*A. firma*
      (Japan) Zone 6
    7. Branchlets densely pubescent, needles rarely more than 1 inch in length (Labra-dor to W. Virginia and Iowa) Zone 3

A. balsamea

      (Allegheny Mts., W. Virginia and Ten-nessee) Zone 4...............*A. fraseri*
      (These two are closely related and difficult to tell apart without cones or without a lens. The under surface of the needles of *A. fraseri* has 8 to 12 lines of stomates in each white band, while that of *A. balsamea* has only 4 to 8 lines in each white band.)
5. Majority of needles not at right angles but pointing toward the tips of the twigs (see Fig. 5b)
  6. Lower side of one-year twigs olive green

A. grandis

    (Vancouver to California and Montana) Zone 6
  6. One-year twigs not olive green

7. Foliage grayish white beneath; needles $\frac{1}{24}$ to $\frac{1}{16}$ inch in width
Note: this is a difficult measurement to make but the point is that the needles of the following two firs are narrower than those of most other species)
  8. Needles dark green. . *A. sachalinensis* (Japan, Kurile Isls.) Zone 2
  8. Needles light green. . . . .*A. sibirica* (Northern Russia to Kamchatka, Turkestan and Manchuria) Zone 2 (These two are difficult to tell apart without a lens. The undersurface of the needles of *A. sachalinensis* has 7 or 8 lines of stomates in each white band while that of *A. sibirica* has only 4 or 5 lines in each white band)

7. Foliage of one year shoots intensely white beneath; needles $\frac{1}{12}$ inch or more in width
  8. Winter buds resinous
    9. Needles mostly more than 1 inch long (1 to $2\frac{1}{4}$ inches) twigs usually grooved. . .*A. spectabilis* (Himalayas) Zone 7
    9. Needles mostly less than 1 inch long; twigs not grooved
      10. Branchlets gray pubescent *A. amabilis* (British Columbia to Oregon) Zone 5
      10. Branchlets brown pubescent. . . . .*A. veitchi* (Japan) Zone 3
  8. Winter buds not resinous
    9. Leaves closely arranged in two ranks like teeth in a comb (see fig. 3b). . . . .*A. alba* (Mountains of Central and Southern Europe) Zone 4
    9. Leaves not in two closely arranged ranks
      10. Needles of one-year twigs very white beneath, the upper ones directed forward and closely appressed to the twigs *A. nordmanniana* (Caucasus Mts. and Asia Minor) Zone 5

10. Needles of one-year twigs merely greenish white beneath, more or less spreading and with a V-shaped depression above, not closely appressed to the twigs

    (Asia Minor, Syria) Zone 5......A. cilicica (These two are difficult to tell apart without the cones. The Nordmann Fir is by far the more common of the two in this country)

3. Foliage dull grayish or bluish green above and below because there are stomatiferous lines on both upper and lower surfaces of the needles

(These can be seen with a lens)

    4. Needles flat in cross section (as in *Picea omorika*)

      5. One-year twigs glabrous

        6. Foliage bluish green................A. concolor (Colorado to California and New Mexico) Zone 4

        6. Foliage a bluish white......A. concolor violacea

      5. One-year twigs pubescent

        6. Twigs ashy gray—bark of trunk gray A. lasiocarpa

    (Alaska to New Mexico) Zone 3

        6. Twigs rusty brown

          7. Foliage bluish green A. procera (A. nobilis) (Washington to California) Zone 5

    4. Needles, at least some of them, quadrangular in cross section, similar to the cross section of those of *Picea glauca*) A. magnifica

(Oregon to California) Zone 5

Abies concolor	120'	Zone 4	White Fir

*HABIT: stiffly pyramidal, rather narrow, branches horizontal
*FOLIAGE: evergreen, bluish green, needlelike
HABITAT: western and southwestern United States
VARIETIES: *conica*—dwarf, pyramidal, slow growing
          violacea—leaves bluish white

One of the best of the firs for planting in northern gardens and thoroughly reliable as far north as Boston, it is noted for withstanding heat and drought better than most of the other firs. It also has the longest needles, and makes an excellent color contrast when planted in front of such evergreens as White Pine

The stiffly upright growths on this fir branch are the reddish flowers which
will eventually develop into cones. The staminate or pollen bearing flowers
are much smaller.

or hemlock. Under good conditions it should grow 1½ feet a year which is
fairly rapid for most evergreens. Because of its habit of growth and even though
the branching is horizontal, it forms a softer looking tree than does the Blue
Spruce, another frequently used conifer in landscape planting.

Abies cephalonica   90′   Zone 5   Greek Fir

*HABIT: stiffly pyramidal, branches horizontal
*FOLIAGE: evergreen, needlelike, dense
HABITAT: Greece
INTRODUCED: 1824
   This has proved one of the better firs in the Arnold Aboretum collection. It
branches right down to the ground, is very dense and vigorous with excellent light
green needles.

Abies firma   150′   Zone 5   Momi Fir

*HABIT: broadly pyramidal, stiff, branches horizontal
*FOLIAGE: evergreen, needlike, dense
HABITAT: Japan
INTRODUCED: 1861
   A good dense fir tree, more stiff in character than some of the others.

Abies homolepis   90′   Zone 4   Nikko Fir

*HABIT: stiffly pyramidal, branches horizontal
*FOLIAGE: evergreen, needlelike, dense
*HABITAT: Japan
INTRODUCED: 1861
   Another one of the best firs for ornamental planting. Easily distinguished
from other firs because of the horizontal decurrent lines along the one year twigs.

Dark green, vigorous—an excellent conifer for use in any landscape where it can be given plenty of room to grow naturally.

Abies koreana   50'   Zone 5   Korean Fir

*HABIT: stiffly pyramidal, horizontal branching
*FOLIAGE: evergreen, needlelike, dark green above and whitish beneath, dense
HABITAT: Korea
INTRODUCED: 1918

This tree grows very well but few trees in this country have reached their mature height. It grows more slowly than some of the others and might be the only one considered for small gardens because of this fact. It is stiff and formal but the whitish undersurface of the needles shows to good advantage.

Abies magnifica   200'   Zone 5   Red Fir

*HABIT: pyramidal, stiff, branches horizontal
*FOLIAGE: evergreen, needlike, dense
HABITAT: Oregon and California

This fir does not do well in situations where there is a great deal of soft-coal smoke in the atmosphere. Where it is hardy, especially on the West Coast, and the soil is rich, it grows into a fine specimen.

Abies pinsapo   75'   Zone 6   Spanish Fir

*HABIT: stiffly pyramidal, branching horizontal
*FOLIAGE: evergreen, needlelike, dense
HABITAT: Spain
INTRODUCED: 1837

This is a beautiful fir under perfect growing conditions.

Abies veitchi   75'   Zone 3   Veitch Fir

*HABIT: stiffly pyramidal, horizontal branching
*FOLIAGE: evergreen, needlelike, dark green above, whitish below, dense
HABITAT: central Japan
INTRODUCED: 1876.

A very fine fir, hardier than most, of special interest because of the interesting white undersurface of the needles.

Acacia baileyana   30'   Zone 10   Cootamundra Wattle

*FLOWERS: light yellow, feathery, ⅛" diameter in racemes 3" long
    TIME: January to March
HABIT: spreading
*FOLIAGE: steel blue, fine texture, leaflets running spirally around the twig, evergreen
*HABITAT: New South Wales

This short-lived tree needs good soil, and given that, proves to be a very attractive small tree of very fine texture and color. It grows very fast and is used to a considerable extent as a street tree in southern California.

The Golden yellow flowers of Acacia decurrens dealbata—a popular tree in
the deep South.

Acacia decurrens dealbata   50′   Zone 9   Silver Wattle

*FLOWERS: clear yellow, fragrant, profuse small flowers in small ball-like clusters
    TIME: March–April
HABIT: vigorous in growth, more or less spreading
*FOLIAGE: very graceful, finely divided, slightly blue to grayish in color, evergreen
HABITAT: Australia

This is the species best known to most gardeners in this country and in
England, for this is perhaps the hardiest of some 400 or more kinds. The small
balls of flowers are only about ¼″ in diameter and are conspicuous only because
of the many stamens in the flowers. It is very rapid in growth and is handsome
indeed, doing well in good soil. It might be the first to be considered of this large
group of exotic trees for the enterprising gardener who lives in the warmer parts
of the South. It is used considerably as a street tree, but like most members of
this genus it is short lived.

Acacia decurrens mollis   50′   Zone 10   Black Wattle

*FLOWERS: small light yellow
    TIME: June–July
HABIT: slender but attractive spreading branches
*FOLIAGE: yellowish when young, fine texture, dull green at maturity
HABITAT: Australia

This species does not require much water and grows quickly but is less
popular than the Silver Wattle and it should be used more.

Acacia longifolia floribunda   20′   Zone 10   Gossamer Sydney Acacia

*FLOWERS: whitish yellow, in spikes or balls 2¼″ long
   TIME: February and March
HABIT: spreading
*FOLIAGE: fine, evergreen
HABITAT: Australia
   Apparently adapted to dry situations and used as a street tree, but like most acacias, it is short lived.

Acacia pendula   25′   Zone 10   Weeping Boree Acacia

FLOWERS: none too prominent, yellow
*HABIT: branches pendulous
*FOLIAGE: fine texture, bluish gray
HABITAT: Queensland, New South Wales
   Valued chiefly for its pendulous habit and not especially for its flowers.

ACER

Those interested in finding shade trees that have proved excellent over a long period of years will find some of the best among the maples. Then too, if you are interested in something new, a shade tree that is neat and compact yet unusual and not much used, you will also find much to choose from among these fine trees. Varied in habit, in rate of growth, in size and leaf character, the maples should always be considered when one is selecting shade trees for street, highway or garden. Some may have their defects, some may not have bright colored flowers or brilliant fruits, but all recommended here have some particular characteristic which makes them outstanding trees for producing shade.

Maples are dense in habit with the exception of one or two recommended solely for growth in wooded areas. Few have conspicuous flowers, but the Red and Norway Maples are two notable exceptions. The fruits of all maples are winged samaras (a small nut with wings, attached usually in pairs), not too conspicuous, yet they are produced in quantity and are colorful in some species like *Acer ginnala*. The autumn color of the American and Asiatic types is a brilliant red or yellow, often both. Some grow to be mighty giants over 100 feet tall while others remain neat and compact at about 20 feet in height. Some are comparatively low and squat like the Japanese Maple, others are tall and columnar like the Sentry Maple and still others are widely rounded like the serviceable Norway Maple.

All maples apparently seem to grow in any good soil; some like the Box-Elder will thrive in the poor dry soils of the Great Plains area of the Midwest. During the growing season most have normally green leaves but some have variegated leaves, some have yellow leaves and some have red or purplish red leaves. They are not infested with any serious disease or insect pests but sometimes have their trouble. Lice on the branches, maple wilt and maple scorch take their toll of leaves when the weather conditions are just right, but usually these troubles do not occur frequently and for the most part can be overlooked. Few trees are more easily grown. The maples are a good group of trees and should be scrutinized carefully.

In order to assist in their general identification, the following grouping could be suggested but it must be stressed that leaves of all trees vary and identifying trees by the lobing of their leaves alone is not always accurate:

1. Leaves not lobed:
   Acer carpinifolium
   Acer tataricum

2. Leaves 3 lobed:
   Acer floridanum
   Acer ginnala
   Acer pensylvanicum
   Acer spicatum

3. Leaves 5 lobed with milky sap at petiole base when broken:
   Acer campestre
   Acer macrophyllum
   Acer platanoides

4. Leaves 5 lobed and no milky sap at petiole base when broken:
   Acer argutum
   Acer palmatum
   Acer pseudoplatanus
   Acer rubrum
   Acer saccharum

5. Leaves 7 (or more) lobed:
   Acer circinatum
   Acer palmatum sometimes and several of its varieties

6. Leaves compound:
   Acer griseum
   Acer mandshuricum
   Acer negundo
   Acer nikoense

Acer argutum   24'   Zone 5

HABIT: branches erect, rather narrow
FOLIAGE: leaves 5 lobed, dense
HABITAT: Japan
INTRODUCED: 1879

Another graceful tree and good for the small property. Since much emphasis is being placed on planting small properties, such trees as this certainly should be considered where small shade trees only are wanted.

Acer campestre   25'   Zone 4   Hedge Maple

*HABIT: rounded
FOLIAGE: dense
AUTUMN COLOR: yellowish
HABITAT: Europe and Western Asia
INTRODUCED: early colonial times

This maple is commonly used in Europe in clipped hedges because of its dense growth. It does not have the vivid autumn coloration of native species but as a clipped hedge or screen it is ideal. Several ornamental varieties have been found and named, chiefly displaying foliage variations, but not sufficiently meritorious to warrant growing them in preference to the species. From Long

Eleven kinds of maple leaves are portrayed here, each easily distinguishable
from the others.
Top row—A. pseudoplatanus, ginnala, campestre, saccharum.
Middle row—griseum, pensylvanicum, negundo.
Bottom row—saccharinum, rubrum, palmatum, platanoides.

Island southward, it makes a dependable screen plant requiring little attention.
It is one of the few maples (along with the Norway) which show a white milky
sap at the base of the leaf petioles when they are pulled off the twig.

Acer carpinifolium   30′   Zone 5   Hornbeam Maple
*HABIT: vase-shaped with many stems from the base
FOLIAGE: dense, bright green leaves (not lobed), similar in size and shape to that
  of the Hornbeam
AUTUMN COLOR: brownish yellow
HABITAT: Japan
INTRODUCED: 1881
    An interesting, clean growing small shade tree that has performed well in
Washington, D.C., as well as in the Arnold Arboretum. It should be added to the
limited group of small shade trees for small properties and may have merit as a
street tree because of its size.

Acer circinatum   25′   Zone 5   Vine Maple
FLOWERS: white and purple, small drooping clusters
  TIME: late April
FRUIT: winged keys or samaras, red
  EFFECTIVE: summer
*HABIT: wide spreading, with several branches from the base

*FOLIAGE: dense
*AUTUMN COLOR: red to orange
HABITAT: British Columbia to California

A native maple of the Pacific coast adapted for use in gardens because of its small, compact size and its ability to grow in partially shaded situations, especially under evergreen. It is somewhat similar in habit to *A. palmatum* except that its stems twist and turn in a most interesting manner, thus giving rise to its name. The wood is very tough—the Indians, according to legend, used the wood to make fish hooks.

| Acer floridanum | 50' | Zone 9 | Florida Maple |

*BARK: very pale gray
FOLIAGE: dense
HABIT: rounded
HABITAT: southeastern United States

Planted in some parts of northern Florida as a shade tree.

| Acer ginnala | 20' | Zone 2 | Amur Maple |

*FRUIT: winged keys or samaras usually red and conspicuous
    EFFECTIVE: summer
*HABIT: upright but rounded, branching dense
FOLIAGE: dense, fine texture
*AUTUMN COLOR: scarlet
HABITAT: central and northern China, Manchuria, Japan
INTRODUCED: about 1860

A dense shrub or small tree with comparatively small leaves about 3" long and extremely hardy. The fruits turn bright red in the summer while the leaves are still green, making an interesting color combination. The scarlet autumn color of the foliage is as brilliant as any of the maples. A good tree for specimen or for screening purposes, requiring practically no care.

| Acer griseum | 25' | Zone 5 | Paperbark Maple |

HABIT: rounded, rather open
*BARK: exfoliating in paper-thin strips
FOLIAGE: rather open, compound leaf, 3 leaflets
HABITAT: western China
INTRODUCED: 1901

Very difficult to propagate in quantity because the embryos in the seeds do not develop. Otherwise, it could easily be one of the most popular maples. The bark is cinnamon-brown and exfoliates in paper-thin strips similar to that of certain birches. This bark characteristic is easily noticeable from some distance away, making this tree of outstanding interest throughout the entire year. It is hoped that a reliable method can be found for propagating this plant on a large scale for it certainly merits wide use.

| Acer macrophyllum | 90' | Zone 6 | Bigleaf Maple |

FLOWERS: small, yellow, in pendulous clusters, 4–6" long, fragrant
    TIME: May

FRUIT: winged keys or samaras in pendulous clusters 4–6″ long
    EFFECTIVE: early fall
HABIT: round-headed
FOLIAGE: dense, leaves the largest of all maples 6–12″ in diameter, coarse
⁎AUTUMN COLOR: a good yellow
HABITAT: Pacific coast from Alaska to California

A very popular tree on the Pacific coast where it thrives. Its unusually large leaves make it an excellent shade tree, and turn a bright yellow to orange color in fall. Unfortunately it does not seem to do well in eastern North America.

Acer mandshuricum   30′   Zone 4   Manchurian Maple

HABIT: rounded head
FOLIAGE: rather open, leaves compound, petioles red
⁎AUTUMN COLOR: red to scarlet
HABITAT: Manchuria, Korea
INTRODUCED: 1904

A close relative of the Box-Elder, this small tree also grows rapidly, has wide spreading branches and the red petioles afford a pleasing color contrast with the dark green color of the leaves. A good small shade tree.

Acer negundo   60′   Zone 2   Box-Elder

HABIT: wide-spreading, rather open
FOLIAGE: open, leaves compound, leaflets 3–5
HABITAT: eastern and central North America
VARIETIES: *variegatum*—leaves with broad white margin, one of the most con-
        spicuous of variegated leaved trees—Silver Leaf Box-Elder
        aureo-variegatum—leaves spotted yellow—Goldspot Box-Elder
        auratum—leaves yellow—Yellow Leaf Box-Elder
        aureo-marginatum—leaves bordered yellow—Goldedge Box-Elder

A very rapid growing maple and recommended only for certain areas of the Midwest where drought and cold make it impossible to grow many other better ornamental trees. In the East the Box-Elder is considered a weed for it quickly seeds itself everywhere. It is very weak-wooded and splits easily in storms. It has no autumn color. The only excuse for using it at all in the East, where much better trees are available, is that it can be used for a very quick (and temporary!) deciduous screen. Also it will withstand dry situations where nothing else but sumacs, Siberian Elm and the Tree of Heaven will grow.

In the West, it is used considerably in shelter belts, especially as a temporary quick-growing screen to protect slower-growing but longer-lived trees in becoming permanently established. The only reason for mentioning the variegated forms is to suggest something a little more colorful and unusual for those areas of drought and cold where few ornamental trees will withstand the cold winters or the terrifically hot, dry summers. For places other than the Great Plains areas and the southwest United States, the Box-Elder might well be omitted from any serious consideration.

Acer nikoense   45′   Zone 5   Nikko Maple

⁎HABIT: round-topped
FOLIAGE: leaves compound, 3 leaflets, rather open

*AUTUMN COLOR: brilliant red or purple
HABITAT: Japan, central China
INTRODUCED: 1881

This is not a fast-growing maple, but it is beautiful at most seasons and so is of interest for planting on the smaller properties.

Acer palmatum   20'   Zone 5   Japanese Maple

*HABIT: rounded and often moundlike
*FOLIAGE: dense, green to red, leaves 5–9 lobed and up to 4" in width
*AUTUMN COLOR: scarlet
HABITAT: Korea, Japan
INTRODUCED: 1820

VARIETIES: *atropurpureum*—leaves mostly 7 lobed, deep red to almost purple throughout the entire growing season. One of the best varieties for red colored foliage—Bloodleaf Japanese Maple.

dissectum—leaves divided almost to the base in 5–9 lobes with each lobe deeply cut, green in color—Threadleaf Japanese Maple.

elegans—foliage green throughout most of the growing season.

ornatum—leaves with extremely deeply cut lobes, red throughout the early summer later turning a bronze green; plant with a somewhat weeping habit, an excellent ornamental specimen—Spiderleaf Japanese Maple

"Oshiu-beni"—leaves with 9 deeply cut lobes, red in spring but a normal green by early summer.

sanguineum—leaves usually smaller than some of the above varieties with about 7 none-too-deeply cut lobes, red throughout the growing season, though sometimes it may turn bronze by mid-summer—Scarlet Japanese Maple.

This is a variable species of shrubs or small trees, very popular in Japan and grown to a considerable extent in this country as well. A Japanese nursery firm listed over twenty-five varieties a few years ago as the "best" of a large number. More recently an American nursery has listed at least fifteen varieties. The leaves have 5–9 lobes, those of some varieties more deeply cut than others, with colors ranging from green to dark red. The nomenclature in the commercial nurseries both here and in Japan is pretty much confused. Some specimens have the desirable trait of holding their deep red color all summer long; others that have bright red young leaves early in the spring, disappointingly turn green in the summer. Some make poor specimens as they grow older because of poor understock on which named varieties are grafted. Then too, many nurseries adopt the questionable practice of growing these from seed and "selecting" the best seedling forms, often giving them accredited varietal names for clons which should be only asexually propagated. This of course only adds to the confusion since many of the seedling forms do not have all the traits of the varieties after which they are named.

These low shrubby maples often grow into small trees and are best used as specimen plants. They should not be jammed into the shrub border. Those with leaves variegated pink, white, yellow, etc., are not to be recommended since they are hard to grow properly.

Acer pensylvanicum   36′   Zone 3   Striped Maple or Moosewood

HABIT: open, indefinite
*BARK: striped white
FOLIAGE: open, leaves large, coarse
*AUTUMN COLOR: yellow
HABITAT: eastern North America
VARIETY: *erythrocladum*—a rare but most unusual type with twigs in winter
colored a brilliant red, almost as brilliant as some of the red stemmed
dogwoods. Originated about 1904.

A tree which does best in partially shaded woods, of value chiefly for its
striped bark of trunk and branches in the winter time. Its open habit of growth,
large and coarse leaves, prevent it from having much appeal as a lawn specimen.
But, on the edge of woodlands or in naturalized plantings it can add a touch of
brightness to what might otherwise be a uniformly colored planting. Because it
is native it should take preference over species which are somewhat similar such
as *A. davidi, capilipes, crataegifolium* and *rufinerve*.

Acer platanoides   90′   Zone 3   Norway Maple

*FLOWERS: small, yellow, appearing in conspicuous clusters before the leaves
TIME: late April
*HABIT: rounded
FOLIAGE: very dense, leaves lobed and bright green
*AUTUMN COLOR: bright yellow
HABITAT: Europe, Caucausus
INTRODUCED: early colonial times
VARIETIES: *columnare*—columnar habit, upright branches—Columnar Norway
Maple
"Crimson King"—leaves a deep purplish red throughout entire spring
and summer and hence superior to var. *schwedleri*.
erectum—narrow pyramidal in outline—Erect Norway Maple
globosum—densely globose in habit—Globe Norway Maple
laciniatum—upright columnar habit, tips of leaf lobes turned up giving
the maple its common name—Eagle Claw Maple
schwedleri—leaves purplish red when young but turning green by
early summer. This has been widely planted in the past but will
probably now be superseded by the much better variety "Crimson
King" which keeps its good red foliage color throughout the entire
growing season, whereas Schwelder's variety loses most of its red
color by early summer—Schwedler Maple

Although a native of Europe, the Norway Maple has become one of the
most commonly planted street and shade trees in the eastern United States. Its
widely rounded habit, and dense foliage make it capable of giving dense shade, in
fact so much so that it is very difficult to grow anything underneath it. The feeding roots are very close to the surface, making the growing of other plants near
it additionally hazardous.

In the spring its yellow flowers appear before the leaves, making the tree
a mass of yellow visible from a mile away. In the fall the leaves turn a clear

yellow, in fact it is one of the best of all shade trees for its yellow autumn coloration.

Because it has been grown for so long, over twenty varieties have been named. The columnar forms are being widely used now in the planting of narrow streets. Schwedler's Maple, with the purplish red leaves in the spring and early summer, has been a widely used favorite, but I think its popularity is on the wane for "Crimson King," a new variety, holds its deep reddish color all summer long. It is one of the few maples, along with the Hedge Maple to show a white milky sap at the base of the leaf petiole when it is pulled from the twig.

Finally, it can be considered a quick screen for it grows more rapidly than other maples, although not as fast as the Siberian Elm or Lombardy Poplar. It has more ornamental and lasting qualities than either.

Acer pseudoplatanus   90′   Zone 5   Sycamore Maple

FRUIT: winged keys or samaras in clusters 5″ long
　　EFFECTIVE: summer
HABIT: wide spreading
FOLIAGE: dense, leaves large and lobed, often coarse
HABITAT: Europe, western Asia
INTRODUCED: early colonial times
VARIETIES: *erythrocarpum*—leaves smaller and lustrous, fruits bright red—Scarlet
　　　　　Fruit Sycamore Maple
　　　　　purpureum—leaves purple on the underside—Purple-Leaf Sycamore
　　　　　Maple
　　　　　worleei—leaves deep yellow, almost orange-yellow when young—
　　　　　Yellow Sycamore Maple

A common old-world tree widely cultivated for centuries, has earned a place for itself in North America. It has no autumn color and so cannot compete with American and Asiatic species in this respect. However, it is one of the best of all trees for withstanding the salt-laden blasts of wind in seashore gardens, where it is highly respected for this peculiar characteristic. Its 5-inch long clusters of fruit are interesting and conspicuous for a greater part of the summer. This is especially true in the red fruited variety *erythrocarpum*. *Acer heldreichi* is similar to the Sycamore Maple with slightly deeper lobed leaves, but is not superior to it as far as I can tell from specimens growing in the Arnold Arboretum. There is a variety in the nurseries of this country and Europe being called "Brilliantissima" the foliage of which is a bright yellow in the early spring, making it most conspicuous.

Acer rubrum   120′   Zone 3   Red or Swamp Maple

*FLOWERS: red, very small but profuse
　　TIME: early April
*FRUIT: winged keys or samaras, bright red
　　EFFECTIVE: late spring
HABIT: round head but sometimes pyramidal or even elliptical when young
FOLIAGE: dense
*AUTUMN COLOR: brilliant red

HABITAT: eastern and central North America

VARIETIES: *columnare*—densely upright in habit, not as narrow as *A. saccharum monumentale* or *A. platanoides columnare,* but an excellent, fast-growing upright type, sometimes densely pyramidal in outline at maturity—Columnar Red Maple

schlesingeri—interesting in that it colors a full month before the species in the fall, otherwise identical with the species. We have grafted this variety on seedlings of some red maples and left some of the shoot of the understock living as well as the scion material to test this early autumn coloring characteristic. Invariably the scion material colors weeks before the shoot from the understock even though both branches are nourished by the same roots.

The Red Maple is commonly seen in low and swampy areas, especially evident in the early spring since its myriads of small red flowers, each inconspicuous in its own right, are produced in such large numbers and bloom so early that they are noticeable for some distance. In many areas, the bloom of the Red Maple is one of the first visible evidences of spring for many people, just as the brilliant fall coloration is one of the first signs of approaching autumn. One reason why the Red Maple colors before most other trees in the fall is that it is native in swamps or low spots where the frosts of fall are felt first. A fast-growing tree, somewhat weak wooded, it is superior to the Silver Maple as a lawn tree, but in areas where snow or ice storms are common it can be expected to break up more easily than Sugar Maples and most oaks.

Acer saccharum 120′ Zone 3 Sugar Maple

HABIT: oval; mature specimens with rounded head
FOLIAGE: dense, leaves lobed
*AUTUMN COLOR: yellow to orange and red
HABITAT: eastern North America
VARIETY: *monumentale*—columnar, dense, but rather slow in rate of growth when compared with columnar varieties of *A. rubrum* and *A. platanoides*—Sentry Maple

Widely grown throughout the eastern part of North America, the Sugar Maple (or Rock Maple as it is sometimes called) is one of the best and most common of our native shade trees. One of the largest, among the measured trees at least, is in West Virginia near Morgantown. It is 110′ tall, has a spread of 75′ and a trunk circumference of 17′6″ at breast height. So they do grow into stately specimens! But even while young they make excellent shade trees requiring very little attention. The sap from these trees, when boiled down sufficiently, yields maple syrup. Every country lad in New England is familiar with the general process of "tapping" the trees in early spring, collecting and boiling the sap to make maple syrup. Most nursery trees are grown from seed, and mature trees do show considerable variation in general outline, some being rounded, others being densely pyramidal or even oval. The Sugar Maple in its fiery red and yellow fall garb is perhaps one of America's most colorful sights. It is more sturdy and breaks up much less in snow, ice and wind storms than does the more brittle Norway Maple.

Acer spicatum   25′   Zone 2   Mountain Maple

*FRUIT: winged samaras bright red
    EFFECTIVE: summer
FOLIAGE: rather open and coarse
*AUTUMN COLOR: orange and scarlet
HABITAT: Labrador to Saskatchewan, south to Georgia and Iowa

    Another extremely hardy maple, found over a wide area of North America, no better than other shrubby maples here suggested but of value for its hardiness and ability to grow in partial shade. This tree requires practically no attention.

Acer tataricum   30′   Zone 4   Tatarian Maple

*FRUIT: keys or winged samaras, red
    EFFECTIVE: summer
HABIT: upright, elliptical
FOLIAGE: dense, fine, bright green
*AUTUMN COLOR: red to yellow
HABITAT: Europe, western Asia
INTRODUCED: 1759

    Another small tree for street planting, well shaped and in need of very little attention. It is perfectly hardy in New England and is grown readily from its profuse seed by commercial nurserymen.

AESCULUS

    The horse-chestnuts and buckeyes as a group have been greatly over-planted in North America. *Aesculus hippocastanum* was brought over to this country by the earliest colonial settlers (possibly some small boy kept it in his pocket, as boys do the world over, when he sailed for the new land) and it has been planted ever since. It is definitely coarse in foliage texture, flower and fruit, and is now considered a "dirty" tree in that it is always dropping something—twigs, flowers, fruits and leaves. Its two weeks of bloom is the only time it is interesting, and even these flowers are large and coarse. A leaf scorch often seriously disfigures *A. hippocastanum* but not *A. glabra* in late summer. In any event none in this genus should be considered for the small property. If and when they are planted it should be where they could be observed several hundred feet away as in large public areas. They make poor street trees for the above mentioned reasons.

x Aesculus carnea brioti   75′   Zone 3   Ruby Horse-chestnut

*FLOWERS: bright scarlet in 6–8″ upright panicles
    TIME: mid-May
HABIT: rounded head, pyramidal when young
FOLIAGE: coarse but more resistant to rust than *A. hippocastanum,* palmately
      compound, 5 leaflets
HYBRID ORIGIN: *A. hippocastanum* x *A. pavia*
ORIGINATED: 1858

    The only difference between this variety and the species (which is widely used) is that in this variety the flowers are slightly larger and a bright scarlet color, while the flowers of the species are more flesh colored. However, since the species is a tetraploid it comes remarkably true from seed. Very conspicuous in flower—but it must be kept in mind that, like all horse-chestnuts, it has coarse foliage, no autumn color, and the fruits are large and coarse creating a nuisance on the ground where they fall.

Aesculus glabra   30′   Zone 3   Ohio Buckeye

FLOWERS: small, greenish yellow in upright panicles 6″ high
    TIME: mid-May
HABIT: rounded head
FOLIAGE: coarse, palmately compound, 5 leaflets
*AUTUMN COLOR: brilliant orange
HABITAT: central United States

    Merely listed here because it is the only one of the horse-chestnuts with a good autumn color. Its flowers are the least desirable of any, its foliage and fruits no better than those of *Aesculus hippocastanum*. Seldom do we have space to plant a tree for autumn color alone and unless the space is available, this tree should be overlooked entirely.

Aesculus hippocastanum baumanni   75′   Zone 3   Baumann Horse-chestnut

*FLOWERS: double flowers ¾″ in diameter, white, in 12″ upright spikes
    TIME: mid-May
HABIT: elliptical when young, massive and rounded at maturity
FOLIAGE: coarse, palmately compound, 5–7 leaflets
ORIGIN: as a sport about 1822 in Switzerland
INTRODUCED: 1838

    The Common Horse-chestnut has been widely used as a street tree and as a specimen in Europe (where it is native) and in America as well. It grows to be a stately tree and is covered with foot-long, upright panicles of conspicuous flowers. Often up to 100 feet in height, it is easily grown and easily propagated from seed. However, it has earned a bad reputation in most places. Its wood is rather weak and its massive branches, broken off by winds, afford excellent spots for infection by rotting fungi, which eventually cause serious damage. Its large compound leaves are coarse in texture, have no autumn color, and in most places are susceptible to a rust disease that seriously disfigures them the latter part of the summer. The fruits (nuts) are large and coarse, are profusely borne, and have no ornamental or economic interest whatsoever (except to small boys who like to collect them) and result in a hazard on street, walk or lawn, wherever they fall. Actually there are many trees superior to the horse-chestnut and these should be used in its place.

    If a horse-chestnut must be used, the Baumann Horse-chestnut should be selected, for it has double flowers and no fruits. Being double, the flowers naturally last longer than do the single flowers of the species. In other ways it is not superior to the species, but the absence of the fruit is quite a point is its favor.

Aesculus octandra   90′   Zone 3   Yellow Buckeye

FLOWERS: yellow in 6″ upright panicles
    TIME: mid-May

HABIT: round headed

FOLIAGE: coarse, palmately compound, 5 leaflets

HABITAT: southeastern United States

Of no particular merit when compared with *Aesculus carnea briotti* but it is the best of the native American horse-chestnuts and might be used as an ornamental tree within the limits of its habitat.

Ailanthus altissima erythrocarpa 60′ Zone 4 Red Fruited Tree of Heaven

FLOWERS: small, yellow, in large pyramidal clusters

TIME: late June

*FRUITS: sexes separate, female has red keys, somewhat similar to those of Maples

EFFECTIVE: August to November

HABIT: rounded but open, often giving very little shade

FOLIAGE: open, coarse

HABITAT: China

INTRODUCED: 1784

No matter where you go in a city, in Boston, New York, Chicago, Washington, or anyone of many other cities in this country or abroad, there is one interesting tree that is continually cropping up in the most unexpected places. It can grow between cement blocks; it seems to thrive on nothing but ashes; it will breathe in air laden with soot, gas and smoke, yet produce an abundance of green foliage; it apparently likes the toughest and most trying growing conditions it can find. This is the Tree of Heaven, a native of northern China which grows better under city conditions in this country than any other tree, native or exotic.

It was first brought to England by Peter Collinson in 1751, and reached the United States late in the same century. At one time it was highly recommended for city planting in this country (and still is in some places) so that it has become widely distributed here in America. It is easy to propagate, either by seeds or root cuttings, and because of its very vigorous growth, has made itself at home in many out-of-the-way places. The large compound alternate leaves can be distinguished from those of the sumacs, because the leaflets have a small point at the base of each near the petiole.

One of the unusual things about this tenacious tree is its fruiting habits. The sexes are separate, that is, the staminate, or pollen-bearing flowers and the pistillate, or fruiting flowers occur on separate trees. The flowers themselves are comparatively small, greenish yellow in color, and borne in large terminal clusters that are very conspicuous. Occasionally there are trees which have both male and female flowers on the same plant, but this is the exception rather than the rule. The staminate or male flowers, when fully open, give off a vile smell, and for this reason the male plant should not be propagated or used in any way.

The fruits produced by the pistillate or female plant are keys somewhat similar to the fruits of the maple except that the seed is in the center of the wing. These wings are slightly twisted at both ends, much like an airplane propeller. When the keys fall off the plant, they whirl around in the air, and if there is any breeze at all they are frequently carried quite a distance before they finally come to rest on the ground. Such seeds insure the dissemination of the tree. They mature about the last of the summer and if collected and dried will sprout readily when sown in a seed flat. The seeds do not require fertilization in order to mature, but if not fertilized they cannot germinate. This is another excellent reason for not using the male plant. The tree is actually becoming a pest in many places and the fewer viable seeds produced, the less the plant will spread. Hence only fruiting plants should be propagated vegetatively by root cuttings.

From an ornamental standpoint, there are four things of importance about this tree, The first, and that for which it is primarily used, is of course its ability to withstand seemingly unfavorable conditions. It grows in wet or dry soil, with apparent disregard for slight changes in soil acidity and other items about which so many of our valued ornamental trees are very particular. It is not susceptible to any serious disease or insect pest, a noble quality particularly for a tree in the city where care is often sadly neglected. Still another rugged characteristic has become apparent as a result of recent hurricanes; the Tree of Heaven can withstand submergence in salt water. I have seen it at Newport, Rhode Island, within about a hundred feet of the ocean in normal times when the hurricane tides covered their roots with sea water for days, yet they sent out normal leaves the following spring and altogether showed little effect of the trying ducking they received, a ducking which all too frequently proved disastrous for many other nearby plants.

In addition to its adaptability, a second important feature is that it does have a well rounded form when several years old. Furthermore, it can be used to create semi-tropical effects in gardens, for if the saplings are allowed to grow about ten feet high and then cut to the ground ever so often, they sprout up vigorously from the base and produce an unbelievable luxuriance of foliage in one year. Finally, the fruits of the female tree are a bright reddish color in the late summer, and lend considerable interest at that time of year—before most other trees bear colored fruits and before the foliage of other trees begins to take on vivid hues in the fall.

On the other hand, this tree should not be recommended for general landscape use. For one thing, its vigorous growth is against it. Because it grows so fast, often several feet a year, the wood is light and weak, readily splitting and breaking in heavy windstorms or when weighted down with snow and ice in the winter. There is nothing particularly beautiful about the foliage. Large compound leaves, like those of the Tree of Heaven, do not have "fine texture." The putrid odor of the male flowers make it objectionable anywhere under any conditions. When both sexes are present, viable seeds are scattered and soon sprout everywhere, making the tree a pest all over the garden. In fact, it is said that there was once a city ordinance in Washington which prohibited the planting of the Tree of Heaven anywhere within the city limits.

Although this strange tree does have its uses, it is practically a weed at present. In the suburbs of large cities, where good garden soil and intelligent care are available and one can grow many different kinds of trees, there is little room for the Ailanthus. But in the crowded streets and alleys of the large cities, in unattractive backyards where nothing else will grow, on city dumps and fill-in areas, in a thousand and one places where "civilization" has encroached upon nature to the extent of nearly eliminating plants—there grows the Tree of Heaven. Its green leaves and bright-colored fruits, its vigorous growth and wide branches seem to be a living proof that nature can find some tree to grow in even the poorest soil. Many a city dweller is unconsciously grateful to the little known plant collector who brought this hardy tree from China.

The hardy form of the Silk Tree, (Albizzia julibrissin rosea) has been growing in the Arnold Arboretum, where it was first introduced, since 1918.

Albizzia julibrissin   36′   Zone 7   Silk Tree

*FLOWER: prominent because of light pink stamens in rounded heads
    TIME: summer
HABIT: flat-topped, spreading, often several trunks
*FOLIAGE: very fine, compound leaves, graceful
HABITAT: Persia to central China
INTRODUCED: 1745
VARIETY: *rosea*—stamens deeper pink color, tree smaller, hardier (Zone 5), introduced by the Arnold Arboretum in 1918 from Korea. One tree has lived out-of-doors ever since, with hardy offspring.—Hardy Silk Tree

This tree of exceedingly dainty foliage and flowers is now threatened in the South with a serious wilt disease which kills the tree. This fungus occurs in the soil and infests the tree through the roots. Many clons are being tried and some have been found to be very resistant to the disease. Fortunately it has not reached trees grown north of Philadelphia and may not affect trees in the northern states at all. The hardy variety is probably like the species in that it is difficult to get established at first. Since vegetative growth is made late in the season it can be killed somewhat during very cold winters.

Although it can be grown on many soils, we have found that it does well on poor, dry, gravelly soils and so has an important use.

Being a legume, the seed is borne in small flat pods. The flowers are conspicuous, not because of petals (which are insignificant) but because of inch-long pink colored stamens, borne in ball-like clusters. The plant has the very desirable trait of opening its flowers consecutively throughout the summer months. The plants growing in Boston start to bloom about July 15th and are continuously in bloom until early September—a long flowering period which cannot be matched by any other northern ornamental tree. The leaves fall at the first frost without changing color.

A splendid ornamental tree, very much worth experimenting with in the North (hardy variety only) until just the right soil and winter protection are found so that it will live over the first few winters and become a sizeable plant. The tree blooms early in life, sometimes when the seedlings are only two to three years old. Propagation is easily accomplished by 3-inch root cuttings made in very early spring, using roots that are ⅓-inch or more in diameter. Smaller roots do not root nearly as well.

ALNUS

Most of the alders have little to recommend them for garden use. They have no special autumn color, no interesting fruits. It is true that the flower catkins are present all winter, but so are those of the birches. They are mostly short-lived trees, with several insects that thrive on them, especially the tent caterpillar.

However, they are well adapted to growing in moist or wet soils and are recommended here solely for this purpose. Where better soils are available, other trees with more ornamental possibilities than the alders should be grown.

Alnus cordata   45′   Zone 5   Italian Alder

HABIT: round head
FOLIAGE: dense, glossy, open
HABITAT: Italy, Corsica
INTRODUCED: 1820
This is considered one of the handsomest of the alders.

Alnus glutinosa   75′   Zone 3   European Alder

HABIT: ovoid to oblong head
FOLIAGE: dark green, leaves fall off green late in the season
HABITAT: Europe to Siberia
INTRODUCED: colonial times
VARIETY: *laciniata*—leaves deeply lobed, fine texture—Cutleaf European Alder
There is not much to recommend this for garden or street use except its adaptability to wet soil conditions. Where it is not needed for this specific purpose, better trees might well be substituted.

Alnus incana   60′   Zone 2   Speckled Alder

HABIT: round head
FOLIAGE: dense, dark green leaves which fall off in the fall while still green
HABITAT: Europe, North America

One of the hardiest of the alders, often shrubby, usually found growing in moist or wet spots. It is suitable for planting in such situations where other trees will not grow. However, in good soils other more ornamental trees might be selected.

Alnus rubra   60′   Zone 4   Red Alder

HABIT: pyramidal
FOLIAGE: dense, dark green
HABITAT: Pacific coast of North America
VARIETY: *pinnatisecta*—leaves deeply lobed, making the foliage of very fine
           texture—Cutleaf Red Alder
A moisture-loving tree for planting on the Pacific Coast. It is very susceptible to attacks of the tent caterpillar.

Amelanchier canadensis   60′   Zone 4   Shadblow Serviceberry
or Downy Serviceberry

*FLOWERS: white, small nodding racemes
    TIME: late April
FRUIT: maroon-purple, berrylike, edible
    EFFECTIVE: early summer
HABIT: upright, often narrow
FOLIAGE: young foilage grayish, open
*AUTUMN COLOR: yellow to red
HABITAT: eastern United States
The tallest of the Amelanchiers, this is admired by many because of the grayish young foliage as it first unfurls in the spring.

x Amelanchier grandiflora   25′   Zone 4   Apple Serviceberry

*FLOWERS: pure white, 1¼″ diameter
    TIME: early May
FRUIT: red to black, berrylike, edible
    EFFECTIVE: early summer
HABIT: wide spreading branches
BARK: light gray
FOLIAGE: dense
*AUTUMN COLOR: yellow to orange
HYBRID ORIGIN: *A. canadensis x A. laevis*
ORIGINATED: 1870
This tree is of interest because it has larger flowers than any of the other serviceberries and occasionally the flower buds and the petals at first are tinged pink. The petals quickly fade white, however. I have seen the variety at one time named *rubescens*, and although the light pink color is very definitely there when the flowers first open, it lasts for such a short time—merely a day or two—that it seems wasted effort to propagate the plant, for in all other ways it is identical with the species. This Apple Serviceberry has been considered by some to be the best of all the native species in this genus.

Amelanchier laevis   36'   Zone 4   Allegany Serviceberry

*FLOWERS: white, small, drooping racemes
FRUIT: red, berrylike
  EFFECTIVE: July
HABIT: spreading branches, often shrubby
*BARK: light gray, smooth
FOLIAGE: young leaves purplish
*AUTUMN COLOR: yellow to red
HABITAT: eastern North America

Not as tall as *A. canadensis* but the flowers are about the same size. Only mentioned with the others because this species is native and widely distributed and makes just as good a small tree as the others. The winter bark of the trunk is especially distinctive.

Aralia elata   45'   Zone 3   Japanese Angelica-tree

*FOWERS: small, white flowers in large pyramidal spikes, sometimes 18" tall
  TIME: August
FRUIT: small black berries
  EFFECTIVE: early fall, but quickly eaten by birds
HABIT: wide spreading, often with several trunks, open
FOLIAGE: dark glossy green, compound leaves up to 2½' long, very coarse, open
AUTUMN COLOR: reddish orange
HABITAT: northeastern Asia
INTRODUCED: 1830

The Devil's Walking Stick, as it is often called, is a peculiar, exotic looking plant, decidedly out of place in most small gardens. It is a spindly growing shrub or small tree, often suckering from the base, the main stems having sharp triangular thorns and large compound leaves sometimes 2½' long that are usually clustered around the ends of the stems. The large feathery spikes of small flowers are produced above the rather horizontal leaves so that they are conspicuous from all sides, and are followed by small black berries which quickly fall in the early autumn.

An unusual tree, conspicuous at all seasons and very difficult to use properly. It grows fairly well in almost any good soil. It is recommended in preference to *A. spinosa* merely because it is the hardiest member of this thorny genus. All do well under city conditions.

Araucaria araucana   90'   Zone 7   Monkey-puzzle Tree

*HABIT: open, whorled branches, unique appearance but producing poor shade
*FOLIAGE: evergreen, leaves sharply pointed scalelike, open
HABITAT: Chile
INTRODUCED: 1795

Not a desirable specimen because of its weird twisted branches, but nevertheless planted because it is the hardiest one of this genus. The ropelike branches twist in various ways, forming an ungainly mass of foliage giving rise to its common name.

The Monkey-puzzle Tree, always a very conspicuous tree.

Araucaria excelsa   100′   Zone 10   Norfolk Island Pine

*HABIT: pyramidal, open, horizontal branches, producing poor shade
*FOLIAGE: evergreen, leaves sharply pointed and scalelike, open
HABITAT: Norfolk Islands

    Another picturesque member of this genus, used only to give unusual effects in the warmest parts of the country. Widely grown in greenhouses, however, as a foliage pot plant.

Arbutus menziesi   75′   Zone 7   Pacific Madrone

*FLOWERS: whitish, small (like those of *Vaccinium*) in pyramidal clusters 3–9″
      tall and 6″ broad
  TIME: May
*FRUIT: red to orange colored berries
  EFFECTIVE: fall and winter
HABIT: open, often with picturesque shape
*BARK: red to cinnamon—older bark peeling off
*FOLIAGE: leaves evergreen 2–6″ long, dark glossy green
HABITAT: British Columbia to California

    An excellent broad-leaved evergreen tree, considered by some of the English gardeners as one of the most beautiful of broad-leaved evergreens. It is certainly not used enough in its native country, one reason being that it is very difficult to transplant, and seedlings not over 18″ tall are about the safest to use and should be put in a permanent growing place. Secondly, it has the bad reputation of always dropping something, leaves, flowers, fruit or bark, throughout the entire year. This can prove disconcerting especially on a well-kept lawn.

The Strawberry Tree (Arbutus unedo) does well on the Pacific Coast.

However, if it is used in the flower border or shrub border, its untidy habits are not noticeable. Its beautiful spring flowers, conspicuous orange colored fruits and cinnamon colored bark, and rich, broad evergreen leaves make it an excellent specimen nevertheless. Unfortunately, like a great many other things, it does not do well in the East, but on the Pacific Coast, gardeners would do well to hunt situations where it could be grown and shown off to best advantage. Not the least of its attributes is its ability to grow in poor dry soils.

Arbutus unedo   10–30′   Zone 8   Strawberry Tree

*FLOWERS: small, white
    TIME: October to December
*FRUIT: strawberrylike, brilliant orange-red berries ¾″ diameter
    EFFECTIVE: October to December
HABIT: with one or several trunks
*BARK: dark, cracking open on larger stems showing the bright red inner bark
*FOLIAGE: evergreen, leaves to 4″ long, lustrous
HABITAT: southwestern Europe
INTRODUCED: long in cultivation
    An interesting, slow-growing shrub or tree, with small flowers turning into red strawberrylike fruits at once which may remain on the tree for months. The dark brown bark cracks open to show the bright red inner bark of the larger stems. It should not be planted in alkaline soils.

Asimina triloba   35'   Zone 5   Pawpaw

FLOWERS: purple, cupshaped, 2" diameter
   TIME: late May
FRUIT: fleshy, yellow to brown pods, 2–3" long, edible
   EFFECTIVE: early fall
HABIT: erect
FOLIAGE: dense, coarse, leaves drooping and 6–12" long
*AUTUMN COLOR: yellow
HABITAT: eastern United States

This tree is rarely seen in cultivation. Its flowers are unique but not conspicuous. It likes good rich soil. The most interesting ornamental characteristic is its drooping leaves, which though large, are always moving in the slightest breeze. The large edible fruits were familiar to and hunted by the earliest American settlers.

Bauhinia variegata   20'   Zone 10   Buddhist Bauhinia

*FLOWERS: lavender to purple, like small orchids, flowers few together in leaf axils
   TIME: winter and spring
FOLIAGE: two lobed or parted leaves
HABITAT: India, Burma

Widely planted in southern Florida and valued chiefly for its orchidlike flowers, partially without foliage in late winter. It is also frequently called Mountain Ebony or Orchid Tree.

BETULA

In general the birches are valued as ornamentals for their interesting bark (white, black, red or yellow), for their early flowers or catkins which, when they enlarge and drop their pollen are one of the first signs of spring, and for their beautiful yellow autumn color. Most are short lived and the wood is easily susceptible to attacks from fungus. The Gray Birch (*Betula populifolia*) has slender trunks that often are weighed down to the ground with ice and snow, yet are resilient enough to spring back in place in the spring. The foliage of some is very susceptible to serious attacks of the birch leaf miner and spraying for these pests must be done at just the right time or the foliage is materially disfigured for the rest of the growing season. Then too, they "bleed" profusely when pruned in the spring so that pruning should be done at other times of the year. The Paper Birch is probably one of the best and most satisfactory of this group as an ornamental.

Betula albo-sinensis   90'   Zone 5   Chinese Paper Birch

HABIT: rounded
FOLIAGE: open
*AUTUMN COLOR: yellow
*BARK: bright orange to orange red, exfoliating
HABITAT: central and western China

INTRODUCED: 1910

Not common in America but of special interest because of its bright orange colored bark, especially noticeable in the winter.

Betula davurica   60′   Zone 4   Dahurian Birch

HABIT: wide spreading branches
*BARK: curling, reddish brown, exfoliating
FOLIAGE: open
*AUTUMN COLOR: yellow
HABITAT: northeastern Asia
INTRODUCED: 1883

Somewhat similar to the River Birch, but in the Arnold Arboretum this species grows remarkably well on comparatively gravelly hillside. Hence it might have merit in situations where the River Birch would not grow. The bark is especially interesting in that it peels or flakes off in regular pieces an inch or so square.

Betula lenta   75′   Zone 3   Sweet Birch

*HABIT: pyramidal and dense while young, round topped at maturity
*BARK: reddish brown to black, cherrylike
FOLIAGE: dense
*AUTUMN COLOR: golden yellow
HABITAT: eastern United States

Although common in the eastern part of the country, this makes an excellent specimen. Its shape, autumn color and cherrylike bark are all in its favor. It is truly handsome, probably the best of all the birches for fall color. The young bark and twigs have an agreeable aromatic taste when chewed, giving rise to the common name.

Betula mandshurica szechuanica   60′   Zone 5

HABIT: open, wide spreading branches
*BARK: white, peeling off in paper-thin sheets
FOLIAGE: leaves thick, blue-green, remaining on tree until late fall
*AUTUMN COLOR: yellow
HABITAT: western China
INTRODUCED: 1872

There are several forms of the Manchurian Birch, but this one from the high mountains of extreme western China is perhaps the best. It approaches our Canoe Birch in size and form, but the twigs are a polished red-brown, and the thick blue-green leaves remain on the tree longer in the fall.

Betula nigra   90′   Zone 4   River Birch

*HABIT: pyramidal
*BARK: reddish brown, exfoliating
FOLIAGE: open
*AUTUMN COLOR: yellow
HABITAT: eastern United States

Commonly found native in lowlands and along stream banks where the soil is moist, often covered with water for several weeks during the course of the year. It is not long lived in the North. The River Birch is valued chiefly for its ability to grow in wet places and also for its beautiful paper-thin, exfoliating bark in the winter time.

Betula papyrifera   90′   Zone 2   Canoe Birch

*HABIT: generally pyramidal
*BARK: white, peeling off in paper-thin sheets
FOLIAGE: open
*AUTUMN COLOR: yellow
HABITAT: north central and northeastern North America

The Canoe, White or Paper Birch, is one of our best native ornamental trees, commonly found in the woods and mountains over a wide area of North America. Indian lore is rich in the legends surrounding the Canoe Birch, for it was this tree, probably more than any other which supplied the coverings for wigwams and huts, as well as the materials from which canoes were made. Now it is one of our best ornamental trees, because of its good foliage and autumn color, and particularly because of its beautiful white bark. It should always be grown with a single trunk. It should be planted in public places with discretion, for the bark-pealing instincts of the public frequently result in the permanent marring of these beautiful trunks. There is nothing more beautiful on the home grounds than one of these trees if it is allowed to grow unscarred. Summer and winter alike, its stately beauty and majestic habit will set it aside as one of our own most beautiful trees. It is superior to any of the other white barked birches, in that its trunk has considerably fewer black markings. This species is not seriously infested by the bronze birch borer which troubles the European species so much.

Betula pendula   60′   Zone 2   European Birch

*HABIT: pyramidal, branches somewhat pendulous in older trees
*BARK: white, exfoliating
FOLIAGE: open
*AUTUMN COLOR: yellow
HABITAT: Europe, Asia Minor
INTRODUCED: colonial times
VARIETIES: *fastigiata*—columnar in habit—Pyramidal European Birch
            gracilis—similar to the variety *tristis* but with laciniate leaves very finely dissected, a graceful specimen—Cutleaf European Birch
            tristis—very slender pendulous branches with round regular head—Slender European Birch
            youngi—gracefully pendulous branches, one of the best forms for the small garden—Young's Birch

Formerly termed *Betula alba* or *B. verrucosa*, this is a short lived but exceedingly graceful tree. The species has slightly pendulous branches, but the varieties are markedly so. The variety *gracilis* is frequently found in catalogues under the name of *laciniata*. I have seen specimens of these varieties 20 feet tall that were simply perfect in every way. However, this species is most susceptible to the bronze birch borer, an insect which bores its way into the trunk high up in the tree, frequently killing the entire top. Since these are all grown with single trunks and are definitely pyramidal in shape, the tree can be ruined in one short growing season. I have seen a cemetery in Ohio where these trees were placed as the feature tree, beautiful specimen 15–20 feet tall which were completely ruined in a very few years by this pest. The entire planting, which had thrived for a dozen years, had to be removed and replaced with other kinds of trees.

The development of new sprays and possible repellents may eventually insure longer lives for these trees, but until that time comes they should certainly not be used to line avenues, and used on private properties only when the owner is fully aware of the quick destruction which can be caused by this pest.

Betula populifolia   30′   Zone 5   Gray Birch

*HABIT: usually with several trunks growing in clumps
*BARK: white with triangular black markings
FOLIAGE: open
*AUTUMN COLOR: yellow
HABITAT: northeastern North America

This certainly should not be confused with the taller, single trunked birches. The Gray Birch is incorrectly named in that its bark is white, with many triangular black markings. It is short lived, grows with several trunks in clumps on poor gravelly soil or even in very wet soil. The trunks are slender and pliable so that in heavy snow or ice storms they are frequently bent to the ground. They have great recuperative powers from such storms, but their trunks are seldom straight, and once broken, disease and rot quickly take its toll. In New England, this tree is frequently severely infested with the birch leaf miner, which quickly skeletonizes the leaf in the early summer unless promptly sprayed. If spraying will not be considered as an almost annual chore one should consider selecting other trees not troubled with this pernicious pest.

Brachychiton acerifolium   60′   Zone 10   Flame Bottle Tree

*FLOWERS: scarlet red in erect trusses
    TIME: July–August
HABIT: fairly rounded, trunk bottle-shaped
FOLIAGE: coarse, drops prior to blooming, leaves lustrous, 10″ diameter, dense
HABITAT: Australia

This tree has a deep tap root and does best in deep soils used principally in the South and in California. The trees of this genus are called "Bottle Trees" because the lower part of the trunk is usually swollen. These are not among the best ornamentals for sub-tropical areas and indeed are frequently considered a nuisance because they are always dropping something (like Eucalyptus) to litter the ground beneath their branches. However, they seem to do well throughout lengthy dry periods.

Broussonetia papyrifera   48′   Zone 6   Common Paper-Mulberry

FLOWERS: female catkins are globular and interesting
    TIME: May
*FRUIT: round, orange to red, ¾″ diameter
    EFFECTIVE: June and July

HABIT: wide spreading, broad rounded head
FOLIAGE: dense, irregularly lobed
*BARK: gray, trunk grows into irregular shapes
HABITAT: China, Japan
INTRODUCED: 1750

A neat tree with irregularly lobed leaves and interesting fruits. The common name comes from the fact that paper is made from the bark in China, the fibres being stuck together with rice paste. The bark has also been used to make cloth, and the sap to make glue in the Islands of Polynesia. In the South it is used as an ornamental and occasionally as a street tree. It does unusually well on poor, sterile, gravelly soil, where other trees will not survive, and seems to do equally well in areas where heat, smoke and dust are prevalent. If the roots are disturbed it has been noted to sucker freely. Not one of the best ornamental trees but a reliable one where growing conditions are difficult.

Buxus sempervirens arborescens   20′   Zone 5   Tree Box

HABIT: dense, rounded
*FOLIAGE: evergreen, dark lustrous green leaves to 1¼″ long, fine texture
HABITAT: southern Europe, northern Africa, western Asia
INTRODUCED: early colonial times

The Common Box in America and its many varieties are usually treated as shrubs. The arborescent variety is merely listed here to bring attention to the fact that it can grow into a small tree, although it does take many years to do so. It is only in parts of the South (Zone 6) where century-old specimens have reached sufficient size to be really classed as trees rather than tall shrubs. Actually this species is more effective ornamentally when grown as a shrub rather than a tree with a single trunk.

Callistemon lanceolatus   30′   Zone 9   Lemon Bottlebrush

*FLOWERS: spikes with bright red stamens
    TIME: February–July
*FOLIAGE: evergreen, leaves 3″ long
HABITAT: Australia

Rugged colorful evergreens, there are some selected strains far superior to others. Seedlings should be avoided if possible as many prove worthless ornamentals. These plants can be grown in dry soil, and since the foliage is fairly ineffective, the plants should be used against a foliage background for the better display of the flowers.

Camellia japonica   45′   Zone 7   Common Camellia

*FLOWERS: conspicuous, large, white to red, single or double, 2–5″ in diameter
    TIME: October–April
HABIT: upright while young, more rounded at maturity
*FOLIAGE: evergreen, lustrous, dark, leathery, leaves to 4″ long
HABITAT: China, Japan
INTRODUCED: 1797

The popular, late-flowering camellia of the South is this species from Japan represented by several hundred varieties now being grown in this country. These

range in color from pure white to a rich, deep red with all the variations in between. Flowers of some varieties are single, some are semi-double and some are
very double. Popular for growing in shaded situations where other plants may
not bloom well. It is interesting to note the large number of varieties which have
occurred within one species. So often, as in roses for example, hybridization between several species has resulted in a large number of varieties, but here the
large number of varieties has resulted chiefly from hybridization within a single
species and also the raising of many bud sports.

The flower forms of these camellias differ considerably and some authors
have divided the varieties into nine different groups or classes. Chief among
these, however, are the single type with one row of no more than six petals with
prominent yellow stamens in the center (var. "Amabilis"); the semi-double type,
variously named, with mature petals around the perimeter of the flower and
many small petals or modified stamens in the center ("Adolphe Audusson"); and
several ramifications of the double form with petals regularly placed in a very
definite arrangement ("C. M. Hovey") or with no apparent petal arrangement
but still very few stamens ("Debutante"); and others very definitely double but
with a center of golden stamens when fully open ("Kumasaka"). The flowers of
some varieties have the general form of roses while others are suggestive of
peonies. The camellia specialist is particular about his selection of just the right
flower type, but for the amateur they are all beautiful and the twenty-five suggested varieties contain some of the best of all the flower types.

The camellia is widely grown from North Carolina to Florida along the Gulf
Coast, and on the Pacific Coast as far north as Seattle. Even when their large
waxy brilliantly-colored flowers are not evident, the C. *japonica* makes a good
evergreen shrub for its foliage alone. The varieties of this species, though they
bloom at different times, come as a group after the varieties of C. *sasanqua* which
bloom from September to October. Most varieties can be grown in normally
good soil of about 6.0 pH or slightly less in the full sun, though many withstand
shade very well indeed. The following popular varieties now being grown in the
South and on the Pacific Coast have been selected to exemplify the wide range
of color and type of flower in this most variable species. (The color notes are
taken from "Camellias in America" by H. H. Hume, 1946, and refer to the
English Horticultural Colour Chart.)

Red varieties:

"Adolphe Audusson"—flowers semi-double, 4″ diameter, turkey red 721 to
rose madder 23.

"Arajishi"—flowers double, 3–4″ diameter and 1½″ high, turkey red 721,
blooms early for this species.

"Aunt Jetty"—flowers double, 4″ diameter, 2″ high, turkey red 721. The
parent plant of this variety in western Florida (Tallahassee) is about 132
years old. It is not apparently injured by cold weather.

"C. M. Hovey"—flowers double, 3¼–4″ diameter and flat, carmine 21, slightly
variegated. This was first raised a century ago by Hovey & Co., of Cambridge, Mass., in 1847, when camellia growing in greenhouses was a
popular industry in New England. This is a splendid type and might well
be considered one of the best and most dependable of all.

"Gloire De Nantes"—flowers double, nearly 4″ diameter by 1½″ high, crimson 22/1.

"Lady Vansittart"—flowers semi-double, 4″ diameter, 1¼″ high, carmine rose 621. Sometimes the flowers are almost variegated, white with carmine stripes, but it is a comparative newcomer to the United States having been introduced here in 1917.

"Mathotiana"—flowers double, 4″ wide and 2″ high; carmine 21/1 with a coloring along the edges of the petals. Flowers are shaped very much like those of a rose.

"Prince Eugene Napoleon"—flowers double, 3″ diameter, 1″ high, rather flat, crimson 22.

"Professor C. S. Sargent"—flowers double, 3–4″ diameter, 2″ high, turkey red 721. It was named after Charles Sprague Sargent, the first Director of the Arnold Arboretum, Boston, Mass. This variety is an excellent one, grows vigorously, is among the hardiest and is sometimes used as an understock on which other varieties are grafted.

Pink varieties

"Debutante"—flowers double, 3″ diameter and 1¾″ high, carmine to carmine rose 621/1. This originated as a chance seedling in Magnolia Gardens on the Ashley River of South Carolina, a show garden where many excellent varieties of camellias are grown. It is free flowering, tall, compact in habit, and the flowers are of a color, size and shape desirable for use in corsages.

Frau Minna Seidel"—flowers double, 2½″ diameter, 1¼″ high, carmine rose 621/3. This is one of the most commonly grown of all camellia varieties, often found under the name of "Pink Perfection." It is vigorous and compact in habit, a reliable sort, and one which might easily be the single selection for a small garden.

"Lady Humes Blush"—flowers double, 2¾″–3″ diameter, 1¼″ high, white blushed pink. This is a slow grower, and though long in this country has not proved as popular as other varieties. It is a good color however and so is recommended in this small selective group.

"Magnoliaeflora"—single flowers, 3½″ wide and 1½″ high, white but blushed a very delicate light pink.

"Otome"—flowers double, 3½″ wide and 1½″ high, carmine rose 623/2 in central part of petals shading to almost white at the margins. This is another excellent type for corsages and the plant produces many fine blossoms.

"Sweet Vera"—flowers double, 4″ diameter, 2″ high, carmine rose 621/1 and slightly lighter at the center, sometimes almost white. The flower petals are marked with red lines and dots.

White varieties:

"Alba Plena"—flowers double, 4″ diameter, often 3″ high and pure white. This is one of the oldest varieties in the United States and is still very popular. It is vigorous and compact and has been known to endure short cold spells of 10°F.

"Amabilis"—flowers single, 3″ diameter, white.

"Imura"—flowers semi-double, 4¾" diameter, white. This originated in the Overlook Nurseries of Crichton, Alabama, from Japanese seed grown there in 1925. It is very much like a water lily in form of the flowers. Some like this variety best of all for its general habit of growth, reliability and delicate floral beauty.

"Purity"—flowers double, 3½" diameter, 1¼" high, white. A widely popular variety with flowers of long lasting quality and desirable for corsages. The petals are slightly wavy and almost like porcelain in texture.

Variegated varieties:

"Daikagura"—flowers double, 4" diameter and 2" high, carmine rose 621 with blotches of white. This early flowering variety is one of the best in its group and was introduced into this country from Japan. Unfortunately it grows slowly and tends to be slightly open in habit.

"Donckelari"—flowers semi-double, 4" diameter, 1½" high, turkey red 721, with some flowers having white markings. Another hardy variety, it was introduced from the Orient by that famous German naturalist Philip Franz von Siebold, who spent several years in Japan beginning about 1823.

"Herme"—flowers double, 3½" diameter and 1¾" high and extremely variegated red and white. This slightly fragrant variety is known under three names: "Herme," "Souv. de Henri Guichard" and "Jordan's Pride." This might be construed as an indication of its extreme popularity.

"Kumasaka"—flowers double, 4" diameter, 1¼" high, carmine 21/1 or variegated with white markings. Only moderately vigorous, it is compact and upright in habit.

"Lady Clare"—flowers semi-double, 4¾" diameter, 1¼" high, carmine rose 621 with some variation of darker colors in the petals. The flowers do not remain in good condition as long as do those of some other varieties.

"Sara-Sa"—flowers semi-double, 4½" diameter, 1½" high, a dull white with narrow broken stripes and dots of red. This is another variety that is popular on the Pacific Coast as well as in the southern United States.

Carpinus betulus   60′   Zone 5   European Hornbeam

FRUIT: small nutlets in leaflike bracts borne in pendulous clusters
    EFFECTIVE: summer and fall
*HABIT: pyramidal when young but rounded at maturity
FOLIAGE: leaves 1½ × 3½" long, dense
    AUTUMN COLOR: yellow
HABITAT: Europe and Persia
INTRODUCED: colonial times
VARIETIES: *incisa*—leaves narrow, deeply lobed—Cutleaf European Hornbeam
            fastigiata—upright habit, an excellent form—Pyramid European Hornbeam
            globosa—densely rounded in outline, almost as if it were sheared— Globe European Hornbeam
            pendula—branchlets pendulous—Weeping European Hornbeam
    This tree is used a great deal in Europe, especially in making hedges and pleached alleès, for it withstands shearing very well. It too may be a little difficult

Carpinus betulus fastigiata an interesting
form of the European Hornbeam.

to move as a large tree. Whenever this fact is known about a species, it is best to
use the smallest possible tree at the start. Several forms of this species are available
and make for considerable variety in this fine foliage plant. Like many other plants
native to Europe, it is not as striking in fall color as its American or Japanese
relatives.

Carpinus caroliniana   36'   Zone 2   American Hornbeam

FRUIT: hard nutlets in leaflike bracts borne in pendulous clusters 3½" long
   EFFECTIVE: summer and fall
HABIT: several trunks, rounded and bushy
*BARK: gray
FOLIAGE: dense, 2½–4½" long
*AUTUMN COLOR: orange to red
HABITAT: eastern North America
VARIETY: *pyramidalis*—should be mentioned. More open in habit than *C. betulus*
      fastigiata but branches all definitely upright in habit of growth. Tree
      in Arnold Arboretum is over 40' tall.

   This native is often called "Blue Beech" or "Ironwood" and is commonly
found in the woods of eastern North America. Small boys know it because the
wood is so tough to chop with an axe; the term "Ironwood" seems sufficient. Unfortunately it is not too easily transplanted but makes an excellent small tree for
the small place. It grows often with several trunks that are not completely
rounded in cross section but more like the outline of the wrist with the fist
clenched tightly. The delicately shaped leaves, splendid autumn color and interesting pendulous clusters of fruits, tend to make it of considerable interest throughout its growing season and its "muscled" trunk and gray bark, as well as its habit of
growth, call attention to the fact that it has merit during its leafless period as well.

Botanists draw attention to minute distinguishing characteristics between a northern form (called var. *virginiana*) and a southern form, but the ornamental purposes one is just as good as the other. It will not withstand clipping as well as *C. betulus*.

Carpinus japonica	45'	Zone 4	Japanese Hornbeam

FRUIT: hard nutlets in leaflike bracts borne in pendulous clusters 2–2½" long
    EFFECTIVE: summer and fall
*HABIT: flat topped
FOLIAGE: leaves larger than other species, 2–4" long, dense
*AUTUMN COLOR: red
HABITAT: Japan
INTRODUCED: 1879

Most of the hornbeams make excellent small trees but are rather slow growing. Because they give good shade, they are well adapted to use on the small property. This species might be considered as having the coarser texture of the three mentioned.

CARYA

The hickories are a sturdy lot of tap-rooted native American trees that have the reputation of being hard to move in larger sizes. Although baseball bats and axe handles are made from their wood, the trees themselves do split rather easily in heavy storms. The fruits are of course known to all those familiar with America's woods, and the bark of some has much ornamental value. The golden brown autumn color is a foliage characteristic of no mean importance. Their rugged habit, interesting form, and comparative freedom from serious pests or diseases, make them of considerable ornamental value in many locations.

Commercial growers who frequently transplant or root-prune their trees in the nursery row are the ones from whom these trees should be bought. Native plants dug in the woods frequently fail to live, for growing in one place for a long time with the roots undisturbed, the delicate feeding roots may be at quite some distance from the tree and be cut off in the digging operation. Also the tap root will be very large. Grown in the nursery, where these roots are cut every few years, feeding roots will be close to the trunk and the tap root will not be too large. In other words, to succeed with hickories, plant them in their final growing place early in life.

Hickory wood makes excellent fuel in fact it is probably the best of our native woods for this purpose. A cord of hickory wood is said to produce as much heat as a ton of coal. The wood has many uses, including baseball bats and shock absorbing tool handles, and the sawdust of green hickory is used by the large meat packing industries for smoking meats. The hickory bark beetle and canker worm seem to be its worst enemies. Although hard to transplant, their excellent habit, beautiful autumn color and general sturdiness make them excellent ornamentals.

Carya cordiformis   90'   Zone 4   Bitternut

HABIT: broad, rounded
FOLIAGE: dense, compound leaves, leaflets 5–9
*AUTUMN COLOR: yellow
HABITAT: central and eastern United States

Not as popular a tree as the other hickories, nor as long lived, but nevertheless a symmetrical specimen if the others are not available to use in its place. The nuts are bitter and of little economic value.

Carya glabra   120'   Zone 4   Pignut

*HABIT: narrow to round
FOLIAGE: dense, leaves compound, 3–9 leaflets
*AUTUMN COLOR: yellow
HABITAT: eastern United States

The Pignut does grow in dry rocky soils, and so can be used in places where the Pecan will not do well. It grows into a tall and handsome tree, but grows slowly and is not recommended as a street or avenue tree. A well grown specimen, well placed, can be just as beautiful in the large garden as can an American Elm. The nuts are small and difficult to crack and so these have little economic value.

Carya ovata   120'   Zone 4   Shagbark Hickory

*HABIT: narrow, upright, irregular
FOLIAGE: none too dense, leaves compound 5–7 leaflets
*AUTUMN COLOR: golden brown
*BARK: flaking off in loose plates
HABITAT: eastern United States

Next to the Pecan, this is the most popular of the hickories for its nuts, and many varieties are available. As an ornamental tree it is the best of the hickories, with its narrow, upright habit, picturesque and open branching habit, and its loosely flaking bark of interest all winter long.

A number of varieties originating in the South and West have been named because this species is the most economically important in the genus for its nuts. Such varieties would include "Davis," "Fox," "Glover," "Goheen," "Kirtland," "Miller," "Neilson," "Whitney," and "Wilcox."

Carya pecan   150'   Zone 5   Pecan

HABIT: massive branches, rounded
FOLIAGE: not too dense, leaves compound, 11–17 leaflets
*AUTUMN COLOR—yellow
HABITAT: south central United States

This is the fastest growing of the hickories and will eventually grow into a massive, large-branched tree of rounded habit. Old trees may be as much as 350 years old. It is found chiefly in rich, moist, bottomlands adjacent to streams and rivers, never in dry soils. There are many clons, grown chiefly for their nuts. The variety "Burlington" produces good nuts and is also the best as a shade tree and seems to be hardy as far north as Ithaca, New York. Over 20 varieties of pecan are

The Shagbark Hickory is a native American, difficult to transplant but an excellent specimen.

listed in current nursery catalogues, some of southern origin, some of northern origin. Among the latter would be "Green River" and "Major."

Carya tomentosa 30' Zone 4 Mockernut

HABIT: upright with round head
FOLIAGE: dense, leaves compound, 5–9 leaflets
*AUTUMN COLOR: yellow
HABITAT: eastern and central United States

Suggested only because it is native in at least a third of the United States and in the open makes a beautiful symmetrical tree. It grows to be 250–300 years old, but like all hickories it is hard to transplant and the smaller the original plant purchased, the easier to transplant. The leaves are fragrant when crushed, and the common name "Mockernut" stems from the fact that the fruits contain so little meat, it is really not worth while to try to dig the meat out.

Cassia fistula   30′   Zone 10   ..   Golden Shower Senna

*FLOWERS: pale yellow in racemes 1′ or more long
    TIME: spring before the leaves
HABIT: rounded but upright
FOLIAGE: coarse
HABITAT: India

The long racemes of golden yellow flowers in the spring make this tree a popular one for ornamental planting.

Castanea mollissima   60′   Zone 4   Chinese Chestnut

HABIT: dense and rounded head
FOLIAGE: dense, coarse
*AUTUMN COLOR: yellow to bronze
HABITAT: China, Korea
INTRODUCED: 1903

Since the advent of the chestnut bark disease over thirty years ago, this is the only chestnut (with suitable nut for eating) apparently resistant to this disease. Now it is being given great impetus by the United States Department of Agriculture and various commercial concerns for planting both as an ornamental and as a nut bearing tree to bring about again the growing of chestnuts in America. Recently three varieties have been introduced by the United States Department of Agriculture for trial, namely, "Nanking," "Meiling" and "Kuling." These were grown from seed introduced from China in 1936 and since that time, at the age of ten years, have produced an average of 75–100 pounds of edible nuts per tree. Chinese chestnuts have proved self-sterile so that at least two different varieties are needed to cross fertilize each other. One single tree, grown alone, will produce only a handful of nuts. The nuts chiefly seen in the market in this country today are imported from Europe and are of the blight-susceptible European species *C. sativa.* Young trees can not compete successfully with vigorous weeds and so the Chinese Chestnut should be grown under conditions of clean cultivation at first. The dense foliage and rounded habit are good qualifications for a shade tree, but it must be kept in mind that to produce nuts one tree is not sufficient.

A word might be said here of our native *C. dentata,* for sprouts are still coming up in the woods throughout the East, and in fact there are trees mature enough to bear many fruits. Suffice it to say that with hundreds of people looking for a blight-resistant native tree, none has been found to date. One may appear somewhere, but the enthusiastic amateur would save the experts time if he would continue to watch his tree in the woods that is "bearing nuts" for another five years. If, after observing it this long it still does not show any branches or twigs that have been killed by disease, then he can call in the experts to investigate. It may still be susceptible even at that!

Castanospermum australe   60′   Zone 10   Moreton Bay Chestnut

*FLOWERS: yellow, in large loose racemes 6″ long
    TIME: spring
FRUIT: pods 9″ long and 2″ broad with large, edible, chestnutlike seeds
    EFFECTIVE: fall
HABIT: unusually wide spreading, often wider than high
*FOLIAGE: evergreen, coarse, compound
HABITAT: Australia
    Of value for its evergreen foliage and conspicuous flowers.

Castanopsis chrysophylla   105′   Zone 7   Giant Evergreen Chinquapin

*FLOWERS: soft fluffy spikes of creamy white flowers
    TIME: summer
FRUIT: prickly burrs
HABIT: pyramidal
*FOLIAGE: evergreen, leaves 2–5″ long, dark green and lustrous above
HABITAT: Oregon to California
    This broad-leaved evergreen is valued for the fact that it grows well on poor, dry soils. It should be much better known than it is within its hardiness limits.

Casuarina equisetifolia   70′   Zone 10   Horsetail Beefwood

FRUIT: cone, ½″ diameter
HABIT: open top, poor shade
*FOLIAGE: leaves are minute scales and in appearance they resemble pines
HABITAT: Australia
    A peculiar tree but widely planted in southern Florida because it grows in all types of soils, can be easily clipped into hedges, and withstands brackish soils and salt water spray, making it a valuable plant for seacoast gardens. It has been used also as a windbreak.

Casuarina stricta   30′   Zone 10   Coast Beefwood

HABIT: slender but unusually rapid in growth
*FOLIAGE: evergreen, in feathery, long jointed sprays somewhat akin to the
    northern native plant known as "Horsetail"
HABITAT: Australia
    These peculiar small trees grow well in sandy seashore situations, but when grown where the prevailing winds are all in one direction they grow one sided very quickly. They will even withstand brackish situations.

Catalpa bignonioides   45′   Zone 4   Southern Catalpa

*FLOWERS: 2″ long, white with yellow and brown markings in upright panicles 7″
    high
    TIME: late June
FRUIT: long beanlike pods, 15″ long
    EFFECTIVE: hanging on until late fall and winter, not especially ornamental

HABIT: broadly rounded
FOLIAGE: leaves ovate, 4" long, coarse
HABITAT: Georgia, Florida and Mississippi

Smaller in height and with leaves less coarse than those of the Western Catalpa, this tree might be considered easier to work into plantings properly. It is famed for its overplanted variety *nana* which is grafted at about 6 to 7 feet high on the species and then allowed to grow with long pendulous branches touching the ground. In order to force dense growth, these are often cut back to a few buds in the winter, making a most unsightly, stubby looking plant. Because of its regularity of growth many people like to use them in conspicuous parts of the lawn, but they are far too conspicuous at all times of year. The enterprising gardener will study available plant materials and select a combination of plants that will give more interesting effects than this unnatural looking variety.

Catalpa speciosa   90'   Zone 4   Northern Catalpa

*FLOWERS: 2" in diameter, creamy white with yellowish and brown markings arranged in upright panicles 6" high
TIME: late June
FRUIT: long beanlike pods, sometimes 18" long
EFFECTIVE: late fall and winter, not particularly ornamental
HABIT: loosely pyramidal
FOLIAGE: leaves heart shaped, coarse, often 12" long
HABITAT: Indiana to northern Arkansas

This common mid-western tree is often called the "Indian Bean" because of its long podlike fruits. The tree withstands hot summers and dry soil but is certainly not adapted for planting on the small place. The habit is large, their leaves, flowers and fruits are large and coarse in every way. For these reasons they are very difficult to work into a planting scheme properly. They are commonly used over a wide area, and in park plantings, they are at their best. Their large conspicuous flowers appear at a time when few other trees have any blossoms at all.

Cedrela sinensis   70'   Zone 5   Chinese Toon

*FLOWERS: greenish yellow to white in pendulous clusters 12" long
TIME: June
HABIT: rounded and dense
FOLIAGE: coarse, compound, similar to that of *Ailanthus*
HABITAT: China
INTRODUCED: 1862

A tree resembling *Ailanthus altissima* but less hardy, although it makes a better ornamental specimen. It has been used as a street tree in Philadelphia with good results. Its compound leaves are coarse and appear like those of *Ailanthus* except that the glandular tooth at the base of each leaflet is missing. The flowers do not have the disagreeable odor of those of *Ailanthus*. However, it usually takes a tree fifteen to twenty years before it produces the first flowers; consequently it can not be considered as a specimen to be planted for its flower alone. It is merely mentioned here as a possible substitute for the *Ailanthus*, if such a tree is really needed. Like the *Ailanthus*, it has no autumn color.

CEDRUS

Three exotic species of the true cedar are here recommended because they grow in different hardiness zones and because they all make excellent specimens. Their picturesque habit of growth is not for a small garden since eventually they will grow over 100′ tall and be well over 40′ in diameter of branch spread. Hence they need a great deal of room. They are fine lawn specimens, needing little attention if they have good soil and have proved popular specimens on both the East and West coasts wherever they are hardy. Except for color and cones, they prove somewhat difficult to distinguish one from the other. *Cedrus deodara* can be distinguished from the other two by its pendulous branchlets and cones which are rounded on top. The other two species are not pendulous but very stiff,

These cones of the Cedar of Lebanon take two years to mature, and are borne upright on the upper side of the branches.

and their cones are either flat or slightly concave on top. *Cedrus libani* has branchlets that are either glabrous or only slightly pubescent and needles 1–1¼″ long, while *C. atlantica* has pubescent branchlets and needles mostly less than 1″ long. These characters are sometimes hard to see, but help in distinguishing one of these species from the other.

Cedrus atlantica   120′   Zone 6   Atlas Cedar

*FRUIT: cones upright on upper side of branches, 3″ long and 2″ in diameter, requiring two years to mature
EFFECTIVE: most of the time
*HABIT: widely pyramidal
*FOLIAGE: evergreen, needlelike, in bunches, silvery to light green
HABITAT: northern Africa
INTRODUCED: before 1840
VARIETY: *glauca*—foliage definitely bluish—Blue Atlas Cedar
As a young tree this is rather difficult to distinguish from *C. libani*, but its

twigs are always more pubescent than those of the other species. As it matures it also develops the flat topped habit of *C. libani,* but its silvery to light green foliage color is distinctive.

Cedrus deodara   150′   Zone 7   Deodar Cedar

*FRUIT: cones upright on upper side of branches 4″ long and 2½″ in diameter
  requiring two years to mature
  EFFECTIVE: most of the time
*HABIT: pyramidal, gracefully pendulous branches
*FOLIAGE: evergreen, needlelike, often in bunches, rather dense
HABITAT: Himalayas
INTRODUCED: 1831

In India the wood of this tree is used for incense. Few coniferous evergreens are as graceful as this tree. The main branchlet is always arching to pendulous, giving a decidedly graceful aspect to the whole tree. When grown from seed, as it usually is, it varies considerably as to color of foliage and habit, several varieties being offered in the trade. It is distinguished from the others because of this pendulous habit and longer needles.

This hardy Cedar of Lebanon is 45 years old and is thriving in New England. It comes from a special hardy strain introduced by the Arnold Arboretum from its native habitat in 1903.

Cedrus libani   120′   Zone 5   Cedar of Lebanon

*FRUIT: cones, upright on upper side of branches, 4″ long and 2½″ in diameter
  requiring two years to mature
  EFFECTIVE: most of the time
*HABIT: narrow pyramidal while young, branches stiffly horizontal
*FOLIAGE: evergreen, needlelike, often in bunches
HABITAT: Asia Minor
INTRODUCED: colonial times

Widely grown throughout the South, it was not until the Arnold Arboretum sent a special expedition to Asia Minor in 1903 to collect seed at the highest altitudes where these trees were native that plants could be perfectly hardy in the northeastern United States. Mature trees are very wide at the base but trees 30 to 40 years of age have about the same dimensions as *Abies concolor*, alhough they are not nearly as dense. The dark green foliage, stiff habit, picturesque and rigidly upright cones, some of which are usually on the tree since they take two years to mature, give this tree a popular interest. Frequent reference is made to it in the Bible, and Solomon's Temple was supposed to have been built with its massive timbers, another reason why considerable interest is shown in it today. It does not produce much shade and certainly is very formal in habit, but apparently has great popular appeal nevertheless in areas where the other two members of this genus are not hardy.

Ceiba pentandra 120′ Zone 10 Kapok, Silk-cotton Tree

FLOWERS: greenish white to pinkish, mallowlike
    TIME: summer
FRUIT: cucumberlike
    EFFECTIVE: early fall
*HABIT: huge buttressed trunk, wide spreading branches at right angles to it
BARK: smooth, gray
FOLIAGE: deciduous, leaves digitately compound
HABITAT: tropics of both hemispheres

One of the most conspicuous trees in southern Florida because of its massive size, profuse flowers and great trunk. The kapok of commerce comes from the silky, lustrous floss about the seeds. A large tree, it needs plenty of space in which to grow properly.

CELTIS

The hackberries (especially *Celtis occidentalis*) are widely planted in the South as street trees. Some have merit, with their foliage and dense habit of growth. The native *C. occidentalis* is susceptible to attacks from either a small mite or a mildew fungus or both, deforming the buds and resulting in a bunch of twigs growing from one place, often called "witches broom" disease. A goodly proportion of these small twigs die each year giving the tree a most unsightly appearance. It is well whenever possible to use species not so troubled with this pest, especially since no effective control measures are known. The fruit is a round drupe, one of the ways of distinguishing these plants from elms, for their leaves are similar. In general they have nothing especially to recommend their use where better and more attractive trees are available.

Celtis australis 75′ Zone 6 European Hackberry

FRUIT: dark purple berry, ½″ diameter
    EFFECTIVE: summer and fall
HABIT: spreading branches, round topped head
FOLIAGE: elmlike

HABITAT: southern Europe
INTRODUCED: 1736

This tree is valued for highway planting in hot, arid sections of the South west, where little soil moisture is available.

Celtis bungeana   45′   Zone 5   Bunch Hackberry
FRUIT: hard black berry ¼″ diameter
    EFFECTIVE: summer and fall
*HABIT: broad, rounded head
*FOLIAGE: lustrous, dark green
HABITAT: China and Korea
INTRODUCED: 1868

In general this species performs the best of those in the Arnold Arboretum. For this reason it is mentioned here even though it is as yet unavailable from commercial sources. The leaves are lustrous, dark green and 1¾–3″ long. It is not apparently infested with the witches broom so troublesome on *C. occidentalis*. The plant at the Arnold Arboretum is easily 45′ tall.

Celtis jessoensis   70′   Zone 5
FRUIT: hard black berry, ¼″ diameter
    EFFECTIVE: summer and fall
HABIT: more open in habit than *C. bungeana*
FOLIAGE: open
HABITAT: Korea and Japan
INTRODUCED: 1892

Not infested with witches broom disease and possibly of value as a substitute for the American Elm. It makes a better and more dense tree than does *C. laevigata.*

Celtis laevigata   90′   Zone 5   Sugar Hackberry
FRUIT: hard black berry ¼″ diameter
    EFFECTIVE: summer and fall
HABIT: spreading branches, sometimes pendulous, round headed
FOLIAGE: fine texture, open
HABITAT: south central and southeastern United States

Recommended because it is a widely found native tree, very resistant to the witches broom disease so seriously infesting *C. occidentalis* and widely used as a street tree in the South where it is native.

Ceratonia siliqua   50′   Zone 10   Carob
*FLOWERS: small red, lateral racemes
    TIME: spring
FRUIT: pods, 1′ long, edible by humans and stock animals
    EFFECTIVE: early fall
HABIT: rounded
*FOLIAGE: dense, glossy, evergreen leaves
HABITAT: eastern Mediterranean region
INTRODUCED: 1854

This can be grown in dry soils and still be expected to do well, one of the reasons why it is extensively cultivated in southern California. Its neat, evergreen foliage makes it a fine shade tree for specimen and avenue planting as well. It has been termed "St. John's Bread," because the seeds and sweet pulp of this tree were supposedly the "locusts and wild honey" St. John ate in the wilderness. Since it has been grown and cultivated for centuries, many varieties have appeared through the years. Some are more susceptible to cold than others.

The Katsura Tree (Cercidiphyllum japonicum) is wide spreading only when allowed to develop several main leaders. An excellent tree free of pest troubles.

Cercidiphyllum japonicum   60–100′   Zone 4   Katsura Tree

*HABIT: rounded, often with several trunks, but narrow when grown with only one
*FOLIAGE: open, fine texture
*AUTUMN COLOR: yellow to scarlet
HABITAT: Japan
INTRODUCED: 1865

A wide spreading tree with foliage very much like that of *Cercis canadensis*, usually growing with several main stems or trunks. The flowers are insignificant, but the small dry fruit capsules on the pistillate trees—the sexes are separate—remain on the tree most of the winter. The rounded leaves are nearly 4″ long. Valued as a shade tree because of its wide spreading habit but also valued because of the rather loose foliage which allows for a great amount of air circulation. It has been termed the largest deciduous tree of China. The variety named *sinense* is merely the Chinese form, practically indistinguishable from the species. An excellent specimen tree of particular value for its graceful leaves which remain unattacked by an insect pest throughout the entire season.

Cercis canadensis   36'   Zone 4   Eastern Redbud

*FLOWERS: small, purplish pink, pealike in clusters
    TIME: mid-May
*HABIT: flat top, irregular
FOLIAGE: heart shaped, fine texture, open
*AUTUMN COLOR: yellow
HABITAT: eastern United States
VARIETY: *alba*—flowers white

A common sight in the eastern United States, especially in the woods of Pennsylvania, Maryland and Virginia when it blooms early in the spring. It is often planted with the Flowering Dogwood, blooming at the same time. The white flowered variety is almost as hardy as the species, while the double flowered variety (*plena*) is not as interesting nor as conspicuous in flower. Some seedlings have come to light with flowers very definitely red rather than purplish pink. It may be that one of these desirable clons will be named in the not too distant future.

Cercis chinensis   40'   Zone 6   Chinese Redbud

*FLOWERS: rosy purple, dense, pealike
    TIME: mid-May
HABIT: often shrublike
FOLIAGE: heart-shaped leaves, fine texture, dense
*AUTUMN COLOR: yellow
HABITAT: central China
INTRODUCED: before 1850

Even though this is a tree in its native habitat, it has proved more or less shrubby in this country and is better grown this way, especially in the North. Its profuse, rosy purple pealike flowers are its chief interest to gardeners. This is actually the tallest of the redbuds, otherwise similar in most respects to *Cercis canadensis*.

Cercis racemosa   30'   Zone 7   Raceme Redbud

*FLOWERS: rosy pink, pealike in pendulous racemes 1½–4" long
    TIME: mid-May
HABIT: flat top
FOLIAGE: rather coarse, open
*AUTUMN COLOR: yellow
HABITAT: China
INTRODUCED: 1907

This species, introduced by the Arnold Arboretum, is distinct in that it has pendulous clusters of flowers which appear on the naked branches (before the leaves) on wood one to several years old.

Cercis siliquastrum   30'   Zone 6   Judas Tree

*FLOWERS: profuse, small pealike, bright purplish rose
    TIME: mid-May
HABIT: flat top

FOLIAGE: heart-shaped, open
HABITAT: southern Europe and Western Asia
INTRODUCED: colonial times

The flowers usually are produced on twigs 2 to 4 years old but sometimes as much as 20 to 30 years old—often 100 flowers on a twig only 5" long. A white variety *alba* of this has been reported but I do not know where it is available in America. In sunny Italy it makes a wonderful display in April or early May.

CHAMAECYPARIS

Two native species and two introduced species constitute the members of this genus as it is used in ornamental planting in America. However, there are many varieties with variations in shape, foliage and habit. They are evergreen like the arborvitaes, but can be distinguished from this group of plants because of small white lines on the under surface of the scale-like foliage which the arborvitaes do not have. They are mostly an attractive lot, easily transplanted, with few insect pests or diseases and many varieties from shrubs to trees.

Chamaecyparis lawsoniana   120′   Zone 5   Lawson False Cypress

* HABIT: slender to broadly pyramidal tree
*FOLIAGE: evergreen, scalelike
*BARK: shredding
HABITAT: southwestern Oregon to northwestern California
VARIETIES: *allumi*—columnar form with steel blue foliage-Scarab Lawson Cypress
  argentea—leaves silvery white—Silver Lawson Cypress
  erecta—a columnar, dense form with bright green foliage. There is a form of this "*erecta glauca*" with blue foliage
  glauca—steel blue leaves, the much advertised variety "Triomphe de Boskoop" is similar—Steel Lawson Cypress
  gracilis—very graceful pendulous form—Fountain Lawson Cypress
  nidiformis—horizontal branches radiating from a dense center
  pendula—branchlets pendulous—Weeping Lawson Cypress

Native over very small corners of two states, often called the Port Orford Cedar, it has been widely distributed in Europe and New Zealand particularly in areas that are continually moist, since it does not like dry weather. Some seventy varieties have been described, for it is a variable species. In areas near its native habitat, or where climate is mild and moisture is always present, the Lawson Cypress and its varieties offer interesting variations for the winter garden.

Chamaecyparis nootkatensis   120′   Zone 4   Nootka False Cypress

*HABIT: narrowly pyramidal
*FOLIAGE: evergreen, dark green and scalelike
*BARK: shredding
HABITAT: southwestern Alaska to Oregon

One of three native *Chamaecyparis* species. It does not have a wide distribution in this country merely because it needs a moist climate in which to thrive. It is not used much even on the Pacific Coast where it is native, but is considered one of the finest where it can be grown.

Chamaecyparis obtusa   120′   Zone 3   Hinoki False Cypress

*HABIT: broadly pyramidal
*FOLIAGE: evergreen, scalelike leaves, dark glossy green, usually dense
BARK: shredding
HABITAT: Japan
INTRODUCED: 1861
VARIETIES: *erecta*—fastigiate, ascending branches—Column Hinoki Cypress
            gracilis—compact, pyramidal, branchlets pendulous—Slender Hinoki Cypress

A slow growing ornamental in both shrub and tree forms, it is a beautiful specimen when properly grown. It needs a moist climate, but there are some of the tree forms doing well in the Arnold Arboretum in Boston. The foliage is usually a dark glossy green, and it might well be considered one of the most attractive in this genus.

Chamaecyparis pisifera   150′   Zone 3   Sawara False Cypress

*HABIT: narrowly pyramidal, branches horizontal, but rather loose and open throughout
*FOLIAGE: evergreen, scalelike, often open
BARK: shredding
HABITAT: Japan
INTRODUCED: 1861
VARIETIES: *aurea*—foliage golden yellow—Golden Sawara Cypress
            This might be discarded as a shrub but there are very few trees of satisfactory yellow foliage in the summer and it might be included for this purpose only. In the winter, the foliage is a very poor color, and the tree should not be counted as an attractive specimen at this time.
            filifera—branchlets threadlike—Thread Sawara Cypress
            plumosa—foliage frondlike but slightly feathery—Plume Sawara Cypress
            squarrosa—foliage very feathery, not flat and frondlike—Moss Sawara Cypress

A variable species with many popular varieties, prone to lose its lower branches rather early in life. Most of these must be gone over annually and the dead branches removed in order to keep the trees in good condition. It should always be kept in mind that this species is a tree even in this country. Too often these plants are used in foundation plantings and put in front of windows without thought of their later development. In a few years time they have naturally grown out of all proportion to other plants in such a planting, often obliterating the view from the windows. They can be kept under control by persistent pruning. This species and its varieties, seem to do about the best of all the *Chamaecyparis* in northern gardens, and to grow well in areas where the moisture-loving Pacific

Coast species will not. As shrubs or trees they are commonly used, their brownish red shredding bark is another interesting feature of older plants.

| Chionanthus virginicus | 30' | Zone 4 | Fringetree |

*FLOWERS: white, feathery, in loose panicles
    TIME: early June
FRUIT: dark blue, grapelike, in clusters
    EFFECTIVE: fall
*AUTUMN COLOR: bright yellow
HABITAT: New Jersey to Florida

    The native Fringetree is just as ornamental if not slightly more so than its oriental relative, *C. retusus*. Its fleecy white flowers are produced in the utmost profusion. Usually the sexes are separate with the staminate flowers being larger. This species is closely related to the lilacs and also must be watched for scale infestations, otherwise it is a splendid ornamental especially as a specimen in the full sun. By some Europeans it is considered the most beautiful and striking of our native shrubs. Its only drawback is the fact that it is one of the last plants to produce leaves in the spring. In fact, they appear so late many people think the plants are dead.

| Cinnamomum camphora | 40' | Zone 9 | Camphor Tree |

FRUIT: black berries about size of a pea but not effective
HABIT: round headed
*FOLIAGE: evergreen, very dense, glossy
HABITAT: China and Japan
INTRODUCED: early colonial times?

    Used considerably in the South as a street tree, it is slow growing, with attractive foliage the entire year except in the early spring. Camphor is distilled from the twigs and leaves, which if crushed, give off a distinctive camphor odor. The lower limbs need some pruning or they will ruin the general tree character.

| Citrus species | Zone 9–10 | Lemon, Orange, Lime, Grapefruit, Tangerine, Kumquat, Satsuma, etc. |

    The citrus species are always possibilities for planting on the small property as dual ornamental and economic trees. Some are more frost resistant than others. Like their northern counterparts, the apples, pears and peaches, they should not be planted solely for ornament, for if their fruits are not cared for by proper and persistent spraying they may easily become unsightly and actually defeat the purpose for which they were planted.

| Cladrastis lutea | 50' | Zone 3 | American Yellow-wood |

*FLOWERS: pendulous clusters of white, fragrant flowers, similar in size and shape
    to those of Wisteria
    TIME: early June
HABIT: rounded
FOLIAGE: dense
*AUTUMN COLOR: orange to yellow

The Coconut, a common tree in the tropical regions of the world. Very seldom does it grow with a rigidly upright trunk.

*BARK: light gray, smooth
HABITAT: North Carolina, Kentucky, Tennessee

An excellent tree for its flowers and foliage, making a handsome specimen. It may not bloom consistently every year, sometimes only becoming covered with flowers every third year. Pruning, when necessary, should be done in early summer since if pruned in spring it tends to "bleed" profusely. An immense specimen tree with pale pink flowers is growing on the grounds of the Perkins Institute for the Blind, at Cambridge, Massachusetts, and would seem to be sufficiently distinctive to be worthy of propagation.

Clethra barbinervis   30′   Zone 5   Japanese Clethra

FLOWERS: white, in horizontal racemes
    TIME: late July
HABIT: wide spreading, irregular, often with several trunks
BARK: brown, shredding, rather attractive
FOLIAGE: open
HABITAT: Japan
INTRODUCED: 1870

This is the first of the clethras to bloom and by some is considered the most beautiful. The racemes are held horizontally, and the plant is larger in every way than *C. alnifolia*, but the flowers are not so fragrant. For some reason or other, *C. barbinervis* has not been susceptible to the severe attacks of red spider often occurring on *C. alnifolia*.

Clethra delavayi   40'   Zone 7   Delavay Clethra

*FLOWERS: white, bell-shaped, ½" wide in horizontally borne racemes 4–6" long
    TIME: July
HABIT: open
FOLIAGE: open, leaves 2½–6" long
HABITAT: western China
INTRODUCED: 1913
    Rare, but about the most beautiful of the clethras.

Trees with alternate, compound leaves include:
1. Sophora japonica
2. Robinia pseudoacacia
3. Sorbus aucuparia
4. Rhus typhina
5. Cladrastis lutea
6. Gleditsia triacanthos
7.. Koelreuteria paniculata
8. Albizzia julibrissin rosea

Cocos nucifera   80'   Zone 10   Coconut

*HABIT: palm tree
FOLIAGE: graceful but coarse, leaves often 15' long
HABITAT: probably southern Florida as well as other tropical regions of the world
    A tree typical to many parts of the tropics, with long crooked or leaning trunk, grown in this country only in southern Florida. Planted as an ornamental here it is grown quickly from seed and may even bear a few nuts in five years' time. L. H. Bailey states that a tree in good soil may produce seventy-five nuts a year but that the average is only about one-third of this. In the landscape of the tropics there is nothing quite as distinctive as the Coconut.

Cornus capitata   40'   Zone 8   Evergreen Dogwood

*FLOWERS: pale yellow bracts, 4–6 in number and 1½–2" long
    TIME: June, July
*FRUIT: red, strawberrylike, 1–1½" diameter
    EFFECTIVE: October, November
*HABIT: round head, similar to *C. florida* but somewhat bushy
*FOLIAGE: evergreen to semi-evergreen, leaves lustrous dark green, leathery,
    bronze in winter
HABITAT: western China
INTRODUCED: before 1900?

A delicate dogwood, unfortunately little seen in this country because of its tenderness, but a handsome tree, nevertheless, in flower and fruit as well. It should be given good soil and a spot to grow in where it will have protection from winds in winter. The fruits are quickly eaten by the birds but are effective for as long as they last.

Cornus controversa   60'   Zone 5   Giant Dogwood

*FLOWERS: small whitish in flat clusters 3–7" diameter
    TIME: late May
*FRUIT: bluish black berries in flat clusters
    EFFECTIVE: August and early September
*HABIT: picturesque horizontal branching in tiers
FOLIAGE: dense, lustrous
AUTUMN COLOR: red
HABITAT: Japan, China
INTRODUCED: before 1880

Unlike most members of the *Cornus* genus the leaves of this plant are alternate. It is not susceptible to the serious twig blight which so seriously injures our native Alternate Leaved Dogwood, *C. alternifolia*. This tree makes an excellent specimen because of its picturesque habit but is rarely seen in gardens. The flowers are small, somewhat similar to those of certain viburnums or the Wild Carrot, but nevertheless are profusely borne and the black fruits are rather prominent.

Cornus florida   40'   Zone 4   Flowering Dogwood

*FLOWERS: bracts white, cluster about 3–5" diameter, true flowers inconspicuous
    TIME: mid-May
*FRUIT: bright red berries in tight clusters
    EFFECTIVE: fall
*HABIT: definitely horizontal branching
*FOLIAGE: dense, lustrous
*AUTUMN COLOR: scarlet
HABITAT: eastern United States
VARIETIES: *pluribracteata*—with 6–8 or more flower bracts—Double Flowering
    Dogwood
    rubra—red flower bracts—Red Flowering Dogwood
    xanthocarpa—fruits yellow—Yellow-berry Flowering Dogwood

This tree is the best ornamental of all the natives growing in the northern United States. It has special interest every season of the year—in spring with flowers; in summer with good foliage not marred by insect or disease; in fall with brilliant red berries and vivid autumn color; in winter because of its picturesque horizontal method of branching. The red flowered variety is striking when in bloom in front of some of the white flowered types. Some trees have been noted in which the tip to tip diameter of the flower bracts is 6½". Thousands of dogwoods have been planted at Valley Forge, Pennsylvania, as a memorial to those who fought in the Revolutionary War. Many towns have adopted this tree as the major plant in recent war memorial planting projects. The New Jersey Highway Commission and cooperating garden club organizations are featuring these trees along certain highways in New Jersey—highways which can easily be most prominent in the future if care is taken of the plants as they develop. Because this tree

The fruits of the Japanese Dogwood (left) differ considerably from those of the native Flowering Dogwood of the Eastern United States (right). Both are attractive when they color red in the fall.

easily starts into growth with the first mild weather, it is impossible to grow it properly in the vicinity of London, England, where its premature attempts of flowering are always nipped by late frosts. Fortunately, it makes an ideal tree in the smaller gardens over a wide area of North America.

Cornus kousa   21'   Zone 5   Japanese Dogwood

*FLOWERS: inconspicuous in small clusters surrounded by large pointed bracts that
       are white to pinkish on occasion
     TIME: mid-June
*FRUIT: raspberrylike, red
     EFFECTIVE: late summer
*HABIT: horizontal branching
*FOLIAGE: dense, lustrous
AUTUMN COLOR: scarlet
HABITAT: Japan, Korea
INTRODUCED: 1875

VARIETY: *chinensis*—practically identical from an ornamental standpoint except that the flower bracts may be slightly longer than those of the species—Chinese Dogwood

Widely grown in gardens now, this plant blooms about three weeks after *C. florida* and so is valued greatly. Its flower bracts are pointed (not rounded and notched as the native species) and often show splotches of pink as they fade. Like the native dogwood, the flower clusters are borne on the upper side of the horizontal branches, so that to be most effective the plant should be looked down on from above. E. H. Wilson said that the form he introduced from China (var. *chinensis*) was superior to the species, but I have been unable to see any marked difference between the species and the variety as they are growing side by side in the Arnold Arboretum, except that the bracts of the species are 1½–2″ long while those of the variety are 2–3½″ long. These differences, however, are not always evident.

Cornus macrophylla   45′   Zone 6   Largeleaf Dogwood

*FLOWERS: yellowish white, small, in clusters 4–6″ in diameter
  TIME: July–August
*FRUIT: bluish black berries
  EFFECTIVE: fall
HABIT: rounded
*FOLIAGE: large leaves, handsome
HABITAT: China and Japan
INTRODUCED: 1827

Sometimes confused with *C. controversa*, the leaves of this species are opposite (those of *C. controversa* are alternate), and about 4–7″ long and as much as 3½″ wide. It is excellent as a foliage plant but its flowers and fruits are not superior to those of *C. controversa*. Its late bloom is an important factor when trees for summer display are needed.

Cornus mas   24′   Zone 4   Cornelian Cherry

*FLOWERS: yellow, small, before leaves
  TIME: early April
*FRUIT: scarlet, edible, ½–¾″ long
  EFFECTIVE: August and September
*HABIT: round, dense, shrublike
*FOLIAGE: lustrous green
*AUTUMN COLOR: red
HABITAT: central and southern Europe, western Asia
INTRODUCED: probably before 1800
VARIETIES: *elegantissima*—leaves variegated with creamy white and tinged red, 4½″ long
  flava—yellow fruit
  macrocarpa—fruit larger than species

One of the earliest blooming of the spring flowering trees and shrubs with flowers before the leaves. A sturdy, vigorous plant, useful as a specimen, small tree or large shrub or as a hedge. Its fruits, which have been used in making preserves, are not too conspicuous for many are hidden by the foliage. The yellow fruiting form is more conspicuous in early summer, but except for color, need not be grown in preference to the species. This plant is unaffected by insect or disease pest, an uncommon but valuable trait.

Cornus nuttalli   75′   Zone 7   Pacific Dogwood

*FLOWERS: flower bracts 4–6, white, 4–5″ diameter (tip to tip), similar to a large
    clematis blossom
  TIME: April
*FRUIT: berries bright red to orange
  EFFECTIVE: summer and fall
*HABIT: pyramidal, often horizontal branching
FOLIAGE: dense
*AUTUMN COLOR: scarlet and yellow
HABITAT: British Columbia to southern California

Many plantsmen consider this the most handsome flowering tree of North America. It is unfortunate that it does not grow well on the East coast but it seems to require the moist, moderate climate of the Pacific coast areas, where it frequently has a second blooming period in August and September. The bracts are normally white but may fade to a rose-pink color that is rather attractive. The "flowers" are larger than those of *C. florida* and often have six bracts instead of four. An excellent specimen for planting on the Pacific coast.

Cornus officinalis   30′   Zone 5   Japanese Cornel

*FLOWERS: yellow, small, before the leaves
  TIME: early April
*FRUIT: scarlet, edible, ½–¾″ long
  EFFECTIVE: August and September
*HABIT: dense, rounded, often shrublike
*FOLIAGE: shiny green
*AUTUMN COLOR: red
BARK: exfoliating in paper-thin strips
HABITAT: Japan and Korea
INTRODUCED: 1877

Probably better for general landscape use than the common *C. mas* because of its very interesting exfoliating bark, hidden by the foliage in the summer, but evident all winter. Aside from this, the two species are similar.

Corylus colurna   75′   Zone 4   Turkish Filbert

FLOWERS: male catkins 2–3″ long
  TIME: winter and spring
HABIT: regularly pyramidal
FOLIAGE: leaves 2½–6″ long, dense
HABITAT: southeastern Europe, western Asia
INTRODUCED: early colonial times

A well shaped ornamental tree, perfectly hardy, of interest because of its form and good foliage. The male catkins appear very early in the season and are another reason why it is grown for early spring display. It is also excellent for planting in dry situations, for in New England during the past dry summers it has remained vigorous and green in situations where maples have dropped some of their leaves for lack of sufficient moisture.

Cotinus americanus   30′   Zone 5   American Smoke Tree

FLOWERS: greenish, feathery masses of fine textured growths appearing like "smoke" from a distance
   TIME: mid-June
HABIT: upright, rather narrow
FOLIAGE: dense
*AUTUMN COLOR: scarlet to orange
HABITAT: southeastern United States

   The fruiting panicles of this are not showy but there is little to surpass it when autumn has touched its leaves a brilliant scarlet to orange. It should be grown only for its fall effect, and in cases where the smaller Smoke Tree (*Cotinus coggygria*) will suffice, this American species can be omitted from further consideration.

CRATAEGUS

   At one time there were 550 species and varieties of *Crataegus* growing in the Arnold Arboretum, a great proportion of them being American natives. Hawthorns are widely distributed over North America and are frequently a common sight in pastures or along old hedge rows or even in valleys where they have crowded out other plants. This great group was one of the particular interests of Charles Sprague Sargent, the first Director of the Arnold Arboretum. As his studies progressed, and those of others as well, it became evident that this is a most difficult group to study and the separation of species and varieties on the basis of minute characteristics is a thankless task, to say the least. Some make meritorious ornamental trees. Many, many others are practically identical, certainly from the landscape point of view, and it seems valueless to continue producing them commercially for this reason. It is at this point that I would like to recommend strongly that the plant growing public become interested in only a *very* few of the best and completely discard the others from planting plans and nursery catalogues.

   All are dense, twiggy trees or bushlike shrubs, with thorns often an inch or more long. They are members of the rose family and as such are susceptible to some of the same serious troubles as scale, lace bug, borers, leaf miner and red spider. In fact most of them are in the group of trees which require annual attention in order to look well, reason enough for using them with discretion in areas where such care may not be forthcoming. Many are difficult to transplant unless properly root-pruned considerably in advance, and since all are extremely thorny, maintenance men always like to give them a wide range and you can not blame them.

   The *Crataegus* are valued for their picturesque shapes, for their dense and thorny habit of growth, some for their glossy foliage, and most for their clusters of small white (sometimes pink) flowers in the early spring, and their bright red fruits (small pomes, often borne in clusters and usually colored bright red or yellowish red, varying from ¼–1″ in diameter) in the fall. Indeed, some have beautiful autumn color. Many have proved amenable to shearing and because of their twiggy habit, dense foliage and sharp thorns, make excellent hedges and barrier plants. The seed usually does not germinate until the second year it is in the ground.

It would seem that the variation among the following fourteen species and thirteen varieties might be sufficiently ample so that these could be the first from which to make selections without encroaching on the tremendously large number of similar types growing in North America today. It should be again emphasized that these trees require annual maintenance to look well, a very important reason why they should not be selected for certain types of planting.

Crataegus arnoldiana   30′   Zone 4   Arnold Hawthorn
*FLOWERS: white, ¾″ diameter
   TIME: early May
*FRUIT: bright crimson, ¾″ long
   EFFECTIVE: middle August to early September
HABIT: rounded, thorny, dense branching
FOLIAGE: dense
HABITAT: New England
This hawthorn has the most conspicuous early fruits of all in the entire group, reason enough for suggesting it here. If early fruits are not desired, other species might be selected.

Crataegus coccinioides   21′   Zone 5   Kansas Hawthorn
*FLOWERS: white, ¾″ diameter, borne in 5–6 flowered clusters
   TIME: mid-May
*FRUIT: dark red, ¾″ diameter
   EFFECTIVE: fall and winter
*HABIT: round headed, thorny, dense branching
FOLIAGE: red when first unfurling in spring
AUTUMN COLOR: orange to scarlet
HABITAT: Indiana to Kansas
A very good hawthorn for foliage as well as fruit.

Crataegus crus-galli   36′   Zone 4   Cockspur Thorn
*FLOWERS: white, ½″ diameter
   TIME: late May
*FRUIT: bright red, ⅜″ diameter
   EFFECTIVE: during most of the winter
*HABIT: round headed, sometimes flat, wide spreading and horizontal branches, thorny, dense branching
*FOLIAGE: lustrous, dense
AUTUMN COLOR: orange to scarlet
HABITAT: northeastern North America

Several of the hawthorns made excellent hedges.

The variety *splendens* is supposed to have leaves that are very glossy and hence more ornamental than those of the species. This species is typical of many hawthorns and as a specimen is truly excellent for its definite horizontal branching habit of growth. Where the glossy leaved variety can be obtained it certainly should be used. This hawthorn also withstands shearing as well as any, making fine hedges.

x **Crataegus lavallei**   21'   Zone 4   Lavalle Hawthorn

*FLOWERS: white, ¾" diameter in many-flowered clusters
  TIME: late May
*FRUIT: brick red to orange red, ⅝" diameter
  EFFECTIVE: fall and winter
HABIT: thorny, spines 2" long, dense branching
FOLIAGE: dense
*AUTUMN COLOR: bronzy red
HYBRID ORIGIN: *C. crusgalli* x *C. pubescens*
ORIGINATED: before 1880

The Lavalle Hawthorn is of particular interest because of its fruits which remain on the tree throughout the winter.

Crataegus mollis   30'   Zone 4   Downy Hawthorn

*FLOWERS: white, 1" diameter
  TIME: mid-May
*FRUIT: pear shaped, red, often 1" in diameter
  EFFECTIVE: late summer and early fall

*HABIT: thorny, rounded, dense branching
FOLIAGE: dense, leaves larger than many other hawthorns
HABITAT: southern Ontario to Virginia and Kansas

This is one of the larger fruiting hawthorns, but because the fruits are so large they might be considered even coarse in some situations.

Crataegus monogyna   30′   Zone 4   Single Seed Hawthorn

*FLOWERS: white, ⅝″ diameter
  TIME: late May
FRUIT: red, ⅜″ in diameter
  EFFECTIVE: fall
*HABIT: rounded head, with slightly pendulous branches, more thorny than *C. oxyacantha*, dense branching
FOLIAGE: leaves 3–7 lobed, dense
HABITAT: Europe, northern Africa, western Asia
VARIETIES: *biflora*—often blooming in mild seasons in mid-winter in England and again in spring. (Sometimes termed *C. monogyna praecox*.) The legend concerning the origin of this plant is related by W. J. Bean in "Trees and Shrubs Hardy in the British Isles": "Joseph of Arimathea, after the crucifixion of Christ, came to England to found Christianity. He went to Glastonbury, where, his exhortations having but little influence on the inhabitants, he prayed that a miracle might be performed in order that they might be convinced of the divine nature of his mission. God granted his prayer, for his staff, on being thrust into the ground, immediately burst into leaf and flower, although it was then Christmas Day. The wonder was repeated on every anniversary of that day.

  "An old tree grew in the vicinity of Glastonbury Abbey until about the beginning of the nineteenth century, to which popular belief attached this legend. The variety is worth growing, not only for the sake of the old legend, but because of its interest in flowering in mid-winter. The flowers are not borne so abundantly as in May, but they have the true hawthorn fragrance . . . "—Glastonbury Thorn

inermis—thornless, excellent mushroom habit. This tree, although subject to the various pests of all hawthorns, might prove an excellent one nevertheless for use along narrow streets. Its bushlike top, especially if it is grafted high on understock with a single main trunk, is dense, well shaped and requires very little pruning. It is not a fast growing tree.

pendula—with pendulous branchlets

pteridifolia—leaves deeply lobed and closely incised

semperflorens—a low shrubby form often flowering continuously until August

stricta—with upright branches, rather narrow but as it grows older it quickly grows out of the narrow habit. The tree in the Arnold Arboretum is 30 feet tall and 8 feet through.

Somewhat similar to *C. oxyacantha* but more thorny, this tree is better for use in hedges. In England there are hundreds of miles of hedges of this one species alone, for it is easily grown, and lends itself well to clipping. It is used much more in hedges than is *C. oxyacantha* and the two species are frequently confused. There is an old saying in England that if the "haws" of the thorns and "hips" of the roses are borne in great profusion, then a hard winter is ahead.

Most of the hawthornes have bright red fruits, borne profusely. This branch is from Crataegus monogyna, a native of Europe and widely used in England in hedge rows.

Crataegus nitida   30′   Zone 4   Glossy Hawthorn

*FLOWERS: white
    TIME: late May
*FRUIT: dull red, ⅜″ diameter
    EFFECTIVE: all winter
*HABIT: round headed, thorny, dense branching
*FOLIAGE: lustrous
*AUTUMN COLOR: orange to red
HABITAT: Illinois to Arkansas

This is another hawthorn with fruits all winter and with several other good attributes as well.

Crataegus oxyacantha   15′   Zone 4   English Hawthorn

*FLOWERS: white, ⅝″ diameter in 5–12 flowered panicles
    TIME: late May
*FRUIT: scarlet ¼–⅝″ diameter
    EFFECTIVE: fall
*HABIT: thorny, branches spreading, round headed, dense branching
FOLIAGE: leaves 3–5 lobes, dense
HABITAT: Europe and northern Africa

VARIETIES: *aurea*—fruits bright yellow

coccinea—flowers red, double

rosea—flowers light rose, single

rosea-plena—flowers light rose, double

ruba—the best in fruit, fruits bright red, ⅜" diameter, flowers single

pauli—flowers double bright scarlet, one of the most showy of all the hawthorns—Paul's Scarlet Hawthorn

plena—flowers double white, few fruits

This is the "May Tree" so often referred to in English literature and is one of the few species of *Crataegus* to have pink to red flowered varieties—reason enough for its wide popularity on both sides of the Atlantic Ocean. The varieties are more grown than is the species itself, at least in North America. The absence of autumn color puts the species at least in a lower class than, say, *C. phaenopyrum* which has brilliant fall color. However there are no other hawthorns with more colorful flowers than some of the varieties of this English Hawthorn.

Crataegus phaenopyrum   30'   Zone 4   Washington Hawthorn

*FLOWERS: white, ½" diameter in many-flowered clusters

TIME: mid-June

*FRUIT: bright red, about ¼" diameter

EFFECTIVE: all winter

*HABIT: broadly columnar, thorny, dense branching, eventually with round head

*FOLIAGE: leaves 3–5 lobes, lustrous, dense

*AUTUMN COLOR: scarlet to orange

HABITAT: southeastern United States

VARIETY: *fastigiata*—columnar in habit, flowers and fruits smaller than species—Pyramidal Washington Hawthorn

If only one hawthorn was to be selected from the many native or exotic types available in North America today, the Washington Hawthorn would be the first one to consider. It is excellent—of interest every season of the year—something which can not be said of the majority of trees grown in gardens and along highways today. Its upright, dense habit, profuse flowers, and brillliant autumn color as well as its solid little red fruits which remain colorful all winter long are its best assets. It has been used as a specimen and lawn tree as well as for highway planting. The dense twiggy growth shields headlight glare from approaching cars (when planted on the middle strip of a two lane highway) throughout the growing season and even in the winter time is sufficiently effective to be desirable. This is one of the last species to bloom in the spring.

Crataegus pinnatifida major   18'   Zone 5   Large Chinese Hawthorn

*FLOWERS: white, about ¾" diameter, in clusters

TIME: late May

*FRUIT: brilliant red, 1" diameter

EFFECTIVE: fall

*HABIT: round headed, thorny, dense branching

*FOLIAGE: lustrous, leaves 5–9 lobed

HABITAT: northern China

INTRODUCED: about 1880

The leaves are often divided down to the mid-rib and its large fruit is so large that it is cultivated and eaten by the Chinese. Charles Sprague Sargent, who studied the *Crataegus* thoroughly for years, once said that it was one of the handsomest species now being grown in America.

Crataegus pruniosa   21′   Zone 4   Frosted Hawthorn

*FLOWERS: white, ¾″ diameter, borne in loose clusters, with rose colored anthers
    TIME: late May
*FRUIT: red to orange, ⅜″ diameter
    EFFECTIVE: fall
*HABIT: rounded, thorny, dense branching
FOLIAGE: dense, bluish green
HABITAT: Ontario to Virginia and Illinois
    The Frosted Hawthorn is a beautiful hawthorn, especially in fruit.

Crataegus punctata   30′   Zone 4   Dotted Hawthorn

*FLOWERS: white, ¾″ diameter in many-flowered clusters
    TIME: late May
*FRUIT: dull red, ¾″ diameter, with small dots
    EFFECTIVE: fall
*HABIT: thorny, dense branching
FOLIAGE: dense
HABITAT: eastern North America
VARIETY: *aurea*—fruit yellow
    The fruits are among the largest of the native American hawthorns and the tree may grow to be twice as broad as it is high. Because it may eventually reach a width of 40′, it might best be used chiefly in park planting.

Crataegus succulenta   15′   Zone 3   Fleshy Hawthorn

*FLOWERS: white, ¾″ diameter in many clusters
    TIME: late May
*FRUIT: bright red, ⅜″ diameter
    EFFECTIVE: fall
HABIT: thorny, dense branching
FOLIAGE: dense
HABITAT: northeastern North America
    This has been considered (by Sargent) to be one of the six handsomest hawthorns in North America and is included here in respect to his expert judgment.

Crataegus viridis   36′   Zone 4   Green Hawthorn

*FLOWERS: white ¾″ diameter borne in flat clusters 2″ across
    TIME: late May
*FRUITS: bright red, ¼″ diameter
    EFFECTIVE: fall and winter
*HABIT: rounded, thorny, spreading and dense branching
FOLIAGE: dense

HABITAT: central and southeastern United States

The Green Hawthorn is particularly valued for planting throughout the area which is its native habitat.

Cryptomeria japonica 150' Zone 5 Cryptomeria

*HABIT: pyramidal with spreading whiplike branches
*FOLIAGE: evergreen, dagger shaped needles
BARK: reddish, shredding off in strips
HABITAT: Japan
INTRODUCED: 1861
VARIETIES: *compacta*—compact, conical, short leaves
　　　　　　elegans—densely branched, bushy—Plume Cryptomeria

The Cryptomeria is hardy in America as far north as Boston. The foliage is somewhat similar to that of the *Sequoiadendron* or the Big Tree of California; the bark is often used by Japanese peasants to shingle the roofs of their houses and is the timber tree of Japan. It is symmetrical while young which gives it special interest and it is not very difficult to grow. The plants grown from seed vary, and several varieties are available all having small cones about ¾" long when they reach maturity. These cones, like those of the other coniferous evergreens, are interesting but can not be depended upon annually since some years very few if any are produced. The much talked of variety *lobbi* does not differ from the species, and the Chinese form *sinensis* is not as ornamental as the species.

Cunninghamia lanceolata 75' Zone 7 Common China Fir

HABIT: spreading branches, pendulous at the tips
*FOLIAGE: evergreen, needlelike 1–2½" long, somewhat similar to that of the more
　　　　　common *Araucaria*
HABITAT: southern and western China
INTRODUCED: 1804

Only of value in the warmer parts of the country, the China Fir has the meritorious quality which few evergreens possess of sprouting from the stump and roots when cut down. In China, this method of quickly reproducing itself by suckers from roots or stumps make this a very important tree for reforestation purposes. The cones are 1–2" long but cannot be depended upon annually.

Cupressus arizonica bonita 35' Zone 7 Smooth Arizona Cypress

HABIT: loosely pyramidal to columnar
*FOLIAGE: fine texture, gray to bluish green, evergreen, scalelike
HABITAT: southern Arizona

This tree has a very poor root system and is very difficult to transplant. Some nurserymen graft it on other understock with better roots, for if this is not done the top may actually outgrow the roots and so cause it to be easily blown over. It should have a dry, light soil in order to grow at its best.

Cupressus bakeri 30' Zone 5 Modoc Cypress

HABIT: rounded and bushy
*FOLIAGE: glaucous, evergreen, scalelike
HABITAT: Oregon

This little-known cypress is the hardiest and should be used considerably more in gardens. The MacNab Cypress of California is very similar but not nearly as hardy.

Cupressus macrocarpa   75′   Zone 7   Monterey Cypress

HABIT: pyramidal when young, broadly rounded when old
*FOLIAGE: evergreen, small scalelike (similar to Junipers)
HABITAT: California coast south of Monterey

The Monterey Cypress is the best cypress for seaside planting and probably best used solely for this purpose, especially as a windbreak against ocean breezes. As a specimen tree or clipped hedge, it withstands salt laden ocean winds better than most other evergreens. At Monterey it has been forced to grow in picturesque habit by the winds off the Pacific Ocean. It grows very rapidly.

Cupressus sempervirens   75′   Zone 7   Italian Cypress

*HABIT: with horizontal or erect branches
*FOLIAGE: dark, evergreen, scalelike
HABITAT: southern Europe and western Asia
INTRODUCED: probably in colonial times
VARIETIES: *stricta*—the columnar Italian Cypress is probably the most popular form for it is extremely narrow in habit, often only a few feet in diameter but 20 feet or more in height. In the group of columnar trees, it is the most rigidly erect and narrowest of them all. It is therefore used a great deal in the gardens of southern Europe for this characteristic—Pyramidal Italian Cypress
horizontalis—with horizontal branches forming a very wide head—Spreading Italian Cypress

Probably the most popular form of this species is the columnar, since there is no other evergreen which grows so tall yet remains so narrow in habit. For purely formal gardens where erect lines are to be emphasized, this tree has no peer. One interesting note on the durability of this wood is the fact that the doors of St. Peter's Cathedral in Rome were supposed to have been made of this wood and were 1100 years old when they were removed, still in sound condition.

Davidia involucrata   60′   Zone 6   Dove Tree

*FLOWERS: many stamens forming a yellow ball 1″ in diameter and 2 bracts, the lower being the longer, as much as 7″ long
TIME: mid-May
HABIT: broadly pyramidal, especially while young
FOLIAGE: dense, rather coarse
HABITAT: western China
INTRODUCED: 1904

This tree was introduced by Ernest H. Wilson and is probably the most widely publicized. The story of how he made a special trip to China to obtain this plant amidst great difficulties, only to find on his return to England that it had been introduced the previous year into France, was one of his major disappointments. Many trees have been distributed in this country—a few are flowering, but many have been disappointingly devoid of flowers. Even in the Arnold Arboretum, the plants bloom only about once in fifteen years, but in Newport, Rhode Island, there is a magnificent specimen which blooms every year. Several plants are performing well on the Pacific coast also. The flower consists of two creamy white bracts, the upper rather small but the lower one pendulous and nearly 7″ long. Between the two bracts is the flower head, rounded, ball-like and yellowish. It is beautiful in flower, but for many gardeners who live in cold areas or who want quick results, this tree may not be worth waiting for, and in fact, the flower buds may not be produced even if the rest of the tree is apparently hardy.

Delonix regia   40′   Zone 10   Royal Poinciana or Flame Tree

*FLOWERS: bright scarlet and yellow, 2–3″ diameter
  TIME: summer
FRUIT: pods, 2′ long and 2″ wide
HABIT: wide branching
FOLIAGE: dense, fine texture, fernlike
HABITAT: Madagascar
  This is probably southern Florida's most popular ornamental flowering tree. The fernlike foliage (deciduous) topped by the brilliant scarlet and yellow blossoms is reason enough why it should be so. It grows rapidly in almost any soil and is one of the sights that a northern visitor to southern Florida rarely forgets, if he is fortunate enough to see a tree in bloom.

Diospyros kaki   40′   Zone 7   Kaki Persimmon

FRUIT: 1½–3″ diameter, fleshy, orange to bright yellow, edible
  EFFECTIVE: early fall
HABIT: rounded head
FOLIAGE: rather dense, leaves 2–7″ long
HABITAT: China, Korea
INTRODUCED: before 1870
  This tree is cultivated only in the subtropical United States in climate similar to that where figs are grown. It has some merit as a shade tree, but can be very difficult as a bearer of edible fruits if only one tree is grown. The species is chiefly dioecious but individual plants have been known which have all three types of flowers on the same tree—perfect, staminate and pistillate. On the other hand, an individual tree has been known to produce a crop of staminate flowers one year, and not produce them again for many years, producing pistillate flowers during the interim.
  The importance of all this is that, in general, this species will not develop fruit (a very few clons may) unless properly fertilized. In California the growers have capitalized on a few "seedless" varieties, i.e., varieties that produce fruits without being pollinized, but the fruits have no seeds. On the other hand, many Florida growers like varieties requiring pollination for they believe it increases the yield. Horticulturists have found some trees fairly dependable pollinizers and of course these are grown.
  In Japan more than eight hundred varieties of this species have been grown and at least one-fourth of these have been termed good varieties. This is the

large persimmon of commerce, but home owners who may wish to plant only one tree would do well to investigate carefully the available varieties before they make their selections. The best information on this score can always be obtained from the nearest state experiment station.

Diospyros virginiana   75′   Zone 4   Common Persimmon

FRUIT: 1½″ diameter, yellow to orange, edible after frost
HABIT: round headed, often pendulous branches
*BARK: deeply cut into regular small blocks
FOLIAGE: dense
AUTUMN COLOR: yellow
HABITAT: eastern and southeastern United States

The Common Persimmon with fruits about 1½″ in diameter is found over a wide area. Sexes are usually separate and plants have been selected producing bigger fruits than others. As a specimen tree (aside from the fruits which are not ornamental) the persimmon has little to offer over many other better kinds of trees.

Elaeagnus angustifolia   20′   Zone 2   Russian Olive

*FLOWERS: silvery outside, yellow inside, fragrant, small
    TIME: early June
FRUIT: yellow coated berries with silvery scales
    EFFECTIVE: early fall
HABIT: widespreading, rather open
BARK: brown, shredding off in long strips
*FOLIAGE: dull gray-green, leaves 1–3½″ long and narrow
HABITAT: southern Europe to west and central Asia
INTRODUCED: early colonial times

The flowers and fruits of this plant are none too conspicuous, but the gray foliage is outstanding and the plant can be used for this one feature. Hardy and vigorous, it grows easily in many kinds of soils and its unique crooked trunk can easily be attractive in its own right, for it is covered with a brown shredding bark which is of considerable interest throughout the winter.

Eriobotrya japonica   20′   Zone 7   Loquat

*FLOWERS: fragrant ½″ diameter in panicles 5–7″ long
    TIME: fall
*FRUIT: orange-yellow, pear shaped, 1½″ long, edible
    EFFECTIVE: spring
HABIT: dense
*FOLIAGE: evergreen, leaves 5–10″ long, leathery
HABITAT: central China
INTRODUCED: 1784

The leathery leaves are very handsome, but in order to do well this shrubby tree requires deep, well-drained soil and full sun. It is grown in certain areas especially for its edible fruits but its rich foliage alone makes it desirable as an ornamental.

Erythea armata   18'   Zone 10   Blue Erythea

HABIT: fan shaped palm
FOLIAGE: silvery blue, fan shaped leaves
HABITAT: Lower California

This is one of the most satisfactory palms in the cooler coastal areas of southern California and this species is even hardy in Texas. Unfortunately it requires considerable moisture and must be watered (and occasionally fertilized) in order to become a specimen tree. Other than this, it requires little care.

Eucalyptus species   Zone 9   Eucalyptus

There are some seventy species and varieties of Eucalyptus offered in the trade today, certainly far more than are needed. These exotic trees are mostly natives of Australia and have taken root so well throughout California that in many sections they are now naturalized. They grow in various soils but unfortunately many have been planted that are inferior or useless. They are rank feeders in the soil, shallow rooted, easily blown over and are always dropping something— bark, leaves or fruit. These interesting evergreens with good foliage, flowers, fruit and bark are best suited to semi-arid regions. The following species, *E. cornuta, ficifolia, globulus, leucoxylon, lehmanni* and *sideroxylon* are only a few which have been used ornamentally as specimens, street trees and windbreaks. If Eucalyptus are contemplated for any kind of ornamental plantings, the entire group should be carefully studied and selections made only after the planting requirements are thoroughly understood. It may well be when the planting problem is analyzed that another kind of tree might actually meet the requirements better than the Eucalyptus. *Eucalyptus gunni* has been found to be the hardiest species both in America and Great Britain.

Eucalyptus ficifolia in flowers. One of many species used on the Pacific Coast.

Eucommia ulmoides   60'   Zone 5   Hardy Rubber Tree

HABIT: rounded
FOLIAGE: elmlike, open
HABITAT: central China
INTRODUCED: 1896

Probably this tree should be included in the secondary list and not mentioned here for it has no outstanding ornamental merits. Its interest to plantsmen is
the fact that it is the only hardy rubber-producing tree for the central and
northern parts of the country. If the leaf, bark or seed is broken and gently pulled
apart, the thin strands of rubber can be seen. From a commercial standpoint,
however, this has little value since the rubber content of the bark is only 3 per
cent of its dry weight and the extraction is difficult. The sexes are separate but
fruiting plants are producing seed now in the Arnold Arboretum.

Eugenia paniculata   40′   Zone 9   Brush-cherry Eugenia

*FLOWERS: white, ½″ diameter with conspicuous stamens, in small terminal
     clusters
   TIME: a good part of the year
*FRUIT: a rose-purple berry, ¾″ diameter
HABITAT: rounded
*FOLIAGE: evergreen, dense, glossy, tinged with red when young
HABITAT: Australia

Widely planted in California and Florida, this is probably the most popular
Eugenia of which there are many. The variety *australis* is more bushy and is
supposed to bloom more or less throughout the year. It will not withstand salt
spray and is susceptible to drought, but responds to shearing well. The excellent
foliage and generous flowers and fruits assist in making this a popular ornamental
tree within its hardiness zone.

Euonymus bungeana semipersistens   18′   Zone 4   Mid-winter Euonymus

*FRUIT: yellowish to pinkish white, opening capsules
   EFFECTIVE: fall and early winter
FOLIAGE: light green, leaves 1½–4″ long, often rather open
HABITAT: China and Manchuria
INTRODUCED: 1902
ADDITIONAL *E. bungeana* VARIETY:
     bungeana pendula—branchlets drooping gracefully—Weeping Euonymus

The variety *semi-persistens* is superior to the species because the abundant
fruits remain on the plant long after the leaves have fallen, thus prolonging its
landscape effectiveness materially. A loose-growing, vigorous shrub with light
green leaves, this plant will grow into a splendid specimen or deciduous screen
in record time. One of the better large shrubs for quick growth. However, it
should be asexually propagated since there are only one or two clons in this
country which fruit well. These should be continued and one of them is growing
in Highland Park, Rochester, New York. Seedlings of this tree have grown
vigorously for eight years, but hardly a fruit has developed.

It should be remembered that most Euonymus are susceptible to infestations
of the Euonymus scale, a serious pest, and unless this can be controlled by
constant care and spraying with the right materials at just the right time, these
plants might well be overlooked entirely. There is nothing quite as disreputable
looking as an uncared for Euonymus, sick and dying from an infestation of scale.

Euonymus europaea aldenhamensis   21′   Zone 3   Aldenham Spindle Tree

*FRUIT: brilliant pink, opening capsules
    EFFECTIVE: fall
FOLIAGE: dark green, leaves 1½–3″ long, dense
AUTUMN COLOR: reddish
ORIGIN: chance seedling at Aldenham, England
INTRODUCED: 1922
OTHER *Euonymus europaea* VARIETIES:
    europaea alba—fruit white—White Fruited Euonymus
    europaea intermedia—bright red fruits
    The varieties *aldenhamensis* and *intermedia* are the most colorfull fruiting of the varieties of the old fashioned, popular Spindle Tree, *E. europaea,* and so should be given preference to the widely distributed European species. Of vigorous growth, all varieties retain their leaves late in the fall and so afford an excellent foliage background for the display of the colorful fruits. These varieties, like other Euonymus, are susceptible to infestations of scale insects (see discussion under *E. bungeana semipersistens*).

Euonymus latifolia   21′   Zone 5   Broadleaf Euonymus

*FRUIT: red to orange opening capsules
    EFFECTIVE: fall
*FOLIAGE: handsome leaves, 3–5″ long, reddish underneath, open
AUTUMN COLOR: red
HABITAT: southern Europe
INTRODUCED: 1730
    This plant has large leaves for a Euonymus and is covered with fruit larger than that of *E. europaeus* and more pendulous but not borne in as great profusion. This species, *E. sanguinea* and *E. sachalinensis* are the first to open their leaves in the spring. It makes an excellent specimen when grown alone. (For scale insects see discussion under *E. bungeana semipersistens*.)

Euonymus sanguinea   21′   Zone 5

*FRUIT: red to orange, opening capsules
    EFFECTIVE: fall
*FOLIAGE: dark green, reddish underneath, leaves 1½–4″ long
AUTUMN COLOR: red
HABITAT: central China
INTRODUCED: 1900
    One of the best deciduous Euonymus from the standpoint of foliage! Its leaves appear as early in the spring as those of *E. latifolia* and at first are reddish, later becoming dark green above and reddish below. This tree has grown exceptionally well in the Arnold Arboretum with vigorous branching and dense foliage, and fruit which opens early and falls quickly, usually before the leaves fall. Because of this and the fact that the fruits are not borne profusely, this species should only be used for its good foliage. (For a discussion concerning infestation of scale insects, see *E. bungeana semipersistens*.)

Evodia danielli   25′   Zone 5   Korean Evodia
*FLOWERS: small, white in large flat clusters
    TIME: early to mid-August
*FRUITS: red to glossy black berries
    EFFECTIVE: September–November
HABIT: open, often shrublike
FOLIAGE: loose, open
HABITAT: northern China and Korea
INTRODUCED: 1905

The Korean Evodia is fast becoming of interest because of its late summer flowers, which come at a time when few woody plants are in bloom. The flower clusters, nearly 6″ across are made up of many small whitish flowers quite similar to the flowers of *Viburnum lentago*. This might be considered a "new" tree for the small garden, especially where late summer bloom and early fall fruits are desirable. As a street tree it will not prove satisfactory, for its wood is comparatively weak and splits easily and apparently it is short lived (15–40 years).

FAGUS

Among deciduous trees, there is nothing quite as majestic or as graceful as the beech. About ten species are recognized in the temperate regions of the Northern Hemisphere, but since they are so similar, only two will be included—our native American Beech and its European relative, *Fagus sylvatica*. Both are beautiful all seasons of the year, something which can not be said of many other trees. They are large trees, with solid round trunks and thin, firm, smooth, gray bark. The European Beech is one of the few European native trees which seem to thrive in North America. The two species are amenable to shearing and have been pruned in several ways, as arbors, hedges, and in pleaching, growing vigorously and fast with many wide spreading branches that frequently sweep the ground.

The feeding roots of these trees are mostly fibrous and near the surface of the soil. Because of this and the deep shade, their low hanging branches create, it is difficult and often impossible to get grass or other plants to grow underneath them. This fact must be known and accepted in advance where they are to be grown.

When these trees are grown properly, they make excellent specimens and really it is not necessary for anything else to grow under them, since their low spreading branches (if not cut off) will completely cover the ground.

The European Beech has slightly darker gray bark than the American Beech and its leaves are not as sharply toothed. There are many varieties of the European (pendulous, fastigiate, colored foliage, cut leaved) but not of the American Beech. The American Beech frequently sprouts profusely from the base of the trunk, while the European type does not.

Because they are fibrous rooted, beeches are easy to move. Their dense foliage and golden autumn color, together with their splendid habit and

The Cutleaved English Beech is a popular favorite everywhere. In the background is the columnar variety, Fagus sylvatica fastigiata.

colorful bark, make them among the best of specimens for ornamental planting. They are not suited for street trees merely because they need so much space in which to grow properly that it is not practical to plant them along streets or highways where space is always at a premium. Where plenty of room is available, either singly or in groups, there are no better trees that can be planted for year-round beauty.

Fagus grandifolia   90'   Zone 3   American Beech

*HABIT: densely pyramidal
FOLIAGE: dense
*AUTUMN COLOR: golden bronze
*BARK: light gray
HABITAT: eastern North America

A splendid native tree, grown over a wide part of this country. Its excellent form, splendid foliage throughout the spring, summer and fall months, and its beautiful light gray bark for winter beauty, lend an ornamental interest every season of the year. The fibrous roots make all beeches notorious surface feeders which means that it is most difficult to grow anything properly underneath their branches. The American Beech should be placed at the top of the list as a splendid specimen tree. It does not withstand city conditions well, however, but is hardier than the European Beech. A grove of native beeches is always a beautiful sight and as a single specimen there is not a tree which will surpass it in year-round beauty.

Fagus sylvatica   90′   Zone 4   European Beech

*HABIT: densely pyramidal
*FOLIAGE: glossy, dark green, dense
*AUTUMN COLOR: bronze
*BARK: dark gray
HABITAT: central and southern Europe
INTRODUCED: early colonial times
VARIETIES: *asplenifolia*—leaves very narrow, often linear—Fernleaf Beech

     atropunicea—leaves purple. There are many forms of this variety vary-
ing in the color of the leaves. The "Copper" Beech is only a form of
this variety, with lighter coppery red foliage. Any group of seedlings
will show quite a variation. The forms, *atropurpurea* and *nigra* are
merely slight variations of the Purple Beech, *atropunicea*. Commercial growers frequently sow the seed of the Purple Beech and
select various forms from among the seedlings, based entirely on
slight variations in color. Since the colors of these trees do vary considerably one should be careful of what is purchased under the
varietal name *atropunicea*. E. H. Wilson said that of all the trees
with colored foliage this was the only one worth planting.—Purple Beech

     fastigiata—fastigiate in habit, often called the Dawyck Beech, this
is one of the best trees of this general type.

     laciniata—leaves narrow, often deeply cut or lobed in somewhat the
same manner as the fronds of a fern. A very beautiful specimen.—
Cutleaf European Beech.

     pendula—pendulous branches, making this one of the most beautiful
trees of the type available for planting in northern gardens.—Weeping Beech

     purpureo-pendula—pendulous branches and purple leaves.—Weeping
Purple Beech

     rotundifolia—very dainty foliage, leaves small, about an inch or less in
length, rounded and borne closely together.—Roundleaf Beech

     tricolor—leaves nearly white, spotted green and with a pink margin.
This variety is really a monstrosity, very deficient in chlorophyll and
usually a weak grower because of this. It is only mentioned here
because there are always gardeners who want to try such plants.

    The English Beech and its varieties should be at the top of everyone's list
of desirable large shade trees. Its dense habit and excellent form, especially in
the variety *pendula*, easily make it one of the most conspicuously graceful
ornamental trees we have.

Ficus carica   30′   Zone 6   Common Fig

FRUIT: figs, pear shaped and greenish to brownish violet
HABIT: wide spreading and rounded, often shrubby
*FOLIAGE: evergreen or deciduous, coarse
HABITAT: western Asia
INTRODUCED: colonial times

    Contrary to popular belief, figs are grown as far north as Long Island, where

A splendid old Weeping Beech at Tiverton, Rhode Island, seventy years old.

they are wrapped carefully and covered for winter protection. Farther south, they are completely hardy and are grown on both coasts. They give a dense shade and their leaves are very large and coarse. If grown for their fruit as well as their ornamental characteristics, there are several varieties available. This tree, if grown in too rich a soil, may not produce much fruit. An application of super-phospate or a root pruning (or both!) are in order to assist fruit bud formation.

Ficus macrophylla   75'   Zone 10   Moreton Bay Fig

HABIT: dense, rounded, at least twice as broad as tall
*FOLIAGE: dense, coarse, but handsome and glossy, evergreen leaves up to 10" long and 4" broad
HABITAT: Australia
INTRODUCED: before 1877
    The famous Moreton Bay Fig tree in Santa Barbara, California, is probably the largest of its kind in America. It was planted in 1877 and has a spread (branches) of 145', and one of the exposed roots 120' from the trunk is 4" in diameter. It is estimated that 9,500 people could stand in its shade at noon. This is one tree that grows twice as wide as it is tall but makes a wonderful evergreen shade tree where space is available. There are many other species of *Ficus*, mostly evergreen, used as ornamental trees in the far South besides this.

Firmiana simplex   40'   Zone 9   Chinese Parasol Tree

FRUITS: borne at the edges of peculiar, leaflike open pods, about 5" long
HABIT: upright
BARK: green

Franklinia alatamaha, named after Benjamin Franklin and found in Georgia
by John Bartram 200 years ago.

FOLIAGE: deciduous, similar to leaves of sycamore, coarse, often 1′ in diameter
HABITAT: China, Japan
An interesting fast-growing tree for the South.

Franklinia alatamaha   30′   Zone 5   Franklinia

*FLOWERS: white, yellow stamens in center, 3″ in diameter
    TIME: September–October
HABIT: upright
FOLIAGE: loose, open, leaves up to 6″ long
*AUTUMN COLOR: brilliant orange to red
HABITAT: Georgia, but not found wild since 1790

John Bartram, one of the early American plant collectors, first found this plant in Georgia in 1770 and later obtained a few plants for his garden in Philadelphia. For some strange reason, no plants have ever been found wild since 1790. All plants now are direct descendants from those few trees Bartram first collected. North of New York, this should not be grown as a tree but as a shrub in order to be better able to combat winter cold. As a tree, it is pyramidal, rather open, but its large white flowers in late summer, followed by its brilliant orange to red autumn color (if it is growing in the full sun) make it an excellent tree for late summer interest. It grows in either acid or alkaline soils but seems to do better in the latter.

FRAXINUS

There are at least sixty species of ash in the northern hemisphere, half of them native of North America, but only a few have proved of value in ornamental planting. The trees are vigorous, rapid growing, with compound opposite leaves, most of which color a brilliant yellow to purple in the fall and are usually fibrous rooted, hence not too difficult to transplant. The wood is tough, usually straight grained, and has been used considerably for this reason. The leaves are opposite and mostly compound. This group of trees is often susceptible to attacks of the oyster scale and must be sprayed occasionally to keep this pest under control. Since there are many other trees which are not so susceptible to scale pests, trees in this group should be selected with discretion. Certainly they are too vigorous to be used on the small property and they frequently become pests by seeding themselves all over the garden.

| Fraxinus americana | 120′ | Zone 3 | White Ash |

HABIT: erect but with rounded top
FOLIAGE: dense, leaves compound
*AUTUMN COLOR: deep purple or yellow
HABITAT: eastern United States

A common tree, often considered a weed because it is reproduced rapidly from seed and quickly reseeds itself over the entire area where a mature tree grows; nevertheless it is a vigorous-growing specimen that provides much of the wood for baseball bats. Its quick growth, vigorous habit and lack of special soil requirements enable it to be used in many a situation, especially in places where better ornamentals would not make such a quick showing. The wood is especially used for handles for tools and agricultural implements. Since it is commonly available all over the East, it is probably used more in landscape planting than any other ash.

| Fraxinus excelsior | 120′ | Zone 3 | European Ash |

HABIT: round headed
FOLIAGE: open, leaves compound
HABITAT: Europe, Asia Minor
INTRODUCED: early colonial times
VARIETY: *pendula*—branches pendulous, making a small, rounded, moundlike tree not much better than the Weeping Catalpa monstrosity, although the texture of the foliage is much finer.—Weeping European Ash

This tree, which is used a great deal in Europe as an ornamental tree, has been planted to some extent in America. Its leaves do not have the attractive autumn coloration of *F. americana*, but drop off the tree while still green.

| Fraxinus oregona | 80′ | Zone 6 | Oregon Ash |

HABIT: narrow, upright to broad
FOLIAGE: dense, compound
HABITAT: British Columbia to California

One of the important deciduous trees of the Pacific coast, often used in landscape work within this region as a shade tree.

Fraxinus ornus   60′   Zone 5   Flowering Ash

FLOWERS: white, small, in dense fragrant panicles 3–5″ long
     TIME: mid-May
HABIT: round head
FOLIAGE: dense, compound, luxuriant
HABITAT: southern Europe, western Asia
INTRODUCED: before 1700

The small flowers, being profusely borne and very fragrant, make this species unique among the ashes. It is a favored shade tree in Europe.

Fraxinus pennsylvanica lanceolata   60′   Zone 2   Green Ash

HABIT: dense and rounded
FOLIAGE: dense
AUTUMN COLOR: yellow
HABITAT: central and eastern North America

This is the most widely distributed ash in North America, growing naturally in nearly half the area. It is a vigorous, well-shaped, dense tree, used in many places throughout its habitat.

Fraxinus velutina   45′   Zone 7   Velvet Ash

HABIT: round headed
FOLIAGE: more or less open
HABITAT: Arizona, New Mexico, Mexico

This tree is of value chiefly in the dry alkaline soils of the Southwest where it has been used a great deal as a street tree. Although it should have fertile soil, it grows fairly rapidly almost anywhere, even in severely alkaline soils, throughout its general habitat.

Ginkgo biloba   120′   Zone 4   Ginkgo or Maidenhair Tree

FLOWERS: inconspicuous but sexes separate
FRUIT: round plumlike, 1″ diameter, the kernel eaten by Chinese but the outside
     flesh of obnoxious odor when ripe
*HABIT: picturesque, wide spreading, open
*FOLIAGE: leaves fan shaped, open
*AUTUMN COLOR: clear yellow
HABITAT: eastern China
INTRODUCED: about 1784
VARIETY: *fastigiata*—with columnar habit—Sentry Ginkgo

Over the two centuries this tree has been grown by the white man in America it has become quite common along highways and as a specimen in gardens. Its picturesque wide fan-shaped branching habit, together with its small fan-shaped leaves have become familiar to many. It should be remembered, however, that the fruiting or pistillate trees (staminate flowers are on one tree and pistillate flowers on another) bear round plumlike fruits, the flesh of which has an obnoxious odor when ripe. Trees in the Arnold Arboretum, grown from seed, were twenty years old and at least 25 high before they had their first flowers! A long wait to determine whether the plants will bear fruit! Nurserymen would do well

A very old Ginkgo in the heart of down town Boston. The Ginkgo is one
of the best trees for withstanding city conditions.

to propagate staminate or non-fruiting trees asexually. It has been stated that
staminate trees are more upright in habit, fruiting trees are more wide spreading,
often with slightly pendulous branchlets. I have not been able to observe this first
hand. This is an excellent tree for street planting or as a specimen tree on a large
lawn, but not a tree for the small property.

The Ginkgo, probably the most ancient of trees now alive, has been growing
on this earth for ten million years as geological records have proven—(from the
Jurassic period on, with various rocks mute evidence that it was at one time native
in what is now North America).

An excellent specimen of the Sentry Ginkgo (Roosevelt Boulevard, Philadelphia, Pa.)

There are clons of the *fastigiata* form that are definitely staminate, making them ideal for street tree planting. One of the most conspicuous (and oldest) of such plantings is along the Roosevelt Boulevard (U. S. Route 1) in northeast Philadelphia, Pennsylvania.

The most important fact of value to every plantsman is that the Ginkgo is not infested with any insect or disease, hence needs no spraying. Trees of low maintenance cost like this are few indeed!

Gleditsia triacanthos   135′   Zone 4   Common Honey-locust

FRUIT: brown pods, 12–18″ long
    EFFECTIVE: fall
HABIT: broad and open
*FOLIAGE: fine texture, leaves singly and doubly compound, very open, leaves
    7–12″ long
HABITAT: central United States
VARIETIES: *elegantissima*—thornless and the dense bushy habit. Of merit for street
        tree planting especially when grafted high on the species as under-
        stock—Bushy Honey-locust
    inermis—no thorns—Thornless Honey-locust
    inermis "Moraine"—patented (No. 836) by the Siebenthaler Nursery
        of Dayton, Ohio, and said to be non-fruiting
A splendid tree for withstanding city conditions, its only drawback is its large, very stiff and branched thorns, sometimes as much as 4″ long. In playgrounds and adjacent to highways this is enough to black-list the tree, since these thorns are dropped or broken off on occasion and afford a rather serious hazard. Otherwise, the tree is a good shade tree, easily transplanted, well adapted to a varying number of difficult growing conditions.

The new "Moraine" Locust, a thornless and seedless variety of the Honey-locust which is being widely recommended as a substitute for the American Elm. It was originally grown by the Siebenthaler Nurseries of Dayton, Ohio. Picture Courtesy of the Siebenthaler Company.

The thornless variety has been widely recommended as a substitute for the American Elm, not because of its shape—which certainly is not similar—but because it can be grown in so many situations. The long twisted pods of the species are interesting for they remain on the tree long after the leaves fall, yet under certain lawn conditions can be troublesome since they must be raked off. It is not subject to borers as is the true Locust (*Robinia*), has no particularly interesting flowers nor autumn color. The new variety "Moraine" developed and patented by the Siebenthaler Nursery Company of Dayton, Ohio, is thornless and is said to be sterile, hence no fruit pods are developed. This observation is based on the original tree which is fifteen years old and 16" in diameter. Since young trees are slightly vase shaped, it is being widely advertised as an excellent substitute for the American Elm.

The Honey-locust can be a long-lived tree. One in Dayton, Ohio, which was cut down recently showed 327 annual rings. The foliage tends to appear late in the spring, and the leaves drop off very early in the fall, giving this tree some value as a lawn tree to allow maximum sunshine to the turf underneath its branches during the cooler weather of the active growing season.

Gordonia lasianthus   60'   Zone 8   Loblolly Bay Gordonia

*FLOWERS: 2½" in diameter, white and fragrant
    TIME: summer, for nearly two months
HABIT: dense, narrow head
*FOLIAGE: evergreen, leaves 6" long, lustrous and leathery
HABITAT: southeastern United States
    This tree is used in the far South especially for its good foliage.

Grevillea robusta   150'   Zone 10   Silk-oak Grevillea

*FLOWERS: golden yellow to orange trusses
    TIME: April
HABIT: upright
*FOLIAGE: evergreen, feathery, 6"–8" long and as broad, white silky on the under surface
HABITAT: Australia
    Often grown in the greenhouse in pots merely as a decorative pot plant, this tree has considerable merit as an ornamental specimen and as a street tree in southern California because it grows in poor sandy soils as well as in deep rich soils.

Gymnocladus dioicus   90'   Zone 4   Kentucky Coffee-tree

HABIT: open, large branches, picturesque
FOLIAGE: open, coarse, leaves singly and doubly compound
HABITAT: central United States
    Although this tree has no conspicuous flowers, no autumn color and rather ugly large pods for fruits, its picturesque large branches and stubby twigs offer considerable interest throughout the winter, noticeable for a good six months of the year anyway. It is not a good shade tree, is often considered a "dirty tree" because it drops its pods and large leaves occasionally, but might be given consideration particularly for its value in the winter landscape.

Halesia carolina   30'   Zone 4   Carolina Silverbell

*FLOWERS: white, bell shaped, ½" long
    TIME: mid-May
FRUIT: dry 2 or 4 winged pods, 2" long
    EFFECTIVE: fall

Halesia monticola, the Silverbell blooms in mid-spring.

HABIT: rounded
FOLIAGE: open
AUTUMN COLOR: yellow
HABITAT: West Virginia to Florida and Texas
Supposedly the hardier of the Silverbells, certainly the smaller, of garden value only when the delicate, pendulous, bell-like flowers are in evidence. These do not remain on the tree very long.

Halesia monticola	90'	Zone 5	Mountain Silverbell

*FLOWERS: white, bell shaped, 1" long
    TIME: mid-May
FRUIT: dry 2 or 4 winged pod, 2" long
    EFFECTIVE: fall
HABIT: pyramidal to round topped
FOLIAGE: coarse, open
AUTUMN COLOR: yellow
HABITAT: Tennessee and North Carolina to Georgia
VARIETY: *rosea*—flowers pale pink—Pink Mountain Silverbell
With larger flowers than the Carolina Silverbell, this species and its variety are planted more because they are more easily seen when in bloom. The pendant flowers, appear all along the twigs of the previous year's growth, making a well-grown tree a uniquely beautiful sight when in bloom. At other times of year, the tree is not meritorious but it has no serious insect or disease pests, an important point to consider where annual maintenance and careful supervision will not be given. Because of its loose foliage and comparatively small flowers, it might best

be used where it can be closely observed, or else planted with an evergreen background of white pine or hemlock.

Hemiptelea davidi   20′   Zone 5   David Hemiptelea

HABIT: rounded, often shrubby, thorny branches
FOLIAGE: dense, leaves ¾–2¼″ long
HABITAT: northern China, Manchuria, Korea
INTRODUCED: 1899

A small tree, rarely used, but which might have considerable merit. It is dense in habit, often shrubby, and producing very prominent thorns that may be 4–5″ long. In northern China it is used as a hedge or screen and so might have use in this country for the same purpose.

Hippophae rhamnoides   30′   Zone 3   Common Sea-Buckthorn

FLOWERS: inconspicuous, sexes separate
     TIME: early April
*FRUIT: bright orange berries ¼″ in diameter borne in large clusters, profusely on pistillate plants
     EFFECTIVE: fall
HABIT: open, rounded, often with lower trunk devoid of branches, spiny twigs
FOLIAGE: leaves willowlike, grayish green on upper surface, silver-green beneath
HABITAT: Europe and Asia
INTRODUCED: colonial times

Grown chiefly for its profuse, bright orange or orange-yellow fleshy fruits, gray and silvery foliage. However, the sexes are separate, pistillate flowers all on one tree and staminate flowers on another. Both must be present to insure fruiting, preferably in a ratio of one staminate plant to every six pistillate plants. The fruit is very acid, not quickly eaten by birds, and remains on the plant a long time. The English think highly of this shrub or small tree, some even saying that it should be present in every garden, probably because of the fact that it not only does well in seashore plantings, but in inland areas as well. For some reason we have had much difficulty in getting it established in the Arnold Arboretum, but once established, it makes a splendid ornamental for fall display.

Hymenosporum flavum   50′   Zone 10   Sweet-shade

FLOWERS: yellow, 1½″ long in terminal panicles, fragrant
     TIME: early summer
HABIT: short branches, often a long bare trunk, pyramidal
*FOLIAGE: evergreen, dark green, coarse
HABITAT: Australia

Frequently selected as a street tree because of its rapid growth. It is closely related to the Pittosporums and often planted in Lower California, where it does not seem to be susceptible to serious insect or disease troubles, and so can be considered in the select group of low maintenance street trees.

ILEX

The hollies comprise a most valuable group of ornamental trees and shrubs, some evergreen and some deciduous. There are those that are native to Asia, many are native to South America, some native to Europe and of course some native to North America. The hollies most commonly thought of when the name is mentioned are the European Holly (*Ilex aquifolium*) and our native American Holly (*I. opaca*), both being small trees and highly valued for their ornamental red berries. Both have been cultivated for such long periods that there are nearly one hundred varieties of each, truly a bewildering number.

Eight of the following species like *Ilex aquifolium* and *I. opaca* have evergreen foliage which makes them more valuable as ornamentals than the two deciduous types. All the types recommended here have bright red or yellow berries and are far more attractive than some shrub types with black berries. The flowers of all species are small and inconspicuous.

Hollies belong to that group of plants with separate sexes, staminate flowers on one plant and pistillate flowers on another. Both must be present in the near vicinity to insure the fertilization of the pistillate flowers. In some regions where hollies are native, wind-blown pollen or even insect-carried pollen may be sufficient so that only the pistillate form of the species need be planted in the garden. Usually the safer method to insure fruiting is to have both sexes in the same garden. Planting a small staminate plant in the same hole with the pistillate plant is another method to insure good fruiting, and pains must be taken, as these plants grow older, to prune the staminate plant to a minimum number of branches. Pollen from one species of holly may fertilize the flowers of another species, but it is essential for the two to be in bloom together. Most of these trees bloom in late May or early June, or at the same time as the Locust and the Yellow-wood. Fortunately, some commerical nurserymen are recognizing the importance of growing the holly sexes separately and it is from these sources that plants should be obtained. There is no positive way to identify the different sexes until they flower.

Hollies are propagated by cuttings and seeds, but the seeds take two years to germinate, sometimes three. The shrubby species are, for the most part, rather rugged individuals and easy of culture; the tree types are a little more difficult because they are not the easiest type of plants to move and must have a ball of soil about the roots if the operation is to prove successful. A normally good garden soil is all they need in which to thrive. If grown in a dry, sandy soil, it might be advisable to mulch the plants with oak leaves or pine needles. Most hollies are comparatively free of insect and disease pests (except possibly the holly leaf miner) and where these troubles exist they can be eliminated by applying commonly available materials.

Ten species are recommended here and each one could easily make a splendid garden specimen within its limits of hardiness. Other species are being grown, but the few here mentioned are certainly among the best.

Ilex aquifolium   70'   Zone 6   English Holly

*FRUIT: bright red berries on female plants, ¼" diameter, on previous year's growth

EFFECTIVE: fall and winter

*HABIT: pyramidal, dense branching

*FOLIAGE: dense, evergreen, lustrous

HABITAT: southern Europe, northern Africa, western Asia

INTRODUCED: early colonial times

VARIETIES: *angustifolia*—small narrow leaves—Narrowleaf English Holly

        argenteo-marginata—leaf margin silver—Silver-edge English Holly

        aureo-marginata—leaf margin golden, leaves with gray-green mottlings —Yellow-edge English Holly

        bacciflava—fruit yellow—Yellow Fruit English Holly

        camelliaefolia—few spines on leaves, fruit large and bright red, foliage colors bronze in winter

        ferox—leaves with short spines on the upper convex end—Hedgehog Holly

        hodginsi—leaves 2½–3¾" long and dark green with prominent spines

Since the English Holly has been grown for centuries, literally hundreds of varieties have been named. These vary according to leaf, size, shape and color, tree habit and also according to fruit characteristics. Some of the interesting foliage forms are male plants. There are several beautiful variegated forms being grown on the Pacific Coast especially for their foliage (and berries) at Christmas time, being grown in commercial orchards, cultivated and maintained like any other orchard, and their branches clipped in the late fall and sold "by the pound." Cut in this way, the larger more lustrous green leaves and the larger berries are superior in every way to those of the native American species, *I. opaca*. On the East Coast the English Holly is grown in ornamental plantings, but seems to grow far better in the moister climate of the Pacific coast.

It will eliminate future disappointments to remember that in order to bear fruits, the pistillate plant *must* have a pollen-bearing plant in the near vicinity.

Ilex cassine   36'   Zone 7   Dahoon

*FRUITS: red berries ¼" diameter, profusely borne in dense clusters (sexes separate)

EFFECTIVE: fall and winter

HABIT: rounded, dense branching

*FOLIAGE: evergreen 1½–5" long, entire and spineless margins, dense

AUTUMN COLOR: purplish green

HABITAT: southeastern United States

This tree is a native in the South in wet soils and is valued for its heavy fruit production. The common name Dahoon may have originated with the Indians. Fortunately, although it grows in moist spots it will also grow in normal soils without excessive moisture, especially when grafted on *I. opaca* understock.

Ilex decidua   30'   Zone 5   Possum Haw

*FRUITS: orange to scarlet berries, ¼" in diameter (sexes separate)

EFFECTIVE: fall and winter

HABIT: spreading branches
BARK: light gray
FOLIAGE: deciduous, lustrous
HABITAT: southeastern United States
Common over a wide area, especially in swamps, its evergreen foliage and willowy growth are its chief assets.

Ilex latifolia   60'   Zone 7   Lusterleaf Holly

*FRUITS: dull red berries, ⅓" diameter in crowded clusters (sexes separate)
      EFFECTIVE: fall
HABIT: rounded
*FOLIAGE: evergreen, dark lustrous leaves 4–8" long
HABITAT: Japan
INTRODUCED: 1840
A handsome dark-leaved evergreen requiring good soil and a shaded situation and regarded by some as being the most handsome broad-leaved evergreen tree in its native land.

Ilex montana   36'   Zone 5   Mountain Winterberry

*FRUITS: orange-red berries, ⅓" diameter (sexes separate)
      EFFECTIVE: fall and winter
HABIT: rather slender
FOLIAGE: deciduous, leaves 2–6" long, open
HABITAT: New York to South Carolina
Red fruiting trees are mostly in demand as ornamentals, especially when they retain their fruits for a long time. This is the reason why this native holly is retained in the desirable list. As a shrub it can be discarded in preference to *Ilex verticillata*.

Ilex opaca   45'   Zone 5   American Holly

*FRUITS: bright red berries on female plants ¼" in diameter on current year's
      growth (sexes separate)
      EFFECTIVE: fall and early winter
*HABIT: pyramidal, dense branching
*BARK: smooth, light gray
*FOLIAGE: evergreen, spiny leaves, not lustrous, mostly dense
HABITAT: eastern United States
VARIETIES: *subintegra*—leaves entire or nearly so and not with spiny margins—
            Whole-leaf American Holly
          xanthocarpa—fruits yellow—Yellowfruit American Holly
This native American Holly is one of the most sought-after trees for Christmas decoration. It is native in wide areas along the eastern seaboard and is frequently transplanted to gardens from the wild. Large amounts of it are collected every year and in some places it is grown merely for the production of fruiting branches which are reaped for the Christmas trade. Individual plants differ widely in leaf size, shape and in size and number of fruits.
This tree prefers good, well-drained soil. If planted in an orchard pattern there should be at least one staminate tree to every ten pistillate trees. On the

small property it might be well to have a pistillate tree onto which is grafted a staminate branch or to have a small staminate plant near the larger pistillate plant.

Between seventy-five and one hundred varieties of the American Holly have been described.[1] Desirable characteristics in holly varieties would include annual bearing, large and bright colored fruits, good foliage, and a good dense habit.

Commercial growers sometimes have their own pet holly tree which they propagate because they are sure of its performance. A very few of the varieties which have acquired wide spread distribution are "Bountiful," "Croonenburg," "East Palatka," "Hume 2," "Lake City," "Mrs. Santa," "Taber 3."

Recently, in Rhode Island I had the pleasure of inspecting several acres of native holly which was being carefully attended, some of which was even being fertilized. All trees were there as nature had planted them, some of them with solid trunks 8" in diameter. There was tremendous variation among these trees. Size and disposition of the fruit varied as much as the luster, size and shape of the individual leaves. Even the habit of the tree varied, some being dense, making excellent ornamental specimens, and others being very open.

This experience with variation proved to me once again that it is impossible to select any of the seventy-five or more varieties now named and offered commercially as being "best." Some may do better on certain soils than others, some will do better in warmer (or drier) climates—it will take years of experimentation and comparison to select the superior clons. The New Jersey Experiment Station at New Brunswick has undertaken a testing of these many varieties. Until results can be accurately reported and selections made, one should be careful about accepting all the claims made for any one clon. It should always be remembered that, from an ornamental standpoint, fruit characteristics are only a part of the picture and that a good habit and a good dense foliage go just as far in making a worthy ornamental specimen.

One of the larger northern outposts of American Holly is at Fort Hancock, Sandy Hook, New Jersey. Here in a one-hundred-acre tract and protected from the grasping hands of individuals seeking Christmas decorations these hollies are growing under government protection. Some are nearly 20" in diameter with the tallest about 55'. It is estimated that some are over 275 years old and may have been growing there in 1609 when Hendrik Hudson first sailed upon the great river now bearing his name. In many places along the Atlantic seaboard—Cape Cod, New Jersey, Delaware and Virginia, native stands are fast being destroyed, but this one, now under government surveillance, it is hoped, will continue to be protected for all time.

Ilex pedunculosa   30'   Zone 5   Longstalk Holly

*FRUITS: bright red on slender stalks nearly 1" long, ¼" in diameter (sexes separate)
EFFECTIVE: early fall to early winter
*HABIT: densely pyramidal
*FOLIAGE: evergreen, lustrous leaves, 1–3" long
HABITAT: Japan
INTRODUCED: 1892

[1] Hume, Harold H. "Evergreen Hollies Native in the United States," Nat. Hort Mag. Vol. 26; 143–179, July 1947.

The Longstalk Holly Ilex pedunculosa, has lustrous evergreen leaves and red fruits, an excellent small slow growing tree, little seen in American gardens.

This is one of the hardiest of evergreen hollies and should be better known, especially in northern gardens. The fruits are often as large as those of *I. aquifolium*.

Ilex pernyi   30′   Zone 6   Perny Holly

*FRUITS: red berries ¼″ diameter, in clusters, (sexes separate)
  EFFECTIVE: late summer and early fall
*FOLIAGE: glossy, evergreen leaf, ½–1¼″ long with a few spines on the margin
HABIT: pyramidal, especially when young
HABITAT: central and western China
INTRODUCED: 1900
  Somewhat similar to the shrubby Chinese Holly (*Ilex cornuta*), it has smaller leaves and when young is very definitely pyramidal in habit. Since there are none too many red fruiting evergreens, this species is kept in the recommended list. The fruits are in conspicuous clusters and borne in the axis of the leaves.

Ilex purpurea   40′   Zone 7

*FRUITS: red berries ¼″ diameter (sexes separate)
  TIME: fall
HABIT: pyramidal, dense branching
*FOLIAGE: evergreen leaves 2½–4″ long, dense
HABITAT: China, Japan
INTRODUCED: 1900
  Not too much is known about this plant in cultivation as yet, but some splendid specimens are being grown in the South, even as far north as Glen Dale, Maryland. In China it grows with *Ilex cornuta* and is greatly admired by the Chinese, especially at New Year's time when great bunches of it are collected for

decorations. The evergreen leaves are stripped off the branches, leaving the brilliant red berries. This plant should be exploited more in America in areas where it proves hardy.

Ilex vomitoria   24′   Zone 7   Yaupon

*FRUITS: bright red berries, ¼″ diameter (sexes separate)
    EFFECTIVE: fall and winter
HABIT: rather loose and open
*FOLIAGE: leaves about 1–1½″ long, lustrous, evergreen
HABITAT: southeastern United States

This is one of the most interesting of the evergreen hollies. Often a shrub, occasionally a tree, it flowers on the previous year's growth with fruiting twigs usually literally covered with fruits. In fact, this might be considered as the holly which produces the most fruit. It stands shearing well and so can be used in hedge making. Large specimens do not transplant easily if collected from the wild.

Jacaranda acutifolia   50′   Zone 10   Sharpleaf Jacaranda

*FLOWERS: 2″ long, blue, borne in great profusion
    TIME: early summer
HABIT: spreading branches
*FOLIAGE: fernlike, very delicate texture
HABITAT: Brazil

This is one of the most popular ornamental trees of the sub-tropical United States and is used a great deal in both southern Florida and coastal southern California. Its abundant clusters of lavender-blue flowers in early summer, together with its delicate fernlike foliage, endear it to many a home owner and make it a valued subject for park and highway planting as well. The tree is without foliage for a short time only, prior to the appearance of its flowers. When used as a street tree it might best be spaced 40′ apart.

JUGLANS

The walnuts are not particularly beautiful specimen trees. They have no interesting flowers and their fruits can be troublesome if the tree grows in a neatly kept lawn. Certainly the fruits could not be considered ornamental. These trees are all tap rooted and the large ones are rather difficult to transplant and they have no autumn color. There are two varieties which have cut leaved foliage which might be considered better than the species as specimens, but as yet, both are extremely difficult to locate commercially. In any event, these trees cannot be considered as specimens for the small property, and should be overlooked where other types of ornamental trees are available. As timber trees, or grown primarily for their fruits, they have their uses.

Juglans hindsi   50′   Zone 8   Hinds Black Walnut

HABIT: round head
FOLIAGE: coarse, compound leaves, dense
HABITAT: central California

On the Pacific Coast this tree is used considerably as a street tree and as understock for *J. regia* because it grows more vigorously.

Juglans nigra   150′   **Zone 4**   Eastern Black Walnut

FRUITS: large nuts, 1–2″ diameter
HABIT: rounded to upright
FOLIAGE: coarse, rather open
HABITAT: eastern United States
VARIETY: *laciniata*—with leaflets finely cut, giving the foliage a truly fine texture. An excellent foliage form, superior to the species from an ornamental viewpoint.

This walnut is only included because of many associations which people have with it throughout its native range. It is too coarse for a street tree and its nuts falling on the road would make driving hazardous. Its flowers have no interesting ornamental value and it has no autumn color. It has been definitely proved that its roots give off a material which is toxic to many other kinds of plants, hence it should not be grown near valued specimens. It should therefore be used as a specimen only where it has plenty of room to grow. Even then, unless the owner has certain sentimental reasons for growing it, there are many other trees which would give better ornamental value in the same space.

There are many commercial varieties of this available, selected because of the size or edible qualities of their fruits. Among the best of these would be "Thomas" (especially for growing in the northern limits of Zone 4); "Ohio" and "Stabler" from Ohio; "Tasterite" and "Snyder" from New York; "Wiard" and "Allen" from Michigan; "Kettler" from Wisconsin; "Clark" from southern Minnesota and "Cresco" from northern Iowa. Over seventy-five varieties are currently listed in the nursery catalogues. The Black Walnut requires a rich, deep soil, slightly alkaline or neutral.

Juglans regia   90′   **Zone 5–6**   English or Persian Walnut

FRUITS: nuts 1½–2″ in diameter
HABIT: broad head, rounded
FOLIAGE: dense, coarse
BARK: silver gray
HABITAT: southeastern Europe and China
INTRODUCED: early colonial times
VARIETIES: "Carpathian"—a geographical form introduced from Poland by Mr. Paul Crath of Toronto, Canada, in 1926. It has withstood temperatures of −40°F in its native habitat. Some of these trees in Canada and the northern United States show promise.
laciniata—a fine, cut-leaved variety of value for its ornamental foliage, superior to the species from an ornamental viewpoint.

A variable species, widely grown commercially in California for its nuts, this tree has merit, where hardy, as an ornamental specimen but as in the case of *Juglans nigra*, the cut-leaved variety makes the better ornamental tree. It is round headed and very dense, and some clons are grown as far north as Boston, Massachusetts. However, it can only be depended on considerably farther south. Some of the varieties are "Breslau," "Broadview," "Eureka," "Franquette,"

"Mayette," "Payne" and "Willson." On the Pacific coast, north of central California, the English Walnut is commonly propagated on *J. hindsi*. When trees are twenty years old or thereabouts, a high percentage of them die due to incompatibility of stock and scion and this trouble is referred to as "walnut girdle ' or "black-line." Other more compatible understock is being sought; one species tried is *Pterocarya stenoptera*. Whether or not this will prove a permanently satisfactory understock remains to be seen.

Juglans sieboldiana cordiformis   60'   Zone 4   Heartnut

FRUITS: nuts 1–1½" long
HABIT: rounded, massive branches
FOLIAGE: coarse
HABITAT: Japan
INTRODUCED: 1863

The Heartnut is here suggested as an ornamental in preference to both the Manchurian Walnut (*J. mandshurica*) and the Japanese Walnut (*J. sieboldiana*) merely because its nuts apparently have a higher economic value. All these trees are rounded in habit with massive branches and coarse compound leaves, but the Heartnut produces nuts that are heart shaped and easily cracked, sometimes even split open with a pen knife. It is not unusual for the kernels to come out whole. Some varieties like "Bates," "Fodemaier" and "Walters" are available, but they have not been producing on a commercial scale for a long enough period for us to know very much about them. If a combination shade- and nut-producing tree is not desired, but merely a shade tree, some other tree would undoubtedly give better all-round satisfaction.

JUNIPERUS

The junipers, like the yews, are unusual among the evergreens in that the sexes are usually separate, and only the pistillate or fruiting trees will bear the small, round blue berries (smaller than a pea) so desirable as a display in the fall and winter. Both male and female plants should be grown in fairly close proximity to each other, and since the flowers are minute, the distinguishing of one sex from the other (except when in fruit) presents a real problem. If the nurserymen would only propagate these sexes asexually and thus keep them straight, it would be splendid, but this is a much slower process usually (and more expensive) than growing these species from seed. Trees can be transplanted in fruit, so that the sexes can be told apart if large plants are to be purchased in the fall.

Most junipers are easily moved with a ball of earth when young but the older they grow the more difficult it becomes to transplant them. The small scalelike foliage of these plants varies considerably, even on trees of the same species and even on the same tree, depending on the age, making identification among them extremely difficult at times. Four native species have been recommended here, chiefly because they are native in different parts of the country and each one has a locale where it grows to best advantage. Taken out of that area, they cannot be expected to do well. Four commonly grown exotic species have also been recommended because of

A magnificent specimen of the Chinese Juniper photographed near Peking, China.

their good adjustment in this country. The junipers prefer alkaline soils, are tall, narrow and dense in habit. The fruits of some species require two years to mature, while others ripen in one year. Incidentally this can be the means of differentiating the native *Juniperus virginiana* from its western counterpart, *J. scopulorum*. There are a large number of shrubs, but comparatively few trees, in this genus.

When junipers are grown in the vicinity of certain plants like the Shad Bush, Hawthorn, native crab apples, etc., some plants will harbor the juniper rust. The fungus has two cycles in its life—one spent on the deciduous plants where it spots and mars the foliage. The other cycle is spent on the juniper where it is manifest in peculiar hornlike red to orange fleshy growths on the foliage, especially in wet weather. This is the teliospore stage. On junipers this can be controlled with spraying, using ferric dimethyl dithio-carbonate (one of the commercial compounds is called "Fermate"); or sodium dinitrocryselate (trade name Elgetol) applied as a one-per-cent spray in very early May has apparently stopped this teliospore development. It does seem difficult to have to remove one or the other hosts of this fungus where it is prevalent, since both are such important ornamental plants. Spraying in this fashion will break the life cycle and remove the fungus as a threat, thus allowing both types of host plants to be grown side by side.

Juniperus chinensis   60'   Zone 4   Chinese Juniper

*FRUITS: sexes separate; female plants with fruits ⅜" in diameter but ripening
    the second year
  EFFECTIVE: fall and winter
HABIT: pyramidal
*FOLIAGE: evergreen, pointed scalelike leaves
HABITAT: China, Japan
INTRODUCED: 1767
VARIETIES: *columnaris*—columnar, silvery green foliage, all the leaves are sharp.
    Introduced by Frank Meyer of the U.S.D.A., Bureau of Plant Industry—Blue Columnar Chinese Juniper
    keteleeri—broadly pyramidal, ascending branches. This has been listed in many references as a form of the native *Juniperus virginiana*, but plants growing in the Arnold Arboretum are obviously forms of *J. chinensis*—Keteleer Juniper
    mas—narrow, dense, conical with staminate flowers
    pyramidalis—narrow, bluish green, compact pyramid. This plant is often grown in the North under the incorrect name of *J. excelsa stricta*, which is only truly hardy in Zone 7.
A variable species with many named varieties being offered in the trade, ranging from ground covers to standard trees. The leaves are of two kinds (as in *J. virginiana*) scalelike and acicular or sharp pointed, the latter often being predominant. The sexes are separate in all junipers and the fruits on the pistillate plants take two years to develop, being slightly larger than the fruits of *J. virginiana*. The general aspect of these plants is a lighter green than our native red cedar, often not quite as dense foliage. I would personally prefer the native species in my garden, but many admire this Chinese native so it is included here merely because it offers variations for planting in Zone 4, where only these two tree types prove reliably hardy.

Juniperus drupacea   60'   Zone 7   Syrian Juniper

*FRUIT: brown to bluish berry, ripening the second year (sexes separate)
  EFFECTIVE: fall and winter

*HABIT: columnar
*FOLIAGE: evergreen, dense, pointed, scalelike leaves
HABITAT: Greece and Asia Minor
INTRODUCED: 1853

The Syrian Juniper is an interesting and handsome juniper (especially in limestone soils) for the southern part of the country.

Juniperus excelsa   60′   Zone 7   Greek Juniper

*FRUIT: round berries, ⅜″ diameter on female plants
    EFFECTIVE: fall
*HABIT: narrow pyramidal
*FOLIAGE: evergreen, usually juvenile foliage or scalelike type, dense
HABITAT: Greece, Western Asia
INTRODUCED: 1836
VARIETY: *stricta*—columnar form with juvenile glaucous foliage. Sometimes this
        name is given incorrectly to *J. chinensis pyramidalis* in northern
        nurseries, but the true *J. excelsa stricta* is not hardy in the North.
        Where it can be grown it is most desirable as a densely compact,
        pyramidal, slow-growing shrub or small tree—Spiny Greek Juniper

Juniperus lucayana   50′   Zone 9   West Indies Juniper

FRUIT: small, blue berries (sexes separate)
    EFFECTIVE: fall
*HABIT: dense, pyramidal, upright, but graceful
*FOLIAGE: evergreen, small pointed scalelike leaves
HABITAT: southern Georgia to Florida

This is a substitute for the native *J. virginiana* (and similar to it) in the warmer parts of the country where the northern species will not grow. It has been considered one of the most beautiful of the junipers.

Juniperus pachyphloea   60′   Zone 7   Alligator Juniper

*FRUIT: reddish brown berries, ½″ diameter (sexes separate)
    EFFECTIVE: fall
HABIT: spreading
FOLIAGE: on young plants the pointed scalelike leaves are a silvery white color
BARK: checkered, very beautiful
HABITAT: Arizona, New Mexico, southwest Texas and Mexico

One of the most ornamental of the native tree junipers but not hardy north of the Middle Atlantic States.

Juniperus rigida   30′   Zone 5   Needle Juniper

*FRUIT: ¼″ diameter, ripening the second year (sexes separate)
    EFFECTIVE: fall and winter
*HABIT: pyramidal, pendulous branchlets
*FOLIAGE: evergreen, loose and open, pointed scalelike leaves
HABITAT: Japan, Korea, northern China
INTRODUCED: 1861

A very graceful, narrowly pyramidal tree with loose and open branches and foliage but with gracefully pendulous branchlets. It would not shear well nor form a good windbreak, but is recommended solely for its graceful appearance as a specimen. *Juniperus formosana,* considerably more difficult to find in America, is similar in every way and need not be planted in preference to *J. rigida.*

Juniperus scopulorum   36′   Zone 5   Western Red-cedar or
                                                                Rocky Mountain Juniper

*FRUIT: bright bluish berries, ¼″ diameter, ripening the second year (sexes separate)
EFFECTIVE: fall and winter
*HABIT: narrowly upright, sometimes devoid of branches at the base as it matures
*FOLIAGE: evergreen, dense, color varies from green to light blue, pointed scale-like leaves
HABITAT: Rocky Mountains from British Columbia to California
VARIETIES: "Chandler Blue"—blue foliage, pyramidal form
            "Hill Silver"—bluish, compact, brightest color during summer months
            viridifolia—bright green foliage, pyramidal form

A variable species, but especially grown in the Rocky Mountain area where it is hardy, and eastward to Illinois it seems to withstand drought conditions much better than does *J. virginiana.* In fact, in the East it does not seem to do at all as well as the native *J. virginiana.* When grown from seed it varies considerably with green, bluish green and greenish blue forms, some being purplish in the fall and winter. Several varieties have been grown rather widely in the trade and many others have been introduced by various individuals, such as "Moonlight," "North Star," "Marshall Silver," etc., most of them being forms selected for the marked color of their foliage.

Juniperus virginiana   90′   Zone 2   Eastern Red-cedar

*FRUIT: female plants have bluish berries ¼″ diameter, ripening the first season, (sexes separate)
EFFECTIVE: fall and winter
*HABIT: densely pyramidal, often columnar
*BARK: shredding in long strips
FOLIAGE: evergreen, scalelike and acicular, varies greatly
HABITAT: entire eastern half of the United States
VARIETIES: *burki*—narrowly pyramidal, steel blue foliage, slightly purplish in winter—Burk Red-cedar
            canaerti—compact pyramidal form, dark green foliage throughout summer and winter, profuse bluish fruits—Canaert Red-cedar
            crebra—the plants usually found in the northern part of its habitat, being much more narrow in habit than the species from Virginia southward—Northeastern Red-cedar
            filifera—broad pyramidal form; slender, divided branchlets and blue gray foliage—Threadleaf Red-cedar
            glauca—pyramidal, dense, light silvery blue foliage—Silver Red-cedar
            pendula—spreading branches but tips pendulous—Weeping Red-cedar
            pyramidalis—columnar, dense—Pyramidal Red-cedar

Kalopanax pictus—a rare tree with large leaves somewhat the shape of those of the Sweet Gum.

> *pyramidiformis*—"Hill Juniper"—pyramidal, foliage green in summer, purplish in autumn and winter—Purple Pyramid Red-cedar
>
> *schotti*—narrowly pyramidal, bright green scalelike leaves—Schott Red-cedar

Native from Florida to Canada and westward to the Rocky Mountains, this is the hardiest and most popular of the tree junipers. Over thirty varieties have been named, for the species varies considerably in form, in color of foliage and in type of foliage. Like other junipers it is dioecious, that is, staminate and pistillate flowers are on separate plants. Consequently if fruiting plants are desired care should be taken in their selection. Even then these trees may fruit once in only two or three years. Some of the clonal varieties are pistillate. The Red-cedar is usually dense and can be pruned easily. Two geographical forms are recognized and easily noticed, those of the South being broadly pyramidal in habit (the true species) and plants found mostly from Pennsylvania northward are much more narrow in habit and not as tall (var. *crebra*).

The Red-cedar grows slowly—trees 16 to 24″ in diameter may be 150 years old. It will grow in most soils but particularly is it noted for the fact that it does well in poor gravelly soils. The wood is of course highly prized for many purposes, chiefly because of its fragrance. The shredding red bark has considerable interest ornamentally. It is a splendid evergreen and available from most nurseries.

The fruits of the large leaved Kalopanax pictus are small and black, borne in round ball-like clusters. They are most attractive to birds in the early fall.

Kalopanax pictus   90′   Zone 4

*FLOWERS: very small in ball-like clusters 1″ in diameter, several clusters making up a large umbel 6–8″ across
    TIME: late July
*FRUIT: small black seeds, quickly eaten by the birds
    EFFECTIVE: early fall
*HABIT: round head, massive branches, open
*FOLIAGE: leaves a similar shape to those of the Sweet Gum, but larger
AUTUMN COLOR: reddish
HABITAT: China, Korea, Japan
INTRODUCED: about 1865
VARIETY: *maximowiczi*—leaves more deeply lobed

This tree should be grown much more than it is. Typically a tall, rounded tree, its large maplelike leaves give it a somewhat tropical appearance, and a deep rich soil with plenty of moisture seems to be much the best for good growth. Some of the younger branches and vigorous shoots have sharp prickles, but most of these disappear at maturity. The small balls of flowers appearing in the late summer are unique, and the small black fruits are quickly eaten by birds. Possibly it is not grown more because the seeds take two years to germinate and there are very few fruiting trees in this country even though the tree has been growing here for almost a century. Many a grower has given up in disgust the first year because no seedlings appear, but by waiting patiently he would find that they germinate nearly 90 per cent the second spring. A good shade tree devoid of insect or disease pests and should be planted more widely.

Keteleeria fortunei   90′   Zone 7   Fortune Keteleeria

FRUIT: cones, 3–7″ long, purplish while young
    EFFECTIVE: fall
*HABIT: pyramidal while young, flat-topped like *Cedrus libani* when mature
*FOLIAGE: evergreen, needlelike
HABITAT: southeastern China
INTRODUCED: 1845
    Akin to the firs, and somewhat of the same general appearance, this tree will withstand somewhat drier situations.

Koelreuteria paniculata   30′   Zone 5   Golden-rain Tree

*FLOWERS: small, yellow, in large upright, pyramidal clusters
    TIME: early summer
FRUIT: light yellowish to brown, bladderlike pods
    EFFECTIVE: fall
HABIT: flat-topped
FOLIAGE: leaves compound, coarse, open
HABITAT: China, Korea, Japan
INTRODUCED: 1763
    This and the Laburnum are the only trees with truly yellow blossoms that can be grown in the Arnold Arboretum. It is quickly and easily grown from seeds and its large conspicuous flower clusters in early summer, followed by its equally conspicuous fruits, make it prominent throughout the summer period when most other trees have few if any flowers or colored fruits. It is being used a great deal in the Ohio Valley, even as a street tree. Because of its weak wood, this might be none too advisable. It has no autumn color and unless desired specifically for its summer bloom, other trees might be used instead which would have a longer life of ornamental usefulness. This much must be said in its behalf, however—it does seem to grow well in a wide range of soils.

Laburnum alpinum   30′   Zone 4   Scotch Laburnum

*FLOWERS: yellow, pealike, in pendulous clusters up to 16″ long
    TIME: late May
HABIT: stiffly upright to vase shaped
FOLIAGE: open
HABITAT: southern Europe
INTRODUCED: probably in colonial times

The Scotch Laburnum is much hardier and the flower clusters much longer than those of the Common Laburnum (*L. anagyroides*) which is really inferior to both this and its hybrid *L. watereri*. The hybrid is probably the better garden specimen but this Scotch Laburnum is recommended because of its hardiness. Without autumn color and interesting fruits, its only claim to fame is the profusion of pendulous golden yellow flower clusters for the two-week period its flowers are open.

x Laburnum watereri   30'   Zone 5   Waterer Laburnum

*FLOWERS: yellow, pealike, in pendulous clusters
    TIME: late May
HABIT: stiffly upright
FOLIAGE: open
HYBRID ORIGIN: *L. anagyroides* x *L. alpinum*
ORIGINATED: before 1864

Often called *L. vossi,* this hybrid has proved justly popular in the trade and is a better plant than its hardier parent, *L. alpinum* because it is more dense in habit and the flowers are larger and a deeper yellow. *L. vossi* is listed as a synonym of Rehder, but European nurserymen have hybrids under both names that are apparently distinct. They claim *L. vossi* makes the better specimen, being more dense in habit of growth.

Lagerstroemia indica   21'   Zone 7   Crape-myrtle

*FLOWERS: bright pink to red, up to 1½" in diameter
    TIME: August
HABIT: upright to rounded, dense branching
*BARK: flaking off in irregular patches displaying a lighter underbark
FOLIAGE: fine texture, leaves privetlike, dense
HABITAT: China, tropical and subtropical countries
INTRODUCED: 1747

Hardy as far north as Baltimore, the Crape-myrtle is grown widely throughout the South, especially for its profuse summer bloom. Its privetlike leaves are not seriously affected with pronounced pest troubles. Blooming on the current year's wood, it is thus amenable to heavy winter pruning when necessary to force compact growth. It blooms over a lengthy period and the crinkled flowers, combined with its vigorous, rounded habit, make it popular. It is difficult to transplant and should have a ball of earth about the roots whenever it is moved. Several varieties of Crape-myrtle are available with white, pink, red, lavender or bluish flowers.

Lagunaria patersoni   50'   Zone 9   Paterson Sugar-plum Tree

*FLOWERS: pale pink, somewhat similar to those of *Hibiscus*
    TIME: May–June
HABIT: pyramidal
*FOLIAGE: dark olive green, evergreen
HABITAT: Australia

This tree is especially useful in seaside plantings and also as a street tree where it is hardy for it is shapely with regularly spaced branches.

LARIX

Stiffly pyramidal in habit yet most graceful in leaf, the larches are among the few deciduous conifers which shed their leaves in the fall and bear cones similar to those of their evergreen relatives. They are easily transplanted and of exceptional beauty in the spring when their small green needles first appear, but they are not used very much because of several pests which can disfigure them quickly. The larch case bearer is one of the most severe pests, for infestations of this insect can ruin the appearance of the tree for all the time it is in leaf, unless controlled by spraying at the proper time. The small worms hatch outside the leaves but eat their way inside when the needles are only half grown. Once inside, no spray reaches them and if applied too soon the spray is not effective. We have found at the Arnold Arboretum that just a difference of three or four days in time of spray application makes all the difference between an effective kill of the pest and normal green foliage the rest of the season, or an ineffective kill and brown, partly-eaten foliage for the remainder of the spring and summer. It is because of this pest and certain serious fungi infestations that larch trees are frequently omitted from plantings.

Their pyramidal habit, often pendulous branchlets, and the very loose and open texture of their foliage giving a very light shade, as well as their striking appearance in leafing out during the early spring, are their chief qualifications for planting.

Larix decidua   100′   Zone 2   European Larch

*FRUIT: cones about 2″ long
    EFFECTIVE: several years
*HABIT: pyramidal and open while young, rather irregular head at maturity
FOLIAGE: deciduous, needlelike, open
HABITAT: northern and central Europe
INTRODUCED: early colonial times
VARIETY: *pendula*—with pendulous branches, very ornamental and graceful

Popularly used in Europe as one of the better larches, it has also done well in the northern United States, probably being planted more than any other. One of its best features is its cones, which remain on the tree several years and give much interest to the entire tree. However, these are not borne until the tree is about twenty years old!

Larix laricina   60′   Zone 1   Eastern Larch (or Tamarack)

*HABIT: very open and pyramidal
FOLIAGE: deciduous, needlelike, open
HABITAT: Alaska and Canada and northern United States

One of the hardiest of all trees in North America—habitually grows in moist wet spots but can also thrive in good normal soil.

Larix leptolepis   90′   Zone 4   Japanese Larch

*HABIT: short horizontal habit, very open pyramidal
FOLIAGE: deciduous, needlelike, open
BARK: peeling off in long strips showing red underneath
HABITAT: Japan
INTRODUCED: 1861

This is the best ornamental among the larches and seems to grow faster than some of the others. However, it is not immune to the various troubles which plague most of the larch species but it is less susceptible to canker disease than is the European and American Larch.

Laurus nobilis   30′   Zone 6   Sweet Bay or Laurel

FLOWERS: greenish white
      TIME: early June
FRUIT: dark green, finally black, berries
      EFFECTIVE: fall
*FOLIAGE: evergreen, leaves to 4″ long, aromatic, dense
HABITAT: Mediterranean region
INTRODUCED: colonial times

This is the famous laurel of ancient history and poetry—cultivated for centuries by the Greeks and Romans. Amenable to shearing, it is often kept closely clipped and grown in tubs especially in formal plantings. The aromatic leaves are used as seasoning for various purposes, and the oil from the fruit is used in making a perfume. It is a splendid small tree yielding dense shade.

Leptospermum laevigatum   25′   Zone 9   Australian Tea Tree

*FLOWERS: white
      TIME: March to May
HABIT: rather ungainly
*FOLIAGE: light green, doing well under marked exposure, evergreen
HABITAT: Australia

This tree will grow in almost pure sand and as it reaches maturity becomes irregular in habit and sometimes very picturesque. However, it will not grow well in heavy soils with poor drainage.

Leucadendron argenteum   30′   Zone 10   Silver Leucadendron

HABIT: distinctive, rounded
FOLIAGE: leaves 6″ long, covered with silvery hairs, dense
HABITAT: South Africa

Probably this tree is grown only in southern California, but is a beautiful small tree, according to Maunsell Van Rensselaer, formerly of the Santa Barbara Botanic Garden, who recommends it highly. In fact, he considers it the most "spectacularly beautiful" tree in Santa Barbara, a city noted for its many beautiful trees. Its soft silvery appearance is unique among woody plants, although it is rather short-lived (25–30 years reported to be its length of usefulness) and difficult to grow properly.

Libocedrus decurrens   135′   Zone 5   California Incense-cedar

FRUIT: cones ¾″ long at tips of branches
  EFFECTIVE: fall and winter
*HABIT: narrowly columnar
*FOLIAGE: evergreen, scalelike, lustrous, branchlets with vertical or "edgewise"
  leaves
HABITAT: Oregon, northern California
  An excellent tree for formal plantings, well clothed with branches to the base of the tree, which should be used considerably more than it is. The leaves are very aromatic when crushed and are borne in vertical planes (instead of horizontal like those of *Thuja plicata*). Practically no foliage pests attack the tree, but in the forests where it is native, mature tree trunks are often infested with dry rot of the heart wood. The wood has been used for pencil slats, cedar chests, moth proof lining of closets and door and window sash, even for cigar boxes. It requires a moist, good soil and provided this, develops into a splendid ornamental tree.

Ligustrum lucidum   30′   Zone 7   Glossy Privet

FLOWERS: white, small pyramidal clusters
  TIME: August
FRUIT: blue-black berries
  EFFECTIVE: September to February
HABIT: upright, branching dense
*FOLIAGE: glossy, mostly evergreen, leaves to 6″ long, dense
HABITAT: China, Korea, Japan
INTRODUCED: 1794
  This, as a shrub, is inferior to *Ligustrum japonicum* with which it is frequently confused. There are several varieties of both in the trade, but since it is the tallest growing privet it can be mentioned here as a very rapid-growing tree, free from insect or disease pests.

Liquidambar styraciflua   125′   Zone 4   Sweet-gum

*FRUIT: round, horned balls, 1″ diameter
  EFFECTIVE: fall
*HABIT: broadly pyramidal
FOLIAGE: star shaped, dense
*AUTUMN COLOR: scarlet
BARK: deeply furrowed, branches often with corky twigs
HABITAT: eastern United States
  The Sweet-gum is an excellent specimen tree, rather difficult to transplant in the large sizes, but once established it has few troubles. It is appearing repeatedly now in use along the parkways and highways of the eastern United States and even in southern California. If given plenty of room in which to develop, few other trees can approach it in symmetrical beauty. The peculiar, ball-shaped fruit remains on the tree for a time after the leaves have fallen.

Liriodendron tulipifera   150'   Zone 4   Tulip Tree
(Tulip or Yellow Poplar)

*FLOWERS: greenish yellow marked with orange, tulip shaped and about the
     same size
   TIME: mid-June
FRUIT: pyramidal, dry pods, 2–3" long
   EFFECTIVE: not particularly effective
HABIT: broadly pyramidal, massive branches
FOLIAGE: dense, leaves uniquely shaped, squarish
*AUTUMN COLOR: yellow
HABITAT: eastern United States
VARIETY: *fastigiatum*—upright in habit
   A common native tree, often growing to tremendous size with many living
specimens estimated to be two hundred years old, it should be given plenty of
room to grow in, otherwise its beauty is not appreciated. The tulip-shaped flowers
appear after the leaves are fully developed and so are none too conspicuous from
a distance, but they are nearly 2½" long, greenish yellow with an orange band
and give the tree its name. Rather easily transplanted, the species is only for the
larger gardens and parks where at least 75' of space can eventually be allotted
each tree, but the fastigiate form does have possibilities for use as a narrow street
tree. These trees are not seriously affected with insect or disease pests.

Livistona australis   50'   Zone 10   Australian Fan Palm

*HABIT: palm tree, orbicular head
FOLIAGE: dense, fanlike, 3–5' in diameter
HABITAT: Australia
   A beautiful palm and one of the hardiest with dark green, fan-shaped leaves
and rounded crown.

Macadamia ternifolia   35'   Zone 10   Queensland Nut

FLOWERS: white in racemes 1' long
   TIME: spring
HABIT: erect, round head
*FOLIAGE: evergreen, leaves in whorls of 3 or 4, leathery and lustrous, spiny, up
     to 1' long
HABITAT: New South Wales
   A slow-growing tree from the tropics which requires a deep rich soil in
which to grow but makes a fine, dense evergreen specimen even in situations
where there is little rainfall. It sometimes grows with several trunks but is usually
clothed with branches from the ground on up.

Maclura pomifera   60'   Zone 5   Osage-orange

FRUIT: large, orangelike, green, 3" diameter
   EFFECTIVE: fall
HABIT: open, irregular, rounded top, thorny
FOLIAGE: loosely open
AUTUMN COLOR: yellow
HABITAT: south central United States

The Osage-orange is recommended only for use in the Midwest where it seems to withstand cold winters and summer drought better than most other trees. It is used chiefly as a windbreak or hedge plant (along fence rows) because of its unusually vigorous growth and stout thorns and its ability to withstand heavy clipping. When planted along a fence row it quickly grows into an impenetrable thorny mass capable of confining stock throughout the year. Other plants outstrip it in ornamental qualifications for general landscape use in the East and far West. The sexes are separate so only the pistillate plants will bear the large fruits from which this species takes its common name.

MAGNOLIA

Like the cherries, this group of plants is valued for its flowers, many of them appearing in early spring before the leaves. Eight of the recommended species are natives of Asia, six are natives of North America and four are hybrids. The flowers are large and conspicuous, white, pink and red to reddish purple, some nearly a foot in diameter, making these the largest in any group of hardy plants in our north temperate area. They have no conspicuous autumn color and their peculiar fruits are only noticeable for a very short time when they are split open revealing the red seeds within. These quickly fall to the ground and shortly thereafter the pod itself withers and falls off. Some species produce more of these fruits than others. The seeds quickly lose their viability which is the reason magnolia seeds should be sown as soon as they are ripe.

Since magnolias are difficult to transplant, they should be moved with a ball of soil about their thick, fleshy roots. They must be handled very carefully and transplanted preferably in the spring of the year in most areas.

The foliage of many magnolias can be considered coarse, yet it is sturdy and seldom attacked by leaf eating insects. Unfortunately some species (especially *M. soulangeana*) are susceptible to a soft scale attacking the young twigs and when this is the case it must be kept rigidly under control or dead branches begin to appear.

Some of the native species (*M. tripetala, fraseri* and *macrophylla*) have unusually large leaves, the last-mentioned sometimes 30″ long, while others (*M. salicifolia*) have leaves seldom over 4″ long. The very coarse texture is not desirable under many conditions, and when grown in an exposed situation the wind can whip the leaves about until they are shredded and unsightly for a greater part of the growing season.

It must be admitted that magnolias are desirable trees and should be considered for many situations where conspicuously flowered types are desired. Some, like *M. soulangeana* do well under city conditions. Most are rather wide spreading with bark that is easily injured and so they are not adaptable as street trees.

There are eighteen species of magnolia trees recommended here with several varieties. This seems an unusually large number, yet they all have a place in certain types of planting. For instance, *M. acuminata, campbelli, grandiflora* and *obovata* are all tall trees over 90′ high at maturity. On the other hand, *M. cordata, salicifolia, sieboldi, soulangeana, stellata, watsoni* and *wilsoni* are all under 30′ high at maturity—well adapted for medium-sized gardens, and each one deserving of use in its own right.

Magnolia loebneri and *M. veitchi* are mentioned because of their rapid growth and early flower production; *M. macrophylla* merely because of its unusually large leaves; *M. virginiana* because of its summer flowers; *M. fraseri* because of its large flowers and *M. denudata* and *M. kobus borealis* merely because they have been widely used and are very beautiful. Thirteen of these species have white flowers, all the more reason for growing those with colored flowers. The group is highly valued and some one of these magnolias will be found in all but the driest and the coldest parts of the country. As flowering trees, none surpass them.

Magnolia acuminata   90′   Zone 4   Cucumber Tree

FLOWERS: greenish yellow, rather inconspicuous, 3″ high
    TIME: early June
FRUIT: pink to red, in peculiar cucumber-shaped shells
    EFFECTIVE: early fall
*HABIT: pyramidal, upright while young, massive with wide reaching branches at maturity
FOLIAGE: leaves large, 5–10″ long, dense
HABITAT: eastern United States

Found native in a wide area, this tree is best used for its foliage and habit. The flowers are cup shaped and greenish yellow but because of their color and since they appear after the leaves are fully developed, they are not at all conspicuous and should not even be considered from an ornamental viewpoint. The leaves are not too coarse; they have no autumn color and they turn brown in the fall before dropping. Mature trees have wide spreading branches that arch and may even touch the ground, but trees even 40 years old are stiff, fairly narrow and upright in habit. It is one of the fastest-growing magnolias and should only be used where it will have plenty of room to develop normally since it does not look well when confined by restrained pruning. This excellent tree grows very vigorously which is one of the reasons why it is frequently used as understock in grafting other magnolias.

Magnolia campbelli   150′   Zone 8–9   Campbell Magnolia

*FLOWERS: shell pink, 8–10″ diameter, fragrant, cup-shaped
    TIME: very early spring
HABIT: few branches, rather open
FOLIAGE: coarse, leaves 6–10″ long
HABITAT: Himalaya

This is a rare plant, hardy in only a small area of this continent, but a huge tree in its native habitat. It does not bloom while young and its flower buds are very tender. Certainly it is worthy of a trial where it is hardy. This plant has come through temperatures of 15° above zero without injury. In fact a recent report from a Seattle nurseryman stated that it survived temperatures of zero to 5°

below on eight successive nights and still showed no injury even to the tips of the branches by April of the following spring.

Magnolia cordata   30′   Zone 5   Yellow Cucumber Tree

FLOWERS: cup-shaped, yellow, 2″ high
   TIME: late May
FRUIT: peculiar cucumberlike pods, splitting open to disclose numerous bright red seeds
   EFFECTIVE: fall
*HABIT: upright but open
FOLIAGE: leaves 3–6″ long, coarse
HABITAT: Georgia

The flowers are certainly more conspicuous than those of *M. acuminata* and the leaves are slightly smaller. Because it is smaller in all its characters this might be the substitute for *M. acuminata* on the small place, especially since it does not grow nearly as rapidly as does the Cucumber Tree.

Magnolia denudata or the Yulan, is an early white flowering magnolia with fragrant flowers.

Magnolia denudata   45′   Zone 5   Yulan Magnolia

*FLOWERS: white, fragrant, 6″ in diameter before the leaves appear, 9 petals
   TIME: early May
*FRUIT: peculiar cucumberlike pods, splitting open to disclose numerous bright red seeds.
   EFFECTIVE: fall
HABIT: rounded
FOLIAGE: dense, leaves 4–6″ long
HABITAT: central China
INTRODUCED: 1789

Many people have learned to know this excellent tree under another name, *M. conspicua*, now superceded by the name *denudata*. It has been cultivated in the gardens of central China since the earliest times—a splendid tree which should not be crowded by other plants but given plenty of room in which to develop. This means it should be allowed a ground space of about 30′.

Magnolia fraseri   45′   Zone 5   Fraser Magnolia

*FLOWERS: creamy white, fragrant, 8–10″ in diameter, 6–9 petals
    TIME: late May
FRUIT: peculiar cucumberlike pods, splitting open to disclose red seeds
    EFFECTIVE: early fall
HABIT: open head, wide spreading branches
FOLIAGE: coarse, leaves 12″ long
HABITAT: southeastern United States

Another large-leaved magnolia. One of these, growing in the Arnold Arboretum, is over 12″ in trunk diameter. However, this species is not dependable in the Boston climate. John Bartram discovered it growing in South Carolina in 1776. The leaves are thinner and smaller than those of the larger leaved *M. macrophylla*. It should be kept in mind, however, that large flowers and coarse foliage do not go to make a really interesting landscape specimen except under unusual conditions.

Magnolia grandiflora   90′   Zone 7   Southern Magnolia

*FLOWERS: white, fragrant, 8″ in diameter, usually 6 petals
    TIME: late May and part of the summer
*FRUIT: peculiar cucumberlike pods splitting open to disclose red seeds within
    EFFECTIVE: early fall
*HABIT: pyramidal, usually dense
*FOLIAGE: evergreen, leaves 5–8″ long and dropping at end of second year
HABITAT: southeastern United States

This magnificent, single-trunked tree is precariously hardy as far north as Philadelphia and Harrisburg, Pennsylvania. There are several varieties, varying in leaf size, length of flowering, and the amount of brown tomentum on the under surface of the leaves. This magnolia is widely planted throughout the South and its evergreen leaves are dried and used in "artificial" florists combinations throughout the entire country. Flowers on well grown specimens may be as much as 12″ in diameter—truly striking. The variety *gloriosa* is said to have flowers 14″ in diameter. The Southern Magnolia is a fine specimen tree but does not take kindly to crowding and should be given plenty of room in which to develop.

Magnolia kobus borealis   75′   Zone 4

*FLOWERS: white, 5″ in diameter before leaves appear, 6–9 petals
    TIME: late April
*FRUIT: peculiar cucumberlike pods, splitting open to disclose red seeds within
    EFFECTIVE: early fall
*HABIT: pyramidal while young, rounded and very open at maturity
FOLIAGE: dense, rather fine texture for a magnolia, leaves 2½–4″ long

HABITAT: Japan
INTRODUCED: 1876
    This magnolia is the hardiest of the Asiatic species but does not bloom freely while young. It may well be that some of the clons of *M. loebneri* will eventually prove superior for they have just as good flowers, probably produced in greater quantity while the plant is still only a few feet tall. However, *M. kobus* seedlings are widely used as understock for grafting other magnolias. This is the fastest growing of the Asiatic magnolia species but may be surpassed by certain clons of the hybrid *M. loebneri.*

x Magnolia loebneri   50′   Zone 4   Loebner Magnolia
*FLOWERS: white, 3″ in diameter, 8–12 petals; before leaves
    TIME: late April
FRUIT: peculiar cucumberlike pods, splitting open to reveal red seeds within
    EFFECTIVE: early fall
*HABIT: pyramidal, rapid growing
FOLIAGE: dense, leaves slightly larger than those of *M. stellata*
HYBRID ORIGIN: *M. stellata x M. kobus*
ORIGINATED: about 1910
    There are several clons of this growing in America, but one which originated in the Arnold Arboretum in 1939 has shown excellent vigor. When the plants were ten years old they were 12′ tall and have been covered with blossoms for several years. It is just as vigorous as *M. kobus borealis* but has the early-blooming qualities of *M. stellata,* and flowers just as large with 8–12 petals.

Magnolia macrophylla   50′   Zone 5   Bigleaf Magnolia
*FLOWERS: creamy white, fragrant, 10–12″ in diameter, 6 petals
    TIME: early July
*FRUIT: peculiar cucumberlike pods, splitting open to reveal red seeds within
    EFFECTIVE: early fall
HABIT: round-headed, open
FOLIAGE: leaves often 20–30″ long and 10″ wide, very coarse
HABITAT: southeastern United States
    The leaves of this tree are the largest of any native tree in temperate North America. It is precisely these large coarse leaves which prevent it from being used extensively in American gardens, for if planted where winds whip them about, they quickly tear and break to such an extent that the tree becomes unsightly. As a novelty, where winds do not continuously mar the foliage, it may find a few enterprising gardeners who will want to grow it, but there are many, many trees much easier to establish.

Magnolia obovata   90′   Zone 5   Whiteleaf Japanese Magnolia
*FLOWERS: white, fragrant, 6″ in diameter, 6–9 petals
    TIME: mid-May
*FRUIT: peculiar cucumberlike pods, splitting open to reveal the red seeds within
    EFFECTIVE: early fall
HABIT: pyramidal, open
FOLIAGE: leaves 8–16″ long, coarse in texture, blue-white beneath

HABITAT: Japan
INTRODUCED: 1865

The native Umbrella Magnolia (*M. tripetala*) is similar to this species but the flowers are inferior to it and have a disagreeable odor, while those of *M. obovata* are fragrant, making this Japanese plant the more desirable ornamental specimen. The leaves of both *M. tripetala* and *M. obovata* are mostly pointed at the base and so easily distinguished from those of *M. macrophylla* which are rounded or somewhat cordate at the base.

Magnolia salicifolia   30'   Zone 5   Anise Magnolia

*FLOWERS: fragrant, white, 5" diameter, 6 petals
   TIME: late April
*FRUIT: peculiar cucumberlike pods, splitting open to reveal the red seeds within
   EFFECTIVE: early fall
*HABIT: closely pyramidal
*FOLIAGE: dense, leaves and bark have lemon scent when bruised, fine texture for
      a magnolia, leaves 2½–4½" long
HABITAT: Japan
INTRODUCED: 1892

This is a splendid tree for its flower and form and particularly nice specimens are being grown in the Morton Arboretum, Lisle, Illinois, and Swarthmore College, Swarthmore, Pennsylvania. The leaves are very narrow for magnolias, not over 1½" wide. It has the desirable trait of blooming while quite young, something which cannot be said of *M. kobus* or its varieties. The flowers have a fragrance similar to that of the Lemon-scented Verbena. So many magnolias spread out into what is often an ungainly rounded habit at maturity that this species is particularly desirable in being so closely pyramidal.

Magnolia sieboldi   30'   Zone 6   Oyama Magnolia

*FLOWERS: white, fragrant, cup-shaped, 4–5" in diameter, scarlet stamens
   TIME: early June
FRUIT: peculiar cucumberlike pods splitting open to reveal the red seeds within
   EFFECTIVE: early fall
HABIT: rounded, open, rather weak in growth
FOLIAGE: rather fine texture, leaves 2–6" long
HABITAT: Japan, Korea
INTRODUCED: about 1865

The beauty of this Japanese species, formerly called *Magnolia parviflora*, is its habit of producing flowers over a period of many weeks not all at once. The numerous crimson stamens clustered about the center of the flower show off very well against the white background of the waxy petals. It does not have very good foliage, when compared with some of the others, hence its flowers alone are its chief claim to fame.

x Magnolia soulangeana   25'   Zone 5   Saucer Magnolia

*FLOWERS: large, white to purple 5–10" diameter, cup-shaped, appearing before
      the leaves
   TIME: early May to late May

Magnolia soulangeana "Speciosa"

FRUIT: peculiar cucumberlike pod, splitting open to disclose the red seeds within
   EFFECTIVE: early fall
HABIT: often shrublike with many main stems, but easily trained to a single trunk
FOLIAGE: leaves 6–8" long, rather coarse
HYBRID ORIGIN: *M. denudata x M. liliflora*
ORIGINATED: about 1820
VARIETIES: "Alexandrina"—flowers 7" in diameter, flushed rose-purple outside, in-
         side of petals pure white; one of larger and earlier varieties
         "Amabilis"—flowers white, very similar to *M. denudata*
         "Andre Le Roy"—flowers 7" in diameter, a darker pink to purplish on
         the outside, white inside, flowers cup-shaped
         "Brozzoni"—larger flowers; color outside paler than "Candolleana" but
         white inside, petals 5½" long, 3" wide. When wide open the
         flowers are 10" across, one of the larger flowering varieties of this
         species.
         lennei—flowers darkest of group but not as dark as those of *M. liliflora
         nigra;* petals 4 to 6" long and 4" wide, flowers rich rose-purple out
         side but white inside, one of the last varieties to bloom.

> *nigra*—flowers colored outside a rich purple, inside whitish. Plant is said to bloom nearly 6 weeks.
>
> *rubra*—(syn. *rustica rubra*) not as dark as variety *lennei* but blooms earlier; flowers 5½″ diameter and more rounded than the species.
>
> *speciosa*—flowers white, 6″ diameter, last to bloom of these varieties.

This popular hybrid originated as a chance seedling in the garden of Mr. Soulange-Bodin at Fromont near Paris, over a hundred years ago. Unlike many other trees, it will bloom when it is still very small, plants merely 2–3′ tall often producing several flowers. Since it is a hybrid species there are many clons, the flowers ranging from white to a deep reddish purple, according to variety. According to some reports, the flowers on a single tree may vary in color somewhat from year to year. Normally, the Saucer Magnolia is as wide as it is high with several main trunks. It is susceptible to rather serious infestations of the magnolia scale so that the spraying of trunks and branches in the early spring with a dormant oil is not amiss. These plants are popular because of their conspicuous large flowers before the leaves appear and eight varieties have been listed merely to show a range in color and size of the flowers and the time of bloom, for some bloom nearly a week earlier than others. These magnolias do not have autumn color and all are rather coarse in leaf texture so that one should consider them carefully before devoting an appreciable portion of a small garden to this species.

Magnolia stellata   20′   Zone 5   Star Magnolia

*FLOWERS: double, white, fragrant, over 3″ in diameter, at least 12–15 petals
    TIME: mid-April
*FRUIT: peculiar cucumberlike pod (2″ long) splitting open to disclose red seeds within
    EFFECTIVE: early fall
*HABIT: branching dense, mounded to shrublike
*FOLIAGE: dark green, leaves 1½–4″ long, fine texture
*AUTUMN COLOR—bronze to yellow
HABITAT: Japan
INTRODUCED: 1862
VARIETY: *rosea*—flower buds pink, flowers fading white at maturity—Pink Star Magnolia

The Star Magnolia is the hardiest and in many respects the most ornamental of the Asiatic magnolias. The flowers have 12–19 petals, are very fragrant and sometimes nearly 4″ in diameter. The long narrow leaves are thick and dark green, turning an excellent bronze in the fall, especially when grown in direct sunshine. The plant is dense, either a shrub or small tree, and is best used as a specimen plant for its branches face the ground well. In the North, near its northern limit of hardiness, it may tend to bloom too early if given a southern exposure, for late frosts frequently mar the blossoms. With a northern exposure the flower opening is retarded somewhat and this proves helpful during those seasons with late frosts.

There is also a variety sold under the trade name of "Waterlily" which is supposedly faster growing than the species and with larger flowers. Then too, reports have just been received about two new clons, each one of which is said to have red flowers rather than the light pink of *M. stellata rosea*. I have not seen normal flowers on either one of these plants but if they are red-flowering forms of *M. stellata*, they may prove to be very popular.

x Magnolia veitchi   40′   Zone 7   Veitch Magnolia

*FLOWERS: pink with 9 petals, 6″ in diameter
      TIME: April, before leaves
HABIT: coarse, open
FOLIAGE: coarse, leaves 6–12″ long, 3–7″ wide
HYBRID ORIGIN: *M. campbelli x M. denudata*
ORIGINATED: Veitch Nursery, England, 1907, first flowered in 1917

This is an interesting hybrid with very brittle branches. Apparently, it has considerable hybrid vigor, for a three-year-old plant grew up to 30′ in height in only eight years. It is well worth growing where it is hardy for it produces flowers even when the tree is very young.

Magnolia virginiana   60′   Zone 5   Sweet Bay

*FLOWERS: white, very fragrant, 2–3″ diameter
      TIME: late May
*FRUIT: peculiar cucumberlike pods splitting open to disclose the red seeds within
      EFFECTIVE: early fall
HABIT: a tree in the South; shrublike in the North
*FOLIAGE: green above, white below, leaves 2½–4½″ long
HABITAT: coastal area of eastern United States

The very fragrant, waxy white flowers appearing in June and early summer, the gray bark and good foliage with leaves white on the undersurface, make this an attractive species. In the deep South this plant is a tree and nearly evergreen, but in New England it is much more shrubby and deciduous. It can be grown well in wet and even almost swampy soils, although it does not require such situations to grow well—an excellent native plant.

x Magnolia watsoni   20′   Zone 5   Watson Magnolia

*FLOWERS: white, fragrant, pink or red stamens, flowers about 5½″ diameter,
          pink sepals
      TIME: mid-June
HABIT: small, rounded, rather straggling
FOLIAGE: leaves 4–7″ long, rather coarse
HYBRID ORIGIN: *M. obovata x M. sieboldi*
ORIGINATED: Japan 1889

This tree is suitable for the small garden but has the habit of being rather open and unruly. It is valued only for its conspicuous fragrant flowers with dense clusters of pink or red stamens in the center of the flower. This, like *M. sieboldi*, has also been formerly incorrectly termed *M. parviflora* and is distinguished from *M. sieboldi* by its larger flowers and larger and more leathery leaves as well as its more robust growth.

Magnolia wilsoni   24′   Zone 6   Wilson Magnolia

*FLOWERS: white, fragrant, 6″ diameter, conspicuous ring of crimson stamens
      TIME: May

FRUIT: peculiar, cucumberlike pods, splitting open to disclose red seeds within
    EFFECTIVE: early fall
HABIT: often shrubby and rather open
FOLIAGE: rather fine texture, leaves 2–4½" long
HABITAT: western China
INTRODUCED: 1908

Cup-shaped, fragrant flowers are the chief attraction of this rare magnolia. Although introduced over forty years ago there is only one nursery listing it at present. It is not superior to other magnolias but in the warmer parts of the country it might have merit for its flowers.

MALUS

The Crab Apples as a group are about our most ornamental flowering and fruiting trees. They should be used a great deal in park and parkway plantings as well as on private grounds. Only one word of caution is necessary—they should not be neglected. All are susceptible to scale infestations and borers, and some are susceptible to fire blight. They should not be planted in long hedges or windbreaks for it is much easier to care for them properly when planted as individuals or in small groups. Actually they require a minimum amount of attention, but spraying, pruning and borer control must be given regularly to insure good growth. Otherwise, they are among our best ornamental trees, which is why over forty species and varieties are suggested in the following pages. Because of their importance it might be of interest to discuss briefly a little bit of their past history and the specific reasons for which we now value them.

History

The first plant which was thought of as a Crab Apple was undoubtedly *Malus pumila*, native of eastern Europe. The fruits of this tree are comparatively small and sour tasting and are of little economic value, though they may be used in preserves or in making cider. However, apples have been known as such since the earliest of times. Cato (3rd century B.C.) knew seven apple varieties and Pliny (1st century A.D.) knew thirty-six apple varieties. Various seedlings of *M. pumila* and *M. sylvestris* occurred with fruits larger than others and these of course were the earliest of apple varieties. Seedlings of *M. pumila* were used as understock on which were grafted scions of the more valued seedlings. In about 1600, the term *Crab Apple* included some of the native *Malus* species noted by Captain John Smith as growing in Virginia, probably *M. coronaria* and *M. angustifolia*. He found the fruit to be small and of bitter taste, but the trees very beautiful in the spring when in flower. Because of the association of the term Crab Apple with these trees bearing small apples, the term was naturally used later when the Siberian Crab Apple was introduced, again when hybrids of this and the common apple appeared, and still later (after 1850) when the Asiatic species of the genus *Malus* were introduced into Europe and North America. Generally speaking, all the crab apples have fruits smaller than those of the common apple, and consequently we have considered the Crab Apple as any member of the genus *Malus* which has fruits two inches or less in diameter.

Most of the botanical species and varieties of the genus *Malus* constitute the wild crab apples of the world. Three are native of Europe—*M. pumila*, *M. sylvestris*, and *M. florentina* (Italy). In North America nine species are native, most of them with green fruits, but others have become naturalized. Seventeen species are considered native of eastern Europe and Asia, most of these being the crab apples with the delightfully colored, small fruits we frequently associate with China and Japan. These species and their varieties, then, constitute the native crab apples of the world. When grown together and promiscuously hybridized, their numerous off-spring present a most diverse group, including hundreds of clons of devious origin. This is the picture we have today. To understand it a little better, let us take a quick glance at early books and nursery catalogues in England and America.

In England there may have been a few hybrids between the native *M. pumila* and the large cultivated apples, prior to 1784. In that year, however, the seeds of the Siberian Crab Apple (supposedly *M. baccata*) were intro-duced to Kew Gardens, and shortly thereafter numerous hybrids began to appear between this and varieties of the common apple. It is not known when *M. spectabilis* was introduced into Europe, but Dr. Fothergill, a famous English physician, was growing it in his spacious garden in 1780. The Siberian Crab Apple undoubtedly was listed in English catalogues about 1800 for William Forsyth in 1802 listed this and the Double Blossom Apple (probably *M. spectabilis*) as being the only two crab apples grown in England at that time. Seven years later the Siberian Crab Apple was offered in France together with several of its varieties. Prior to 1768 no crab apples were listed in treatises of English pomology, so it is safe to surmise that after this date a few hybrids of *M. pumila* and the cultivated apples may have been offered as crab apples, but that crosses of the cultivated Apple and *M. baccata* did not begin to appear until shortly after 1800. By 1826, over thirty crab apples, including several American species, were listed in English nurseries.

In America we can presume that the Siberian Crab Apple was intro-duced shortly after 1784, since John Bartram offered it for sale from his nursery in Philadelphia in 1814. Only one Crab Apple was listed by the Prince Nursery of Flushing, Long Island, in its catalogue of 1790 and that was the Virginia Crab Apple. By 1831 this same nursery offered the Siberian Crab Apple, "large" and "small," the Amber Crab Apple, which undoubtedly was a yellow fruiting *M. baccata*, and the double flowering Chinese Crab Apple, *M. spectabilis*. The Siberian Crab Apple "large" may have been either *M. prunifolia* or x *M. robusta*. The appearance of these exotic crab apples undoubtedly was the signal for many amateur experiments in hybridization, in which large fruiting apple varieties were crossed with the smaller fruiting Siberian. By 1835 "Montreal Beauty" was being offered by the Prince Nursery, it having originated in Quebec some time prior to 1833. At any rate, this was the time at which exotic crab apples were beginning to be grown, hybridized and offered for sale by American nurseries. Though *M. baccata* and *M. prunifolia* were introduced into America early, the majority of the Asiatic species did not reach here until after 1850, and some not until after 1900.

It is probable that crab apples were not grown in large number by the eastern colonists for the larger fruiting apple varieties were perfectly hardy from Maine southward, and these were most important economically. A few crab apples were needed for jellies and conserves, and it is probable that in the older colonies, as people had more leisure, they became interested in planting crab apples here and there purely for ornament. Certainly this was not done to any great extent.

The colonists alone were not responsible for disseminating European apple varieties in North America. The Indians undoubtedly did a great deal of it from the time the European apple first arrived in this country. Apples were apparently carried by the Indians and early traders to all parts of the country, and frequent mention has been made in early literature of Indian settlements with apple and peach orchards. There was the eccentric missionary, John Chapman, better known as "Johnny Appleseed," who roamed the frontiers of Ohio and Indiana planting seeds and seedlings in hundreds of different places. It may be that what we now consider to be x *M. soulardi* (*M. pumila* x. *M. ioensis*) had as one of its parents a seedling planted by this somewhat erratic person.

In the colder parts of Vermont and New Hampshire, it became increasingly apparent that the Apple varieties of those times were not completely winter hardy, but that the introduced Siberian crab apple was extremely so. With the westward movement of settlers, and the desire to establish the Apple everywhere, it became evident that many apple varieties would not survive the extremely cold Midwest climate when the Siberian Crab Apple would. This knowledge brought about feverish activity in sowing the seed of apples—any apples—in order to find trees that would prove hardy. Downing wrote in 1845 that because of its remarkable hardiness, many individuals were experimenting with *M. baccata* and many crosses were being grown. However, he listed only *M. baccata* and *M. spectabilis* in his book published in 1845, though later in another edition (1869) crab apples were of sufficient importance in this country so that he listed thirty-seven varieties. Some of these may have been introduced from Europe, but several certainly originated in North America. Both "Brier" and "Gibb" originated in America some time between 1860 and 1870 as the result of crossing the Siberian Crab Apple with common Apple varieties of those times. It is of interest to note that of the thirty-seven varieties Downing listed, at least five are being grown today, namely "Hyslop," "Montreal Beauty," "Orange," "Soulard" and "Transcendent."

By 1862 some of the Asiatic crab apples were reaching America. *Malus floribunda, sieboldi, x micromalus and halliana parkmani* all were being grown in this country prior to 1865. In 1892 Professor Charles S. Sargent, Director of the Arnold Arboretum went to Japan and sent several Asiatic crab apples back from the Orient, including one which was named after him, *M. sargenti*. A few years later, E. H. Wilson, also of the Arnold Arboretum, sent several back from his various expeditions to China and Japan. Among these was *M. toringoides*, one of the handsomest of all in fruit, sent to this country in 1904. Hundreds of other varieties have been introduced since. They are now widely distributed over the United States and Canada. Because of the ease with which cross fertilization takes place, new hybrids are continually appearing and there is always the possibility of a new hybrid being decidedly worthwhile.

Reasons for Growing Crab Apples

1. **Flowers.** The crab apples have many uses both ornamental and economic. In the first place, they are planted for their beautiful flowers which usually appear in May before the lilacs bloom. The majority of the species and varieties have single flowers, but there are some with semi-double and double blossoms comparing favorably with the double flowering oriental cherries, though the flower clusters are not as large. The colors range from pure white to dark purplish red, with many variations of pink and red between the extremes. Consequently, there is a wide range of color in the flowers, and within the limits noted, varieties can be selected for one particular color which may fit in with the planting scheme better than another. Not the least of the assets of the crab apples are their beauty in bud. Even though the flowers of many are pure white, the buds may be pink or even red and white. As the flowers open, this color may gradually fade to white. In some varieties the color of the flower buds and of the flowers is identical.

Most varieties have flowers which are very fragrant—another valued asset. *Malus baccata* and its varieties are exceptionally so and this characteristic adds materially to the effectiveness of these plants when in bloom.

2. **Fruits.** The fruits range in size from that of a small pea, up to two inches in diameter, and the colors from pure red to pure yellow with all intermediate shades and combinations. Many of the species native to this country have green fruits which are not of particular ornamental value. The fruits of some varieties begin to show color in early August, while almost all have colored fruits during the month of September. After that, the fruits of many varieties begin to fall, while those of a few varieties may remain on all fall and even well into the winter. These bright colored fruits are decidedly ornamental and make the crab apples bearing them doubly valuable since there are two seasons during which these plants are of

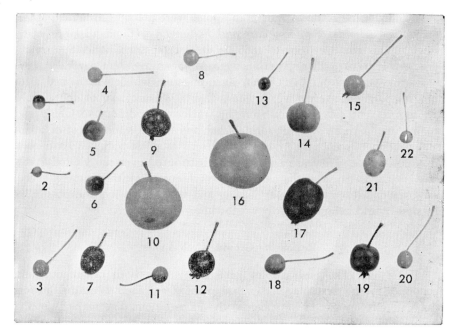

The varieties and species of Crab Apples vary considerably in size and color. Here are fruits from 22 varieties (the large fruit in the center of the picture is about one and a quarter inches in diameter.)

1. M. sargenti
2. M. sieboldi
3. M. hupehensis
4. M. "Katherine"
5. M. brevipes
6. M. toringoides
7. M. robusta persicifolia
8. M. halliana spontanea
9. M. "Hopa"
10. M. coronaria
11. M. zumi calocarpa
12. M. "Makamik"
13.. M. atrosanguinea
14. M. robusta
15. M. "Dorothea"
16. M. soulardi
17. M. "Dolgo"
18. M. arnoldiana
19. M. purpurea
20. M. baccata
21. M. prunifolia rinki
22. M. floribunda

ornamental interest. The oriental flowering cherries cannot boast two seasons of effective beauty.

3. **Habit.** The crab apples in general are small trees less than twenty feet tall. A few are standard trees, while others are round and moundlike in habit, more like large shrubs. A few have very pendulous branches, and are comparable to the Weeping Cherry so popular in American gardens. One of the trees (*M. baccata columnaris*) is columnar in habit, at least while young. Others are supposed to be, but apparently as they grow older the weight of the fruits they bear forces the upright branches to a more horizontal position. Thus, with columnar, pendulous, moundlike, small- and tall-growing varieties available, there is considerable variation of habit which can be utilized in planting.

4. **Foliage Color.** The majority of the crab apples have leaves that are a normal green, but some have leaves that retain a reddish to bronze color

throughout the entire growing season. These colors are not brilliant, but nevertheless are sufficiently evident so that the plants can be used to splendid advantage. The color of the foliage is just enough red, bronze or dark green to make these varieties stands out from surrounding plants while at the same time blending pleasingly with them. There are other varieties which have young foliage conspicuously colored, but in these the color usually disappears after the leaves reach maturity.

Contrary to general belief, there are a few of the crab apples which do have autumn color. It depends largely on the climatic conditions of an area, and when temperature, sunshine, exposure and even soil conditions are just right during the early fall, autumn coloration on certain types of plants can be expected. One of the most important factors is a southwestern exposure, for then the warm rays of the sun late in the afternoon will warm the leaves and a quick drop in temperature immediately after sunset (approximately to 45°F.) may bring autumn coloration. Only a few varieties of the genus *Malus* have been known to color materially in the fall, but these should be noted and this characteristic might be made use of in planting.

5. **Wildlife Preservation.** Certainly the crab apples should be considered in this category. Their fruits are most attractive to many kinds of birds, and because of the ability to hold their fruits long into the winter, certain varieties are excellent as sources of food for wildlife. "Bob White" is one example. It is a hybrid and came to the attention of members on the staff at the Arnold Arboretum because it held its fruits all winter. In the fall, when birds eat the fruits of other crab apples, none touch the hard fruits of this variety. However, in January and February, after the fruits of most other plants fall to the ground and after successively cold days freeze the fruits of "Bob White" and they become somewhat softened, then they are sought out especially by the pheasants. On a day in February, I counted six pheasants eating the fruits from this tree at one time and when one realizes that this tree is only a few hundred feet from one of Boston's main automobile arteries, and for that matter the entire Arboretum is surrounded by built up "city," one can understand the value of this variety in offering food at a time when other natural food is practically unobtainable.

6. **Economic Uses.** Crab apples replace apples in the colder portions of the Midwest and the Provinces of Canada where winter temperatures are so low that the ordinary Apple varieties do not prove hardy. One of the recently introduced economic varieties of crab apples has withstood temperatures of 59° below zero. In the past many varieties have been bred solely for this purpose, and even now some new varieties are appearing from certain of the Canadian Government experiment stations. Of course, in such areas it is those crab apples with the largest fruits which are of value. A number of these are now being grown, but the demand for them is, of course, limited to certain very cold areas.

Even though ornamental crab apples are grown purely for their ornamental properties, some people do like to experiment with making jelly from the fruits. A few years ago fruits of fourteen different species of Malus were made into jellies by one of the staff members of the Arnold Arboretum. The fruits of *M. purpurea, glabrata, lancifolia,* and *coronaria* made good jelly with fair pectin content. Some were improved by the addition of a few fruits of *M. purpurea* for additional coloring. Fruits of *M. sargenti, floribunda, baccata, micromalus* and *zumi* made rather poor jelly because the fruits were so small they did not yield much juice. Usually the larger the fruits, the easier it is (and the more practical as well) to obtain sufficient juice to make good jelly.

Disease and Insect Pests

Crab apples are susceptible to the various troubles of the common apple, namely, fire blight, scale and borers. The scale insects are kept in check by a dormant spray of some miscible oil applied any time between the middle of February and early April. Lime sulfur can be used, but since Crab Apples are frequently growing in prominent places, it might be inadvisable because of the discoloring effect on the trees themselves and on adjacent shrubbery or buildings.

Apparently the Oriental Crab Apples are not severely infested with fire blight. Varieties which have been hybridized with the common Apple (this refers particularly to certain "economic" Crab Apples bred for their large size) may suffer from this pernicious disease. "Transcendent" is one variety which has been notably susceptible to the disease in southern Canada and has been discarded in many places for this reason. There is little that can be done in the matter of controlling fire blight except to cut out infested branches or trees, sterilizing the tools afterward and burning the affected parts at once. Often an unusually heavy application of nitrogenous fertilizer will cause excessive vegetative growth and then fire blight may become pronounced. This may be somewhat alleviated by correspondingly heavy applications of phosphorus and potash fertilizers.

Several borers infest all apple and crab apple trees, especially the flat-headed and the round-headed apple tree borers. There are no paints which are known (as yet) to be thoroughly effective as deterrents, hence about the only method of control is to examine the bases of young trees in the spring and fall for fresh borings, and to eradicate the borers at once. This can be done by digging them out with a knife, killing them by forcing a wire up the hole, or by inserting a few drops of paradichlorobenzene in the hole and stopping it up at once. However, D.D.T. applied as a sticky spray to the trunks of peach trees at certain times is helpful in controlling peach and locust borers and it may prove applicable for controlling apple tree borers as well.

Certain crab apples, notably *M. ioensis plena,* are susceptible to the cedar rust disease, serving as alternate hosts with the Junipers. In the

Crab Apples leaves vary as illustrated by these nine examples:
Top row—M. toringoides, spectabilis, sargenti
Middle row—M. sieboldi, pumila halliana
Bottom row—M. baccata, purpurea, atrosanguinea

late summer the leaves become covered with disfiguring brown blotches. Spraying with colloidal sulfur has proved effective, using five to six applications seven to ten days apart, beginning before the first expected rains after the leaf buds have opened. Also a trade fungicide called "Fermate" has proved very effective in the control of this disease.

Fortunately, the oriental crab apples do not appear to be susceptible to this disease, and this very important fact should be noted in making selections of varieties for planting. It is equally important to notice that oriental crab apples do not appear to be severely troubled with fire blight. At least this has proved the case in the Arnold Arboretum, where the collection is adjacent to a severely infested group of pear trees.

It is not necessary to spray the fruits of crab apples if they are merely to be ornamental on the tree. If, however, the fruits are to be used for any economic purpose, it may be necessary to follow the apple spray schedule recommended for each particular region by the state agricultural experiment stations.

x Malus arnoldiana   20′   Zone 4   Arnold Crab Apple
*FLOWERS: bud rose-red; flower phlox pink outside fading to white inside, 2″
          diameter, fragrant
     TIME: early May

*FRUIT: ⅝" diameter, yellow and red
   EFFECTIVE: September and October
*HABIT: mounded, dense branching
FOLIAGE: dense, fine texture
HYBRID ORIGIN: *M. floribunda x M. baccata*
ORIGINATED: 1883
   Originated as a chance seedling in the Arnold Arboretum and one of the best in flower, especially because of its deep red flower buds which contrast well with the light pink to white of the opening flowers.

x Malus atrosanguinea   20'   Zone 4   Carmine Crab Apple

FLOWERS: bud crimson, flower rose madder and 1¼" diameter
   TIME: mid-May
FRUIT: ⅜" diameter, dark red, not ornamental
   EFFECTIVE: late August to late October
*HABIT: mounded, almost shrublike, dense branching
FOLIAGE: dark green, dense, glossy
HYBRID ORIGIN: *M. halliana x M. sieboldi*
ORIGINATED: before 1889
   This hybrid is used a great deal in Japan and introduced into America from Japan by the Arnold Arboretum. When it is in full bloom, the flowers are a rich carmine but they fade to a rather unsightly pink just before they fall. One of the smaller trees, good for contrast with some of the taller white flowering varieties. The foliage of this species is about the best of any Crab Apple.

Malus baccata   50'   Zone 2   Siberian Crab Apple

*FLOWERS: white 1–1½" diameter, very fragrant
   TIME: early May
*FRUIT: red or yellow, ⅜" diameter, varies considerably
   EFFECTIVE: late August to late October
HABIT: vigorous, upright, narrow head, dense branching
FOLIAGE: dense
HABITAT: northeastern Asia
INTRODUCED: before 1800
VARIETIES: *gracilis*—white flowers 1⅜" in diameter, more dense than the species with the tips of the branches slightly pendulous. The leaves are smaller also, giving the entire tree a more refined appearance. Commercial growers will continue to offer the species because it grows readily from seed, but this and the following variety are really superior and should be used instead where possible.
   mandshurica—flowers white, 1½" in diameter, appearing in late April making this the first of the Crab Apples to bloom.
   Actually a standard tree, one of the hardiest of all the *Malus*, used considerably in hybridizing in an effort to obtain hardier apples of commercial sizes, especially for the prairie provinces of Canada. Many varieties of this widely distributed species have been described, some very meagerly indeed. The point to keep in mind is that since these are readily grown from seed by the commercial grower, the sizes of flowers and the sizes and colors of the fruits will vary con-

siderably. If a particular type is wanted, make certain the plants have been asexually propagated from the desired specimen. It is one of the taller crab apples and so should not be used on small properties. On the other hand, in parks or other large areas it has its place especially as a background tree for other crab apples since its flowers are always white and profusely borne.

x Malus "Bob White" 20′ Zone 4

*FLOWERS: buds cherry color, flowers fade to white, 1″ in diameter, fragrant
    TIME: early May
*FRUIT: ⅝″ yellow
    EFFECTIVE: all winter
HABIT: rounded, dense branching
FOLIAGE: dense, fine texture
HYBRID ORIGIN: clon of *Malus zumi*
ORIGINATED: before 1876
    Of interest because the fruits remain on the tree all winter and afford food for the birds at times when snow covers most of the available food.

Malus brevipes 15′ Zone 5 Nippon Crab Apple

*FLOWERS: whitish, ¾″ diameter, fragrant
    TIME: early May
*FRUIT: red, ⅜″ diameter
    EFFECTIVE: late August to mid-November
*HABIT: mounded, dense branching
FOLIAGE: dense, fine texture
ORIGIN: unknown, cultivated since 1883
    Chiefly valued because it is small, dense and rounded and because its fruits turn color in early August, thus making a conspicuous color combination with the green foliage considerably before the fruits of most of the other crab apples color.

Malus coronaria charlottae 30′ Zone 4 Charlotte Crab Apple

*FLOWERS: double (18 petals), 2″ diameter, pink buds and flowers
    TIME: late May
HABIT: rounded, wider at base than top
FOLIAGE: dense
HABITAT: discovered about 1902 by the husband of Mrs. Charlotte M. de Wolf, Waukegan, Illinois, and named after her.
    This is a better form than the species because of its double flowers, but it must be admitted that, like other crab apples native to North America, it is susceptible to disfiguration from the Juniper rust, and its fruits when produced are not ornamental, merely because they are large and green. The more recently introduced variety *nieuwlandiana* is somewhat similar but sources for it are very difficult to locate. This tree has short, thornlike side branches.

x Malus "Cowichan" 40′ Zone 4

*FLOWERS: 1¾″ diameter, purplish red
    TIME: early May

*FRUIT: purplish red, 1½″ diameter
    EFFECTIVE: late August to mid-October
HABIT: rounded
FOLIAGE: dense
AUTUMN COLOR: reddish
HYBRID ORIGIN: *M. pumila niedzwetzkyana* open pollinated
ORIGINATED: 1920, named in 1930

This tree is one of the better "Rosybloom" crab apples, so named by Miss Isabella Preston of the Dominion Experimental Station, Ottawa, Canada, who was responsible for collecting the seed and naming twenty-two selected forms. Of these, four have been selected in later years as the best at the Ottawa Station, namely, "Cowichan," "Makamik," "Rosseau" and "Sissipuk." The variety "Cowichan" is valued because it blooms well every year and bears good fruit from which jelly can be made. All these four varieties are improvement over *M. pumila niedzwetzkyana,* for on this species the fruit is nearly 2¼″ in diameter, so large that it should be sprayed at frequent intervals (like commercial apples) or the fruit will be very disfigured by insects and disease. In any event, the fruit is so large that it is really out of the crab apple class—and at the same time is too small for a commercial apple!

The flowers of most of the "Rosybloom" crab apples, like their parent, have the disconcerting habit of fading rapidly to a washed out reddish color that is not particularly desirable, but when they are approaching full bloom, there certainly is nothing quite like them.

x Malus dawsoniana   35′   Zone 4   Dawson Crab Apple

*FLOWERS: white, 1–1¼″ in diameter
    TIME: early May
FRUIT: elongated, 1″ long, only ½″ diameter, yellow-green and reddish
    EFFECTIVE: early September to late November
HABIT: rounded, sometimes upright or oval
FOLIAGE: dense
*AUTUMN COLOR: red and yellow
HYBRID ORIGIN: *M. fusca x M. pumila*

The fruits of this crab apple are longer than wide, and the autumn color is an excellent red and yellow, especially when it is growing in the full sun. This autumn color has been noted both in the Arnold Arboretum and in the parks of Rochester, New York, where this species has been growing for many years. Since few crab apples have such autumn color, it was included in the group to be recommended. Otherwise, it has no particular merit since other varieties are superior to it in flower and fruit as well.

Malus "Dolgo"   40′   Zone 3

*FLOWERS: white, 1¾″ in diameter, fragrant
    TIME: early May
*FRUIT: bright red, 1¼″ diameter
    EFFECTIVE: August
HABIT: rather open but vigorous
FOLIAGE: dense

ORIGINATED: grown from seed collected in Russia by Dr. Niels E. Hansen in 1897

Dr. Niels E. Hansen, formerly Professor of Horticulture at the South Dakota Agricultural Experiment Station, has been particularly interested in producing hardier fruits for over half a century. This crab apple was one he introduced in 1917, especially because of its early fruits which color and ripen in August, before the fruits of most other *Malus* species and varieties color. It is a vigorous grower, recommended as being particularly hardy and adaptable for growing in the Prairie Provinces of Canada where many other crab apples fail. Its fruits make excellent jelly, thus it is included with the "dual purpose" group (see page   ).

x Malus "Dorothea"   25'   Zone 4

*FLOWERS: semi-double (16 petals), 1⅝–2" diameter, crimson to tyrian rose, with
    rose-opal colored buds
  TIME: mid-May
*FRUITS: bright yellow, ½" diameter
  EFFECTIVE: fall until early winter
HABIT: rounded, dense branching
FOLIAGE: dense, fine texture
HYBRID ORIGIN: *M. halliana parkmani x arnoldiana*
ORIGINATED: found as chance seedling in Arnold Arboretum, May 17, 1943

This seedling was first noted in bloom when it was 5' high. The foliage resembles the Parkman Crab Apple somewhat, while the fruit resembles that of *M. arnoldiana*. It is one of the very few semi-double flowered crab apples which also bear fruit, and particularly beautiful fruit. It is named after my older daughter, Dorothea, and is a valuable addition to the crab apple group. Another very important characteristic is the fact that it bears flowers and fruits annually, something which unfortunately can not be claimed of many crab apples. Also it blooms early in life; young plants grafted one year frequently bloom the next.

x Malus "Exzellenz Thiel"   20'   Zone 4

*FLOWERS: pink buds, followed by white flowers, 1¾" diameter
  TIME: early May
*FRUIT: red and yellow, ¾" diameter
  EFFECTIVE: late August to late October
HABIT: rounded, pendulous branchlets
FOLIAGE: dense
HYBRID ORIGIN: clon of *Malus scheideckeri*
ORIGINATED: Spaeth Nursery in Germany about 1909

Of value merely because of its pendulous branchlets

Malus "Flame"   25'   Zone 2

*FLOWERS: pink buds, flowers fading white
  TIME: early May
*FRUIT: bright red, ¾" diameter
  EFFECTIVE: late August to mid-November
HABIT: rounded
FOLIAGE: dense

ORIGIN: about 1920 as a chance seedling at the University of Minnesota State Fruit Farm, Excelsior, Minnesota

"Flame" has proved a valuable ornamental in the colder areas of Minnesota where it is perfectly hardy anywhere in the state and so has value in such areas where other crab apples may not prove hardy.

Malus floribunda   30'   Zone 4   Japanese Flowering Crab Apple

*FLOWERS: buds deep pink to red, flowers gradually fading white, 1–1½" diameter, fragrant
   TIME: early May
*FRUIT: yellow and red, ⅜" diameter
   EFFECTIVE: late August to mid-October
*HABIT: rounded and densely branched
FOLIAGE: dense, fine texture
HABITAT: Japan
INTRODUCED: 1862

This standard ornamental flowering tree has performed very well indeed all over its hardiness range in America since it was introduced. It grows readily from seed, makes vigorous growth and blooms while comparatively young. It is dense and rounded in habit with branches facing the ground well on all sides. A new variety, "Snowbank," so named because of its profuse crop of flowers annually, is probably a form of *M. floribunda*. Other crab apples may surpass it in color, size of flower, or fruit, but none are more dependably beautiful year in and year out.

Malus "Frau Luise Dittman"   30'   Zone 4

*FLOWERS: double (10–12 petals), pink, 1¼" in diameter
   TIME: mid-May
*FRUIT: yellow, 1" diameter
   EFFECTIVE: late August to early September
HABIT: rounded
FOLIAGE: dense
ORIGINATED: in Germany about 1909, introduced to the United States by the Morton Arboretum, Lisle, Illinois, in 1925

This *Malus* is mentioned because of its double flowers and yellow fruits— very few crab apples have this combination which adds greatly to their ornamental usefulness.

Malus halliana parkmani   15'   Zone 5   Parkman Crab Apple

*FLOWERS: double (15 petals), neyron rose color, 1¼" diameter
   TIME: early May
FRUIT: dull red, ¼" diameter
   EFFECTIVE: September to mid-November
HABIT: upright, almost vase-shaped, dense branching
FOLIAGE: fairly open, lustrous, leathery
INTRODUCED: 1861 from Japan where it was cultivated—a garden plant of unknown origin

A very beautiful, double, pink crab apple, the least hardy of over 150 kinds growing in the Arnold Arboretum. The foliage is dark glossy green, but the fruit is very small, dull in color and hence not too noticeable. This is very definitely not one for two seasons of interest, but many who have come to like this old-fashioned variety will not want to part with it for one of the hardier varieties. It carries the names of two men responsible for introducing it as well as some other interesting and valued Japanese plants. Dr. George R. Hall was a doctor who practiced medicine in the foreign settlement of Shanghai, China, in 1861, and he also travelled widely in Japan. He sent this Asiatic garden specimen to his good friend Francis Parkman of Boston who grew it for the first time in America.

Malus halliana spontanea   15′   Zone 5

*FLOWERS: deep pink buds and flowers white, 1⅜″ diameter, fragrant
    TIME: early May
FRUIT: red ⅜″ diameter
    EFFECTIVE: September to mid-November
*HABIT: wide spreading and vase-shaped, very dense and twiggy
FOLIAGE: dense, fine texture
AUTUMN COLOR: red and yellow
HABITAT: Japan
INTRODUCED: 1919 by the Arnold Arboretum

    This crab apple is recommended chiefly for its uniformly rounded outline with dense twiggy branches as well as its brilliant autumn color (when grown in full sunshine) which few crab apples possess.

x Malus "Hopa"   30′   Zone 4

*FLOWERS: China rose color, 1½″ diameter, fragrant
    TIME: early May
*FRUIT: orange and red, ¾″ diameter
    EFFECTIVE: late August to mid-October
HABIT: rounded, vigorous
FOLIAGE: dense
HYBRID ORIGIN: clon of *M. adstringens*
ORIGINATED: 1920 by Niels E. Hansen, Professor of Horticulture, South Dakota
    Agricultural Experiment Station, Brookings, South Dakota

    Widely grown by nurserymen now because it combines profuse flowers and colorful fruit with the very important feature that the fruits are sufficiently large (and good) to be used in making preserves. Hence it is one of the few "dual purpose" types.

Malus hupehensis   24′   Zone 4   Tea Crab Apple

*FLOWERS: deep pink buds, flowers gradually fading white, to 1½″ diameter, fragrant
    TIME: early May
FRUIT: greenish yellow to red, ⅜″ diameter
    EFFECTIVE: September and October
*HABIT: vase-shaped, decidedly picturesque

The Tea Crab Apple, Malus hupehensis, with a picturesque method of branching was first brought to America by the Arnold Arboretum in 1900.

FOLIAGE: loose and open

HABITAT: China

INTRODUCED: by the Arnold Arboretum 1900

The Tea Crab Apple is the most picturesque of all because it is vase-shaped in habit with long reaching single branches growing from the trunk and spreading out like the ribs of a fan. In bud and flower it is beautiful and its marked habit is clearly evident every season of the year. The flowers are produced on small spurs or short branches up and down the entire length of the long straight branches; the fruits are small and not especially colorful.

Malus ioensis plena   30′   Zone 2   Bechtel Crab Apple

*FLOWERS: double (33 petal), buds and flowers pink, 2″ diameter, fragrant

    TIME: late May

FRUIT: green, 1⅛″ diameter, few produced

HABIT: round-headed, open

FOLIAGE: leaves rather large and coarse, susceptible to spots of juniper rust

ORIGIN: discovered in a fence row by E. A. Bechtel of Staunton, Illinois, between 1840 and 1850

INTRODUCED: 1888

A very popular crab apple during the past fifty years, its place is now being taken by several of the exotic oriental crab apples because all native species belong to the group often seriously infested with the unsightly brown spots of the cedar apple rust. This can be controlled by excessive spraying if Red-cedars must be grown in the near vicinity of the crab apples, but the species native to the

Orient are not susceptible. Then, the Bechtel Crab Apple has only a few fruits and these are green; not at all ornamental, while several of the double flowering orientals (and their hybrids) have brightly colored red or yellow fruits.

It must be admitted that it is beautiful when in full bloom; its flowers look like small rambler roses and it blooms late after most of the other crab apples have passed. All in all, however, I think that several of the newer varieties will take its place.

x Malus "Katherine" 20' Zone 4

*FLOWERS: double (20 petals), light pink fading white, 2¼" diameter
    TIME: mid-May
FRUIT: dull red, ¼" diameter
    EFFECTIVE: fall and early winter
HABIT: loose and open
FOLIAGE: dark green
HYBRID ORIGIN: *M. halliana x M. baccata*
ORIGINATED: as a seedling in Durand Eastman Park, Rochester, New York, about
      1928

This seedling was first noted by B. H. Slavin of the Rochester Park System where the original plant still grows. I named it after Mr. Slavin's daughter-in law, Katherine Clark Slavin, and the Arnold Arboretum introduced it in 1943. "Katherine" has unusually large double flowers, followed by small red fruits. It is more open in its branching habits than many members of this genus. This tree, however, may be an alternate bloomer—it is simply covered with flowers and fruits one year (with very little vegetative growth) and produces very few flowers the next year. This observation is made from our oldest tree, but if it is evident in others, it will be a serious black mark on the record against this very beautiful ornamental specimen.

x Malus magdeburgensis 30' Zone 4 Magdeburg Crab Apple

*FLOWERS: single and semi-double (5–13 petals), rose madder color, 1½" diameter
    TIME: early May
FRUIT: yellow-green and red, 1¼" diameter
    EFFECTIVE: August and September
HABIT: rounded, open
FOLIAGE: dense
HYBRID ORIGIN: *M. spectabilis x M. pumila*
ORIGINATED: before 1900

Since both its parents are tall-growing species, this beautiful flowering tree may eventually develop into one of the tallest of the double flowering crab apples.

x Malus "Makamik" 40' Zone 4

*FLOWERS: 1⅝" diameter, China rose color
    TIME: one of latest of Rosybloom crab apples to flower, early May
*FRUIT: purplish red, ¾" diameter
    EFFECTIVE: fall and throughout the winter

HABIT: rounded
FOLIAGE: dense
HYBRID ORIGIN: *M. pumila niedzwetzkyana* open pollinated
ORIGINATED: 1920, named 1930

This has been considered one of the better of "Rosybloom" crab apples at the Dominion Experimental Farms where it originated. (See note under *Malus* "Cowichan.")

x Malus micromalus   20′   Zone 4   Midget Crab Apple

*FLOWERS: pink, 1½″ diameter, fragrant
    TIME: early May
FRUIT: red to greenish red, ½″ diameter
    EFFECTIVE: September to mid-October
*HABIT: upright, dense
FOLIAGE: dense
HYBRID ORIGIN: *M. spectabilis x M. baccata*
ORIGINATED: about 1856

The Midget Crab Apple is splendid in flower and its shape is densely upright. Its fruits are not as conspicuously colored as those of some other species and it also tends to produce its flowers only in alternate years. When a well-grown specimen is once seen in full bloom, however, it is one of those sights rarely forgotten.

x Malus "Oekonomierat Echtermeyer"   15′   Zone 4

*FLOWERS: purplish red, 1½″ diameter
    TIME: early May
*FRUIT: reddish purple, 1″ diameter
    EFFECTIVE: September
*HABIT: semi-weeping
FOLIAGE: bronze green
HYBRID ORIGIN: *M. pumila niedzwetzkyana x M.* "Exzellenz Thiel"
ORIGINATED: Spaeth Nurseries, Germany, 1914

Interesting because of its graceful, semi-pendulous habit, it should be grafted or budded rather high on upright understock to be most effective. A plant now in the trade called "Pink Weeper" is synonymous with this variety.

x Malus "Prince Georges"   25′   Zone 4

*FLOWERS: double, 2″ diameter, 50 petals, light pink
    TIME: late May
HABIT: upright, dense
FOLIAGE: dense, rather coarse
HYBRID ORIGIN: *M. ioensis plena x M. angustifolia*
ORIGINATED: 1919

Seeds of this crab apple were collected in the Arnold Arboretum by the Division of Plant Exploration and Introduction of the U.S. Dept. of Agriculture in 1919, and in 1930 scions from one of the resulting seedlings were returned to the Arnold Arboretum. The flowers have more petals and the leaves are narrower than those of *M. ioensis plena*. Also it apparently is not as much troubled with disease as is the Bechtel's Crab Apple, although the flowers are similar. It is named after the county in Maryland where it was first grown by the United States Department of Agriculture.

Malus prunifolia rinki   20′   Zone 3   Chinese Pearleaf Crab Apple

*FLOWERS: pink, 2″ diameter, fragrant
  TIME: early May
FRUIT: green and red about 1″ diameter
  EFFECTIVE: late August to mid-September
HABIT: dense branching
FOLIAGE: dense
HABITAT: eastern Asia
INTRODUCED: 1850
  Because of its large flowers, this crab apple is popular among the Chinese as well as the American gardeners.

x Malus purpurea aldenhamensis   25′ Zone 4 Aldenham Purple Crab Apple

*FLOWERS: semi-double, 5–8 petals, 1¾″ diameter, purplish red
  TIME: early May
*FRUIT: purplish red, 1″ diameter
  EFFECTIVE: late August to late October
HABIT: rounded, dense
*FOLIAGE: dark reddish green, sometimes slightly bronze, especially as it first appears in the spring, dense
HYBRID ORIGIN: *M. pumila niedzwetzkyana x M. atrosanguinea?*
ORIGINATED: 1920—introduced to America 1923
  Superior to the Purple Crab Apple because of a larger number of petals, hence a longer period effective in flower. It frequently blooms a second and even a third time.

x Malus purpurea lemoinei   25′   Zone 4   Lemoine Purple Crab Apple

*FLOWERS: single and semi-double, 1½″ diameter, Tyrian rose, the deepest color of any of the varieties of this species
  TIME: early May
*FRUITS: purplish red, ⅝″ diameter
  EFFECTIVE: late August to late October
HABIT: dense
*FOLIAGE: dark green to almost purplish green
HYBRID ORIGIN: *M. pumila niedzwetzkyana x M. atrosanguinea*
ORIGINATED: in the Lemoine's Nursery, France, 1922
  At the time this is being written, Lemoine's Crab Apple has the darkest flowers of any of the *Malus* species. It is decidedly ornamental, and is prominent anywhere. It is far superior to *M. purpurea* or *M. pumila niedzwetzkyana* because of the darker colored flowers and also because they do not fade nearly as much.

x Malus "Redfield"   30′   Zone 4

*FLOWERS: carmine bud and flowers fading to a dull pink
    TIME: early May
*FRUIT: red, 1⅜″ diameter, flesh red
    EFFECTIVE: September
HABIT: dense
FOLIAGE: dense, reddish green
HYBRID ORIGIN: Wolf River Apple x *M. pumila niedzwetzkyana*
ORIGINATED: 1924
INTRODUCED: 1938

    This introduction was made by the New York Agricultural Experiment Station of Geneva, New York, and is of economic value because of its fruits.

x Malus "Redflesh"   25   Zone 4

*FLOWERS: spirea red color, 1¾″ diameter
    TIME: early May
*FRUIT: red, 1½″ diameter
    EFFECTIVE: September
HABIT: dense
*FOLIAGE: bronzy green
HYBRID ORIGIN: a clon of *M. soulardi*
ORIGINATED: 1928

    Dr. Niels E. Hansen of South Dakota was responsible for introducing this large-fruited, red-fleshed "dual purpose" crab apple; the fruits can be used in making preserves.

x Malus "Red Silver"   30′   Zone 4

*FLOWERS: China rose color, 1½″ diameter
    TIME: early May
*FRUIT: purplish red, ¾″ diameter
    EFFECTIVE: September
HABIT: dense
*FOLIAGE: reddish green, noticeable throughout the growing season
HYBRID ORIGIN: clon of *M. adstringens*
ORIGINATED: 1928

    Dr. Niels E. Hansen of Brookings, South Dakota, also introduced this crab apple which is another splendid ornamental in flower, and the fruit of which makes good jelly. Its most pleasing attribute is the dark reddish green color of the foliage which is noticeable throughout the spring and summer.

x Malus robusta   40′   Zone 3   Cherry Crab Apple

*FLOWERS: white, sometimes slightly pink, 1¾″ diameter, fragrant
    TIME: early May
*FRUIT: red and yellow, ¾–1½″ diameter
    EFFECTIVE: September and October
HABIT: oval-shaped, dense branching
FOLIAGE: dense

HYBRID ORIGIN: *M. baccata x M. prunifolia*
ORIGINATED: about 1815
VARIETY: *persicifolia*—excellent red ornamental fruits, ¾" diameter, that remain
   colorful on the tree until the first of the year.—Peachleaf Crab Apple
 Since this is a so-called hybrid species, every one of the progeny of this
cross is a clon. In the Arnold Arboretum there were growing at one time nearly
twenty clons of this cross, varying considerably in size of flowers and size and
color of the fruits. One of the best was a white-flowering clon with fruits about
an inch in diameter, deep red on the side exposed to the sun and yellow on the
shaded portion. One should be very careful in buying plants offered under this
name because of this considerable variation.

x Malus "Rosseau"   40'   Zone 4

*FLOWERS: 1¾" diameter, China rose color
 TIME: early May
*FRUIT: rosy red, about ½–1" diameter
 EFFECTIVE: late August to mid-October
HABIT: rounded
FOLIAGE: dense
HYBRID ORIGIN: *M. pumila niedzwetzkyana* open pollinated
ORIGINATED: 1920 named 1930
 An annual bearing "Rosybloom" crab apple (see note under Malus
"Cowichan") valued because its fruits are a little more colorful than others of this
group.

Malus sargenti   8'   Zone 5   Sargent Crab Apple

*FLOWERS: pure white, ½" diameter, fragrant
 TIME: mid-May
FRUIT: dark red, ¼" diameter
 EFFECTIVE: fall
*HABIT: mounded, the lowest of all *Malus* species, dense branching
HABITAT: Japan
INTRODUCED: 1892
 The only crab apple small enough to be considered a shrub, this may grow
twice as broad as high, is dense and moundlike and is covered with pure white,
fragrant blossoms in mid-May. The fruit is comparatively small for the crab
apples but colors before the leaves drop in the fall making an excellent red-green
color combination, and they may remain on the plant long in the fall, especially
if there are not too many birds in the vicinity.

x Malus scheideckeri   20'   Zone 4   Scheidecker Crab Apple

*FLOWERS: double (10 petals), pale pink, 1½" diameter
 TIME: early May
FRUIT: yellow to orange, ⅝" diameter
 EFFECTIVE: September
HABIT: upright
FOLIAGE: dense

HYBRID ORIGIN: *M. floribunda x M. prunifolia*
ORIGINATED: before 1888 in the Scheidecker Nursery, Germany

Malus sieboldi arborescens   30′   Zone 5   Tree Toringo Crab Apple

*FLOWERS: pink buds, flowers fading white, ¾″ diameter, fragrant
  TIME: mid-May
*FRUIT: yellow to red, ½″ diameter
  EFFECTIVE: late August to mid-November
*HABIT: mounded, dense branching
FOLIAGE: dense
HABITAT: Japan, Korea
INTRODUCED: 1892

Not particularly outstanding but mentioned here only because of its late bloom, for it is one of the last to flower. If time of bloom is not a factor in the selection of varieties, this one might well be overlooked.

x Malus "Sissipuk"   40′   Zone 4

*FLOWERS: 1⅛″ diameter, purplish red
  TIME: mid-May
*FRUIT: ¾″ diameter, purplish red
  EFFECTIVE: fall and throughout the winter
HABIT: rounded
FOLIAGE: dense
HYBRID ORIGIN: *M. pumila niedzwetzkyana* open pollinated
ORIGINATED: 1920 named 1930

Another of the "Rosybloom" crab apples (see under "Cowichan"). It is an annual bearer and since the fruit remains all winter it has considerable merit in the winter garden. It is the last of the selected "Rosybloom" crab apples to bloom.

Malus spectabilis riversi   24′   Zone 4   River's Crab Apple

*FLOWERS: pink, double (9–20 petals), 2″ diameter
  TIME: early May
FRUIT: green, 1¼″ diameter, not effective
HABIT: open
FOLIAGE: open
ORIGINATED: in an English nursery before 1872 as a variety of *M. spectabilis*
  which has never been found in nature
INTRODUCED: before 1883

Malus spectabilis and its varieties are undoubtedly considerably mixed up in the trade. The species has never been found outside of cultivation and the flowers and is often termed *"roseo-plena"* in the trade. The latter has pure white, Considerably superior in flower are the two double-flowered varieties, *M. spectabilis riversi* and *M. spectabilis albi-plena*. The former has large many petaled flowers and is often termed *"roseo-plena"* in the trade. The latter has pure white, double flowers. Both are excellent in flower but have poor fruits. It may well be that some of the newer hybrids, like "Katherine" and Dorothea" which have double flowers and brightly colored fruits, may supersede these two old-fashioned favorites.

Malus toringoides   25′   Zone 5   Cutleaf Crab Apple

*FLOWERS: white, ¾″ diameter, fragrant
   TIME: late May
*FRUIT: pear-shaped, ¾″ diameter, yellow on shaded side, red on sunny side
   EFFECTIVE: late August to late November
*HABIT: upright, pyramidal, branching dense
FOLIAGE: dense
HABITAT: western China
INTRODUCED: 1904
    One of the last to bloom and one of the best in fruit, the fruit remaining on the plant in splendid condition until after the first hard freeze. E. H. Wilson used to consider this the best of all species in fruit, but it must be admitted that there are several superior to it for their colorful flowers.

x Malus zumi calocarpa   Redbud Crab Apple

*FLOWERS: pink buds, followed by white flowers 1″ diameter, fragrant
   TIME: early May
*FRUIT: bright red, ½″ diameter
   EFFECTIVE: late August to February
HABIT: pyramidal, dense branching
FOLIAGE: dense
HYBRID ORIGIN: *M. baccata mandshurica x M. sieboldi*
HABITAT: Japan
INTRODUCED: 1892
    One of the best crab apples for ornamental fruit, some of which remain on the plant far into the winter.

Maytenus boaria   35′   Zone 9   Chile Mayten Tree

HABIT: branchlets pendulous
*FOLIAGE: evergreen, dense and light green
HABITAT: Chile
    This evergreen makes a beautiful specimen and is highly recommended by many as a street and avenue tree as far north as San Francisco in California. It is also used in seashore plantings.

Melaleuca leucadendron   40′   Zone 10   Cajeput Tree

*FLOWERS: creamy white in spikes 6″ long
   TIME: June to October
HABIT: slender and upright
*BARK: gray, thick and soft, peeling off in thin strips
*FOLIAGE: pale green, evergreen
HABITAT: Australia

The Chinaberry (Melia azedarach) grows easily and rapidly from seed and is widely distributed in the South. Especially does it do well in adverse growing conditions.

Fast growing, resistant to grass fires and the effects of salt water spray, this tree has many uses in both southern Florida and California. Apparently it does not suffer from poor drainage. The flowers with very long and exposed stamens give the general effect of a bottle brush, characteristic of the other members of this genus. In places where the soil is moist, it may reseed itself vigorously and quickly become a weed.

Melia azedarach   45′   Zone 7   Chinaberry

*FLOWERS: lilac colored clusters, 5–8″ long, fragrant
    TIME: April to May
*FRUIT: yellow berries, ½″ diameter
    EFFECTIVE: fall and winter
*HABIT: round-headed, branching dense
FOLIAGE: dense
HABITAT: Himalaya
INTRODUCED: colonial times
VARIETY: *umbraculiformis*—branches more or less densely upright, tree with a flattened head.—Umbrella Chinaberry

A common tree throughout the South and, in fact, naturalized throughout all tropical and subtropical countries. It grows rapidly from seed and blooms early in life, quickly yielding a dense shade. It seems to do very well in the hottest of summers, as well as in dry soil. The fruits are very much sought after by the birds. However, it must be admitted that it is not a clean tree, that it is continually dropping fruits or leaves, and its seedlings quickly come up wherever it grows well. Where it can be used, it is always dependable for giving shade, but it is rather short-lived.

Metasequoia glyptostroboides   100'   Zone 6?   Dawn Redwood

FRUIT: small cones
*HABIT: upright
FOLIAGE: loose, open, deciduous, needlelike
HABITAT: Szechuan, China
INTRODUCED: 1948

This Metasequoia, known prior to 1945 only in Mesozoic paleobotanical records, was found in China and identified that year. Three years later the Arnold Arboretum received viable seeds of this interesting tree and distributed them in all parts of the world. It is as old as *Ginkgo biloba* but aside from its interesting background may not prove to be as good an ornamental. The needles are deciduous—about the same size as those of a hemlock—and it can be propagated by softwood or hardwood cuttings. In its first three winters in cultivation it has withstood the out-of-doors as far north as Boston but it will take some time before its real hardiness is known. This tree has probably been growing and repropagating itself for fifty million years or more. It is showing a remarkable rate of growth, which, if it continues and the tree is hardy, may give it considerable value to gardeners. In Santa Barbara, California, this tree grew 5 feet in one year

Morus alba   45'   Zone 4   White Mulberry

FRUIT: similar in size and shape to blackberries, white, pinkish or purplish, ½–1" long, sexes usually separate
   EFFECTIVE: early summer
*HABIT: round-topped, dense
FOLIAGE: bright green, often irregularly lobed
HABITAT: China
INTRODUCED: colonial times
VARIETIES: *pendula*—slender, pendulous branches, frequently planted for its form—Weeping Mulberry
         tatarica—supposed to be the hardiest form, with fruit less than ⅓" long—Russian Mulberry

None of the mulberries should be considered good for general ornamental planting and all might well be placed in the discard list. The trees have no particular autumn color. The fruits are profusely borne and are very attractive to all kinds of birds. If grown by pavement or paved road the falling fruit causes a continual litter. The hanging branches become very troublesome, if the tree is planted along streets, and require frequent maintenance to keep them trimmed back to reasonable proportions.

The White Mulberry varies considerably as far as its foliage is concerned and has been cultivated by the silk worm industry for centuries. It was brought to this country in colonial times in an attempt to establish the silk industry here, especially in the plantation areas of the southeastern United States. This never did prove profitable, but every now and then great publicity is given to these "silk worm" trees and many gardeners are urged to grow them. The White Mul-

berry and its varieties are merely included here because so many people are
interested in them, not because they measure up to better ornamental trees.

Myrica californica   30′   Zone 7   California Bayberry

*FRUIT: small, purple berries, sexes separate
    EFFECTIVE: fall and winter
HABIT: upright shrub or tree
*FOLIAGE: lustrous evergreen, bronze colored, leaves to 4″ long
HABITAT: Washington to California
    Easily grown and valued especially on the Pacific Coast for its berries and
evergreen leaves.

Myrica cerifera   36′   Zone 6   Southern Wax-myrtle

*FRUIT: small gray berries, sexes separate
    EFFECTIVE: fall and winter
HABIT: rather open, irregular in shape
*FOLIAGE: evergreen, leaves to 3″ long
HABITAT: New Jersey to Florida and Texas
    This is the southern counterpart of the northern Bayberry (*Myrica pensyl-
vanica*) and is taller growing and more dense, tending to be evergreen in the
South. A good ornamental, probably not too dependable as a tree.

Nyssa sylvatica   90′   Zone 4   Black Tupelo or Black Gum

FRUIT: a small blue berry, sexes separate
    EFFECTIVE: midsummer, but usually hidden by foliage
*HABIT: pyramidal with somewhat pendulous branches, branching dense
*FOLIAGE: dense, leaves lustrous and leathery
*AUTUMN COLOR: brilliant scarlet to orange
HABITAT: eastern United States
    An excellent ornamental, native over the greater part of the eastern United
States, especially growing in swampy places. It is one of those trees difficult to
transplant so that small specimens, especially dug with a ball of soil about the
roots, are the most likely to succeed after transplanting. The dense, dark green,
lustrous foliage turns a gorgeous autumn color in the fall and its pyramidal habit,
somewhat similar to that of the pin oak, makes it a desirable ornamental specimen.
The sexes are separate, the flowers are inconspicuous but the fruits are dark blue,
about the size of small cherries. Strangely enough it is specimens from this tree
which are sent to the Arnold Arboretum more frequently than any other for
identification, especially when it is in fruit.

Olea europaea   25′   Zone 9   Common Olive

FRUIT: olives, purple
*HABIT: densely rounded in poor soil, open and asymmetrical in good soil
*FOLIAGE: evergreen, gray-green, silvery beneath, distinctive
HABITAT: Mediterranean Region
INTRODUCED: colonial times?

Probably best used as a tree for dry soils since it tends to keep its excellent shape here best. The fruit, not frequently borne in Florida for some reason, can become a nuisance by littering the ground. This economic tree grown in orchards on a commercial scale can also be used on the home grounds and has been used considerably in California as a street tree.

Ostrya virginiana   60′   Zone 4   Hop Hornbeam

FRUIT: bladderlike pods in pendulous clusters, 1½–2½″ long
    EFFECTIVE: summer and early fall
HABIT: pyramidal
FOLIAGE: rather dense
AUTUMN COLOR: yellow
HABITAT: eastern North America

The Hop Hornbeam is of interest because it is fairly free from serious insect and disease pests and is a nice medium-sized tree (usually under 40′) for ornamental use. The clusters of bladderlike fruits are evident throughout the summer. However, experience has shown that it grows slowly and is rather difficult to transplant.

Oxydendrum arboreum   75′   Zone 4   Sorrel Tree or Sourwood

*FLOWERS: small, white, in slightly pendulous racemes
    TIME: mid-July
*FRUIT: dried capsules
    EFFECTIVE: far into the winter
*HABIT: pyramidal
*FOLIAGE: lustrous, dense, leathery
*AUTUMN COLOR: brilliant scarlet
HABITAT: eastern and southeastern United States

This is one of the superior ornamental trees especially while it is young and can be kept clothed with branches from top to bottom and grown in a situation where it is exposed to full sunshine. Its leaves are similar in size and shape to those of Mountain-laurel; they are lustrous and effective throughout the growing season. The late summer flowers, brilliant autumn color and graceful pyramidal habit give this tree additional interest every season of the year.

Parkinsonia aculeata   30′   Zone 9   Jerusalem Thorn

*FLOWERS: yellow, fragrant, in loose axillary racemes
    TIME: early spring
HABIT: open
BARK: green
FOLIAGE: thin, wiry, leaves fine texture, often 1′ long
HABITAT: tropical America

Of little use as a shade tree because of its open habit and peculiar foliage, this tree nevertheless has been used considerably as an ornamental because of its good flowers. It also can be clipped and formed into an excellent hedge, especially effective because of its numerous, inch-long thorns. It is used also in California as a street tree where it grows well in light sandy soil.

Parrotia persica   50′   Zone 5   Persian Parrotia

*HABIT: widely spreading, rounded, with several trunks
FOLIAGE: dense, leaves somewhat similar to those of the witchhazels
*AUTUMN COLOR: brilliant scarlet to orange and yellow
*BARK: mottled gray and white
HABITAT: Persia
INTRODUCED: 1840

An excellent tree for foliage, it usually grows with several trunks from the base and has leaves somewhat similar to those of the Witchhazel but more lustrous. The flowers, appearing before the leaves, are insignificant, but the interesting bark flakes off in patches leaving a colorful trunk like that of the stewartias or *Pinus bungeana* giving it special interest in winter. Also, the branches tend to be more or less horizontal and covered with leaves all in one plane. When allowed to grow with branches to the ground, older specimens can become very graceful indeed. This tree is not apparently infested with any serious insect or disease pest and might well be grown considerably more than it is.

Paulownia tomentosa   45′   Zone 5   Royal Paulownia or Empress Tree

*FLOWERS: large pyramidal clusters (up to 10″ high) of fragrant violet flowers
    TIME: mid-May
FRUIT: dried capsules 1½″ long
HABIT: rounded head, open
FOLIAGE: dense, leaves very large, sometimes 2–3′ in diameter, coarse
HABITAT: China
INTRODUCED: 1834

This very rapid-growing tree is similar to the Catalpa in habit, with very large leaves and fragrant lilac colored flowers, funnel-like and up to 2″ long in large conspicuous clusters. Its texture is coarse, but it does give dense shade. The picturesque and pubescent flower buds are present all winter long, and as a result are frequently killed or severely injured by cold winters in the vicinity of Boston and New York. Otherwise, it is a striking tree especially when in flower, for these appear before the leaves. In England, several of these plants are grown close together, heavily pruned each year, resulting in vigorous shoot growth of up to 12′ in a season with leaves up to 3′ across. This method of forcing over vigorous growth has little merit except for producing an oddity. In Japan the wood was formerly used for making sandals, clogs and even the musical instrument known as the lute.

Phellodendron amurense   45′   Zone 3   Amur Cork Tree

FLOWERS: small, whitish in panicles
    TIME: early June
*FRUIT: round black berries, ½″ diameter, in clusters
    EFFECTIVE: fall
*HABIT: wide, open, massive branches
*BARK: deeply fissured, corklike
FOLIAGE: loose, open, appears late

The rugged Amur Cork Tree, Phellodendron amurense, is perfectly hardy in the North. It has wide spreading branches and deeply furrowed bark, making a good shade tree.

AUTUMN COLOR: yellow, but leaves dropping quickly
HABITAT: northern China
INTRODUCED: about 1856

There has been some misunderstanding about the *Phellodendron* species, because C. S. Sargent stated back in 1905 that *P. sachalinense* was best under cultivation. This statement has since been copied by many authors. The fact of the matter is that of the five species growing in the Arnold Arboretum *P. amurense* has been outstanding and C. S. Sargent himself noted this in 1924. The other species are similar but *P. amurense* has the large branches of picturesque habit and corky bark which is of interest all winter. Like other species in this genus the sexes are separate and only pistillate plants will bear the numerous clusters of black berries. The autumn color is only of passing interest since the leaves quickly drop once they have turned yellow. It is a vigorous-growing tree and easily and quickly grown from seed (seedlings are continually sprouting up all over the Arnold Arboretum—more so than any other plant) and the roots are fibrous, making it easy to transplant. This wide-spreading tree produces only light shade and is of little interest in flower, but of particular interest in winter because of the massive branches and interesting bark.

There is a slight difference in branching habit among the various species of *Phellodendron*. *P. lavallei* is taller; *P. sachalinense* is more regularly vase-shaped than the irregular branching habit of *P. amurense*.

There has been some interest in times past relative to the cork-producing qualities of *Phellodendron* species, but it is not nearly as thick as that of *Quercus suber* or even *Q. variabilis* (which is nearly ½" thick), and as a consequence probably has little economic value.

Phoenix reclinata   25′   Zone 10   Senegal Date Palm

*HABIT: tall trunk, rounded top
FOLIAGE: featherlike compound leaves, long and gracefully arching
HABITAT: Africa

Next to the true date, the best palm tree from Africa for ornamental purposes is the Senegal Date Palm. It is used in southern California as a street tree of some merit for it is most graceful in habit and fairly rapid in growth, but the fruits are not edible. *Phoenix rupicola* is considered even more graceful and refined than this species.

Photinia serrulata   36′   Zone 7   Chinese Photinia

FLOWERS: white, small, in flat heads, 6" in diameter
    TIME: mid-May
*FRUIT: bright red berries
    EFFECTIVE: fall and early winter
*FOLIAGE: evergreen, dark lustrous green, leaves to 8" long
HABITAT: China
INTRODUCED: 1804

This very vigorous tree may become too leggy unless occasionally restrained. The new foliage is a reddish bronze, a brilliant color and considered by some to be sufficient reason to recommend it. If new growth is occasionally cut back, new shoots will be forced so that the young foliage can be evident for a considerable part of the growing season. The tree requires well drained soil and not too much moisture, especially during the summer. However, its lustrous evergreen leaves are really its best display.

Phyllostachys bambusoides   70′   Zone 7–8   Japanese Timber Bamboo

The Japanese Timber Bamboo is not to be considered as an ornamental tree, but a clump of this vigorous bamboo in the right place can be most interesting. This real timber bamboo is one of the tallest species growing in North America.

PICEA

Spruces are native in most of the mountainous regions of North America. Some of the species which have been introduced from Europe and Asia have proved better from an ornamental viewpoint than our natives. Practically none grow old gracefully, that is, as they mature they begin to lose their lower branches. As forest trees, this may be an ideal trait, but for specimen trees in good plantings it is not. As young trees they look splendid, some retaining their needles for six to eight years, making their foliage very dense, and they are as symmetrical as any other evergreen, but the person who is planting for permanence should not be led astray by their youthful appearance. The Red Spruce (*Picea rubens*), Black Spruce (*P. mariana*) and White Spruce (*P. glauca*) are the three most widely distributed natives. The White Spruce has been used in ornamental plantings considerably in the past, merely because it was readily available and easily grown from seed, but it does not mature into a fine ornamental as do some of the others, although several varieties of this species do have good habits. The Red and Black Spruces do not mature into good ornamentals either.

The native Colorado Spruce of the Rocky Mountains is very stiff in habit, while the Norway, Serbian, Oriental and Brewer's spruces are quite the opposite, having graceful more or less pendulous branchlets giving them considerable merit in ornamental plantings. Like many other conifers the spruces are definitely pyramidal in outline and mostly more stiff and rigid in habit than the more soft-textured pines. They vary also in the color of their foliage, in soil requirements and in hardiness.

Some are seriously attacked by the red spider and spruce gall aphids—ample reason why they are not planted in some areas. Each of the species recommended has its peculiar qualifications for landscape plantings but where other trees can be used, the spruces as a group might be overlooked.

For assistance in identification, the keys on page 250 will be of some help. It should prove advantageous in distinguishing spruces from other evergreens to note that the spruces have needles that are square in cross section (except four species) while the hemlocks and firs have needles that are flat. This, and the fact that the leaf bases of all spruces are tenacious and remain on the twigs long after the needles have dropped, making the twigs very rough to the touch. Spruce species frequently resemble one another very closely, making accurate identification difficult indeed. This is just one more reason why a comparatively small number of the species need be recommended for growing as ornamental specimens.

Simple Foliage Key to the Spruces

(Native or Available in North America)

The key which follows is prepared solely for the determination of material which is fresh. It cannot be used with dead material. Such a key has its good points and its bad points—good because the obvious characteristics such as color of foliage and twigs are utilized, and it can be used in the field without the aid of a lens (in most cases); bad because the key is only usable for the period of a few days after the branches have been taken from the living tree.

The key is offered for the individual who is not a trained botanist, and it should not be used as a means of final identification, for standard texts and illustrations should be consulted. In using the key merely go to the first number. If the statement there applies to the specimen, proceed to the next **higher** number until the tree is identified. If the statement there does not apply, go to the following group headed by the same number and proceed as above.

It is interesting to note that there are only seven species of spruce native to North America, and all are included in this key. There are about twenty-two species available in the trade, all of which are included in the key, as well as ten varieties in addition. There are about twenty-six varieties of *Picea abies* offered by various nurseries, and the differences among these are frequently so slight, especially in the younger stages of plant development, that it is impossible to make a satisfactory key for them. Consequently, it has only been possible to list the dwarf varieties of *P. abies* as a group.

Needles borne singly, leaf bases persistent.................... *Picea* and *Tsuga*
  1. Needles without distinct petioles (See Fig. 11 Page 340)......*Picea* species

abies—Norway Spruce	*mariana*—Black Spruce
abies vars. some 26 varieties available in the trade	*obovata*—Siberian Spruce
	omorika—Serbian Spruce
asperata—Dragon Spruce	*orientalis*—Oriental Spruce
bicolor—Alcock Spruce	*polita*—Tigertail Spruce
breweriana—Brewer Spruce	*pungens*—Colorada Spruce
engelmanni—Engelmann Spruce	*pungens argentea*—Silver Spruce
glauca—White Spruce	*pungens bakeri*—Baker Spruce
glauca albertiana—Alberta Spruce	*pungens glauca*—Blue Colorado Spruce
glauca conica—Dwarf Alberta Spruce	*pungens kosteriana*—Koster Spruce
	pungens moerheimi—Moerheim Spruce
glauca densata—Black Hills Spruce	*purpurea*—Purple Cone Spruce
	rubens—Red Spruce
glehni—Sakhalin Spruce	*schrenkiana*—Schrenk Spruce
jezoensis—Yeddo Spruce	*sitchensis*—Sitka Spruce
koyamai—Koyama Spruce	*smithiana*—Himalayan Spruce
	wilsoni—Wilson Spruce

  2. Needles on current year's growth mostly at right angles to twig; also see Fig. 6. (Note: in no specimen are all needles exactly at right angles to the twig. Some needles always point towards the end of the twig, hence making an angle less than a right angle. However, the plants in the group with needles at right angles should have more than 50 per cent of their needles at right angles to the twig. In case of reasonable doubt, certain plants can be located again under the second No. 2—"needles mostly at an angle considerably less than a right angle."
    3. Needles ½" long or less
        4. Needles showing intense white lines when observed from tip looking towards base of branch; branchlets pubescent
                                                              P. mariana
          (Labrador to Alaska; Wisconsin and Michigan) Zone 2
        4. Needles not showing intense white lines, plant a low dense pyramid of tightly compact light green foliage: branchlets glabrous...............................*P. glauca conica*

Figure 6. Tip of one year shoot of Picea pungens showing a majority of the needles nearly at right angles to the twig.

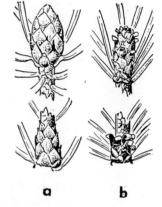

Figure 7. End bud and base of one year shoot of Picea polita (a) and Picea abies (b); showing the tight fitting scales on bud and shoot base of P. polita as compared with those of P. abies.

a   b

3. Needles mostly more than ½" long
    4. Terminal bud lustrous, dark brown, prominent about ¼" long; its tight fitting scales remaining snugly tight fitting and blackish at base of branchlets for several years....*P. polita* (Japan) Zone 5
    4. Terminal but not lustrous nor as prominent, light brown. The scales, if they remain at the base of the current year's branchlets are curled and indistinct, not snugly tight fitting
        5. Foliage of one-year twigs definitely blue

P. pungens glauca
P. pungens argentea
P. pungens moerheimi

The only way to tell these three apart is to determine the degree of blue color. *P. pungens glauca* is the least blue, *P. pungens argentea*, the typical "Koster's Spruce" of the trade, is next, and *P. pungens moerheimi* is the deepest blue.

Note: (Visualize the blue of *P. pungens argentea*— the typical "Koster's Spruce" of the trade, sometimes incorrectly named *Kosteri* or *Kosteriana*) and the green of the Norway Spruce. These are the two sharp color divisions. Plants with foliage a color between these two extremes comes under the second No. 5—"Foliage bluish to grayish green"

5. Foliage bluish to grayish green
    6. Needles rigid, extremely sharp to the touch, one-year shoots strong and vigorous often 6–10" long
        7. Needles frequently curved....*P. asperata* (West China) Zone 5
        7. Majority of needles straight....*P. pungens* (Wyoming to New Mexico) Zone 2
    6. Needles not so rigid, extremely sharp to the touch, one-year shoots not so vigorous
        7. One-year twigs greenish gray....*P. wilsoni* (Central and West China) Zone 5
        7. One-year twigs yellowish to orange-brown
                                    P. glauca
            (Canada and northern U.S.) Zone 2
    5. Foliage uniformly green. Usually most of the needles of this species are not at right angles to the twigs but sometimes on very vigorous shoots they are..*P. abies* (North and Central Europe, naturalized in Eastern U.S.) Zone 2
2. Needles on current year's growth mostly at an angle considerably less than a right angle with the twig; i.e., needles pointing towards the tip of the twig.
    3. Foliage of current year's shoots uniformly blue. (Note: Visualize the blue of *P. pungens argentea* (The typical "Koster's Spruce" of the Trade) and the green of the Norway Spruce. These are the two sharp color divisions. Plants with foliage a color between these two extremes come under the second No. 3—"Foliage bluish to grayish.")
        4. One-year twigs densely pubescent, noticeable without a lens...................................*P. engelmanni* (British Columbia to Arizona) Zone 2
        4. One-year twigs glabrous

Figure 8. Tip of one year shoot of Picea engelmanni showing a majority of the needles at less than right angles to the twig.

5. Plant with rigid, horizontal branches

P. pungens bakeri

5. Plant with pendulous branchlets *P. pungens kosteriana* (Not to be confused with the Silver spruce, *P. pungens argentea,* which does not have pendulous branchlets)

3. Foliage of current year's growth bluish to grayish or whitish; especially when viewed from tip of branch, looking toward base of branch; green when viewed from above the branch

4. Needles ¾" or less in length

5. One-year twigs greenish gray............*P. purpurea* (West China) Zone 5

5. One-year twigs yellowish to brown

6. Needles flat in cross section

7. Winter buds resinous

8. Branchlets glabrous and horizontal, foliage intensely white when viewed from underneath the branch

9. Needles pungent, ½–1" long

P. sitchensis (Alaska to California) Zone 6

9. Needles not pungent, ½–¾" long

P. jezoensis (Manchuria and Japan) Zone 4

8. Branchlets pubescent, usually markedly pendulous; foliage not intensely white when viewed from beneath

P. breweriana (Oregon to northern California) Zone 5

7. Winter buds not resinous; branchlets pubescent....................*P. omorika* (southeastern Europe) Zone 4

6. Needles angular in cross section, usually 4-sided

7. Two- and three-year-old twigs black on upper side of branch at least, giving a dark appearance to the tree; needles sharp; branchlets pubescent...........*P. mariana* (Labrador to Alaska, Wisconsin to Michigan) Zone 2

Figure 9. Cross section of needle of Picea omorika (below) and Picea glauca (above).

7. Two-year twigs usually light brown; branchlets glabrous, needles blunt
P. glauca densata
P. glauca
(Canada and northern United States)
Zone 2............P. glauca albertiana
5. One-year twigs definitely a red-brown
6. Cones 2¼–4¾″ long..................P. bicolor
(Japan) Zone 4
6. Cones 2–3″ long......................P. glehni
(Japan) Zone 3
(Here is a case where differentiation between
these two species without lens and without fruit
is difficult; the differences are largely those of
degree. The white markings on the upper surface
of the needles of P. bicolor are more intense,
whereas the pubescence of the branchlets and
the dark green color of the branchlets of P.
glehni is more marked)
4. Needles more than ¾″ long
5. Needles flat in cross section
6. Branchlets glabrous; foliage intensely white
when observed from underneath branch
P. sitchensis
(Alaska to California) Zone 6
6. Branchlets pubescent; usually markedly pendulous; foliage not intensely white when observed
from underneath branch........P. breweriana
(Oregon to northern California) Zone 5
5. Needles angular in cross section, usually 4-sided
6. Winter buds resinous.............P. smithiana
(Himalayas) Zone 6
6. Winter buds not resinous........P. schrenkiana
(Central Asia) Zone 5
3. Foliage uniformly green
4. The majority of the needles ½″ or less in length
5. Needles flattened against branchlets; a markedly
uniform dark glossy green above and below
P. orientalis
(Caucasus and Asia Minor) Zone 4
5. Needles not flattened against branchlets except in
some P. abies varieties which are dwarf shrubs and
not trees; nor a marked uniform glossy green above
and below except sometimes in P. rubens
6. Plants usually low, dense, dwarf shrubs
P. abies varieties
(Note: some 26 dwarf varieties are offered in
the trade.)
6. Plants not low, dense, dwarf shrubs, but trees

    7. One-year twigs yellowish, foliage gray-
     green..........................*P. glauca*
      (Canada and northern U.S.) Zone 2
    7. One-year twigs reddish brown; foliage green
     8. Needles only slightly glossy, branch-
      lets pubescent
       (Nova Scotia to North Carolina)
       Zone 2.................*P. rubens*
     8. Needles not glossy, branchlets glabrous
             P. koyamai
      (Japan and Korea) Zone 4
  4. The majority of the needles at least ½″ and usually approaching ¾″ in length
    5. Foliage dark green, branchlets usually orange
     6. Terminal bud lustrous, dark brown, prominent,
      about ¼″ long; its tight fitting scales remaining
      snugly tight fitting and blackish at base of
      branchlets for several years; foliage decidedly
      harsh to the touch....................*P. polita*
      (Japan) Zone 5
     6. Terminal bud not lustrous; the scales, if they
      remain at the base of the current year's branch-
      lets, are curled and indistinct, not snugly tight
      fitting; foliage not harsh to the touch
      (North and Central Europe, escaped in U.S.)
      Zone 2...........................*P. abies*
    5. Foliage grayish green, one-year twigs yellowish
     6. Needles usually rigidly upright on the upper side
      of the branchlets; needles dense, even on four-
      year-old branchlets; tree open in habit
             P. glauca
      (Canada and northern U.S.) Zone 2
     6. Needles usually appressed or held closely along
      the upper side of the branch, not upright; needles
      sparsely borne; tree dense and conical in habit
             P. obovata
      (Northern Europe to Kamchatka and Man-
      churia) Zone 2

Figure 10. Side view of shoot of Picea obovata (above)
and Picea glauca (below) showing the difference in the way the needles are borne
on the twig.

Picea abies   150′   Zone 2   Norway Spruce

FRUIT: pendulous cones 4–6″ long
    EFFECTIVE: fall and winter
*HABIT: pyramidal, pendulous branchlets, stiff while young but often graceful at
        maturity
*FOLIAGE: evergreen, needles dark green mostly less than 1″ long, dense
HABITAT: northern and central Europe
INTRODUCED: colonial times
VARIETIES: *pyramidata*—a narrow, slender pyramid in habit—Pyramidal Norway
        Spruce
        columnaris—narrow and columnar in habit—Columnar Norway Spruce
        nigra—very densely branched, pyramidal, needles dark green—Black
        Norway Spruce

The Norway Spruce has been considerably overplanted in North America, certainly in the eastern part of the country. It does not mature gracefully. Older specimens are thin and open at the top, seeming to require more summer moisture than is available in the East. As young specimens they grow vigorously and well—the obvious reason why so many have been used. But once the top begins to become thin and open (after about thirty years) no amount of soil moisture or fertilizer can correct it.

Young plants are usually stiff and upright, but as they grow older, the branches grow wider and more horizontal or even pendulous, while the branchlets themselves become actually pendant, making a very graceful tree. The large conspicuous cones, the largest of any spruce are always an added interest in a fruiting year. Unfortunately, none of the coniferous trees can be counted on to produce profuse fruits every year, for they vary markedly, some years bearing practically none.

The Norway Spruce has a natural inclination to throw "sports," and because of this tendency and the centuries during which it has been cultivated, many "sports" or varieties have arisen, which of course are maintained by asexual propagation. Some of these are very dwarf, others are trees with varying habits.

Picea asperata   75′   Zone 5   Dragon Spruce

*HABIT: pyramidal
*FOLIAGE: evergreen, stiff needles, light green to light bluish, dense
HABITAT: western China
INTRODUCED: 1910

Somewhat similar to the Norway Spruce in general appearance while young, this tree is finding a place for itself in seaside planting where it does better than most spruces. The needles of this species remain on the tree approximately seven years, the main reason why the foliage is so dense. Aside from this it probably is no better than some of the other recommended species.

Picea breweriana   120′   Zone 5   Brewer Spruce

*HABIT: pyramidal, long whiplike pendulous branches, graceful
*FOLIAGE: evergreen needles
HABITAT: southern Oregon and northern California

Used in certain areas of the Pacific Coast, rather rare in the East where it does not do well in cultivation. Of interest because of its long pendulous branches. Apparently this tree needs cool moist atmosphere of the higher altitudes along the northern Pacific coast in order to do well, but where it can be grown it makes an excellent ornamental specimen.

Picea engelmanni   150'   **Zone 2**   Engelmann Spruce

*HABIT: densely pyramidal
*FOLIAGE: evergreen, needles bluish green, dense
HABITAT: southwestern Canada to Oregon

This tree is one of the better spruces for ornamental planting, particularly for its light bluish needles and dense habit. Like many other spruces, it does not grow old gracefully and eventually loses many of its lower branches. The time at which this happens depends on several factors including soil and climate. There is a tree in the Arnold Arboretum 25 feet tall and still clothed with branches to the ground.

The best of the spruces for ornamental planting is the graceful Serbian Spruce (Picea omorika).

Picea glauca densata   40'   **Zone 2**   Black Hills Spruce

*HABIT: dense, pyramidal
*FOLIAGE: evergreen, needles green to bluish, dense
HABITAT: Black Hills of South Dakota

One of the hardiest of the spruces, dense and compact in habit and slow in growth. Even small trees have this characteristic habit. Some plants have foliage as blue as that of the Colorado Blue Spruce. This is certainly more attractive than is the White Spruce which has been overplanted merely because it is easy to grow and makes a good growth in a short period.

Picea omorika   90′   Zone 4   Serbian Spruce

*HABIT: dense, narrow and pyramidal with short ascending branches and often
       pendant branchlets, graceful
*FOLIAGE: evergreen, needles whitish on the underside, dense
HABITAT: southeastern Europe
INTRODUCED: about 1880

One of the best spruces for landscape planting. It has done very well indeed
in the Arnold Arboretum since it was first introduced there seventy years ago. Its
dense habit, and very beautiful glossy green needles, which show much of their
whitish under-surfaces as they move in the wind, make it decidedly beautiful the
entire year. Some of the trees have pendant branchlets which add materially to
their beauty. The Serbian Spruce can be termed almost columnar in habit, for old
plants in the Arnold Arboretum 60 feet tall have a branch spread of no more
than 15 feet at the base. This is one of the few spruces with needles flat in cross
section like hemlock, and not 4-sided as are the needles of most other spruces. If
only one spruce is to be chosen for a planting this should certainly be considered
first.

Picea orientalis   150′   Zone 4   Oriental Spruce

*HABIT: densely pyramidal, branchlets often pendulous, graceful
*FOLIAGE: evergreen needles, smallest of the spruces, glossy, dark green, dense
HABITAT: Asia Minor
INTRODUCED: 1837

A most graceful and compact tree with very dark green foliage. It grows
slowly and frequently has pendulous branches. This also can be considered one of
the best of the spruces, but it is susceptible to the destructive action of the spruce
bud worm more than some of the other species. Also, in New England at least, it
may suffer browning of foliage in late winter more quickly than some of the
others. If proper spraying is practiced and winters are not too cold and dry, this
can easily become a splendid ornamental tree. Its needles are smaller than those
of most spruces so that its fine texture adds materially to its other desirable
qualifications.

Picea polita   90′   Zone 5   Tigertail Spruce

*HABIT: pyramidal, stiff
*FOLIAGE: evergreen needles, very stiff and sharp, dense
HABITAT: Japan
INTRODUCED: 1861

The rigid spiny needles of this tree, standing out at right angles from the
twig, differentiate it quickly from all other spruces. The dark green foliage and its
stiff method of branching make it an acceptable tree for specimen planting, at
least while it is young.

Picea pungens   100′   Zone 2   Colorado Spruce

*HABIT: stiffly pyramidal
*FOLIAGE: evergreen, stiff, green to bluish, dense

HABITAT: Rocky Mountains, Utah to New Mexico

VARIETIES: *argentea*—foliage silvery white. It is this variety which is widely distributed in the trade as "Koster Blue Spruce." The true Koster Blue Spruce is *P. pungens kosteriana* with pendulous branches and a horizontal trunk (unless it is staked to force it to grow in a treelike manner.)—Silver Colorado Spruce

coerulea—leaves bluish white—Cerulean Colorado Spruce

glauca—leaves bluish green—Blue Colorado Spruce

kosteriana—foliage bluish white, pendulous branches, originally propagated by the Koster Nurseries of Boskoop, Holland. The main trunk of this tree tends to be prostrate and must be staked to grow in treelike fashion. Actually this is the real Koster Spruce but is found infrequently in the trade as such.—Koster Weeping Blue Spruce

moreheimi—compact, dense-growing form with very blue foliage—Moreheim Spruce

The Colorado Blue Spruce and its varieties make ideal plants from the standpoint of the commercial grower, and that is why so many plants are grown. They grow quickly from seed, vary considerably in color and make dense, pyramidal young plants that are desirable in various types of planting. Nurserymen should propagate the varieties asexually (by grafts or cuttings) rather than always by seed and merely making selections from the seed bed on a color basis alone.

The important fact to remember is that these plants, like most other spruces, do not grow old gracefully. They lose their lower branches, often early in life. Then, too, they are susceptible to the ravages of the spruce gall aphid which causes the tips of the branches to die. This pest can be controlled by proper spraying. Fifteen-or twenty-foot specimens of Blue Spruce do have branches to the ground but as they grow taller some of the lower branches die out and the trees quickly become unsightly. In other words, this is an ideal tree while young, retaining its needles for seven to eight years, making the foliage very dense. Such a tree is popular among commercial growers and available everywhere, but it will not grow into maturity gracefully. Plan on using it only while it is at its best and replacing it after twenty years with something else. This spruce requires more spraying (to control spruce gall aphids) than any other and in fact requires more than most other evergreens.

Because of its stiff growth habit and pronounced color, it always stands out prominently wherever it is used. Placing these trees properly in the landscape is really very difficult. All too often we see them brazenly spotted in the geometrical center of the lawn, destroying any possible beauty in that area for all time.

Picea smithiana   160'   Zone 5   Himalayan Spruce

*HABIT: broadly pyramidal, branchlets pendulous

*FOLIAGE: evergreen needles

HABITAT: Himalayas

INTRODUCED: 1818

A handsome tree with wide spreading branches and pendulous branchlets of considerably wider habit than many other spruces. Worthy of trial, but the young growth starts very early; hence it should not be planted where there is the possibility of late frosts in the spring.

PINES

There are sixty-eight different kinds of pines listed as being commercially available from one source or another in North America—truly a large number. The thirty species and varieties discussed in the following pages are not all good trees, some being listed merely because they grow in trying situations where little else is dependable, but there is a reason for growing each one of them. Some can be numbered among the very best ornamental trees available for park purposes as well as gardens, and in fact many have been used for planting along our major highways. A great many of these trees have interesting bark (*P. bungeana, densiflora, sylvestris*); others will grow in dry soil where few trees will grow (*P. banksiana, canariensis, rigida, virginiana*). The following will grow under the trying conditions of the seashore (*P. pinaster, radiata, thunbergi*). A picturesque habit is reason enough for growing a few (*P. densiflora, flexilis, rigida, sylvestris*), and *P. densiflora oculus draconis* is just a plain curiosity. Each one of the remaining group has its good points.

A large number of pines have been relegated to the secondary list. Surprisingly enough many of these have very poor foliage in the winter—either yellowish or brownish—not at all a beautiful green as is the native White Pine. This poor winter color is not what should be expected of an evergreen, hence these trees do not have much to offer from an ornamental viewpoint.

Another interesting point is the fact that the needles on some of the trees remain on longer than others. Spruce, firs and yews may keep their needles for five years or longer but this is the exception rather than the rule in pines. For instance, the needles of *Pinus strobus* remain on only about two years. Sometimes the needles of *P. tabulaeformis* and *P. rigida* remain on only one year. On the other hand, the needles of *P. flexilis* remain on the tree about four years and those of *P. bungeana* remain on the tree about five years.

Pines as a group are more neutral in outline than either spruces or firs. They mass well together forming a neutral background, something which cannot be claimed for the precisely pyramidal spruces and firs. All in all the pines are among the very best ornamental trees, and since the selection is so varied, a pine of some kind can be grown in almost every part of the country.

Simple Key to the Pines

(Native and Exotics, Available from Nurseries in North America)

This simple key is offered chiefly for the benefit of the amateur who is frequently confronted with difficult keys which he finds unnecessarily complicated. All measures of leaf length should be considered as approximate only. On one individual tree needles may vary in length from 2″ to as much as 8″ but in the key the length given would be 4 to 6″, meaning that mature needles—not the young ones which are elongating, nor the ones on weak or on overvigorous branches—are mostly within the 4 to 6″ length. If this is clearly understood by those using this key, it will undoubtedly prove helpful in the identification of most of our commonly grown pines.

The key is designed to be used chiefly with living material, hence the color of the foliage and the general habit of the tree sometimes plays an important part. Occasionally, as in differentiating between *Pinus strobus* and *P. monticola,* the two species are so much alike that cone characters are used, but these are resorted to only when absolutely necessary, for many a tree which one would like to identify is not graced with cones at the time one wishes to identify it. Habitats are given, because sometimes such information may prove helpful in assisting in plant identification.

There is no excuse for avoiding a simple key such as this one, merely because of a lack of thorough botanical training. It is understandable, and if used with a full knowledge of its limitations, it can prove most helpful. In using the key merely go to the first number. If the statement there applies to the specimen, go to the next **higher** number until the tree is identified. If the statement there does not apply, go to the following group headed by the same number and proceed as above. Identifications made by the use of any "short" key, and this one in particular, should not be considered final, but should be further checked against a complete description in some standard text, and available illustration.

Needles in bundles of 2 to 5, rarely solitary, enclosed at the base by a deciduous or persistent sheath..*Pinus*

1. Needles 5 in a sheath

albicaulis—White Bark Pine	*parviflora*—Japanese White Pine
aristata—Bristle-cone Pine	*parviflora glauca*
cembra—Swiss Stone Pine	*peuce*—Balkan Pine
flexilis—Limber Pine	*pumila*—Japanese Stone Pine
griffithi—Himalayan Pine	*strobus*—Eastern White Pine
koraiensis—Korean Pine	*strobus fastigiata*
lambertiana—Sugar Pine	*strobus nana*
monticola—Western White Pine	*torreyana*—Torrey Pine

2. Needles usually less than 1½″ long and smooth margin..*Pinus aristata* (California to Colorado) Zone 5
2. Needles usually 1½-2″ long
   3. Bark of trunk brown to creamy white, needless rigid and stout, margin smooth.............................*Pinus albicaulis* (British Columbia to California) Zone 3
   3. Bark of trunk, needles more flexible
      4. Needles bluish green, often twisted, intensely white underneath, leaf margin finely serrulate, i.e., rough to the touch
        Pinus parviflora

(Japan) Zone 5

    4. Needles intensely bluish green......*Pinus parviflora glauca*

    4. Needles light green, not twisted

        5. Mature twigs glabrous, needles smooth..*Pinus flexilis* (Alberta to California) Zone 4

        5. Mature twigs pubescent; leaf margin finely serrulate, i.e., rough to the touch...............*Pinus pumila* (Japan) Zone 3

2. Needles mostly 2½–4½″ long; leaf margin serrulate, i.e., rough to the touch

    3. Mature twigs glabrous

        4. Plant shrubby, not treelike............*Pinus strobus nana*

        4. Branches upright, tree dense

            5. Needles stiff.........................*Pinus peuce* (Balkan Mts.) Zone 4

            5. Needles soft and flexible......*Pinus strobus fastigiata*

        4. Branches horizontal, tree more open

            5. Cones usually 2–4¾″ long; twigs glabrous or only slightly pubescent....................*Pinus strobus* (Eastern United States and Canada) Zone 3

            5. Cones usually 4¾–10″ long; twigs pubescent when young...........................*Pinus monticola* (British Columbia to Idaho and California) Zone 5 (These two species are difficult to tell apart with the naked eye, except that the habit of *P. monticola* is more narrow and dense and the needles stiffer than are those of *P. strobus*)

    3. Mature twigs pubescent

        4. Tree densely upright, pyramidal in habit......*Pinus cembra* (Alps of Europe) Zone 4

        4. Tree not as above, more open

            5. Needles lustrous, dark green........*Pinus koraiensis* (Japan, Korea) Zone 3

            5. Needles dull green

                6. Terminal bud blunt almost globular, cones 12 to 20″......................*Pinus lambertiana* (Oregon to California) Zone 5

                6. Terminal bud sharply pointed, definitely not globular, cones 4–10″.............*P. monticola* (British Columbia to Idaho and California) Zone 5

2. Needles 4½–8″ long.....................................*P. griffithi* (Himalayas) Zone 5

2. Needles 8–12″ long.....................................*P. torreyana* (Southwestern California) Zone 9

1. Needles 3 to 4 in a sheath only occasionally 5; leaf margin smooth

1. Needles 3 to 4 in a sheath only occasionally 5; leaf margin smooth

    Zone 9 Parry Pinyon Pine....................*P. cembroides parrayana*

1. Needles 3 in a sheath

    attenuata—Knob-cone Pine

    bungeana—Lace-bark Pine   *ponderosa*—Ponderosa Pine

    canariensis—Canary Pine   *radiata*—Monterey Pine

    coulteri—Coulter Pine   *rigida*—Pitch Pine

    jeffreyi—Jeffrey Pine   *sabiniana*—Digger Pine

    palustris—Longleaf Pine   *taeda*—Loblolly Pine

   2. Needles mostly 2–5″ long

      3. Leaf sheaths deciduous, bark of older twigs smooth, bark of trunk flaky with white or yellow patches........*Pinus bungeana* (China) Zone 4

      3. Leaf sheaths not deciduous, bark of older twigs very rough, bark of trunk dark brown to black

        4. Foliage dark green, cones usually 2–4″ long..*Pinus rigida* (eastern United States and Canada) Zone 4

        4. Foliage bright or bluish green; cones 3–7″ long

          5. Bark on upper part of trunk and branches smooth

                           Pinus attenuata

        (Oregon to California) Zone 8

          5. Bark on upper part of trunk and branches rough

                           Pinus radiata

        (S. California) Zone 8

   2. Needles mostly 5–10″ long

      3. Winter buds resinous

        4. Twigs fragrant when broken; cone 3 to 6″; foliage dark green, branchlets orange-brown..........*Pinus ponderosa* (Eastern and Central U.S.) Zone 5

        4. Twigs not fragrant when broken; cones 9 to 14″; foliage bluish green...............................*Pinus coulteri* (California) Zone 8

      3. Winter buds not resinous

        4. Foliage bluish green

          5. Needles stout, bark cinnamon red, cones 6–12″

                           Pinus jeffreyi

        (Oregon and California) Zone 5

          5. Needles slim, bark red brown, cones 3–6″..*Pinus taeda* (New Jersey to Florida and Texas) Zone 6

        4. Foliage dark green; cones 5–12″............*Pinus coulteri* (California) Zone 8

   2. Needles 8–18″ long

      3. Foliage gray bluish green

        4. Needles slender, drooping...............*Pinus sabiniana* (California) Zone 6

        4. Needles stiff, erect........................*Pinus coulteri* (California) Zone 8

      3. Foliage green

        4. Needles mostly 8–10″ long, light green and lustrous

                          Pinus canariensis

        (Canary Islands) Zone 10?

4. Needles mostly 12" or more long, dark green.. *Pinus palustris*
(Southeastern United States) Zone 7

1. Needles 3 and 2 in a sheath
    caribaea—Slash Pine
    cembroides—Mexican Pinyon Pine
    echinata—Shortleaf Pine
    ponderosa scopulorum—Rocky Mountain Ponderosa Pine
    tabulaeformis—Chinese Pine
    2. Needles less than 2" long........................*Pinus cembroides*
        (Southern California and Arizona) Zone 9
    2. Needles more than 2" long
        3. One year twigs greenish to purplish, covered with glaucous bloom
                                                            Pinus echinata
            (Eastern United States) Zone 5
        3. One-year twigs yellow-brown to brownish
            4. Terminal bud very resinous....*Pinus ponderosa scopulorum*
                (Rocky Mountain Region) Zone 4
            4. Terminal bud not resinous or only slightly so
                5. Needles 2–7" long; cones 1½–2" long
                                                        Pinus tabulaeformis

Thirteen species of pine leaves and fruits are portrayed here

1. Pinus strobus
2. Pinus cembra
3. Pinus flexilis
4. Pinus parviflora
5. Pinus bungeana
6. Pinus rigida
7. Pinus virginiana
8. Pinus thunbergi
9. Pinus sylvestris
10. Pinus densiflora
11. Pinus banksiana
12. Pinus nigra
13. Pinus resinosa

(China) Zone 5
  5. Needles 8–12″ long; cones 3–6½″ long.*Pinus caribaea*
     (Southeastern U.S., Bahamas, Honduras) Zone 8

1. Needles 2 in a sheath

banksiana—Jack Pine
densiflora—Japanese Red Pine
densiflora oculus—*draconis*
densiflora umbraculifera
echinata—Shortleaf Pine
mugo—Swiss Mountain Pine
mugo compacta
mugo pumilio

nigra austriaca—Austrian Pine
pinaster—Cluster Pine
pungens—Table Mountain Pine
resinosa—Red Pine
sylvestris—Scotch Pine
tabulaeformis—Chinese Pine
thunbergi—Japanese Black Pine
virginiana—Virginia Pine

2. Needles ¾–3″ long
   3. Foliage with each needle marked with a yellow band
                              Pinus densiflora oculus-draconis
   3. Foliage bluish green, bark of upper trunk red
                              Pinus sylvestris and vars.
      (Europe) Zone 2
   3. Foliage green
      4. Plant usually shrubby, with several branches from the base
         5. Needles ¾–2″ long, bark black..*Pinus mugo* and vars.
            (Central Europe) Zone 2
         5. Needles 3–5″, bark red to reddish
                              Pinus densiflora umbraculifera
      4. Plant a tree with a central leader
         5. Needles 1¼–3″ long
            6. Branchlets usually with glaucous bloom, often
               greenish to purplish or yellowish
               7. Foliage bluish green, cones usually not per-
                  sistent, bark of upper trunk red; leaves
                  flexible...................*Pinus densiflora*
                  (Japan) Zone 4
               7. Foliage bright green, cones persistent, bark
                  of upper trunk black; leaves stiff
                              Pinus virginiana
                  (Eastern United States) Zone 4
            6. Branchlets without glaucous bloom, orange to
               yellow
               7. Vigorous shoots often with more than one
                  whorl of branches on the current year's
                  growth
                  8. Needles more than 1″ long; cones not
                     prickly and straight....*Pinus pungens*
                     (Southeastern U.S.) Zone 5
                  8. Needles often less than 1″ long; cone
                     prickly, curved......*Pinus banksiana*
                     (Northeastern U.S. and Eastern
                     Canada) Zone 2

7. Vigorous shoots with only one whorl, of branches on the current year's growth

8. Winter buds white or whitish to light yellow..............*Pinus thunbergi* (Japan) Zone 4

8. Winter buds dark brown
Pinus tabulaeformis (China) Zone 5

2. Needles 3–8" long

3. Winter buds resinous

4. Needles slender and flexible, breaking when bent
Pinus resinosa (Northeastern U.S. and Eastern Canada) Zone 2

4. Needles stout and stiff, not breaking when bent
Pinus nigra austriaca (Central Europe) Zone 4

3. Winter buds not resinous (or only slightly so in *P. tabulaeformis*)

4. Buds stout, up to 1" long; branchlets bright reddish brown
Pinus pinaster (Portugal to Greece) Zone 8

4. Buds less than ½" long

5. Bark of upper trunk red............*Pinus densiflora* (Japan) Zone 4

5. Bark of upper trunk black

6. One-year twigs with glaucous bloom, green to purplish......................*Pinus echinata* (Eastern U.S.) Zone 5

6. One-year twigs without glaucous bloom, yellow to brown

7. Winter buds dark reddish brown
Pinus tabulaeformis (China) Zone 5

7. Winter buds light yellow to white or whitish.................*Pinus thunbergi* (Japan) Zone 4

Pinus banksiana 75' Zone 2 Jack Pine

HABIT: open broad head, often shrubby
*FOLIAGE: evergreen, 2 needles in bundle, mostly 1" long, open
HABITAT: northern and northeastern North America

Not among the best ornamental pines for the needles frequently are yellowish in the winter and remain on the tree only one or two years. Its only qualification for consideration here is the fact that it is one of our hardiest pines and will do well on dry, sandy banks, where most other evergreens (and deciduous plants as well) will fail. Because of its loose and open habit of growth it is not recommended for planting in good soil where better pines might be used.

Pinus bungeana   75′   Zone 4   Lace-bark Pine

*HABIT: often with several trunks, rounded to pyramidal
*BARK: exfoliating in irregular plates, exposing the light, creamy colored inner
      bark
*FOLIAGE: evergreen, bright green, 3 needles in a bundle 3″ long, dense
HABITAT: northwestern China
INTRODUCED: 1846

A rather slow-growing, dark green foliage tree, with excellent possibilities as a specimen plant because of its habit of growth and interesting bark. Very young plants will show the characteristic exfoliating bark when the branches are only an inch in diameter. Also, this tree has the most desirable trait of holding its needles about five years, longer than most pines. Consequently, this excellent specimen pine should be planted considerably more than it is. Its picturesque habit of growth with several major trunks is also one of its desirable points. It was named after Alexander von Bunge, a Russian author of St. Petersburg who recorded much about the plants of northern and northeastern Asia before he died in 1890.

Pinus canariensis   80′   Zone 8   Canary Pine

HABIT: picturesque, round-headed but often pyramidal, open
*FOLIAGE: evergreen, lustrous needles, 3 in a bundle, 9–12″ long
HABITAT: Canary Islands
INTRODUCED: about 1850?

This tree is only of value in California and the extreme southern states. It is very picturesque with its long needles, and grows rapidly especially in dry rocky situations where it does better than *P. radiata*.

The Swiss Stone Pine (Pinus cembra) is slow growing and dense, a fine small evergreen tree.

Pinus cembra   75′   Zone 2   Swiss Stone Pine

*HABIT: dense, tightly pyramidal, not round-topped until fully mature
*FOLIAGE: evergreen, 5 needles in a bundle, 2½–4¼″ long, soft texture
HABITAT: central Europe and northern Asia
INTRODUCED: before 1875

A very slow-growing pine frequently disappointing for this reason. Never theless, it makes a tightly molded pyramidal specimen while young, often well suited to formal planting. It retains its needles for about three years and they are the same shade of green as are those of *P. strobus*. It is of interest to note that this is proving hardy at Dropmore, Manitoba, Canada.

Pinus coulteri   75′   Zone 7   Big Cone Pine or Coulter Pine

HABIT: loose and open
*FOLIAGE: evergreen, needlelike, 3 in a bundle, 6–8″ long, coarse
HABITAT: California

This tree of loose habit and sparse foliage has been used in California plantings. It is not common in cultivation but is very striking in its somewhat gaunt branching. It takes its name from the fact that the cones are sometimes 14″ long.

Pinus densiflora   100′   Zone 4   Japanese Red Pine

*HABIT: horizontal branches, irregular head
*BARK: orange-red, even on the older branches
*FOLIAGE: bright bluish green, needles 2 in a bundle, 3–5″ long
HABITAT: Japan
INTRODUCED: 1854
VARIETIES: *umbraculifera*—low umbrellalike—Tanyosho Pine
             oculus-draconis—each leaf marked with two yellow lines making the general effect interesting and colorful—Dragon's Eye Pine

A picturesque tree, no better ornamentally than some of the other pines native to this country, but of a distinct flat-topped habit. The specific name comes from the fact that the flowers are borne in dense clusters, which of course are followed by numerous cones. The foliage turns a yellowish green to pale green in the winter and the needles are retained for only two years but the bark is certainly interesting throughout the year.

Pinus flexilis   45–75′   Zone 2   Limber Pine

*HABIT: narrow and pyramidal while young, broad and round-topped, branches horizontal, often slightly pendulous, open to dense
*FOLIAGE: evergreen, 5 needles in a bundle, 1½–3″ long, fine texture
HABITAT: western North America

A desirable ornamental pine, often called the Rocky Mountain White Pine, is widely spread over the mountains of the Pacific Coast area with a tendency to become flat-topped as it grows older, the foliage remaining on the tree about four years. It is slow in growth, for individual trees may be over two hundred years old before the trunk will reach a diameter of 9 inches. The largest tree

An interesting form of the Japanese Red Pine called the Tanyosho Pine
(P. densiflora umbraculifera)

in the Arnold Arboretum is only about 30 feet tall and was planted in 1884. Unless its habit is desirable, it is not as good and vigorous an ornamental as *Pinus strobus,* but as a perennial small specimen on the small place it certainly has its advantages.

Pinus griffithi (*excelsa*)   150'   Zone 5   Himalayan Pine
*HABIT: graceful, wide-spreading, dense
*FOLIAGE: evergreen, blue-green, 5 needles in a bundle, 5–7" long, soft texture
HABITAT: Himalaya
INTRODUCED: 1827

A beautiful, fast-growing, wide-spreading tree which eventually may have a spread of 40 to 50 feet. It seems to do best in a sandy loam, but has been seriously injured in the Arnold Arboretum during the past years by winter cold and severe winds. The long, drooping, blue-green needles give it a graceful appearance. It does well in the vicinity of Philadelphia and of Seattle, where the climate and growing conditions seem to be exactly to its liking. This is a large tree, but where space is available to display this plant properly, it is an excellent pine to use.

Pinus halepensis   60'   Zone 9   Aleppo Pine
HABIT: open, round-topped
*FOLIAGE: evergreen, needlelike, leaves 2 (rarely 3) in a bundle, 2½–6" long
HABITAT: Mediterranean Region

INTRODUCED: early colonial times

Where better growing conditions are available, this pine should not be used—recommended only for seashore plantings.

Pinus jeffreyi   120′   Zone 5   Jeffrey Pine

HABIT: pyramidal, often spreading or even pendant branches, open
*BARK: cinnamon red to brown
FOLIAGE: evergreen, 3 needles in bundle, 5–8″ long, pale bluish green
HABITAT: Oregon to California

Somewhat similar to *Pinus ponderosa* but its needles are bluish green. This tree is only of value as an ornament on the West coast.

Pinus koraiensis   90′   Zone 3   Korean Pine

*HABIT: pyramidal, dense
*FOLIAGE: evergreen, needles 3 or 5 in bundle, 2½–4″ long
HABITAT: Japan, Korea
INTRODUCED: 1861

This is a slow-growing tree, and although it eventually grows very tall, it makes an excellent tree for small gardens because of its slow growth. It is truly handsome with dark green foliage all winter and could be planted a great deal more than it is.

Pinus nigra   90′   Zone 4   Austrian Pine

*HABIT: densely pyramidal, wide spreading and rounded top, stiff
*FOLIAGE: evergreen, dark green, 2 needles in a bundle, 3½–6½″ long
HABITAT: central and southern Europe, Asia Minor
INTRODUCED: 1759
VARIETIES: *austriaca*—needles supposed to be slightly shorter than the species, mostly about 3–4″ long. Actually this and the species are so nearly identical ornamentally that this varietal name might be dropped.
pyramidalis—narrow pyramidal form with closely ascending branches—Pyramid Austrian Pine

A fast-growing species, with very stiff needles, making a splendid specimen in several forms, with dark green glossy foliage. It makes an excellent windbreak or screen and should grow well in limestone soils. Certainly it does well in acid soils. There is actually little difference between the species and the variety *austriaca*, the latter being a geographical variety with slightly shorter needles. Most of the Austrian pines in this country are grown from seed anyway so that a certain amount of variability is to be expected. This is an excellent, stiffly-formed tree, well adapted to specimen planting, and holds its needles for three years.

Pinus parviflora   90′   Zone 5   Japanese White Pine

*HABIT: densely pyramidal, wide spreading
*FOLIAGE: evergreen, bluish to dark green, 5 needles in a bundle, 1½–2½″ long
HABITAT: Japan
INTRODUCED: 1861

The Japanese White Pine is an excellent ornamental pine with short, often slightly-twisted needles (remaining on the tree two years), forming brushlike tufts at the end of the branchlets. One plant in the Arnold Arboretum is 60 feet tall and almost as broad! Consequently, it needs plenty of room for future expansion.

Pinus pinaster	90'	Zone 7	Cluster Pine

HABIT: pyramidal, sometimes pendant branches
*FOLIAGE: evergreen, 2 needles in bundle, often twisted and glossy green, 5–9" long

This pine is often called the Maritime Pine because it is well adapted to seaside planting. It is difficult to transplant so that young seedlings should be used whenever possible. If sand dune areas at the seaside are to be planted, this pine certainly merits first consideration where it proves hardy.

Pinus pinea	80'	Zone 9	Italian Stone Pine

HABIT: broad and flat-topped at maturity, picturesque
*FOLIAGE: evergreen, needlelike, 2 in a cluster, 8" long
HABITAT: Mediterranean Region

The Italian Stone Pine is a slow-growing, picturesque pine, often with umbrellalike branches. The seeds are large, nearly ½" long and are edible.

Pinus radiata	60'	Zone 7	Monterey Pine

HABIT: irregular, open
*FOLIAGE: evergreen, needles 3 in bundle, 4–6" long and bright green
HABITAT: southern California

This tree is especially valued for seaside planting.

Pinus resinosa	75'	Zone 2	Red Pine or Norway Pine

*HABIT: stout spreading branches forming a broad pyramidal head
*FOLIAGE: evergreen, dark green and lustrous, 2 needles in a bundle, 4–6" long, soft texture
BARK: reddish brown
HABITAT: north central and northeastern North America

This is a fine ornamental pine as well as a valued timber tree. I have seen splendid trees in the Finger Lakes Parks of central New York State that were two hundred years old and still in perfect condition. The long needles are flexible and thus differ from the stiff needles of the Austrian Pine. The bark of the trunk and some of the larger branches is reddish—an interesting, desirable feature. In some sections of the country, the pine bud moth is a serious pest on the Red Pine, disfiguring its branching habit to a considerable extent, but this pest is easily controlled by timely spraying.

Pinus rigida	75'	Zone 4	Pitch Pine

HABIT: very open
*FOLIAGE: evergreen, needles 3 in a bundle 2–4" long
HABITAT: eastern North America

The Pitch Pine is not an ornamental tree and is used only for planting on dry and rocky soil where little else will grow. Old mature trees are very picturesque with their open branching, and cones remain on the trees for several years, but the needles drop after the first year or two and the remainder turn brownish in the winter. If good soil is available, much more attractive trees could be selected.

Pinus strobus   100′–150′   Zone 3   Eastern White Pine

HABIT: rounded or pyramidal, picturesque at maturity
*FOLIAGE: evergreen, needles 5 in bundle, 2½–5½″ long, soft and flexible
HABITAT: eastern North America
VARIETIES: *fastigiata*—narrowly upright and columnar in habit—Pyramidal White
        Pine
        glauca—foliage light bluish green—Blue White Pine
        pendula—branches pendulous, a most graceful looking pine even
            though the branches are stiff and lack the pleasing flexibility of a
            Cedrus deodara or Picea omorika—Weeping White Pine

The second tallest pine native in North America (the Sugar Pine, *P. lambertiana* is tallest)—a top-notch ornamental evergreen tree, fifth in importance among the timber trees of North America now, although at one time it was the most important.

The delicate, soft green, graceful foliage of the White Pine is unsurpassed by that of any other hardy northern tree except possibly the hemlock. In the fall it drops its three-year-old needles like many another evergreen, but the foliage that remains stays a soft green throughout the long winter months. In fact, the normal green of White Pine foliage year in and year out makes this tree one of the most valuable for background foliage in any landscape planting, be it large or small.

White Pine may grow 10 feet in ten years and 25 feet in twenty years if it is in good soil. Young trees are dense and often pyramidal in habit but the older the tree grows the more picturesque it becomes—with flat top and a missing branch here and there until at a ripe old age these trees are the most conspicuous (and beautiful) in almost any landscape.

Easily transplanted, the White Pine also withstands shearing, but this must be done in just the right way. On close inspection of any branch of White Pine, it will be noticed that the needles are not distributed evenly along the current year's growth, but bunched near the tip. There is a portion of every twig with no needles. This is the place not to cut. Every snip with the pruning shears should be in the middle of the twig where needles are, leaving some of the needles on the twig. At the base of these, new buds will quickly form. If, on the other hand, the cut is made where there are no needles, then that part of the twig will die back to the previous year's growth. This is a rather important sidelight on pruning or shearing White Pine, for when not done properly, pruning this tree can do more harm than good.

Currants of many types carry the dread white pine blister rust, the reason there is considerable legislation regulating the transport of five-needled pines and currants as well.

Fortunately for the small property owner, White Pine can be restrained by proper pruning and so will not grow out of scale. For landscape work on small properties, in parks along major highways and for many other purposes the White Pine is one of the best and most serviceable evergreen trees in eastern North America.

| Pinus sylvestris | 75' | Zone 2 | Scotch Pine |

*HABIT: open, pyramidal while young but round-topped and irregular when old
*FOLIAGE: evergreen, bluish green needles twisted and 2 in bundle, ¾–3" long, stiff
*BARK: red on older trunks and branches
HABITAT: Europe to Siberia
INTRODUCED: probably colonial times

A valued timber tree in Europe, but although extensively planted as a timber tree in America, it has not proved successful. As an ornamental it is valued for its bluish green foliage and very picturesque open habit at maturity, as well as its red trunk and older branches. It cannot be considered a good shade tree, but for displaying unique form and color among the pines it is outstanding. Many horticultural varieties have appeared as is so often the case, especially with native European plants which have been cultivated for centuries. The varieties *rigensis* (with very red bark) and *watereri* (low dense form with steel blue needles) are the only ones being grown to any extent in this country, but there is a beautiful specimen of the variety *fastigiata* growing in Durand-Eastman Park, Rochester, New York. It would seem that there might be an opportunity in this country for some of the other varieties so cherished in Europe.

| Pinus thunbergi | 90' | Zone 4 | Japanese Black Pine |

HABIT: dense, spreading, often pendulous branches
*FOLIAGE: evergreen, dark green, 2 needles in bundle, 3–5" long, stiff, open
HABITAT: Japan
INTRODUCED: 1855

The best pine, possibly the best evergreen, for planting along the seashore in the northeastern United States, is the Japanese Black Pine. It has done very well on Nantucket and Martha's Vineyard where other plants have failed, for it withstands seashore conditions and even a small amount of salt water spray. Its large, grayish white terminal buds can be used to distinguish it from some of the other pines. The Japanese have trained this type into many grotesque forms. Even naturally it grows rather irregularly, but young and vigorous plants should find many uses in seaside gardens. Better pines are available for better growing conditions.

| Pinus torreyana | 45' | Zone 8 | Torrey Pine |

HABIT: spreading and ascending branches but open
*FOLIAGE: evergreen, needlelike, 5 in a bundle, 8–12" long
HABITAT: southern California

This tree is only of merit in dry situations where better pines will not grow. In good soils, other trees certainly should be selected.

| Pinus virginiana | 45' | Zone 4 | Virginia or Scrub Pine |

HABITS open, branching sparse, often with very wide top, stiff
*FOLIAGE: evergreen, needles in bundle of 2, 1¼–3" long
HABITAT: eastern United States

This tree is not an ornamental tree and is used only for planting in poor, dry soils where other pines will not grow.

Natural growing palms and pleached sycamores are used in this planting
in Golden Gate Park, San Francisco, California.

Pistacia chinensis   50′   Zone 9   Chinese Pistache

*FRUIT: small, red in dense clusters, but sexes are separate with male and female
     flowers on different trees
   EFFECTIVE: fall
HABIT: broad-rounded, short trunk
FOLIAGE: beautiful, fine texture, male trees more dense
*AUTUMN COLOR: red and orange
HABITAT: China
INTRODUCED: 1921

First introduced into America by that intrepid plant explorer for the U. S.
Department of Agriculture, Frank L. Meyer, it is akin somewhat to *Rhus* or
Sophora. It is slow growing, effective on small properties, withstands both heat
and drought. The seed yields an oil used in cooking, and the Chinese have been
known to boil the leaf buds and eat them. It is free of insect and disease pests
which is an added advantage. The species *P. vera*, yielding the edible pistachio
nuts of commerce, is frequently grafted or budded on roots of this Chinese
species. In Florida, this species has performed very well as a shade tree.

Pittosporum eugenioides   40′   Zone 10   Tarata Pittosporum

*HABIT: oval-shaped, sometimes columnar, sometimes pyramidal
*FOLIAGE: evergreen, yellowish green
HABITAT: New Zealand

This is probably used more as a shrub than as a tree in the warmer areas of
the country since it does well under shearing.

Pittosporum rhombifolium   80′   Zone 10   Diamond Leaf Pittosporum

FRUIT: bright orange berries in large clusters
    EFFECTIVE: mid-winter
HABIT: symmetrical, rounded
*FOLIAGE: glossy, evergreen, leaves 3–4″ long
HABITAT: Australia

A good tree for parkway planting in the southwestern United States where it is hardy and one of the most popular street trees in Santa Barbara, California.

x Platanus acerifolia   100′   Zone 5   London Plane Tree

FRUITS: in pendulous ball-like clusters, 2 rarely 3 in cluster
    EFFECTIVE: fall and winter
HABIT: wide-spreading branches, open
*BARK: exfoliating in flakes, under-bark light colored often yellowish
FOLIAGE: large, maplelike, leaves 5–10″ wide, coarse
HYBRID ORIGIN: *P. occidentalis x P. orientalis*
ORIGINATED: probably before 1700

This tree is very resistant to the twig blight so troublesome to our native *P. occidentalis*. It grows with a tall straight trunk, the older trees sometimes having trunks over 20 feet in circumference. Both this species and *P. orientalis* are easily clipped and have been grown as clipped screens and arbors, both in this country and abroad. However, their coarse leaves and vigorous growth seem to detract from their use in this way, especially since there are other materials of much finer texture available. It is of interest to note that the young twigs of both these European Plane trees are densely covered with hairs at first, which are gradually shed during the summer. Sometimes a nasal irritation is brought about by these hairs when they are abundant in the summer. As a street tree, both this species and the Oriental Plane tree are planted annually by the thousands.

Platanus orientalis   90′   Zone 6   Oriental Plane Tree

FRUITS: in pendulous ball-like clusters, 3 or more in a cluster
    EFFECTIVE: fall and winter
HABIT: thick trunk, broad round head, open
*BARK: exfoliating in flakes, under-bark greenish white
FOLIAGE: large maplelike leaves, 4–8″ wide, coarse
HABITAT: southeastern Europe and Asia Minor
INTRODUCED: colonial times

This species is much less susceptible to the serious twig blight disease so troublesome to the native Sycamore, *T. occidentalis*. It has been planted as a shade tree since ancient times and grows almost as large a size as the London Plane Tree. The native *T. occidentalis* can usually be distinguished from this and *T. acerifolia* in that the latter have two or more balls of fruit in a cluster while the native *T. occidentalis* has only one. This oriental species, if let alone, will frequently grow with several trunks from the base and reach a great old age, some big trees in England being said to be three hundred and even four hundred years old. This compares favorably with similar trees of *P. occidentalis* in Pennsylvania and Maryland known to have been growing in William Penn's time (1632). As street trees these too are in great demand and have been widely used. However, they do grow big and unless placed on large avenues or along highways with plenty of room, they will grow too large to serve their purpose properly. This can become a very important problem, for overly large street trees growing in cramped situations can become very costly to maintain properly.

Platanus racemosa   120′   Zone 7   California Plane Tree

FRUITS: in pendulous ball-like clusters, 2–7 in a cluster
    EFFECTIVE: fall and winter
HABIT: usually several trunks in picturesque form, open, irregular
*BARK: exfoliating
FOLIAGE: maplelike leaves, coarse
HABITAT: southern California
    Of value chiefly in the warmer climates for its irregular, often gnarled, habit of growth.

Podocarpus elongatus   70′   Zone 10   Fern Podocarpus

FRUITS: fleshy, purplish ⅓″ long
    EFFECTIVE: fall
HABIT: dense
*FOLIAGE: leaves 2″ long and ⅛″ broad, evergreen, fine texture
HABITAT: South Africa
    Fern Podocarpus is used only in the subtropical areas of the country.

Podocarpus macrophyllus   60′   Zone 7   Yew Podocarpus

FRUITS: purplish, fleshy, ½″ long
    EFFECTIVE: fall
HABIT: horizontal branches, pendulous branchlets
*FOLIAGE: dense, needlelike (similar to yews but larger) 4″ long, narrow, dark
    green
HABITAT: Japan
INTRODUCED: 1804
    This tree has foliage similar to the yews except that the needles are longer and wider. It is grown from North Carolina southward, making a popular hedge plant in this country as well as in Tokyo Gardens where it is clipped into many different shapes. This is the most common of the Podocarpus species in America at this time.

Poncirus trifoliata   35′   Zone 5–6   Hardy-orange

*FLOWERS: white, 2″ in diameter, very fragrant
    TIME: late April
FRUITS: yellow, like a small orange, 2″ in diameter
    EFFECTIVE: fall
HABIT: open and rather indefinite, thorny
FOLIAGE: leathery, dark green, open
HABITAT: North China, Korea
*INTRODUCED: 1850

The Hardy-orange is frequently used as a hedge in the South because of its dense growth and prominent spines and also because it will withstand shearing well. Its small white flowers faintly reminiscent of orange blossoms do not remain effective very long, but its leathery dark green leaves and its small, bitter tasting oranges, are its chief ornamental characteristic while the dense growth, too, is of importance. Hardy in protected places as far north as Boston, it can be depended upon to weather all winters south of Philadelphia. It is a unique plant, not among the best of ornamental specimens, but nevertheless serviceable in some situations (especially in acid soils where it grows well) and once established in the right situation it proves to be a vigorous grower. It is not worth much as a shade tree or as a street tree for its large thorns and fruits could easily prove a traffic hazard.

POPULUS

In the past, poplars have entered into America's landscape plantings on a wide scale, chiefly because they are vigorous growers. Some have been widely used in street tree plantings in our larger cities merely because they grow well under adverse conditions. However, it soon became known that they are voracious feeders; roots lifted side walks and street paving, and have entered and seriously clogged water pipes and sewers, causing considerable damage to such installations. Because of this, they have become unpopular in recent years and many cities have an ordinance against planting them along city streets.

Incidentally the best method of controlling roots in the sewer is to allow 5 pounds of copper sulfate crystals dissolved in water to go down the drain slowly and flush no more wastage down for several hours. This might be done once a month until free flowage occurs. The four 1-pound applications per year may be sufficient to keep the roots killed. This also applies to killing roots of elms and willows clogging local sewers.

Then too, these trees are weak-wooded and brittle and break very easily during heavy snow and wind storms. The Lombardy Poplar, long valued for its columnar upright habit, has been a good plant in landscape work until it was found that mature trees frequently developed a trunk canker at maturity for which there is no adequate cure. As a result, trees were carefully tended for years, only to die back at the top when they were finally beginning to prove effective for their habit. Also broken branches and wounds on trunks may develop in serious "bleeding" cankers which are difficult to cure. This combined with the fact that flowers and fruits are of little ornamental value and frequently become a nuisance, have been responsible for their gradual disappearance from the landscape picture in areas where other trees can be grown.

Poplars are very rapid growers and therefore can be used as "fillers" until better trees become well established. Some, like the White Poplar (P. alba), withstand very dry growing situations and so can be used in parts of the Midwest where few other ornamentals can withstand the trying growing conditions. The commercial grower likes to include them in his catalogue for they are very easy to propagate and in good soil make a saleable tree in one year's time. In fact, dormant cuttings can be put in the soil outdoors in the spring and with a reasonable amount of water can be expected to root in place. Not all species will respond to this treatment. People interested in growing wood for paper pulp have been experimenting with these trees for many years and have found that branches with flower buds from male and female trees can be brought into the greenhouse in early February, placed in water, the flowers forced to open and the female plants pollinized and seed will set at once. This seed can then be sown and a small seedling will result that same year. Some of the hybrids so formed have been known to grow as much as 21 feet in two years' time. Consequently, there will always be a demand for poplars.

Twelve species are recommended here for specific uses. Their universal shortcomings should always be kept in mind, and when possible, plants with better ornamental qualifications should be chosen. For specific purposes, or for use in certain areas with poor growing conditions, they may have their place.

Populus alba   90′   Zone 3   White Poplar

HABIT: irregular, rather open
*BARK: whitish gray
*FOLIAGE: upper side of leaves grayish green, lower side white and very pubescent making an interesting color contrast
AUTUMN COLOR: red to reddish, but not too pronounced
HABITAT: Europe and Western Siberia
INTRODUCED: colonial times?
VARIETIES: *nivea*—leaves especially white on under surface—Silver Poplar
pyramidalis—columnar in habit, probably originating in the wild about 1841—Bolleana Poplar
richardi—upper surface of leaves dull yellow—many plants with yellow leaves make inferior landscape specimens but this, with its leaves of white under surface, seems to be a rather colorful combination and not objectionable—Richard's White Poplar

The White Poplar makes a good specimen where there is room for growing it properly for it is a wide-spreading tree. It is the only poplar with lobed leaves (at least on vigorous shoot) and downy under surface of the leaves. Its tendency to have red autumn color, even though this is not as pronounced as in the maples and some other trees, is a point in its favor for Fall display. This excellent columnar variety is a good substitute for the Lombardy Poplar and is not so susceptible to the trunk canker that mars the Lombardy Poplar at maturity. It can well be considered one of the most ornamental of the columnar trees.

x Populus berolinensis   75′   Zone 2   Berlin Poplar

*HABIT: ascending branches, almost columnar in habit
*FOLIAGE: open, bright green
HYBRID ORIGIN: *P. laurifolia x P. nigra italica*
ORIGINATED: prior to 1870

The Berlin Poplar is a very hardy tree and recommended for areas where the winters are very cold and the summers very hot, such as on the great prairie areas of the western part of North America. Otherwise, it will not compete well with better ornamental trees available for eastern planting.

x Populus canadensis eugenei   150′   Zone 5   Carolina Poplar

HABIT: wide-spread, open
FOLIAGE: glossy leaves, coarse
HYBRID ORIGIN: *Populus deltoides x P. nigra*
ORIGINATED: about 1832 in France

This poplar must be mentioned here because it has been so widely used in the past. However, it is *not* recommended for use. In fact, many communities have passed legislation prohibiting its use as a street tree because its roots are sufficiently vigorous to seek out water pipes and drains, making their way into them and quickly clogging them. It is a "dirty" tree, dropping catkins, bud scales and leaves at various times of the year. It is also weak-wooded, like all poplars, and twigs are continually breaking and littering streets and lawns. There are many superior trees which should be used in its place. The original tree, nearly one hundred years old, was measured a few years ago at 150 feet in height and 38 feet in trunk circumference at base .

Populus candicans   90′   Zone 4   Balm of Gilead

HABIT: wide- and large-spreading branches
FOLIAGE: rather open
HABITAT: origin unknown
INTRODUCED: prior to 1800?

This tree is very wide-spreading and is often confused with *P. tacamahaca*. Unless a wide-spreading tree is desired, this might well be omitted from consideration.

Populus deltoides   90′   Zone 2   Eastern Poplar
                                                 (Cottonwood)

HABIT: wide-spreading, large open branches
FOLIAGE: dense
HABITAT: Quebec to Texas

The Eastern Poplar is suggested only from the Midwest throughout the area where it is native, for it seems to withstand hot climate and drying winds provided its roots can tap sufficient sources of soil moisture.

Populus fremonti   90′   Zone 7   Fremont Cottonwood

HABIT: large, wide-spreading branches
FOLIAGE: loose, open, coarse
HABITAT: California and Arizona

This is recommended only for the dry, alkaline soils of the southwestern part of the country where it is difficult to get any trees to grow. Another species, *P. wislizeni* has been used for similar purposes in Texas and New Mexico.

Populus lasiocarpa   60′   Zone 5   Chinese Poplar

HABIT: round-headed, open
*FOLIAGE: leaves large (6–10″), bright green with red midrib and petiole
HABITAT: central and western China
INTRODUCED: 1904
   One of the most beautiful poplars

Populus maximowiczi   90′   Zone 4   Japanese Poplar

HABIT: wide top, open branching
BARK: grayish
FOLIAGE: dull green, rather coarse
HABITAT: Japan
INTRODUCED: before 1890
   This very beautiful poplar is recommended here because it is the first of
the poplars to unfold its leaves in the spring. This characteristic combined with
its 2½–5″ long leaves, light colored bark and vigorous habit give it qualities that
might be desired under certain circumstances.

Populus nigra italica   90′   Zone 2   Lombardy Poplar

*HABIT: columnar, dense
FOLIAGE: dense, leaves very wide at base
ORIGINATED: before 1750 as a clon of *P. nigra* which is a native of Europe and
          western Asia
INTRODUCED: 1784
   This commonly planted tree is not recommended, except possibly as a very
short-lived tree. As it matures it often acquires a canker disease in its upper
branches and trunk for which there is no cure, and this of course utterly destroys
its symmetry. There are other columnar poplars which are almost as fast growing,
and other columnar trees which, although they may not grow as tall as the
Lombardy Poplar, are more permanent. Consequently, avoid using this tree or
use it as quick growing temporary screen, to be removed after a more permanent
screen has had time to become thoroughly established.

Populus simoni   50′   Zone 2   Simon Poplar

*HABIT: rather narrow, dense
FOLIAGE: leaves small and bright green
HABITAT: northern China
INTRODUCED: 1862
VARIETY: *fastigiata*—narrowly pyramidal in outline, not exactly columnar but
          nearly so—Pyramidal Simon Poplar
   A handsome poplar which has been used in ornamental plantings in America
—its light green foliage, rather narrow habit and vigorous growth are its prime
qualities. The fastigiate variety makes a good substitute for the Lombardy Poplar,
although it is not as columnar in habit. The extreme hardiness of the species is
another very important attribute which should be emphasized.

Populus tacamahaca   90'   Zone 2   Tacamahac Poplar

HABIT: ascending branches, rather erect
FOLIAGE: leaves fragrant as they unfold in early spring
HABITAT: northeastern and north central North America

A poplar native over a wide area of North America which has small claim for ornamental use.

Populus tremuloides   90'   Zone 1   Quaking Aspen

HABIT: loose and open
*BARK: gray to actually white
*FOLIAGE: leaves small but attached by flat, weak petioles, causing the leaves
      to move in the slightest breeze
*AUTUMN COLOR: yellow
HABITAT: North America, coast to coast

The Quaking Aspen is probably the most widely distributed tree in nature on the North American continent. It should not be considered as a specimen tree for it is too loose and open. Planted in groups or groves, however, or in natural wooded areas, it really comes into its own. There is no sight more beautiful in the Rocky Mountains (or anywhere else for that matter) than a mountainside covered with these trees in their full autumn regalia. Although it does grow nearly 100 feet tall, it is frequently encountered much smaller than this, for it is one of the first trees to sprout up after fire has destroyed a coniferous forest. Usually the larger the tree, the whiter the trunk, and the more susceptible to disease troubles and breakage from storms.

Prosopis glandulosa   50'   Zone 8   Honey Mesquite

FLOWERS: yellowish orange, in racemes, attractive to bees
      TIME: November
HABIT: loose, irregular top, short trunk
FOLIAGE: bright green, feathery
HABITAT: southwestern United States

This tough-wooded, slow-growing, drought-resistant tree will not withstand temperatures much below zero.

PRUNUS

The cherries, apricots, plums and peaches constitute a large group of trees, native in the northern temperate regions of the world and ranging in size from the 15 to 20 foot Oriental double flowering cherries, to the more than 90-foot height of our native Black Cherry. They are mostly small to medium-sized trees, of particular interest because of their early spring flowers. The flowers of the Asiatic species and varieties appear in early spring before the leaves and are usually borne profusely; those of the native American types and European types bloom a little later, the flowers appearing with the leaves. It is these Europeans and American natives which have very small flowers in racemes, while the Asiatic types have much larger flowers in clusters or sometimes borne singly or in two's.

Many of the flowers are single, either pink or white, but there is that very important group of double flowered Asiatic cherries without which our spring displays would look sad indeed.

Since this group bears its flowers comparatively early in the season, its fruits also appear early, when the leaves are fully developed. As a result, many of the fruits are completely hidden and so have little landscape value, and turn red before they ripen, then blue or black at maturity, when they are quickly eaten by the birds. The double flowered cherries, of course, do not bear fruits.

A few of these trees have autumn color and those few should be used and recommended, for this brings them into the select group of trees that are of interest two seasons of the year. In addition, several have interesting, shiny bark (typical of many cherries) and this is of much ornamental value, especially in the winter landscape. In fact, some of the species have three seasons of interest for this very reason.

The flowers range in size from the small ¼-inch type apearing in racemes on the bird cherries to the giant 2½-inch size of some of the double flowered peaches and oriental cherries. Each one has a special use in the landscape.

As a group, the *Prunus* are susceptible to various troubles affecting other rosaceous plants, chiefly borers and scale. Canker worm and other leaf eating insects seem to like the foliage to such an extent that it should be sprayed once every year in order to keep such pests under control.

The *Prunus* are all of comparatively easy culture but should have full sun in order to bloom their best. Because of the much publicized planting around the Tidal Basin in Washington, D.C., the opinion has been expressed that the cherries, at least, must be planted near water. This conception is erroneous. Most of the group are short-lived trees normally, but will grow in any good soil with a normal supply of soil moisture. In cold areas, sun scald of the trunks of some species takes its toll in cold winters, and heavy winds, snow or ice storms can always be expected to cause some damage to the branches for they split very easily. Consequently, fifteen to twenty years is a normal life-expectancy for them as a group, but some species like *P. serotina* will live considerably longer.

Prunus amygdalus   24′   Zone 6   Almond

*FLOWERS: pink and white 1–2″ in diameter
   TIME: February or March
HABIT: bushy
FOLIAGE: dense
HABITAT: western Asia, northern Africa
INTRODUCED: colonial times

This is mentioned merely because it blooms very early in the spring. Other than this, it might very well be overlooked since flowering peaches have been developed to a greater extent than the Almond.

Prunus armeniaca 30' Zone 5 Apricot

*FLOWERS: single white or pinkish 1" in diameter
    TIME: late April
FRUIT: yellowish red cheek, 1¼" diameter
    EFFECTIVE: early summer
HABIT: rounded head
FOLIAGE: loose, open
HABITAT: western Asia
INTRODUCED: before 1875
VARIETY: "Charles Abraham," double, deep pink flowers

This hardy apricot blooms early in the spring before the leaves appear. In some areas in the northern United States, the flowers appear so early that they are killed by late frosts. As an ornamental tree, it is not one of the best because of its very early bloom. However, many plantsmen are trying to grow certain clons of it like "Scout," "Henderson," "Zing," and others. In order to insure proper pollination, several clons should be grown in close proximity to each other.

This is the apricot so much grown in southern California and other areas on the Pacific coast. There are many varieties grown in those areas especially for their fruits. All considered, this apricot is an inferior ornamental plant which might easily be replaced by better trees—its chief value is of course economic. The Japanese Apricot, *Prunus mume,* is better for flowering purposes.

Prunus avium plena 60' Zone 3 Double Flowered Mazzard Cherry

*FLOWERS: white, double, 1½" diameter with as many as 30 petals
    TIME: early May
HABIT: tall and pyramidal, dense
FOLIAGE: dense, rather coarse
INTRODUCED: before 1878

This splendid tree has been in North America nearly seventy-five years but it is still seldom seen. Its beautiful double white flowers are not borne profusely but they remain effective for a very long time—nearly a week longer than those of the single flowered Mazzard Cherry, which is of course widely planted for its fruits. All Mazzard cherries do best when grown in the full sun, for in the shade only a very few flowers appear.

x Prunus blireiana 24' Zone 5 Blireiana Plum

*FLOWERS: double, light pink, 1" diameter
    TIME: early May
HABIT: rounded, dense branching
*FOLIAGE: reddish purple (actually garnet brown of the Royal Horticultural
    Society's Colour Chart)
HYBRID ORIGIN: *P. cerasifera atropurpurea x P. mume*
ORIGINATED: 1895

If double flowers are desired, with fewer fruits and certain longer bloom, this hybrid or some of its clons might be desirable in place of the other purple-leaved plums (*P. cerasifera* vars.) The foliage is about the same color as the others and just as effective. The variety *moseri* has been grown a great deal but its flowers are slightly smaller and for this reason it might be discarded. This, like other purple-leaved plums, needs considerable pruning to keep it in good growing condition. It is not as vigorous in growth as the Pissard Plum and has been recorded as having foliage slightly lighter than that of the Pissard Plum but as they grow side by side in the Arnold Arboretum the foliage color seems to be identical. Its purplish red fruits are not effective merely because they are approximately the same color as the foliage.

Prunus campanulata   24'   Zone 7   Taiwan Cherry

*FLOWERS: rose-colored, single, 1" diameter
    TIME: early spring
FRUIT: red
    EFFECTIVE: early summer
*HABIT: small bushy tree, dense branching
FOLIAGE: lustrous
HABITAT: Japan, Formosa
INTRODUCED: 1899

In southern and central California where this cherry grows well, it blooms two weeks before any of the others.

Prunus cerasifera atropurpurea (*pissardi*)   24'   Zone 3   Pissard Plum

FLOWER:: pink, ¾" diameter
    TIME: late April
HABIT: upright, dense branching
*FOLIAGE: reddish purple, (actually garnet-brown of the Royal Horticultural Society's Colour Chart)
HABITAT: originally found in Persia
INTRODUCED: about 1890
OTHER VARIETIES of *P. cerasifera:*
    nigra—flowers single, pale pink, ⅝" diameter, leaves very dark purple—Black Myrobalan Plum
    woodi—flowers single, light pink, ¾" diameter, leaves dark purple remaining so all summer—Woods Myrobalan Plum

Prunus cerasifera itself is not a needed ornamental tree. Its several purple leaved varieties are, however, greatly in demand in certain sections primarily because of their reddish purple foliage which remains a reddish purple throughout the entire growing season. The species is considerably variable, many varieties and clons have appeared on the market. "Thundercloud" is one clon that has done well and might be recommended. The fruits of most are edible but small and not effective from a landscape point of view. The double flowered, *P. blireiana* is better than any *P. cerasifera* varieties in flower, and the double flowers last longer on the tree also.

From the standpoint of purple foliage, I have tried to see marked differences among our plants at different times of the year, but have failed to do so. In fact, I have grown a series of *P. cerasifera nigra* plants side by side with a similar series of *P. blireiana* "Newport," treated them with different fertilizers over a period of several years, and failed to see any differences in the leaf color which remained a reddish purple throughout the spring, summer and fall.

All these plums seem to withstand the hot, often dry, summer of the Chicago area very well. They need constant pruning to correct a bad habit of cross branching. They are small, compact and colorful over a long period and hence are of interest to a large group of small property owners. If grown in the full sun they develop the leaf color to its vivid hue but in shade or partial shade they are not nearly as colorful.

Prunus cerasus   30′   Zone 3   Sour Cherry

*FLOWERS: single, white, ¾–1″ in diameter
     TIME: early May
FRUIT: red to blackish cherries
     EFFECTIVE: early summer
HABIT: rounded, open
FOLIAGE: light green
HABITAT: western Asia, southeastern Europe
INTRODUCED: colonial times
VARIETY: *rhexi*—with double white flowers 1½″ diameter—Rhex Sour Cherry

Usually grown for its fruits but listed here because of its extreme hardiness, for it is one of the hardiest of the Asiatic cherries. Its double flowered variety *rhexi is* therefore usable much farther north than is the double flowered form of *Prunus avium.* It has been noted that this is one of the few fruit trees suitable for growing in shaded locations.

Prunus conradinae semiplena   30′   Zone 6   Double Conradina Cherry

*FLOWERS: white to pale pink, fragrant, double, 1″ in diameter, in clusters
     TIME: mid-May
FRUIT: red, egg-shaped, ⅓″ long
     EFFECTIVE: early summer
HABIT: rounded
FOLIAGE: dense
HABITAT: central China
INTRODUCED: 1907

This species is highly valued in England because of its very early flowers often by early March, but the semi-double flowered variety is more desirable since the flowers remain effective longer.

x Prunus "Hally Jolivette"   15′?   Zone 5

*FLOWERS: pink buds, white, double, 1¼″ diameter
     TIME: early May
HABIT: rounded and dense branching
FOLIAGE: fine texture
HYBRID ORIGIN: *Prunus subhirtella x P. yedoensis* crossed back on *P. subhirtella*
ORIGINATED: 1940 by Dr. Karl Sax, of the Arnold Arboretum, Boston, Massa-
          chusetts

This new hybrid has merit because its very double flowers do not open all at once but the buds open consecutively over a ten to twenty day period. This gives it considerable ornamental value. It also blooms very early in life, usually when only two years old, and has a dense rounded habit similar to *Prunus subhirtella*. Its exact mature height is not yet known but will probably reach 15 to 20 feet.

Prunus lusitanica   6–60′   Zone 7   Portugal Laurel

*FLOWERS: white, ½″ diameter, in racemes 10″ long
    TIME: May
FRUIT: purplish cherries
    EFFECTIVE: summer
HABIT: bushy with dense branching
*FOLIAGE: evergreen, glossy, leaves to 5″ long, dense
HABITAT: Spain and Portugal
INTRODUCED: early colonial times

An extremely serviceable, glossy leaved evergreen for southern gardens which may grow into tree form or be confined as a shrub. As an evergreen background or clipped hedge, it has many uses.

Prunus maacki   45′   Zone 2   Amur Chokecherry

*FLOWERS: small white, in racemes 2–3″ long
    TIME: mid-May
HABIT: rounded, dense branching
BARK: brownish yellow, flaking
FOLIAGE: dense
HABITAT: Korea, Manchuria
INTRODUCED: 1878

This differs from the other bird cherries in forming its flower clusters on the previous year's growth, not the current year's, and is ornamental because of its bright colored bark peeling off in thin strips like that of the birch. Also, it is among the hardiest of trees. It should be considered only for areas with unusually low winter temperatures.

Prunus maximowiczi   48′   Zone 4   Miyama Cherry

*FLOWERS: white, single
    TIME: late May
HABIT: rounded, dense branching
FOLIAGE: dense
*AUTUMN COLOR: scarlet
HABITAT: Korea, Manchuria
INTRODUCED: 1892

The brilliant autumn color of this tree makes it one of the few oriental cherries of ornamental interest two seasons of the year.

Prunus mume   30′   Zone 6   Japanese Apricot

*FLOWERS: single pink, fragrant
    TIME: early May
HABIT: round-headed
FOLIAGE: loose, open
HABITAT: Japan, China

INTRODUCED: 1844

VARIETIES: *albo-plena*—flowers double, white, flowering early; introduced 1934—
Double White Japanese Apricot

"Bonita"—flowers double, crimson

"Dawn"—large, double, shell pink flowers; introduced 1925

"Peggy Clarke"—double, deep rose flowers; introduced 1941

pendula—with pendulous branches—Weeping Japanese Apricot

"Weeping Red"—flowers red, fragrant, branches pendulous; introduced 1926

Most of the flowering apricots belong in this group. They are similar to the flowering peaches but are slightly less hardy, hence have a more limited use. Usually these are small trees, considerably under the 30 feet given as the height of the species. Many varieties, found in nurseries are unnamed seedlings of this species and to avoid disappointment it might be well to observe them in flower in the nursery before selection.

Prunus nipponica   18′   Zone 5   Nipponese Cherry

*FLOWERS: white to pale pink, single

TIME: late April

*HABIT: bushy and dense branching

FOLIAGE: dense

*AUTUMN COLOR: yellow, orange to crimson

HABITAT: Japan

INTRODUCED: 1915

This ornamental cherry of dense habit has much to recommend it for general planting and it might possibly be preferred to some of the other cherries because of its foliage which turns a brilliant yellow to orange autumn color.

Prunus padus   45′   Zone 3   European Bird Cherry

*FLOWERS: small white, fragrant in drooping racemes 3–6″ long

TIME: early May

FRUIT: small black cherries, ¼″ diameter

EFFECTIVE: July

HADIT: open

FOLIAGE: rather open

HABITAT: Europe, northern Asia, Japan, Korea

INTRODUCED: colonial times

VARIETIES: *commutata*—individual flowers ½″ in diameter and blooms nearly three
weeks before other varieties—Harbinger European Bird Cherry

plena—flowers large and double, remaining in flower longer than
any variety. One of the best varieties—Double European Bird Cherry

spaethi—flower clusters somewhat pendulous, one of the better varieties
in collections at Arnold Arboretum—Bigflower European Bird Cherry

watereri—this has proved the best single flowered variety in Europe
with racemes of blossoms 8″ long—Longcluster European Bird
Cherry

The European Bird Cherry is superior to our native *Prunus virginiana* as an ornamental because the flowers and fruits are larger, it has better foliage, and is less susceptible to attacks from tent caterpillars. Particularly is it conspicuous as one of the first trees to produce leaves in the spring, an important trait which has earned it much praise.

Prunus pensylvanica   36′   Zone 2   Wild Red Cherry or Pin Cherry

FLOWERS: small white, in short racemes or clusters
    TIME: early May
*FRUIT: small red cherries, ¼″ diameter
    EFFECTIVE: late August
HABIT: open
BARK: red, shining
FOLIAGE: open, fine texture
*AUTUMN COLOR: red
HABITAT: eastern and central North America

This cherry is short lived, and should not be used as a specimen, but proves splendid on the border of woodlands or actually in the woodlands. It is beautiful in early spring when in full flower (when the leaves are only half grown) and again when the fruits are colored a brilliant red. The birds eat the fruits readily and are responsible for distributing the tree over a wide area. This is one of the first "nurse" trees to appear after certain hardwood forests are cut over, and although it does not live long, nevertheless yields ample shade until the longer-lived young trees of other species become fully established.

Prunus persica   24′   Zone 5   Peach

*FLOWERS: single, pink, 1–1½″ diameter
    TIME: late April
FRUIT: red or yellow peaches
HABIT: rounded
FOLIAGE: dense
HABITAT: China
INTRODUCED: early colonial times (probably even before 1696)
VARIETIES: *albo-plena*—flowers double, white, 1½″ diameter—Double White Peach
           atropurpurea—leaves reddish, flowers single, pink—Bloodleaf Peach
           "Burbank"—flowers double, pink
           "Cambridge Carmine"—flowers very bright red
           "Camelliaeflora"—flowers double, red
           "Double Cerise"—flowers double, deep pink, latest to bloom
           "Helen Borchers"—flowers clear pink, 2½″ diameter
           "Iceberg"—flowers white
           "Peppermint Stick"—flowers double, white, mottled with pink stripes
           "Red Pep"—flowers double, red

The common peach is colorful enough where it is grown commercially and when in bloom in large orchards attract many people. One can hardly visualize the peach used as a specimen lawn tree, for there are many other ornamentals far superior to it in many ways. Often enough, one tree is used in the rear of the grounds or near the vegetable garden, chiefly planted for its fruits. The peach is troubled with several diseases and insect pests and is particularly troubled with borers in the trunk. Because of this, it should only be planted when provision will be made to control such pests persistently and completely.

The varieties are mentioned here because many people, after seeing a small tree or branch in bloom, visualize an entire 20-foot tree covered with the blooms. Unfortunately, in the majority of cases, these large flowering varieties make very poor trees. They are weak and easily susceptible to the inroads of pest troubles. They might better be considered as shrubs, kept heavily pruned and hence relegated to a hidden part of the garden. They should be pruned immediately after flowering in such a way as to force out much new growth, for it is only on this new growth that flower buds will be formed for the next year. The more vigorous the growth the better the blossoms. Hence, in order to have profuse blooms the following year, the majority of flowering branches are cut back after blooming is completed. Plants treated this way are rather unsightly for some time afterward.

These trees have colorful and large flowers, but require special care and culture in order to produce good ones. Because of this, they are not considered good specimens, but rather, plants to be forced in a particular way to produce proper blooms.

| Prunus sargenti | 75' | Zone 4 | Sargent Cherry |

*FLOWERS: single, deep pink, 1¼″ diameter
    TIME: late April
*HABIT: upright but rounded top, dense
BARK: typical cherry bark, dark and lustrous
FOLIAGE: dense
*AUTUMN COLOR: red
HABITAT: Japan
INTRODUCED: 1890
VARIETY: *columnaris*—narrowly upright and columnar in habit

Probably the finest of all the cherry trees, both as an ornamental and as a timber tree, for in Japan it has been used a long time for its excellent timber. The oldest tree in America which was growing in the Arnold Arboretum and propagated from the first seed introduced into this country in 1890, had to be taken down a few years ago after being badly smashed during a severe summer storm. This species is a standard tree, far more hardy than most oriental cherries, and is covered with deep pink, single flowers in the early spring. As soon as these fall, the young foliage begins to appear a very colorful bronze, later turning green as the leaves mature. It is one of the few cherries to have a vivid red, autumn color and of course its bark is of interest all winter.

This makes a splendid specimen tree, possibly a little too large for the small property, but where there is room for it on the home grounds, in parks or as a street tree, it makes a perfect ornamental for beauty as well as dense shade.

| Prunus serotina | 90' | Zone 3 | Black or Rum Cherry |

*FLOWERS: single, white, in terminal drooping racemes
    TIME: late May
*FRUIT: small black cherries, but effective while red
    EFFECTIVE: August
*HABIT: branches partly drooping

*FOLIAGE: dense, leaves lustrous and peach shaped
HABITAT: eastern and central North America
VARIETY: *pendula*—with fully pendulous branchlets, a very graceful form—
        Weeping Black Cherry

This is certainly the best of the native American species of *Prunus* for ornamental planting. Only one other, the Pin Cherry (*P. pensylvanica*), has been added to the recommended group. This Black Cherry, with its long, lustrous peachlike leaves, slightly pendulous branches and dense foliage is an excellent tree for general foliage purposes. The small white flowers, in 4–5½" long, profuse racemes are followed by conspicuous red fruits, eventually turning black. Very few large trees of this species are left standing in the East now, for its wood has been highly prized in furniture-making since colonial times.

Prunus serrula   30′   Zone 5

FLOWERS: single, white
    TIME: early May
HABIT: wide spreading, often with several trunks
*BARK: brilliant glossy red
FOLIAGE: open
HABITAT: western China
INTRODUCED: 1908

The best of all the cherries as far as ornamental bark is concerned—the brilliant lustrous, dark red color of this bark makes the tree of interest throughout the year, especially during the winter. It is very difficult to find commercially.

Prunus serrulata—most varieties   20–25′   Zone 5–6   Oriental Cherry

FLOWERS: single and double, white to pink, ½–2½" in diameter
    TIME: early to mid-May
HABIT: low trees, usually upright
FOLIAGE: coarse
HABITAT: cultivated in Japan for centuries

Most of the cultivated varieties of oriental cherries found in Japanese and Chinese gardens have been relegated to this species. The Japanese have named over 120 varieties but only about 50 are probably grown in this country; many of these are barely distinguishable one from the other by the average gardener. Most are small trees (under 30 feet in height) although the species itself reaches 75 feet in height. They have proved very popular in America and many featured plantings of them have been made on the Atlantic and Pacific coasts.

The flowers are either white or pink, single or double, but most appear before the leaves or with them. Some of the varieties have fragrant flowers, and other things being equal, it is these varieties that certainly should be given preference over the varieties without fragrant flowers. This is a very important factor.

There has been a long controversy concerning the best type of understock on which to graft these varieties. *Prunus sargenti* was highly recommended for a long time. William H. Judd, formerly Propagator at the Arnold Arboretum for over thirty years, decided after long experience with both *P. sargenti* and *P. avium* that the latter was superior as an understock. It always "works" better than *P.*

sargenti and this has been borne out also by others, including R. E. Horsey formerly of the Rochester Park Department.

The recommended varieties are not all among the hardiest of the Oriental Cherry group. Paul Russell in his excellent publication "The Oriental Flowering Cherries" (United States Department of Agriculture, Circular 313, March 1934) lists the following five as the hardiest:

Prunus sargenti
Prunus serrulata "Fugenzo"
Prunus serrulata "Kwanzan"
Prunus serrulata "Shiro-fugen"
Prunus subhirtella

Mr. Russell also divides the varieties of *Prunus serrulata* and other species into the following general groups and those recommended here are listed accordingly:

Trees with pendulous branches—*P. subhirtella pendula*
Trees with fastigiate branches—*P. serrulata* "Amanogawa"
Trees with spreading or upright branches
   Trees with flowers greenish yellow—*P. serrulata* "Cyoiko," "Ukon"
   Trees with flowers white, single or nearly so—*P. serrulata* "Jo-nioi," "Taki-nioi," "Washino-o"
   Trees with flowers white, semi-double or double—*P. serrulata* "Shirotae"
   Trees with flowers pink, single or nearly so—(none recommended here)
   Trees with flowers pink, semi-double or double—*P. serrulata* "Botan-zakura," "Kwanzan," "Shogetsu" and *P. sieboldi*

This classification shows the variation which is evident among the varieties of this interesting species.

VARIETIES: "Amanogawa"—the only truly fastigiate oriental cherry worth growing. Usually not over 20 feet tall, flowers 1¾ inches semi-double, light pink and fragrant. The varietal name means "milky way" an indication of its floriferous blooms. David Fairchild is credited with first introducing this variety from Japan in 1906. It is interesting to note that a very high percentage of the seedlings of this tree are identical with the mother plant in form and flowers.

"Botan-zakura"—a small tree with spreading or upright branches. The flowers are semi-double, pale pink, often 2 inches in diameter with 6–15 petals, and fragrant. When it is possible to grow some of these oriental varieties that are truly fragrant, it would seem that those which are not might be discarded.

"Fugenzo"—This popular variety is also found in nursery catalogues under the name of "James H. Veitch" and also "Kofugen." The Japanese name translated means "goddess on a white elephant." The flowers are as much as 2½ inches in diameter, rosy pink fading to a light pink, double with about 30 petals, blooming at about the same time as "Kwanzan." It is rather wide spreading in habit.

Paul Russell in his excellent work on the Oriental Flowering Cherries notes that it was known to the Japanese five hundred years ago and is still widely planted. It is often confused with "Shiro-fugen" but the flowers of this last variety fade.

"Gyoiko"—The Japanese name means "imperial yellowish costume" showing that the flowers are actually yellowish green. This variety is certainly unusual, but not objectionable, and adds considerable interest to every flowering collection in which it appears. It grows about 20′ tall, the flowers are semi-double and about 1½ inches in diameter with about 15 petals. The variety "Ukon" is similar but the flowers are slightly larger.

"Jo-nioi"—E. H. Wilson, who knew the oriental cherries very well, claimed that this variety was the most fragrant of all—reason enough why it should prove popular. The flowers are mostly single, white and about 1½ inches in diameter. It is upright and slightly spreading in habit, reaching a mature height of about 18 feet. It is similar to "Taki-nioi" but differs slightly in habit.

"Kwanzan"—This is probably the most popular and the most hardy of all the double flowered oriental cherries. The deep pink, double flowers are 2½ inches in diameter and have 30 petals. They are borne on a fairly upright growing tree about 12 to 18 feet tall. The young foliage, as it first appears, is a bright reddish copper color, adding considerably to the colorful display of this tree in early spring. Probably the best display is at Washington, D.C., along the Tidal Basin where nearly two hundred trees of this one variety alone are growing.

"Shirotae"—with double or semi-double pure white flowers, often called the finest of all the double, white, oriental cherries. Its name means "snow white." The flowers are 2½ inches in diameter and fragrant. The petals (about 12) are slightly ruffled giving the flowers a pleasing appearance. (There is no double white with as many petals as "Kwanzan.")

"Shogetsu"—some consider this one of the handsomest of the double flowered cherries. The tree grows about 15 feet tall, is broad and flat topped. The flowers are double (about 30 petals) very pale pink, often with a white center and are up to 2 inches in diameter.

"Taki-nioi"—the Japanese varietal name means "fragrant cascade." This tree seldom grows over 12 feet tall, is fragrant, and blooms at about the same time as "Kwanzan." The flowers are single and white but very fragrant, up to 1¼ inches in diameter.

"Washin-o"—This variety has single, white flowers, 1½ inches in diameter, that are very fragrant. It grows about 20 feet tall with wide-spreading and upright branches.

Prunus sieboldi   24′   Zone 5   Naden Cherry

*FLOWERS: semi-double, light pink almost white, fragrant, 1½″ diameter
   TIME: early May
HABIT: dense and often upright
HABITAT: cultivated in Japan
INTRODUCED: 1864

The Naden Cherry is the first of the double-flowered oriental cherries to bloom, the reason why it is recommended here.

Prunus subhirtella   30'   Zone 5   Higan Cherry

*FLOWERS: single, light pink, 1½" diameter
    TIME: late April
*HABIT: rounded, dense branching
FOLIAGE: small, fine texture
HABITAT: Japan
INTRODUCED: 1894
VARIETIES: *autumnalis*—flowers semi-double, ¾" diameter, appear in fall as well
        as spring—Autumn Higan Cherry
        "Moni-figari"—deep red buds, double shell-pink flowers
        pendula—branches pendulous, introduced about 1842—Weeping Higan
        Cherry
        pendula flore plena—with weeping habit and double flowers—"Yae-
        shidare"

This is one of the earliest of the oriental cherries to bloom (always before the leaves appear) and one of the most floriferous as well. The gracefully weeping variety (*pendula*) was probably the first one to come to this country. The old Ellwanger and Barry Nursery of Rochester, New York, listed it in their catalogue in 1846. The species itself varies considerably in form and color of the flowers, giving rise to such ill-named freaks as "P. subhirtella ascendens pendula rubra flore plena."

Prunus yedoensis   48'   Zone 5   Yoshino Cherry

*FLOWERS: single, white to pink, 1" diameter, slightly fragrant
    TIME: late April
*HABIT: flat topped, bushy
FOLIAGE: dense
HABITAT: cultivated in Japan
INTRODUCED: 1902
VARIETY: *perpendens*—with irregularly pendulous branches

It is this species which constitutes the majority of the famous trees about the Tidal Basin in Washington, D.C. where about nine hundred were planted in 1912 as part of the cherry collection presented by the Mayor of Tokyo to the city of Washington as a gift of friendship. To do their best, they should be planted 30 to 40 feet apart which precludes their extensive use on the small property. Although often considered a hybrid, they will breed true from seed. It is widely planted in Tokyo where over fifty thousand trees of this one species were growing a few years ago. It is quick growing, rather short lived and like most other *Prunus* is best displayed by planting in front of some dense evergreens, for the flowers appear very early before the leaves. This species was first introduced into America by the Arnold Arboretum. One of the most floriferous of all oriental cherries, it can be grown from seed or cuttings, or grafted on *Prunus avium* as the understock.

Pseudolarix amabilis (*kaempferi*)   120'   Zone 5   Golden Larch

*FRUIT: unusual cones borne upright on the upper side of the branches
    EFFECTIVE: summer and early fall, the cones falling apart by late October
*HABIT: very broad and pyramidal with horizontal branches, open

FOLIAGE: needles 1½ to 2½″ long, deciduous, open
*AUTUMN COLOR: golden yellow
HABITAT: eastern China
INTRODUCED: 1854

The Golden Larch is one of the most beautiful exotic trees. Originally found by Robert Fortune as ornament pot-plants in China; eleven years later he found it growing naturally in a monastary garden. Unfortunately it has never become popular in America, possibly because it is not a tree for the small garden, since trees even up to 30 to 40 feet are almost as broad as they are tall! Also it is very likely that seed sources, especially in this country are very limited. Our trees have a good crop of seed only about every three or four years. On large estates or in

The cones of the Golden Larch, Pseudo-larix amabilis, are most interesting in the fall. They open, shatter, and fall to the ground by November.

parks it can quickly become a beautiful specimen, interesting because of its beautiful foliage throughout the spring and summer. In the late summer, when the cones begin to mature, these too are interesting, and in the fall its beautiful golden yellow, autumn color is very outstanding even though it is of short duration. Its unique habit of growth and wide-spreading horizontal branches add to its beauty throughout the winter months. As far as I know (it has been growing in the Arnold Arboretum since 1871) it has no serious insect or disease pests, another very important item in its favor.

Pseudotsuga taxifolia   300′   Zone 4–6   Douglas-fir

*FRUIT: pendulous cones, 2–4½″ long
   EFFECTIVE: fall and winter
*HABIT: densely pyramidal, branching horizontal
*FOLIAGE: evergreen, needlelike, dense
HABITAT: Rocky Mountains and Pacific coast

VARIETIES: *compacta*—compact conical form, short needles

> *glauca*—this is the Rocky Mountain form, hardy in Zone 4 and the best form for northern gardens. This type is more compact with slightly more ascending branches than the species. Foliage bluish green.
>
> *pendula*—branchlets pendulous
>
> *viridis*—the form typical of the Pacific coast regions and not as hardy as variety *glauca*

Second only to yellow pine in volume of lumber produced annually, the greater part of these trees are in Washington, Oregon and northern California. It is the slower-growing form found in the mountains of Colorado and surrounding mountain states that constitute the hardy ornamental tree of northern gardens. Mr. F. L. Skinner of Dropmore, Manitoba, Canada, has a form hardy under his very trying conditions in Zone 2. The coastal form is not nearly as hardy. Both forms vary considerably as to general outline, color of foliage and habit, because few of these are grafted and most are grown from seed. On the Pacific coast where moisture is sufficient the tree will grow 35 feet in twenty-five years, which is rather rapid for an evergreen. The needles remain on the tree a considerable time after it is cut, allowing it to be used for Christmas trees in large numbers where it is native. Also, it withstands pruning and shearing well and so can be used in hedges. About the only serious pest it has, in eastern gardens at least, is a white mealy bug which is easily controlled. It is readily distinguished from all other evergreens by its unique pendulous cones, and its long pointed terminal buds with many scales, as well as by its soft needles. The Douglas-fir can be considered one of our best native evergreen ornamental trees, not superior to the hemlocks, possibly, but certainly well up near the top of the list.

Pterocarya fraxinifolia   90′   Zone 5   Caucasian Wing-nut

FLOWERS: female catkins 12–20″ long

TIME: early spring

*FRUIT: drooping racemes of light green, winged nuts

EFFECTIVE: summer

HABIT: wide spreading, open

*FOLIAGE: handsome dark green, 8–24″ long, compound

HABITAT: Caucasus to northern Persia

INTRODUCED: 1850

This peculiar and interesting tree is not common but has considerable interest during the summer, at a time when most other trees are uninteresting, because of its long racemes of fruits. It is closely related to *Carya* and *Juglans* and requires moist soil.

Pterostyrax hispida   45′   Zone 5   Fragrant Epaulette Tree

*FLOWERS: in pendulous panicles, 4½–9″ long, creamy white, fragrant

TIME: June

HABIT: open head, slender spreading branches

FOLIAGE: open, coarse

HABITAT: Japan

INTRODUCED: 1875

This is an interesting tree, unusual because of its pendulous flower panicles, but very difficult to find commercially. It should not be used in preference to more easily obtained trees but it does make an interesting out-of-the-ordinary specimen.

Pyrus calleryana   30′   Zone 5   Callery Pear

*FLOWERS: white, 1″ diameter
       TIME: early May
FRUIT: russet colored, about ½″ long
HABIT: more or less pyramidal
FOLIAGE: dense
*AUTUMN COLOR: red to glossy scarlet
HABITAT: China
INTRODUCED: 1908

The only reason the Callery Pear is mentioned at all is because it is least susceptible to fire blight and so has earned a place for itself in fruit tree breeding, even though it is less hardy than *P. ussuriensis*. If a pear tree is not needed, certainly there are better ornamentals than either of these.

Pyrus ussuriensis   50′   Zone 4   Ussurian Pear

*FLOWERS: white, 1½″ diameter
       TIME: early May
FRUIT: greenish yellow, 1½″ long, not effective
HABIT: more or less pyramidal
FOLIAGE: dense
*AUTUMN COLOR: glossy scarlet
HABITAT: northeastern Asia
INTRODUCED: 1855.

Chiefly of merit for its vigorous, dense growth, good foliage and brilliant autumn color, this tree is the hardiest of all pears. Its fruits are practically worthless, however, and certainly are not ornamental, although varieties of it are cultivated in Korea, Manchuria and northern China. Of course, it has been used in breeding experiments with pears, but apparently pears are susceptible to a "black-end disorder" when worked on it as an understock. As a flowering tree, this Ussurian Pear is the best of the pears because the flower buds are frequently tinged pink and open gradually to white. It is suggested here only because it is the hardiest of the pears and is one of the least susceptible to fire blight. If a pear is not needed, certainly there are better ornamentals than either this or *P. calleryana*.

QUERCUS

The oaks are among the most dependable of our ornamental trees. Some are native in most of all but the arid regions of North America. Thirty are recommended here (twenty-four species and six varieties), although fifty or more are listed as being grown commercially in American nurseries and offered for sale. Undoubtedly there are still others that are used locally where they are native. The members of this genus are valued for their ɔturdy growth, many for their brilliant autumn color, some for their ever-green leaves and most of them for their large size or the definite shapes which they take at maturity.

Unlike the willows, their wood is strong and they do not split easily in summer storms or as a result of winter's snow and ice. Some live to a great old age, the live oaks of the South certainly being in this group, some of these having trunks as much as 35 feet in diameter, breast high, and having a branch spread of well over 100 feet. Six of the species (*agrifolia*, *chrysolepis*, *ilex*, *laurifolia*, *suber*, and *virginiana*) have evergreen leaves, four of these being native in the South.

It is interesting to note that of the twenty-four species recommended here only two are native in the Orient, three are native of Europe and the rest are natives of North America. The European species have no autumn color, as is the case with many European natives, but most of the rest of the species have excellent fall color.

Only two of the entire group have a mature height under 50 feet (*acutissima* and *marilandica*), most of the others growing to be 75 feet or more in height. All in all, this is a group of truly big trees, and few should be given space in the very small garden. They may grow satisfactorily for a while, but sooner or later they grow out of proportion to such a small area. Unfortunately, the oaks are susceptible to various troubles including borers, oak gall insects, twig girdlers and various leaf diseases. The oak wilt now destroying trees in the north central United States presents a serious threat to these trees, but until more is known about it—the method of its spread, its distribution and rapidity of increase—we should not become fatalistic in our outlook on the situation, but should continue to plant oaks and take good care of them.

As specimen shade trees in large lawns and parks and as street trees, this group includes some of the best types available from all parts of the world for growing in North America today.

Quercus acutissima   45'   Zone 6   Sawtooth Oak

*HABIT: very wide-spreading branches, round head
FOLIAGE: chestnutlike, lustrous, dense
HABITAT: China, Korea, Japan
INTRODUCED: 1862

An excellent specimen of this exotic tree is growing on the grounds of the United States Department of Agriculture Plant Introduction Station at Glenn Dale, Maryland. This tree needs plenty of space for lateral development for it grows nearly as broad as it does high. (See page 306)

Quercus agrifolia   90'   Zone 9   California Live Oak

*HABIT: round-headed, spreading branches
*FOLIAGE: evergreen, hollylike
HABITAT: California

This tree is used chiefly near the California coast, where it is native.

Quercus alba   90'   Zone 4   White Oak

*HABIT: broad round head, wide-spreading branches
*FOLIAGE: dense
*AUTUMN COLOR: purplish red to violet-purple
HABITAT: eastern United States

The "Mighty Oak" is significantly exemplified in the White Oak, for massive specimens 150 feet high and some as much as eight hundred years old have been recorded. Older specimens are almost perfectly rounded in outline and usually blessed with thick and sturdy horizontal branches. The White Oak is difficult to transplant because of a very strong tap root and when compared with the Red Oak, rather slow in growth, two reasons why some look upon it with disfavor. Its wide-spreading branches, usually spaced far apart, make it possible to string electric wires through it easily with a minimum of disfiguring pruning. Also, the dead leaves frequently remain on the tree a good part of the winter. Hence, it makes an excellent specimen tree needing plenty of room (80 feet or more) in which to mature properly. Where fast growth is essential, other trees might be substituted, but for majestically mature beauty no tree can surpass a well-grown White Oak.

Quercus bicolor   60'   Zone 3   Swamp White Oak

HABIT: narrow, round-topped, open head
FOLIAGE: dense
AUTUMN COLOR: yellow-brown to red
HABITAT: eastern and central North America

This is an excellent tree for moist or wet soils, somewhat similar to *Q. alba* but the leaves are coarser and the tree itself is not as refined.

Quercus borealis   75'   Zone 4   Red Oak

*HABIT: broad, round-topped when old, pyramidal when young
*FOLIAGE: dense, usually lustrous
*AUTUMN COLOR: red
HABITAT: northeastern and central North America

The Red Oak is one of the most popular of all the oaks for ornamental planting. It transplants easily, something which cannot be said of all oaks, and grows vigorously. It withstands city conditions, is clean in habit and makes one of the best street or avenue trees which we have. Botanists have arbitrarily distinguished a variety *maxima* as being larger and more widely distributed, but for ornamental purposes it is certainly identical with the species. The Red Oak is the most rapid-growing of all the oaks and certainly worthy of consideration for landscape planting.

Quercus cerris   100'   Zone 6   Turkey Oak

HABIT: broadly pyramidal
FOLIAGE: dark green, small, open, no autumn color, fine texture
HABITAT: southern Europe, western Asia
INTRODUCED: 1735

An interesting ornamental tree, with leaves 2 to 4 inches long, comparatively small for the oaks.

Acorns are not always present to aid in the identification of the oaks but
here are 15 species with a leaf and acorn of each:
Top row—Quercus velutina, robur, variabilis, borealis and marilandica
Middle row—Quercus glandulifera, imbricaria, macrocarpa, palustris and bicolor
Bottom row—Quercus alba, montana, arkansana, coccinea and dentata

Quercus chrysolepis	60'	Zone 7	Canyon Live Oak or Golden-cup Oak

*HABIT: wide-spreading head, often pendulous branchlets
*FOLIAGE: evergreen
HABITAT: Pacific coast

This Oak is often considered the most beautiful of the oaks native in California, but only planted in that region as an ornamental.

Quercus coccinea	75'	Zone 4	Scarlet Oak

*HABIT: open and round-topped head
FOLIAGE: rather lustrous but open
*AUTUMN COLOR: brilliant scarlet
HABITAT: eastern and central United States
VARIETY: *splendens*—foliage slightly more glossy than species—Knaphill Oak

Many might consider this tree as of secondary importance to some of the other oaks for one very important reason—it is hard to transplant. Possibly it should not be recommended. Arborists often say that they have more difficulty moving it than most trees. However, it must be said in its favor that it grows naturally over nearly a third of the United States and has a loosely open habit which most of the oaks (especially *Q. palustris* and *borealis*) do not. Its lustrous foliage and brilliant autumn coloration make it attractive for all types of land-scape use. It should be given the greatest care when it is being transplanted. An oak that is very similar is *Q. shumardi* (Shumard Oak) native in the central part of the United States. This oak is proving to be an excellent street tree (though not as hardy as the Scarlet Oak) in areas where it is naturally hardy and should not be overlooked as a substitute for the Scarlet Oak where this would seem advisable.

Part of the Veteran's Highway as it leaves Boston was planted with the Scarlet Oak in the central strip (it is four-lane highway) where the trees neces-sarily have little room and the Pin Oak on either side of the roadway where they have been given plenty of room—an interesting way of using these two species in parkway planting. The Scarlet Oak is more open, gives less shade and in parkway planting is certainly easier to see through since the branching is not as dense as in the Pin Oak.

Quercus falcata   75′   Zone 5   Spanish Oak or Southern Red Oak

*HABIT: rounded head but upright, with stout spreading branches
FOLIAGE: rather open
AUTUMN COLOR: dull orange to brown
HABITAT: southeastern United States

Growing over a wide area of the southeastern United States, the Spanish or Southern Red Oak grows as far north as New Jersey and Pennsylvania. Surpris-ingly enough this tree is perfectly hardy in the Arnold Arboretum where a speci-men 75 feet tall with a trunk 2 feet in diameter has been doing well for over half a century. Since it is a native, it has been used frequently in landscape planting.

Quercus garryana   90′   Zone 6   Oregon White Oak

HABIT: round-headed, ascending branches
FOLIAGE: dense, similar in size and shape to that of *Q. alba.*
HABITAT: Pacific coast

This White Oak is the most important oak for timber purposes on the Pacific coast. As an ornamental it is used only within its habitat, and does well on dry or gravelly soils.

Quercus ilex   60′   Zone 9   Holly Oak (Holm Oak)

HABIT: rounded head, broad spread
*FOLIAGE: evergreen, leaves green, 1½–3″ long and 1″ broad, dense, fine texture
HABITAT: southern Europe
INTRODUCED: colonial times

The Holly Oak has been a popular tree in southern Europe for centuries and it has proved itself one of the best of the evergreen oaks, especially in plantings near the seashore where the atmosphere is continually moist. It can be clipped easily into various forms and makes an excellent shade tree. The leaves are vari-able in shape, about 1 inch broad. This tree, however, has the bad habit of dropping the previous year's foliage in late spring, making the lawn underneath unsightly for some time. This can easily be circumvented, of course, by planting a ground cover underneath in which such falling leaves can settle without being conspicuous.

The Shingle Oak, Quercus imbricaria, makes an excellent clipped hedge or screen.

Quercus imbricaria   75'   Zone 5   Shingle Oak

*HABIT: pyramidal while young, round-topped when old, open
*FOLIAGE: lustrous, laurellike, often remaining on the tree far into the winter
*AUTUMN COLOR: yellowish to russet
HABITAT: central United States

    When well cared for and well grown, the Shingle Oak can easily be one of the most beautiful of all the oaks. Its leaves are similar in size and shape to those of the Mountain-laurel, and a lustrous dark green on the upper surface. After turning a rich yellow to russet in the fall, the leaves may remain on the trees all winter long. This is amenable to shearing and makes excellent hedges, especially the larger sizes for windbreaks and screens. Even though a native of the Ohio Valley, it is unfortunately difficult to find in commercial nurseries.

Quercus kelloggi 90' Zone 7 California Black Oak

HABIT: open, rounded head, stout spreading branches
FOLIAGE: dense
HABITAT: Oregon to California
This tree does well in dry, sandy or gravelly soils on the Pacific coast and is supposed to live to a ripe old age of two hundred to three hundred years.

Quercus laurifolia 60' Zone 7 Laurel Oak

HABIT: dense, round-topped
FOLIAGE: half evergreen, lustrous, dark green
HABITAT: southeastern United States
This tree is used considerably as a street tree in the southern United States.

Quercus marilandica 30' Zone 6 Black Jack Oak

HABIT: irregular, stout branches
FOLIAGE: leathery and glossy
AUTUMN COLOR: brown or yellow
HABITAT: eastern and central United States
This slow-growing tree is well adapted for planting on poor, dry, sterile soil. At maturity it is only a small tree and can hardly be considered a tree until after ten to fifteen years of growth. It has splendid foliage but should only be considered for planting in poor soil situations where more ornamental oaks would not grow.

Quercus montana 90' Zone 4 Chestnut Oak

HABIT: dense, round head
FOLIAGE: dark geen
AUTUMN COLOR: dull orange
HABITAT: eastern North America
The Chestnut Oak is a good tree for planting in rather dry, rocky soil and is probably surpassed in beauty by other oaks in good soil. Nevertheless it is superior to Q. *muhlenbergi* because of its better foliage and so can be included here especially for planting in rather dry situations.

Quercus nigra 75' Zone 6 Water Oak

HABIT: conical or round-topped, slender branches
FOLIAGE: fine texture, small leaves
HABITAT: southeastern United States
A tree frequently used in the Southeast, apparently is very easily transplanted and makes a good street tree where it is hardy.

Quercus palustris　　　　　75′　　　　　Zone 4　　　　　Pin Oak

*HABIT: pyramidal with drooping branches, dense branching
*FOLIAGE: fine texture
*AUTUMN COLOR: scarlet
HABITAT: central and mid-eastern United States

One of the most picturesque of the oaks because of its peculiar habit of growth. The upper branches are upright, the middle branches are horizontal and the lower branches are pendulous, giving the tree a beautiful pyramidal outline. The limbs are small, not massive as in the White Oak, but are numerous, and mature foliage is very dense. Usually found in nature in moist bottom lands, the Pin Oak is easily moved because of its fibrous root system, (it has no tap roots), but is sometimes rather difficult to grow in a location where the soil is alkaline. It is one of the few trees in the East which show a chlorotic condition of the foliage when the soil is not just right. This condition is quickly cured (though often only temporarily) by spraying soluble iron salts on the foliage or injecting them into the tree trunk itself.

This tree makes an excellent specimen as a lawn tree but should never be used as a street tree unless it is placed at least 20 feet from the roadway. It is certainly a mistake to plant it as close to the road as a Red Oak, for instance, since the pendulous limbs obstruct traffic. These are cut off and before long the limbs that were horizontal begin to acquire a pendulous habit and then these too must be removed. It seems that there are always hanging branches to be cut out of a Pin Oak when it is not given sufficient room for normal lateral growth. Allowed to grow naturally with sufficient space so its pendulous branches can sweep the ground, there is no more beautiful or graceful tree.

Quercus phellos　　　　　50′　　　　　Zone 5　　　　　Willow Oak

*HABIT: round-topped to conical, dense branching
*FOLIAGE: fine texture
AUTUMN COLOR: yellowish
HABITAT: eastern seaboard and Gulf States

The Willow Oak has what is perhaps the finest texture foliage of any, with leaves 2½ to 5 inches long, narrow and pointed at both ends more or less like those of a willow tree, and the side branches are slender like those of the Pin Oak. It is included here because of the fine texture of its foliage and because it is used widely for ornamental planting and as a street tree throughout its native habitat, one of the principal reasons being that it is easy to transplant because of shallow roots.

Quercus robur　　　　　75–150′　　　　　Zone 5　　　　　English Oak

HABIT: open, broad head, short trunk
FOLIAGE: rather open
HABITAT: Europe, northern Africa, western Asia
INTRODUCED: colonial times
VARIETIES: *asplenifolia*—leaves deeply cut, fernlike, fine texture—Spleenwort Eng
　　　　　lish Oak
　　　　　atropurpurea—leaves dark purple—Purple English Oak

concordia—leaves are a bright yellow, especially when they first appear
  in the spring. However, in very hot sun the leaves may scorch.--
  Golden Oak

fastigiata—columnar in habit with form similar to that of the Lombardy
  Poplar. An excellent ornamental—a great majority of the seedlings
  raised from acorns sown from this tree have the same columnar
  habit as the parent.—Pyramidal English Oak

pendula—branches pendulous—Weeping English Oak

Widely planted in Europe, many varieties of this species have been noted.
It is not entirely satisfactory in the Arnold Arboretum. True, large trees will grow,
sometimes a foot in trunk diameter, and then will die suddenly within a year, due
to no other apparent cause than unsuitable climate or winter cold. It is widely
distributed in American gardens and the fastigiate variety is even more popular.
Like many a native European plant, this tree does not have a vivid autumn color,
for the leaves drop off late in the fall while still green. Quercus petraea is very
similar but does better in drier soils and holds its leaves longer in the fall.

| Quercus suber | 60' | Zone 7 | Cork Oak |

*HABIT: round-topped head, short trunk, massive branches
*FOLIAGE: evergreen, small leaves, fine texture
HABITAT: southern Europe, northern Africa
INTRODUCED: colonial times

Thomas Jefferson was probably one of the first Americans to realize the
merits of the Cork Oak, but it was not until about 1858 that some of the first
successful Cork Oak plantings were made from seed distributed by the United
States Department of Agriculture. This tree is ornamental because of its large
branches, rounded habit and evergreen foliage. Because of the fact that the
United States uses in excess of 150,000 tons of cork annually, most of it imported
from the Mediterranean Region, American sources were scrutinized rather carefully during the World War. Many mature cork oaks were found in perfect condition in this country. One of these trees yielded 1,050 pounds of cork a few years
ago when its bark was stripped off.

As the result of an extensive cork-planting program conducted by the Crown
Cork and Seal Company of Baltimore, Maryland, and certain state and federal
agencies, thousands of trees have been set out during the past decade. There are
now well over one hundred thousand Cork Oaks growing in the United States,
chiefly in California and the southern states as far north as Baltimore County,
Maryland.

The outer bark is first stripped off the tree when it is about fifteen years old
and then at seven- to twelve-year intervals thereafter for at least 100 years or
more. The inner living cambium tissue is not injured in this process. The grade of
cork improves for the first three strippings and remains fairly uniform thereafter.
The virgin bark must be removed before the high-grade cork is produced.

Cork trees require full sun and seem to thrive in semi-arid soil. The economic
interest in this new American-grown crop, combined with the fact that the tree
does have good ornamental possibilities, should give the planting of cork trees
momentum in those regions of the South peculiarly adapted to its growth, where
winter temperatures do not fall below zero, and average rainfall approaches
amounts equal to those in the cork-growing areas of Spain and Portugal.

Quercus variabilis   75′   Zone 5   Oriental Oak

HABIT: fairly open but still yields good shade
BARK: yellowish gray, deeply furrowed and decidedly corklike
FOLIAGE: dull green, similar to that of *Castanea crenata*
HABITAT: northern China, Korea, Japan
INTRODUCED: 1861

This tree is of particular interest because of its outer bark which is very corklike. In fact, in some regions of China the bark does have economic value, supplying a poor grade of cork. However, this cork layer is only about ½ inch thick, and the chances are the tree will have little economic use in any country where *Quercus suber* can be grown in the warmer regions.

Quercus velutina   100–150′   Zone 4   Black Oak

*HABIT: rounded and dense
*FOLIAGE: lustrous, dark green
*AUTUMN COLOR: red
HABITAT: eastern and central United States

This species is not frequently planted as an ornamental tree, probably because its deep tap root makes it difficult, especially in the larger sizes. The branching system is not as rugged as that of *Q. alba,* nor are they as wide spreading, but it is one of the largest growing of all the hardy northern oaks. The inner bark is yellow and the terminal winter buds pubescent, the chief means by which it can be distinguished from *Q. borealis.* If lustrous leaves and tremendous height are desired, this certainly is the species to use. Otherwise, some of the other species might do as well.

Quercus virginiana   60′   Zone 7   Live Oak

*HABIT: very wide spreading, nearly horizontal branches
*FOLIAGE: evergreen in southern part of its range, deciduous only near its northern
        limits, fine texture
HABITAT: southeastern United States

This massive oak is one of the impressive sights of the coastal gardens of the South Atlantic Gulf States. One of the largest trees on record has a trunk circumference of 38 feet and a spread of 168 feet even though it is only 75 feet high. The leaves are comparatively small and narrow (about 2–5 inches long) and are usually evergreen. However, near its northern limit in Virginia the leaves are often deciduous. The typical habit of one of these trees is easily twice as broad as it is high and densely rounded in outline.

It is easily transplanted when young and has long been popular in the South as a shade and street tree. In Texas, it has withstood temperatures of 10° below zero without any injury to the wood, although the leaves have been killed.

Quillaja saponaria   60′   Zone 10   Soapbark Tree

FLOWERS: white, ½″ in diameter
    TIME: spring
HABIT: open

The Saw-tooth Oak (Quercus acutissima) has lustrous green leaves and a
well rounded shape.

*FOLIAGE: evergreen, open, lustrous
HABITAT: Chile
The Soapbark Tree is sometimes used as an ornamental tree in southern
California, especially because of its evergreen foliage.

Ravenala madagascariensis   30′   Zone 10   Madagascar Traveler's Tree

*HABIT: upright palm, open, like a huge fan
FOLIAGE: coarse but picturesque, leaves often 15′ long
HABITAT: Madagascar
This striking and unusual tree, closely related to the banana, is only used
in subtropical areas for picturesque effects. The common name comes from the
fact that it stores a palatable watery fluid at the base of the leaves which can be
used as a substitute for water where this is not available to the weary traveler.
Its peculiar fanlike shape sets it apart from other trees.

Rhamnus davurica   30′   Zone 2   Dahurian Buckthorn

*FRUIT: shiny black berries, ¼″ diameter
  EFFECTIVE: fall
HABIT: indefinite
*FOLIAGE: lustrous
HABITAT: North China, Manchuria and Korea
INTRODUCED: 1817

This is not a particularly desirable ornamental, but a vigorous grower in almost any normal soil. The lustrous green leaves, and fruit which attracts many kinds of birds are about its only important characteristics.

Rhododendron maximum 12–36' Zone 3 Rosebay Rhododendron

*FLOWERS: rose colored to purple-pink, spotted olive-green to orange
  TIME: late June
HABIT: rounded and irregularly open
*FOLIAGE: dark green, evergreen, leaves 5–10" long
HABITAT: eastern North America
VARIETIES: *album*—flowers white
  purpureum—flowers deep pink to purple

This native species is perhaps the hardiest of all the evergreen rhododendrons, and certainly the tallest and most treelike of those hardy in the North. Its flowers are not as large as those of *R. catawbiense* but are free of the objectionable magenta color. They appear after the leaves of the current year's growth are well expanded. The new foliage hides the flower clusters to a considerable degree. The Rosebay Rhododendron, then, is of value for its hardiness, for its tall habit of growth, for its long leaves, but when flowers alone are considered, there are many species and hybrids far more satisfactory. It requires semi-shade to do well and is frequently used in gardens in the northern United States merely as part of an evergreen shrub background for more ornamental plants. Seldom is it used in gardens as a tree, although it sometimes reaches tree proportions in its native habitat. There are many other rhododendrons growing to tree size, but not until very recently have these been introduced to America. Nearly thirty have been noted as trees, one (*R. giganteum*) described as the tallest of all reaching 90 feet in height in its native habitat. However, these are still all so rare in America that none have grown to tree size and so will not be considered here.

Robinia pseudoacacia 75' Zone 3 Black Locust

*FLOWERS: white, pealike, in pendulous clusters, fragrant
  TIME: early June
FRUIT: dry pods
HABIT: open, few branches, upright
FOLIAGE: open
HABITAT: eastern United States
VARIETIES: *decaisneana*—flowers light rose colored—Decaisne Locust
  dependens—pendulous branchlets
  inermis—thornless—Thornless Black Locust
  rectissima—Shipmast Locust

The variety *rectissima*, native on Long Island, has recently been brought into prominence by the superior lasting-qualities of its wood. It grows with a single straight trunk and the lateral branches are not very long. It is considerably more resistant to borers than is the species, and its wood is excellent for fence posts. Mr. Henry Hicks on Long Island has authenticated records of posts having been in the ground 125 years and still being in good condition. Posts of this wood last nearly twice as long as do those made from the species. The United States Department of Agriculture is recommending this strongly for fence posts for lasting duration and it is being grown in the eastern United States for this specific purpose.

semperflorens—flowering throughout the summer—Perpetual Black Locust

umbraculifera—branches form a dense rounded head—Umbrella Black Locust

There are at least three types, some with single straight trunks, others with irregular trunks and still others with a fan-shaped habit of branching. Locusts are valued for their late spring flowers (after the foliage is fully developed) and for their ability to grow in poor, sterile and dry soils. They are legumes and do have small nitrogen nodules on their roots; their small, stipular thorns (except *inermis*) are omnipresent and rather effective in vigorous young growth.

Like many another native tree, they are frequently planted throughout their native habitat, but there are two serious pests which frequently disfigure them, namely, the locust borer, and the locust leaf miner. The borer, once it gets into the trunk and large branches, can create much havoc and seriously reduce the vigor and beauty of the tree. Control is difficult once the borers are inside the trunk, but spraying with a 12 per cent DDT solution at the time the insects are hatching on the bark (late summer and early fall) seems to be effective.

The locust leaf miner, once it becomes established, can skeletonize the foliage of the entire tree, or even groves of them, in the late summer. This can be controlled by spraying the foliage with poison at the proper time. The point to remember is that in areas where these pests are known to be prevalent, locusts are going to require persistent maintenance care in order to be satisfactory ornamental trees. The shade they yield is practically negligible.

Robinia viscosa   36′   Zone 3   Clammy Locust

*FLOWERS: pink, pealike, pendulous clusters
FRUIT: dry pods
HABITAT: southeastern United States

The Clammy Locust is sometimes used because of its pink flowers.

Roystonea regia   70′   Zone 10   Royal Palm

*HABIT: palm tree
FOLIAGE: graceful
HABITAT: Cuba and southern Florida

The most graceful of the palms planted in the southeastern United States is the Royal Palm. The lower leaves droop and the central leaves are upright, always swaying gracefully in any breeze. The trunk is swollen slightly in the center and then tapers gracefully above and below—a typical tree in the subtropical part of Florida, and because of its plumelike leaves, uniquely suitable to avenue planting in the tropics where it is very popular.

Sabal palmetto   90′   Zone 8   Palmetto

*HABIT: palm with tufted growth of leaves at top of trunk
FOLIAGE: coarse, fan-shaped
HABITAT: North Carolina to Florida

The Royal Palm, hardy in only the subtropical area of the United States.

This is the tree the Seminole Indians of the Florida Everglades call the "Cabbage Palmetto," for it affords timber for the construction of their houses, fibre for tying things, leaves for thatching roofs and the young buds when cooked are eaten and taste like cabbage. It is the dried leaves of this palm which are cut and distributed so widely in religious services on Palm Sunday. The fanlike leaves are 5 to 6 feet long and 7 to 8 feet across, partially divided into long narrow segments. Of course if the terminal bud is removed, the tree dies. This tree is typical of the landscape of the southeastern coastal sections of the United States and it is used for ornamental and street tree planting as well. The Palmetto is one of the hardiest of the palms.

SALIX

There are over three hundred species of willows in the northern temperate regions of the world, some of them trees and many shrubs. A few trees are ornamental and are listed here, but there are many characteristics common to this group which should be thoroughly understood before any one is selected for planting. Many are extremely difficult to identify—even the expert taxonomist throws up his hands in despair when confronted by a pile of herbarium specimens for determination. They have hybridized a great deal so that many hybrids have occurred only to further confuse the identification picture.

In the first place, the flowers of most willows (except the so-called "Pussy Willows") are not ornamental. The sexes are separate, and male catkins occur on one tree with female catkins on another. Incidentally, this does not make the identification of the species any easier. As a rule, the foliage is of a fine texture and most of the leaves might be considered "small." The species are twiggy in habit, with many fine branches continually in motion in almost any breeze.

As a group, they flourish in moist situations and here is where they are best used in gardens. Because of their affinity for water, however, their roots can readily seek out openings in drains or sewers and quickly clog them as easily as those of the Carolina Poplar (see page 277). The Weeping Willows, in particular, have become associated with plantings by ponds, and of course the shrubby types are frequently found in nature in moist soils. All can be readily propagated by cuttings.

The wood of all willows is very weak and cracks easily. This is one of the most important reasons why they should not be used as street or avenue trees. It has been done, probably in many places, but the cost of maintenance far outstrips any possible value added to real estate when such plantings are made.

In many areas, willows are troubled with several serious diseases and with insect pests as well, both important reasons why they require much maintenance. All in all, willows should only be planted in moist situations where vigorous growth and corresponding good foliage is assured, and only after the serious consideration of other kinds of trees that might be used to take their place. For this reason, only eight willow tree species have been suggested for possible consideration here. Many more could have been included but the fewer that are planted, especially along public rights of way, the less expense to everyone responsible for their care.

Admittedly, there is nothing as beautiful and graceful in the northern part of the country at least, as a well-grown Weeping Willow. As will be noted in the following discussions, some may prove superior to others, but certainly there is no other tree like the Weeping Willow for northern planting. A careful selection should be made from among the four types of Weeping Willows suggested, in order to best fit the situation under consideration.

The weeping willows have been considerably mixed in the nurseries and gardens of this country for well over fifty years, and probably will continue to be that way. They are certainly the most graceful of all northern trees, reason enough why they are grown. It is unfortunate that they have become confused, particularly in the trade, for they can be distinguished one from the other in most cases, even in the nursery row when they are nothing more than rooted cuttings. Since some are hardier than others, and some make better weeping specimens than others, it would seem advisable for all commercial growers to work up correctly-named stock.

A study of these plants was begun at the Arnold Arboretum several years ago when three different nurseries had sent in material for identification during one week. Material of these weeping types was requested from twenty of the leading nurseries in the East and the Midwest, then lined out in the nurseries of the Arnold Arboretum and grown for several years. This study pointed out the great confusion concerning nomenclature which now exists, since at least a third of the specimens we received were misnamed.

It is unfortunate that the Babylon Weeping Willow, for some reason or other, has become accepted in the minds of many people as the only weeping willow. As a matter of fact, several types of weeping willows are being grown in the trade under the name of *Salix babylonica* and it must be admitted that there are actually six willow trees in this category. The Babylon Weeping Willow is hardy in only about the lower third of the United States. In more northern areas the hardier species should be grown.

The most hardy is the Golden Willow (*Salix alba tristis,* often incorrectly termed *S. vitellina pendula*). Of the remaining four, one is a native of China and probably not much distributed in this country (*S. matsudana pendula*), and the other three are hybrids, each having *S. babylonica* as one of its parents. It is this affinity which is causing the confusion in identification.

Salix sepulcralis (often termed *S. salamoni*) is the least pendulous of these three *S. babylonica* hybrids and so is not recommended here as one of the truly "weeping" willows. The Thurlow Weeping Willow (*S. elegantissima*) and the Wisconsin Weeping Willow (*S. blanda*) are both grown and recommended, but the latter is probably the less desirable since, in mature specimens, its branchlets are not as long as are those of the Thurlow Weeping Willow.

Of all these the most pendulous are *S. babylonica, S. alba tristis* and *S. elegantissima,* easily distinguishable one from the other. *Salix matsudana pendula* is probably not distributed much in America, and *S. sepulcralis* is the least pendulous of all. The Wisconsin Weeping Willow, *S. blanda,* is a very popular one also because of its good growth and lustrous leaves.

In order to assist in the identification of these four weeping willows which are here recommended, the following key is offered. It does not always prove accurate but at least may help to assist in the proper identification of these very closely related species:

1. One-year old twigs definitely yellow and pendulous, red very little if any on upper side of young twigs, young leaves hairy above and below. .S. *alba tristis*
2. Young twigs yellowish green and reddish on upper side, leaves less than ⅝" in width and glabrous; branchlets very pendulous—one-year rooted cuttings grow almost prostrate on the ground, petiole ⅜"................S. *babylonica*
3. Twigs distinctly green, growth much more upright, leaves ⅝–⅞" in width and glabrous
    a. Leaves lustrous above, 1-year twigs reddish to brown........S. *blanda*
    b. Leaves not lustrous above, 1-year twigs green..........S. *elegantissima*

Salix alba   75′   Zone 2   White Willow

HABIT: spreading branches, loose and open
FOLIAGE: fine texture
AUTUMN COLOR: yellow
HABITAT: Europe and northern Africa to central Asia
INTRODUCED: colonial times
VARIETIES: *chermesina*—twigs bright red—Redstem Willow

  tristis—extremely hardy, this Golden Weeping Willow is a gracefully beautiful tree in its own right, hardy throughout the northern United States and southern Canada. It is available in the trade, erroneously, under three different names, S. *vitellina pendula,* "Niobe" and *S. alba tristis.* Old established trees in the Arnold Arboretum do not have branches "sweeping the ground" but some of the younger trees, planted in good soil about Boston, are 25 feet tall, have branches that are definitely pendant for at least 15 feet and these do "sweep the ground." Dr. L. H. Bailey has noted a S. *babylonica aurea* which name may have been picked up from an incorrect listing in a nursery catalogue or introduced from Europe many years ago. Certainly if there were a form of S. *babylonica* with pendulous yellow twigs, it would be practically impossible to tell it from S. *alba tristis.*

  E. H. Wilson has suggested the fact that possibly there are two forms of S. *blanda* one with yellowish shoots called "Niobe." It is apparently certain that there are two forms of yellow-twigged weeping willows in the trade, even though our best taxonomic botanists classify them both under S. *alba tristis.* One has much longer pendulous branches than the other—Golden Weeping Willow

  vitellina—with yellow twigs—Yellowstem Willow

This can be considered one of the best of the upright willows for landscape planting. Most willows (except the weeping varieties) are not recommended for planting because of their weak wood and susceptibility to attacks, and rather severe ones, from several serious diseases and insect pests. Consequently, for special locations such as by the water or where the varieties with colored winter twigs seem desirable, this species could be used.

Salix amygdalina   30′   Zone 4   Almondleaf Willow

HABIT: round head
FOLIAGE: leaves peachlike, 2–4″ long
HABITAT: Europe and Asia
INTRODUCED: before 1875?

The Almondleaf Willow is not common in ornamental plantings, but its narrow leaves, resembling those of peaches, give it some value. Also, it is used a great deal in Europe in making baskets, for the wood of young branches splits easily, is pliant, and can be readily woven. In this day and age when special hobbies are much in vogue, this willow might find some value if planted in a back corner of the property and grown solely for this purpose. Probably even better for basket-making is *Salix viminalis,* but unfortunately this is rather difficult to obtain from commercial sources in North America. Both are being grown in several arboretums and botanic gardens and like all willows can be easily rooted from cuttings.

Salix babylonica   30′   Zone 6   Babylon Weeping Willow

*HABIT: long pendulous branches, the best of the weeping willows
*FOLIAGE: fine texture
HABITAT: China
INTRODUCED: 1730
VARIETY: *crispa*—leaves folded and spirally curved, not especially ornamental

This is the best of the weeping willows and where it is hardy this should be given first choice. The specific name was first given it by Linnaeus when it was found in the region of the Euphrates River in Babylon, but botanical exploration centuries later proved that it was a native of China. Apparently, it is another of those plants like *Syringa persica* which was deposited along the old trade route from China to Egypt. It has been a popular tree for centuries, being very much in the public eye about 1823, when Napoleon, exiled to the Island of St. Helena, used to sit under one of these trees and contemplate his better days. In fact, he loved this particular specimen so much that he was buried under it and cuttings from it were later in great demand all over the world.

Being a willow, it is naturally a fast-growing and weak-wooded tree, easily susceptible to breakage from ice or snow. It is not hardy in New England where it is frequently tried, only to winter-kill miserably during the first really hard winter that strikes it. When propagated from cuttings it can be distinguished easily from other willows for the first year or two, for it lies almost prostrate on the ground.

x Salix blanda   40′   Zone 4   Wisconsin or Niobe Weeping Willow

*HABIT: wide-spreading head, long pendulous branchlets
*FOLIAGE: fine texture
ORIGIN: S. babylonica x S. fragilis
INTRODUCED: before 1830?

Probably a clon of the same cross as *S. elegantissima*, the true Wisconsin Weeping Willow, is probably the less desirable specimen because its pendulous branches are only half as long as those of the Thurlow Weeping Willow, although more lustrous. Whether or not the term "Niobe" is a synonym is a matter for much discussion. E. H. Wilson has remarked that there were two forms of *S. blanda*, "one with yellowish twigs called Niobe." Whether or not this is true, all specimens of "Niobe" which I have been able to acquire from many nursery sources, have proved to be *S. alba tristis*. As previously noted, possibly there are two clons of this variety.

Salix caprea   27′   Zone 4   Goat Willow

*FLOWERS: small composite heads or catkins about 1″ long
     TIME: March
HABITAT: Europe to northern Asia and north Persia
INTRODUCED: early colonial times

This species is the best of the "Pussy Willows," because it has the largest catkins. The sexes in willows are separate and the male of this species has those long gray fluffy catkins that eventually sprout many bright yellow stamens as they mature. The catkins of the female plant eventually have greenish colored pistils that are not nearly as pretty as those of the male. This willow is a vigorous shrub or small tree of little interest the rest of the year, but the catkins come so early in the season that there may be room in the large garden for this plant to serve just this one purpose. Larger catkins are frequently obtained by cutting the plant to the ground every three years, thus forcing it into vigorous growth. The native *Salix discolor* of the United States is also common in woods and swampy places over the eastern United States, but its catkins are smaller than those of *S. caprea.*

Salix elaeagnos   15'   Zone 4   Elaeagnus Willow

HABIT: slender branched, round head
*FOLIAGE: grayish, feathery
AUTUMN COLOR: yellow
HABITAT: southern Europe and Asia Minor
INTRODUCED: before 1850

This tree is interesting because of its grayish feathery foliage. However, where this characteristic is wanted, the true *Elaeagnus angustifolia* might better be used since it is not so susceptible to attack from pests.

x Salix elegantissima   40'   Zone 4   Thurlow Weeping Willow

*HABIT: long pendulous branchlets
FOLIAGE: fine texture
ORIGIN: unknown, possibly *S. babylonica x S. fragilis*
INTRODUCED: about 1860

The Thurlow Weeping Willow is the best substitute for the Babylon Weeping Willow in the North. Although the pendulous branches are not as long as those of *S. babylonica,* they are twice as long as those of *S. blanda.* This latter species does have lustrous leaves, lacking in the Thurlow Weeping Willow. Other than these two differences, these weeping willows are very much alike, both probably have the same parents.

Salix pentandra   60'   Zone 4   Laurel Willow

HABIT: rounded
*FOLIAGE: lustrous dark green leaves about the size of those of the Mountain-laurel
HABITAT: Europe
INTRODUCED: colonial times?

This is one of the best of the willows for ornamental planting, especially because of its dark green, lustrous foliage and its brownish shiny twigs. When subjected to the ravages of insect attack which is a failing of most willows, it appears as the most dilapidated tree in the garden or along the highway, but cared for properly, it makes an excellent specimen.

The Laurel Willow has been used occasionally as a street tree. This is a mistake, for all willows are in the "high maintenance" group of trees requiring costly spraying and pruning every year in order to look well.

Sambucus coerulea   45'   Zone 5   Blueberry Elder

*FLOWERS: yellowish white, small in large flat clusters 7" in diameter
    TIME: late June
*FRUIT: blue-black but whitened by a heavy bloom
    EFFECTIVE: late summer
HABITAT: Pacific coast of United States and Canada
    The fruit of this plant has a whitish blue appearance which is most attractive and makes this popular for planting on the Pacific coast. It is very vigorous and when cut back it may grow as much as 3 to 12 feet in one year. However, as a tree, the wood is weak and susceptible to breakage in severe storms.

Sapium sebiferum   40'   Zone 9   Chinese Tallow Tree

*FRUIT: milk-white seed adhering to central part of capsule long after it is open
    EFFECTIVE: fall
HABIT: spreading, unsymmetrical trunk divided into several large branches
FOLIAGE: light and lustrous green, poplarlike
AUTUMN COLOR: deep red and yellow
HABITAT: China, Japan
    With the general ornamental aspects of a poplar, the Chinese Tallow Tree has been planted in the southern part of the Gulf States and in lower California. The Chinese use the waxy coating about the seeds for making candles and soap. This tree is remarkably free of insect and disease pests and is adaptable for planting in a wide variation of soils.

Sassafras albidum officinale   60'   Zone 4   Sassafras

FRUIT: bluish black berry under ½" in diameter, with a red stalk
    EFFECTIVE: early fall
*HABIT: short, sparsely-spaced branches, long trunk
FOLIAGE: irregularly shaped, often like one- or two-fingered mittens
*AUTUMN COLOR: brilliant orange to scarlet
HABITAT: eastern and northeastern United States
    The Sassafras is widely distributed, familiar to most people interested in native trees because of its irregular mitten-shaped leaves, their aromatic odor when crushed, and brilliant autumn coloration. The sexes may be separate, some trees may have both staminate and pistillate flowers on the same tree and in still others the flowers may be perfect. The tree often grows in poor gravelly soils and is rather difficult to transplant, at least when it is large. When it grows in groups, as it often does on the border of woodlands or along old fence rows, it tends to be narrow and upright, but grown individually out in the open it makes a fine tree. The oil of sassafras is distilled from the roots and the bark, and it was from these that sassafras tea was made by the early settlers.

Schinus molle   40'   Zone 9   California Pepper Tree

*FRUIT: red berries in abundant clusters
    EFFECTIVE: fall
HABIT: wide-spreading branches, rounded top

FOLIAGE: feather-shaped, compound leaves 9″ long
HABITAT: Peru

The California Pepper Tree is an excellent highway or street tree in California and widely planted there. Sturdy in growth, the pendant branchlets often reach the ground, and in rather arid conditions it seems to thrive even though given little attention on poor soils. It is susceptible to black scale (plant is banned near orange orchards in some sections for this reason) and has the bad reputation for dropping litter on well-kept lawns; otherwise it is a fine plant.

Schinus terebinthifolius   40′   Zone 9–10   Brazil Pepper Tree

*FRUIT: small, bright red
    EFFECTIVE: winter
HABIT: rounded
*FOLIAGE: evergreen, attractive, 4–8″ long and compound
HABITAT: Brazil

This tree is used chiefly in Florida as a lawn or avenue tree and is called the Christmas-berry Tree because its fruits are conspicuous in mid-winter for quite some time. It grows well and very rapidly in dry areas.

Sciadopitys verticillata   120′   Zone 5   Umbrella Pine

FRUIT: cones 3–5″ long
    EFFECTIVE: fall
*HABIT: densely pyramidal, often narrow
*FOLIAGE: evergreen, needles 3–5″ long, dark green
HABITAT: central Japan
INTRODUCED: 1861

This very beautiful tree, easily grown and not susceptible to any serious disease, is valued for its dense habit and very dark green foliage, especially while young. Twenty to thirty of the needles are arranged in whorls about the twigs, somewhat similar to the arrangement of ribs of an umbrella, from which similarity it gets its common name. These needles remain on the tree two to three years before falling off, and one of its good points is that it keeps its lower branches for a long time and so makes a splendid lawn specimen. Although growing tall in Japan, it is rather slow-growing in this country and plants fifty years old in the Arnold Arboretum are still only 25 feet tall. It should have good soil and not be planted in hot, dry situations.

Sequoia sempervirens   365′   Zone 7   Redwood

*HABIT: narrow, open, straight and massive trunk
*FOLIAGE: evergreen, open, somewhat like that of hemlock
HABITAT: southern Oregon and California

In its native habitat along the Pacific coast, the Redwood is very interesting because of its massive beauty. Here giant trees measuring up to 365 feet in height grow in groves so dense that sunlight seldom filters through. The trunks may measure as much as 75 to 80 feet in circumference. The bark is very thick and dense, serving as an excellent insulation against fire and disease. The wood is red and solid, used considerably for furniture and the exterior and interior

The Japanese Umbrella Pine (Sciadopitys verticillata), makes an excellent specimen evergreen.

finishing of houses. The small needles remind one very much of those of hemlocks. These are the tallest trees on the North American continent and considerable work has been done in order to preserve certain groves north of San Francisco along the "Redwood Highway," and prevent them from being destroyed for their lumber.

Sequoiadendron giganteum (*Sequoia gigantea*) 300' Zone 6 Giant Sequoia

*HABIT: narrow, open, straight massive trunk
*FOLIAGE: evergreen, open
HABITAT: California

The Giant Sequoias drawf everything about them.

The Giant Sequoias are probably the oldest trees in the United States, some often estimated to be three to four thousand years old. These do not grow quite as tall as the Coast Redwood but they grow greater in trunk diameter. The General Sherman Tree of Sequoia National Park in California is 37 feet in diameter at its base and 17 feet in diameter at 120 feet above the base—estimated at nearly four thousand years old—the largest tree in bulk of trunk, at least in North America. This is the hardier of the two sequoias. The most northern tree on the East coast is a splendid 70-foot specimen at Bristol, Rhode Island. Other trees have been grown, one reaching 60 feet in height on Cayuga Lake in

The Japanese Pagoda Tree, Sophora japonica, is valued for its late summer bloom.

central New York, only to be killed outright by the severe winter of 1933–34. They have never permanently survived in the Arnold Arboretum although they have been tried many times. This is not a tree for the small garden!

Sophora japonica   75′   Zone 4   Japanese Pagoda Tree

*FLOWERS: white, pealike in large pyramidal upright clusters
    TIME: August
HABIT: rounded, wide branching
FOLIAGE: rather open, leaves compound, somewhat like those of the Locust
HABITAT: China, Korea
INTRODUCED: 1747
VARIETY: *pendula*—with pendulous branches, seldom flowering but frequently used as a formal specimen—Weeping Japanese Pagoda Tree
    This is a good shade tree with alternate compound leaves a dark green color. The common name comes from the fact that it is frequently used around Buddhist temples in the Orient. It is also considerably used there as a wide-spreading street tree, with several desirable qualities. It blossoms in late summer, with large pyramidal clusters of yellowish pealike flowers that are most conspicuous. A yellow dye is made from the flowers and buds merely by baking them in an oven until they turn brown and then boiling them in water. It is the last of the larger trees to bloom in the fall, and so is greatly desired as an ornamental. One excellent quality is its apparent ability to withstand city conditions, certainly a desirable trait. Old trees have much the same general rounded habit as the White Ash. The yellowish pods, following the flowers, frequently remain on the

tree all winter. A desirable large tree, it should be used considerably more than it is.

SORBUS

The mountain-ashes are excellent ornamental trees except for one serious drawback. In some parts of the country, especially the East, they are frequently seriously infested with borers near the base of the trunk, which materially weaken the trees and eventually may kill them. The old-fashioned method of probing for the borers with a wire is time-consuming but feasible. Protective paints may work, but what will probably prove to be the most practical method of controlling all such borers is an application of a 12 per cent spray of DDT to the trunks just prior to the time the borer insect eggs are known to hatch (April to June) and again about three weeks later. This seems to be proving effective not only on these, but locust, peach and apple borers as well, when applied at the proper time.

On small properties one or two trees frequently can be used, but the property holders should never plant them unless they are fully cognizant of the borer problem and will take steps to control it continuously. Once forgotten or omitted for a year or two, borers can get into the trunk and have sufficient time to destroy it completely. A large tree, grown and carefully cared for during a period of fifteen to twenty years is a beautiful thing and its quick loss due to short neglect is most disheartening. These things should be kept in mind when using the mountain-ash, especially in the East. On the Pacific coast, in Seattle and Portland, are many fine streets lined with mountain-ash, apparently unaffected from the ravages of the borer. Gardeners in this area are most fortunate!

Also, all *Sorbus* are susceptible to San Jose Scale and sometimes to sun scald of the trunk and larger branches. They seem to grow better in limestone soils than in strictly acid soils—a rather important observation.

Aside from this defect, the *Sorbus* group has good specimen trees to offer. The leaves of some are simple (*S. alnifolia*) but most are compound. The flowers are small, white and produced in large flat clusters like those of some viburnums or Queen Anne's Lace. The brilliant orange to red fruits (about ¼ inch in diameter) appear in large clusters about 3 to 5 inches in diameter and remain colorful for weeks.

The Korean Mountain-ash (*S. alnifolia*) appears to be least affected by borers, hence it would seem that this species might be widely used. The flowers are borne in great numbers, and I think it might be considered best in this respect. Then too, the leaves are simple and not compound, making for finer texture of the foliage, and the autumn color is a brilliant orange to scarlet. All in all, this unfortunately rare tree in America, has been overlooked during the past for the more easily obtained European Mountain-ash. When people once become acquainted with this species, I am sure it will gain favor rapidly.

Sorbus alnifolia   60'   Zone 5   Korean Mountain-ash

*FLOWERS: small, white, in flat clusters
   TIME: late May
'-FRUIT: scarlet to orange berries, ⅜" in diameter
   EFFECTIVE: fall
HABIT: rounded at maturity, pyramidal and upright while young, branching dense
FOLIAGE: bright green, dense, lustrous, leaves not compound
*AUTUMN COLOR: orange to scarlet
HABITAT: Japan, central China, Korea
INTRODUCED: 1892

   This is one of the most successful of the flowering trees introduced by the
Arnold Arboretum from Japan and it requires practically no attention. It makes
a truly beautiful specimen, dense and well rounded from top to bottom. Why it is
not better known and grown I do not know. It certainly is deserving, particularly
as a tree at its best during the autumn months when fruit and foliage coloration
are pronounced. A splendid tree that might easily be considered the best of the
mountain-ashes and the least susceptible to borer attack in our experience in
Boston. Well worth growing as a vigorous (eventually a rather large) specimen.

Sorbus aria   45'   Zone 5   White Beam Mountain-ash

FLOWERS: small, white, in flat clusters 2–3" in diameter
   TIME: late May
*FRUIT: scarlet red berries, ⅓–½" long, specked with brownish dots
   EFFECTIVE: fall
HABIT: rounded, rather open
FOLIAGE: leaves not compound, 2–4" long, handsome bright green above and
     covered with a white feltlike pubescence beneath
AUTUMN COLOR: reddish
HABITAT: Europe
INTRODUCED: before 1830?
VARIETY: *decaisneana*—the best variety, with larger leaves and fruits than any of
     the several others which have been named. Its leaves are sometimes 7
     inches long and 3 to 4 inches wide with fruits as much as ⅝ inch in
     diameter—Decaisne Mountain-ash

   A common tree in Europe and in England where it does very well on the
chalk cliffs and other limestone soils. The fruits are most colorful but are unfortunately quickly eaten by the birds as soon as they are ripe. A splendid ornamental, not seen much in gardens in this country but certainly worthy of being
grown more. It is especially desirable (but not in areas where much smoke or
soot is in the atmosphere) because of the white, pubescent under surface of the
leaves, giving the foliage a delightful contrasting color.

Sorbus aucuparia   45'   Zone 2   European Mountain-ash or
                                               Rowan Tree

*FLOWERS: small, white flowers in flat clusters 3–5" in diameter
   TIME: late May
*FRUIT: berries bright red, ¼" in diameter in large clusters
   EFFECTIVE: fall

HABIT: erect while young, spreading and gracefully open at maturity
FOLIAGE: compound leaves, rather open
*AUTUMN COLOR: reddish
HABITAT: Europe to western Asia
INTRODUCED: early colonial times
VARIETIES: *asplenifolia*—the leaflets doubly serrate, a graceful clon—Cutleaf European Mountain-ash
   edulis—fruit slightly larger than that of the species and used for preserves in Europe—often called the Moravian Rowan, native or Czechoslovakia.
   fastigiata—upright in habit of growth—Upright European Montain-ash
   pendula—with pendulous branches, not particularly graceful—Weeping European Mountain ash
   xanthocarpa—with yellow fruits
  By far the most popular of the mountain-ashes in North America, this has been grown and admired since colonial times and is even naturalized up in Alaska! Its conspicuous flowers, bright colored fruits and autumn color make it of considerable interest for several seasons of the year. Like most other members of the *Sorbus* group, it is very susceptible to borers, especially low down on the trunk. Unless the borer problem is not meticuously prevented, the Mountain-ash should not be grown in avenues or in large numbers where the elimination of a few trees might destroy the general effect (See discussion under *Sorbus*.)

Sorbus decora   30′   Zone 2   Showy Mountain-ash

FLOWERS: small, white, in flat clusters 2–4″ in diameter
  TIME: late May
*FRUIT: bright red berries, nearly ½″ in diameter, in clusters
  EFFECTIVE: early fall
HABIT: shrubby tree
FOLIAGE: compound leaves with usually about 15 leaflets
HABITAT: southeastern Canada and northeastern United States
  This tree has larger and more conspicuous fruits than its close relative, *S. americana*, hence is better for ornamental use.

Sorbus discolor   30′   Zone 5   Snowberry Mountain-ash

FLOWERS: small white flowers in flat clusters
  TIME: late May
*FRUIT: small white berries ⅜″ in diameter, in clusters
  EFFECTIVE: fall
HABIT: rounded, open
FOLIAGE: leaves compound, 11–17 leaflets rather open
*AUTUMN COLOR: red
HABITAT: northern China
INTRODUCED: 1883
  The plant growing in the Arnold Arboretum has white fruits but several descriptions of this species by reliable botanists seem to be confused as to the color, listing it variously as from yellow to pink. Of course, it may well be that it varies considerably in this respect.

Sorbus decora, one of the better species of Mountain-ash.

Sorbus folgneri   24'   Zone 5   Folgner Mountain-ash

FLOWERS: white, small, rather inconspicuous, in many-flowered clusters about 4"
      in diameter

   TIME: late May

*FRUIT: red berries, ½" long, in clusters

   EFFECTIVE: fall

HABIT: variable but usually with gracefully spreading branches

FOLIAGE: leaves single (not compound), 2–3" long, dark green above but woolly
      tomentose and white below

*AUTUMN COLOR: russet-red

HABITAT: central China

INTRODUCED: 1901

VARIETY: *pendula*—with pendulous branches, not particularly graceful—Weeping
      Folgner Mountain-ash

   This species can be considered even handsomer than S. *alnifolia,* although it
is a considerably smaller tree. The fruits are slightly egg shaped and its habit of
growth is very graceful. It is particularly interesting because of the white woolly
under surface of the leaves which adds an element of considerable interest
especially in the wind.

   It may well be that red spider and certain other insects damaging the under
surface of the leaves of Sorbus in general are held in considerable check by the
woolly surface of the leaves of this particular species.

Spathodea campanulata   70'   Zone 10   Bell Flambeau Tree

*FLOWERS: short terminal racemes of scarlet flowers 4" long, cup shaped

   TIME: winter

FRUIT: 8" long and 2" wide, dry capsules

   EFFECTIVE: winter

HABIT: erect

*FOLIAGE: evergreen in Florida but deciduous in parts of California, leaves com-
      pound, may be 2' long

HABITAT: tropical Africa

This is a most conspicuous tree in flower, a vigorous grower and seems to do best in fertile, well-drained soil but it will not survive the frosted areas.

Stenolobium stans   20′   Zone 10   Florida Yellow Trumpet

*FLOWERS: bright yellow, 2″ long, bell-like in large terminal clusters
    TIME: late fall
FRUIT: long narrow pod
HABIT: shrubby small tree
FOLIAGE: leaves compound
HABITAT: Florida and South America

This tree is planted considerably as an ornamental in the milder parts of Florida and California and has considerable merit for its fall-produced, conspicuously colored flowers.

Some Stewartias have larger flowers than others. Here are the flowers of four species:
upper left—S. koreana
upper right—S. ovata grandiflora
lower left—S. pseudo-camellia
lower right—S. monadelpha

Stewartia koreana   45′   Zone 5   Korean Stewartia

*FLOWERS: white, 3″ in diameter with yellow conspicuous stamens
    TIME: July
*HABIT: pyramidal, dense
FOLIAGE: dense
*AUTUMN COLOR: orange-red
*BARK: flaking, varicolored
HABITAT: Korea
INTRODUCED: 1917

Smaller growing than *S. pseudo-camellia* but with larger flowers and just as interesting winter bark, this Korean Stewartia is very difficult to find in gardens. The conspicuous, early summer flowers, make it a useful small tree for bloom when few trees are in flower. The striking bark, irregularly flaking off in pieces, the older darker bark on the outside of the trunk breaking off to disclose the inner, lighter colored bark beneath it, is somewhat similar to the bark of the Sycamore or *Pinus bungeana.*

It is unfortunate that this excellent specimen is extremely difficult to find in nursery catalogues for it has been flourishing in the Arnold Arboretum, where it is perfectly hardy, ever since 1917 when it was first introduced.

Stewartia pseudo-camellia   60′   Zone 5   Japanese Stewartia

*FLOWERS: white, 2½″ in diameter, cup shaped
    TIME: early July
HABIT: pyramidal
FOLIAGE: bright green
AUTUMN COLOR: purplish
*BARK: flaking bark on older branches and trunk
HABITAT: Japan
INTRODUCED: 1874

    The flower is very similar to that of a single Camellia to which all stewartias are closely related, hence the specific name of this species. The flaking bark is more colorful than that of the other stewartias, being red and peeling off in large flakes. It is difficult to discard any stewartia, for they bloom during several weeks in the summer at a time when few woody plants are in flower. However, this has the smallest flowers of any.

Styrax japonica   30′   Zone 5   Japanese Snowbell

*FLOWERS: white, about ¾″ in diameter, pendulous, bell shaped
    TIME: early June
HABIT: very wide-spreading branches, flat top, often twice as wide as high
FOLIAGE: fine texture
HABITAT: China, Japan
INTRODUCED: 1862

    This wide-spreading shrub or tree, rather dense, with graceful, small, waxy white, pendulous flowers in early June makes an excellent specimen because of its curving horizontal branches and good dark green leaves. The interesting thing about the bloom of this plant is that the flowers appear after the leaves are fully developed, but the leaves are firmly held on the upper side of the branches and the pendulous flowers are clearly evident on the underside of all the small twigs and branches so that their effect is not dimmed by the foliage at all.

Styrax obassia   30′   Zone 6   Fragrant Snowbell

*FLOWERS: fragrant, white, ¾″ in diameter, produced in terminal racemes 6–8″
    long
    TIME: early June
HABIT: ascending branches, dense
FOLIAGE: large, leaves 3–8″ long, coarse texture
HABITAT: Japan
INTRODUCED: 1879

Styrax japonica, the Japanese Snowbell.

It is unfortunate that the flowers of this handsome tree are partly hidden by the large leaves, but even with this slight defect the tree is an excellent ornamental in flower. I have never observed any autumn coloration of the foliage.

Symplocos paniculata   35'   Zone 5   Asiatic Sweetleaf

*FLOWERS: white, fragrant, small, in small clusters
   TIME: late May
*FRUIT: bright blue berry, ¼" in diameter
   EFFECTIVE: October
HABIT: shrubby, wide-spreading and dense branches
FOLIAGE: open
HABITAT: Himalaya to China and Japan
INTRODUCED: 1875

This tall, wide-spreading, dense shrub or small tree, is chiefly of merit for its bright, pale blue berries about ¼" in diameter, but they do not remain on the plant more than a week after they have reached the peak of their color. The small, white, profuse flowers are fragrant, but these too do not remain effective long. Because of these short periods of interest it is better to use other plants for growing in the limited space of the small garden. On large estates or in parks, where space is available for unique plants, this might be a good selection.

Syringa amurensis japonica   30'   Zone 4   Japanese Tree Lilac

*FLOWERS: small, creamy white, in large pyramidal heads sometimes 6" high
   TIME: mid-June
HABIT: pyramidal, rather open
FOLIAGE: leaves larger than those of the common lilac, almost coarse

*BARK: trunk and older branches with cherrylike bark
HABITAT: Japan
INTRODUCED: 1876

This Japanese lilac is a tree that can be grown with a single trunk and it is of special value because of the late bloom of the flowers. The shiny cherrylike bark is interesting in the winter, the large leaves and conspicuously vigorous habit is striking in the spring and summer, and the large, creamy white, pyramidal flower clusters make it an outstanding plant, either as a specimen or in a group as screen or windbreak. The variety differs from the species in being more treelike in habit, taller and slightly later to flower. It is susceptible to borers and scale infestations which must be kept in check if it is to be a well grown plant. For this reason it should not be used as a street tree where annual maintenance and close surveillance are necessities. This is the only native Japanese tree which F. L. Skinner can grow in the severe climate of Dropmore, Manitoba, Canada.

This excellent pendulous specimen of the Bald Cypress could be grown more than it is.

Taxodium distichum 150' Zone 4 Common Bald Cypress

HABIT: narrowly pyramidal while young, broadly rounded at maturity
FOLIAGE: deciduous, needlelike, very open
HABITAT: southeastern and south central United States

This beautiful tree, hardy as far north as Boston where there is a specimen 80 feet tall in perfect condition, has foliage somewhat like that of hemlock but is deciduous. The foliage appears late in the season—in fact it is the last tree to send out its leaves in the Arnold Arboretum in Boston. In nature it is found in swampy areas, and of course is famed for its "knees" on large woody growths coming up from the roots, sometimes as much as 6 feet tall. Its wood is highly valued for its great water-resisting properties, for it will not rot, even when standing in water for long periods of time. Because of its light, feathery foliage, it cannot be considered a good shade tree, and because of its great height it is not a good tree for the small property. In parks or large estates, it makes a distinctive specimen.

TAXUS

The yews are the darkest green of all evergreen shrubs and trees and, without question, the most striking. They flourish in many kinds of soils and withstand clipping and pruning, thus making perfect hedges and screens as well as excellent specimens. Their bright red, fleshy fruits are conspicuous during the fall. It is fortunate that they are represented by a large number of varieties ranging in size and shape so that they can be used for a number of garden purposes.

The yew has been known and valued for centuries, records having shown that pieces of wood of the English Yew, *Taxus baccata,* have been found under glacial deposits in England.

Two principal species provide the ornamental varieties for American gardens, namely, *T. cuspidata,* the Japanese Yew, and *T. baccata,* the so-called English Yew. There are yews in England which must be a thousand years old, their trunk circumferences being at least 30 feet. Robin Hood and his Merry Men used stout cudgels made from yew, as were their long bows and cross bows. Even before this, spears were made from this sturdy wood, for a spear is known to have been dug from underneath a peat-deposit bog in England and is estimated to have been over three thousand years old.

These excellent evergreens are rather slow in growth when compared with deciduous trees, with wood that is hard and close grained. The yews resemble each other so much that a few botanists have suggested in the past that there is only one species. *T. baccata,* and that all other yews are merely geographical varieties of this.

Poisonous properties of the yews have been recorded. Caesar writes that Cativolcus, King of Eburones, poisoned himself by drinking the juice of the yew. The toxic material is probably an alkaloid named taxine, a heart depressant, present in the leaves, and to a lesser extent in the twigs and bark. Although many cases of cattle poisoning have been reported where cattle eat the foliage, there are instances where the branches have been lopped off in the pasture with no ill effects. Illness and death among western cattle have frequently been attributed to their eating large quantities of the foliage and twigs of *T. brevifolia.* While the seed or stone in the fruit is poisonous, the fleshy pulp of the fruit, the only part of the plant that might be eaten by humans, is not poisonous.

Many a yew has failed to produce the decorative, colorful fruits and therefore caused disappointment. This is because the sexes are separate, the staminate flowers on one plant, the pistillate flowers on another. Both are necessary to insure fruiting. One staminate plant is sufficient for every six or eight pistillate or fruiting plants. If a specimen-fruiting plant is desired, it can be placed in the spot with the staminate plant nearby in an inconspicuous or partly hidden location. If a group of fruiting plants is desired, the staminate plant may be hidden in the center of the group and kept fairly inconspicuous by clipping.

Of course the female plant can be identified in fruit, but the sexes can be distinguished one from the other at other times of the year as well—in fact, a greater part of the growing season. The flowers are open for a very short time only in the early spring when the identification of the sexes is easy. However, the staminate flower buds of the yew are rounded and hanging from the underside of the terminal year's growth. The pistillate flower buds are smaller, not nearly as obvious, and very definitely pointed. These differences are marked and easily noted a greater part of the growing season. With little practice one can be proficient at telling these apart.

There are approximately forty species and varieties of yews being grown in the United States, although not all are available from nurseries. Of the seven species grown, the Chinese Yew, *T. chinensis,* and the Pacific Yew, *T. brevifolia,* are little seen in cultivation and are not here recommended.

The English Yew is the least hardy. Although certain varieties—with some winter protection—can be safely grown as far north as Boston, yet *T. baccata* is not dependably hardy north of New York. Since it has been carefully grown for hundreds of years, it is only natural to expect that a number of forms have originated and have been propagated. The Japanese species has been grown extensively outside Japan for less than half a century and consequently comparatively few varieties of it are to be found in commercial nurseries in this country up to this time.

In the Old World the English Yew is widely distributed from England to North Africa and western Asia. It grows as a tree, from 30 to 60 feet high, with needles usually two-ranked and blunt at the end. Over thirty varieties have been named but some are difficult to obtain in this country and several are closely similar. The yews are all comparatively slow growing, but particularly well adapted for hedges and topiary work. In England topiary work has been a hobby with gardeners for centuries and many splendid examples of painstaking pruning are to be seen about the countryside there.

In all probability, the most famous variety of the English Yew is *T. baccata stricta,* popularly called the Irish Yew. Two pistillate trees were found on a farm in Ireland about 1780, differing from the ordinary English Yew in having several leaders all densely upright in habit of growth. Even the needles on the twigs were arranged differently from the English Yew, distributed around all sides of the twig rather than being two-ranked in a flat spray. It is from cuttings of these two trees that the Irish Yew has been propagated. It is highly valued for its upright habit of growth and is excellent for formal planting.

Another popular variety is the Westfelton Yew, *T. baccata dovastoni,* a tree with erect trunk and horizontal branches, with branchlets pendulous. This plant makes an excellent specimen. It was first raised in Shrewsbury, England, in 1777. It has long been a popular form and it may be of interest to know that there is a form with yellow foliage.

Not all varieties of the English Yew are trees. For instance, the variety *adpressa* is a wide-spreading low shrub with needles only half as long as those of the species. Fortunately, this variety is a fruiting form. The Spreading English Yew, *T. baccata repandens*, is a low, almost prostrate form, grown considerably in northern United States where it is apparently more hardy than any other variety of English Yew. If clipped and restrained, it may grow three feet or so in height, with the young branchlets decidedly pendulous. If allowed to grow unrestrained, it becomes very prostrate in habit and literally creeps along the ground.

The Japanese Yew, *T. cuspidata*, was first introduced into this country in 1861, by Dr. George R. Hall, a doctor who practiced medicine in the foreign settlement of Shanghai for a number of years. Later he became interested in collecting plants in both China and Japan, and in sending them back to the United States. This plant has shown its good qualities time and time again and now is being grown by the majority of American nurseries. It has proved itself hardy under trying winter conditions; although not foolproof, it can be grown where many other evergreens cannot. The nomenclature of the varieties of this plant is still greatly confused.

In Bailey's "Cyclopedia" published in 1917, and in numerous other articles written before and since that time, it has been pointed out that *T. cuspidata* is a tree. Hence, the variety erroneously listed in many nursery catalogues as *T. cuspidata capitata* actually is *T. cuspidata*. However, this misunderstanding of names has probably been augmented by the fact that there is a variety of *T. cuspidata* which has spreading upright branches, forming a low center, and in cross section looks broadly V-shaped. Practically every nursery has it and practically every nursery calls this *T. cuspidata*. To alleviate confusion, this form has been named *T. cuspidata expansa*. It is readily known that when seed of *T. cuspidata* is sown, many interesting seedlings will appear, varying considerably in shape and height, and a certain proportion of them will have this desirable spreading upright shape.

Fortunately, these dignified evergreens are comparatively free of serious pests. Occasionally an old plant may be attacked by the strawberry root weevil and the needles will begin to drop. This may frequently be controlled by the use of poison baits for the beetles, and pyrethrum sprays on the ground for the grubs that do the damage. D.D.T. is also proving practicable in the control of this pest.

For specimens, for hedges, for backgrounds, for any one of many uses, the yews are excellently well suited and because of their large number and variety of shapes and sizes, it is not exaggeration to say that there is a yew for every garden where evergreens can be grown.

Taxus baccata   60'   Zone 6   English Yew

*FRUIT: fleshy, single-seeded, red berry (sexes separate)
    EFFECTIVE: fall
HABIT: pyramidal, dense branching
*FOLIAGE: evergreen, lustrous, dark green, needlelike
HABITAT: Europe, northern Africa, western Asia
INTRODUCED: early colonial times
VARIETIES: *dovastoni*—upright in habit with horizontal branches and dark green
        foliage—Westfelton Yew
        elegantissima—vigorous wide-spreading bush with main branches
        mostly horizontal with young foliage striped yellow—Elegant Eng-
        lish Yew
        erecta—upright in habit but much wider in growth than Irish Yew—
        Broom Yew
        stricta—rigidly columnar and upright in habit, one of the most pic-
        turesque of all varieties—Irish Yew

Over thirty varieties of the English Yew have been listed and the above are
perhaps the most prominent.

One of the oldest English Yews in America, over 200 years old, in Williamsburg, Virginia. George Washington is supposed to have proposed to Martha Custis under the branches of this tree.

Taxus cuspidata   50'   Zone 4   Japanese Yew

*FRUIT: red, fleshy berries
    EFFECTIVE: fall
HABIT: pyramidal, dense branching
*FOLIAGE: evergreen, needlelike, dark
HABITAT: Japan and Korea
INTRODUCED: 1855

The Japanese Yew is one of the best narrow-leaved evergreens for ornamental purposes. Many varieties are being grown in this country chiefly as shrubs. (See discussion under *Taxus* concerning the popular commercial variety often termed *T. cuspidata capitata.*)

x Taxus media   40′   Zone 4   Intermediate Yew

*FRUIT: fleshy, one-seeded, red berry
    EFFECTIVE: fall
HABIT: broadly columnar to narrowly pyramidal, dense branching
FOLIAGE: evergreen, needlelike
HYBRID: *T. cuspidata x T. baccata*
INTRODUCED: about 1900

About 1900 a new species of yew originated as a result of a cross between the English and Japanese Yews. Mr. T. D. Hatfield, Superintendent of the famous Hunnewell Estate in Wellesley, Massachusetts, had grown a number of seedlings which were given the specific name of *T. media*. This hybrid is broadly pyramidal, frequently has a central leader and grows into tree form. The hardy qualities of the Japanese Yew and the ornamental qualities of the English Yew are merged in this plant to give an excellent ornamental evergreen.

THUJA

The arbor-vitaes as a group are evergreen trees with flat scalelike leaves, two of the species, at least, being quite variable with many different varieties, mostly shrubby. The four species here recommended are trees, and grow in more or less dense pyramids of foliage, at least while they are young. The American Arbor-vitae and its forms seem to require considerable atmospheric moisture, or they will not do well at all. The same is true of the Oriental Arbor-vitae. The other two seem to grow better where there is less moisture in the atmosphere, but even these cannot be depended upon in dry situations.

There are some forms of these arbor-vitaes with colored foliage, but these are not at all satisfactory in the winter for their leaves frequently turn a sickly yellowish or brownish color. The same is true even of *Thuja occidentalis* itself under certain conditions. The other three species maintain their foliage in rather good condition throughout the winter, reason enough why they are valued as evergreens.

It should be emphasized here, again, that all evergreens drop some of their leaves every year, usually in the fall, and arbor-vitaes are no exception. There is no cause for alarm when dead leaves are observed on these plants in the fall of the year when the leaves of all deciduous plants are colorful. Browning of the foliage may, however, develop at other times of year, and when this happens the cause should be quickly determined. As a group they are sometimes infested heavily with red spider, but this can be controlled if caught before it does too much damage.

As a group then, and as trees, these plants are to be considered as slow-

Arborvitae, where it grows well it will make an excellent hedge or screen.
This is on the famous Hunnewell Estate in Wellesley, Massachusetts.

growing evergreens, rather stiff in habit, with foliage not nearly as soft in texture as that of the pines and hemlocks. As trees they are used primarily as stiff accent points in the landscape.

Thuja occidentalis   60′   Zone 2   American Arbor-vitae

HABIT: almost columnar
*FOLIAGE: evergreen, scalelike, flat
HABITAT: eastern North America

VARIETIES: *douglasi pyramidalis*—dense, broadly columnar—Douglas Arbor-vitae

fastigiata—more narrow and columnar than other varieties, with very short lateral branches

This native species has many slow growing forms that are mostly shrublike in character. They are often used in foundation plantings and seem to do best in areas with considerable atmospheric moisture. In nature these trees are always found in moist woods, often near or beside water. The species and most of the varieties have the undesirable trait of turning brownish in the winter, sometimes markedly so, hence it fails to give a display of good green foliage when it is needed most. This is especially true of those forms with colored foliage—the reason why none are recommended here.

Thuja orientalis   **50′**   **Zone 6**   Oriental Arbor-vitae

*HABIT: pyramidal, open
*FOLIAGE: evergreen lustrous, scalelike, usually arranged in planes, the edges of which face the outside of the plant
HABITAT: northern China, Korea
INTRODUCED: before 1737
VARIETIES: *bakeri*—foliage bright green, seems to withstand hot, dry locations—Baker Oriental Arbor-vitae

"Bonita"—cone shaped, leaves tipped yellow

flagelliformis—branches drooping and threadlike—Weeping Oriental Arbor-vitae

meldensis—narrow pyramidal form, irregular in habit—Melden Oriental Arbor-vitae

stricta—dense, pyramidal habit—Pyramidal Oriental Arbor-vitae

texana glauca—pyramidal, blue-green foliage—Texas Blue Arbor-vitae

This is a very popular evergreen with many garden varieties which vary in habit and color of foliage. The species is a graceful and symmetrical tree, easily distinguished from other *Thuja* species because its fruits or cones have characteristic hooks on them. In China, at New Year's celebrations, sprays of this fragrant evergreen are used to symbolize long life and happiness. One of the more commonly used evergreens throughout the South, this has many shrub forms.

Thuja plicata   **180′**   **Zone 5**   Giant Arbor-vitae

*HABIT: pyramidal, narrow
*FOLIAGE: evergreen, scalelike, lustrous
AUTUMN COLOR: bronze
HABITAT: Alaska to northern California and Montana
VARIETIES: *atrovirens*—foliage very dark green

fastigiata—columnar in habit—Columnar Giant Arbor-vitae

This arbor-vitae is the best native for the colder parts of the country because its foliage does not turn brown in the winter as does the foliage of most of the *T. occidentalis* varieties. Commercial growers in the northeastern United States have learned that it is necessary to use seed collected from plants high in the mountains of Montana and Utah, for plants grown from seed collected on the Pacific coast have not proved hardy in the East. The Giant Arbor-vitae is a splendid tree, large or small, and can be kept restrained at almost any height by proper clipping.

Thuja standishi   40′   Zone 5   Japanese Arbor-vitae

*HABIT: spreading branches, broadly pyramidal
*FOLIAGE: evergreen, scalelike
HABITAT: Japan
INTRODUCED: 1860

This handsome tree is considerably more spreading in habit than the arbor-vitaes native to America and hence of value for this characteristic. The foliage does not turn brown in the winter as does that of *T. occidentalis*. However, the winter foliage of *T. plicata* is superior, at least in New England.

Thujopsis dolabrata   45′   Zone 6   Hiba False Arbor-vitae

HABIT: pyramidal
*FOLIAGE: evergreen, somewhat similar to that of Arbor-vitae, lustrous, dense
HABITAT: Japan
INTRODUCED: 1861

The Hiba False Arbor-vitae is somewhat similar to the arbor-vitae and develops into a beautiful, dense tree when grown in good soil with plenty of moisture. It is of no particular merit in preference to the arbor-vitaes.

TILIA

The lindens are among the best of our shade trees, especially the exotic species. They are widely used for ornament as specimens and especially are they valued as street trees. The seven that are most commonly used can be differentiated one from the other in the following ways:

1.* Leaves large (3–6″ long) and coarse, tree of open habit........*T. americana*
2. Leaves silvery pubescent beneath, very distinct
   3. petioles shorter than half the leaf blade...................*T. tomentosa*
   3. petioles longer than half the leaf blades...................*T. petiolaris*
4. Leaves 2–5″ long, tree of dense habit
   5. Brown hairs in axils of veins on undersurface of the leaves....*T. cordata*
   5. Leaves shiny above.......................................*T. euchlora*
   5. Leaves slightly hairy on both sides........................*T. euchlora*
   5. Leaves very thin in texture, much more so than any of
     the others...*T. europaea vulgaris*

These lindens are the street trees of the Northern Hemispheres, highly valued in Europe as well as America. Some of the species are better than others for this purpose, but all have been used. Lindens have slightly heart-shaped leaves that are unequally developed at the base. They have small pendulous flowers in early summer, that are not especially ornamental

* Read down. If the specimen does not meet the first characteristic try the next in sequence, and so on to the end. This is merely a suggestive key of some merit, but only for the amateur. For positive identification see some precise botanical key in an accepted botanical text.

but are deliciously fragrant. The round, hard fruit, borne on a unique leafy bract remains on the tree until winter, and the seeds often take two years to germinate.

It has been our experience here in the Arnold Arboretum where different lindens have been growing side by side for half a century that the European species are the more vigorous and handsome trees. The American lindens have coarse leaves and do not have a good color late in the season, but turn brownish. The Asiatic lindens are not much better. The European lindens, on the other hand, keep their good color and occasionally the leaves even turn yellow before they fall.

As street trees they are superb, but they must be sprayed occasionally since leaf-eating insects feed voraciously on their foliage. As specimens, there are few trees superior to the Silver Linden or the gracefully beautiful Pendant Silver Linden. All lindens should be known to those responsible for selecting trees for planting, since they are such highly valued and serviceable foliage trees.

| **Tilia cordata** | 90′ | Zone 3 | Little-leaf Linden |

FLOWERS: small yellowish to whitish, rather inconspicuous but unusually fragrant
    TIME: early July
*HABIT: densely pyramidal
*FOLIAGE: dense, compact, giving perfect shade, leaves 1½–3″ long
HABITAT: Europe
INTRODUCED: probably early colonial times

Usually a slow-growing small tree, considerably under the mature height at which it is sometimes seen in Europe. It is the last of the lindens to flower, with heart-shaped leaves often broader than they are long, very dark green above and pale beneath. Because of its dense habit and tightly pyramidal form it makes an excellent shade and street tree. The foliage is of finer texture than the much larger leaved native, *Tilia americana,* and so it is valued. However, if a fast-growing street tree is desired, one of the other lindens might best be used. This, like some of the other lindens, has grown unusually well under adverse city conditions, making it one of the best street trees for urban conditions. Also, this species is growing as far north as Dropmore, Manitoba, Canada, demonstrating its ability to withstand low temperatures very well and making this the hardiest of those lindens here recommended.

| **x Tilia euchlora** | 60′ | Zone 5 | Crimean Linden |

FLOWERS: small, yellowish, rather inconspicuous but very fragrant
    TIME: early July
*HABIT: graceful, somewhat pendulous branches
*FOLIAGE: dense, leaves 2–4″ long, bright green and glossy
HYBRID ORIGIN: *T. cordata x T. dasystyla?*

One of the best of the lindens, it should be used more than it is. A graceful tree with glossy, bright green foliage and fairly vigorous growth, it has many good points for use as a shade tree.

x Tilia europaea   120′   Zone 3   European Linden

FLOWERS: small, yellowish, rather inconspicuous but very fragrant
    TIME: early July
*HABIT: rounded, dense
*FOLIAGE: leaves 2½–4″ long, dense
HYBRID ORIGIN: *T. cordata* x *T. platyphyllos*
INTRODUCED: probably in colonial times

    Ernest H. Wilson used to say that this common hybrid was better than either parent and the best of the lindens for shade on city streets. I agree that it is better than the Large Leaved Linden, but the Littleleaf Linden (*T. cordata*) certainly has some qualities not found in *T. europaea*. It used to be termed *T. vulgaris*, a name still used in many places. It is reproduced largely by "stooling" or suckers and has the unfortunate habit of sprouting readily from the base of the trunk. These suckers must be removed, for if they are not, they soon completely hide the trunk! It is also very susceptible to attacks of plant lice, which mar the foliage. I believe that Wilson's estimate of it was made before other lindens had a sufficient opportunity to prove their qualities in this country. It would seem that others might be considered first before this one is finally selected for planting.

Tilia petiolaris   75′   Zone 5   Pendent Silver Linden

FLOWERS: small and yellowish, rather inconspicuous but very fragrant
    TIME: mid-July
*HABIT: drooping branches forming a narrow head
*FOLIAGE: silvery white underneath, on long petioles, fluttering about in the
    smallest breeze, leaves about 2–4½″ long
HABITAT: probably southeastern Europe
INTRODUCED: 1840

    Closely related to the Silver Linden (*T. tomentosa*) but considered more exquisite because of its pendent branches. It is too bad this beautiful specimen tree is not grown more in America. Its very distinct weeping habit and lovely leaves that are white, downy underneath, make it the most beautiful and graceful of all the lindens for specimen use. Bees seem to find the flowers either narcotic or actually poisonous, as they can be found in large numbers on the ground under such trees. Also, because of the dense pubescence on the under surface of the leaves, this tree should not be grown in urban areas where there is a large amount of smoke, for soot and dust collect on these leaves and make them rather unsightly. But in the open, away from sooty areas, this is without question the most beautiful of the lindens particularly adapted for use as a specimen shade tree.

Tilia platyphyllos   120′   Zone 3   Big-leaf Linden

FLOWERS: small and yellowish, rather inconspicuous but very fragrant
    TIME: early July
*HABIT: rounded to pyramidal in outline
*FOLIAGE: leaves 2–5″ long and as wide, dense, somewhat coarse in texture
HABITAT: Europe
INTRODUCED: colonial times
VARIETY: *fastigiata*—narrow and columnar in habit—Columnar Big-leaf Linden

The Silver Linden, Tilia tomentosa, is valued for the silvery white under-surface of its foliage. The sweet scented flowers of all lindens appear in early summer.

Possibly not as commonly grown in this country and Europe as *T. europaea,* the Common Linden, it is still a shapely tree and does not produce the swollen burls on which sprout so many shoots, as does the Common Linden. The leaves are the largest of any of these recommended European Lindens, making it somewhat coarse in texture.

Tilia tomentosa   90′   Zone 4   Silver Linden

FLOWERS: small and yellowish, rather inconspicuous but very fragrant
    TIME: mid-July
*HABIT: broad, compact, pyramidal, dense
*FOLIAGE: leaves green above, white and pubescent below, about 2–4″ long
HABITAT: southeastern Europe to western Asia
INTRODUCED: colonial times
    Another beautiful specimen tree with erect branches, lacking the pendulous habit of *T. petiolaris* but nevertheless a beautiful tree in its own right. Its very definite outline makes it appear as if it has been clipped, and its beautiful leaves which are white underneath, are always of interest. Here again, however, these leaves being covered with pubescence underneath do collect particles from the air so that the trees should not be grown where there are large amounts of dust and soot. When the leaves are blown in the wind and the under surfaces are clearly seen, this tree is beautiful indeed. It has been reported that the flowers of this tree also are in some way injurious to bees.

Torreya nucifera   75'   Zone 5   Japanese Torreya

FRUIT: a plumlike ovoid, 1" long, greenish, ripening the second season, and the
     seed is edible
*HABIT: pyramidal, often ovoid head with spreading branches
*FOLIAGE: yewlike
HABITAT: Japan
INTRODUCED: about 1860

Very similar to yews in habit and leaf, the Japanese Torreya is frequently
confused with them. This is the hardiest of the three species. *Torreya californica*,
the California-nutmeg, might be used where native in California, and *T. taxifolia*
(the Stinking Cedar because the foliage has a disagreeable odor when crushed)
used in Florida where it is native. These Torreyas are found very infrequently
in gardens, but they may have merit where hardy, especially *T. nucifera*, since it
grows farther north than the others in areas where evergreens are most desirable
winter plants.

TSUGA

The hemlocks can easily be considered the most graceful and beautiful
of narrow leaved evergreen trees but they will grow only in areas where
water is abundant a greater part of the year. Native on both sides of the
continent, the species of the Pacific coast (*T. mertensiana* and *T. heterophylla*) do not grow well in the East. The Canada Hemlock, native in the
eastern and northeastern United States, is the most diversified species, with
many variants showing differences in foliage, habit and method of growth.
The Carolina Hemlock makes just as good an ornamental, perhaps doing
slightly better than its northern relative in the cities, and the dense, dark
green Japanese Hemlock should be grown a great deal more than it is.
All have profuse small and pendulous cones, but these are not always produced every year.

All are easy to transplant, provided, of course, they are planted in good
soil; all withstand and even thrive under stiff shearing. Hemlocks do not
grow well in the city. The leaves of the Canada Hemlock remain on the
tree three or four years; those of the Carolina Hemlock a year longer. In
view of the excellent ornamental qualities of the Japanese Hemlock (*Tsuga
diversifolia*), it should be noted that needles appear sometimes on eight- to
ten-year-old wood. This is why their foliage appears so dense. Although
all species withstand shade, they grow best in the full sunlight. Mr. Charles
F. Jenkins in Germantown, Philadelphia, has made a hobby of collecting
hemlocks and now has about fifty different species and varieties growing
in his "Hemlock Arboretum."

Foliage Key to the Hemlocks

(Native or Available in North America)

Needles borne singly, leaf bases persistent....................*Picea* and *Tsuga*
   1. Needles narrowed at base to form distinct petioles...........*Tsuga* species
      This character must be clearly interpreted. Sometimes when the needle of a

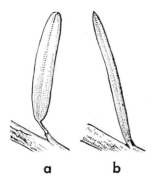

Figure 11. Needle of hemlock (a) with petiole and
spruce (b) without petiole.

a   b

spruce is pulled off, a small portion of the twig bark also comes off, looking
like a petiole unless observed with a lens. The needles of all spruces are
without petioles, their leaf-blades being attached directly to the twig.

    2. Needles with white lines on under surface only, cones less than 2
       inches long.
        3. Needles noticeably blunt and notched at tip.
            4. One-year branchlets pubescent..............*T. diversifolia*
                                      (Japanese Hemlock)
          (Japan) Zone 5
            4. One-year branchlets glabrous.................*T. sieboldi*
                                        (Siebold Hemlock)
          (Japan) Zone 5
        3. Needles not noticeably notched at end but rounded
            4. Many of the needles on vigorous one-year shoot wider at
               base than at the tip; i.e., gradually tapering from base to
               tip; needles mostly two ranked, in one plane, and with a
               very fine serrulate margin (when examined with a lens);
               cones ¾" or less in length. *T. canadensis* (Canada Hemlock)
                  (Nova Scotia and eastern United States) Zone 4
            4. Majority of needles on vigorous one-year shoots not tapering
               but about as wide at base as at tip; needles in several planes
               about twig; needle margin of *T. caroliniana* entire and *T.*
               heterophylla is serrulate (when examined with a lens).
               Cones longer than ¾"

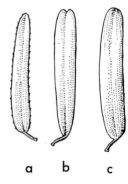

Figure 12. a. Tsuga canadensis. The very fine serrulate mar-
                gin can only be seen with a lens.
        b. Tsuga sieboldi
        c. Tsuga caroliniana

a   b   c

          5. One-year twigs orange-brown, cones 1–1½″ long
              (Southeastern United States Zone 4..*T. caroliniana*
                             (Carolina Hemlock)
          5. One-year twigs pale yellowish brown; cones ¾–1″ long
                    T. heterophylla (Western Hemlock)
              (Alaska to Idaho and California) Zone 6
     2. Needles with white lines on upper and lower surfaces, cones 2″ or
        more in length.................*T. mertensiana* (Mountain Hemlock)
        (Alaska to Idaho and California) Zone 5

Tsuga canadensis   **90′**   **Zone 3**   **Canada Hemlock**

HABIT: long, slender, horizontal to sometimes drooping branches forming a
    pyramidal head
FOLIAGE: evergreen, needlelike, dense
HABITAT: northeastern North America
VARIETIES: *atrovirens*—leaves very dark green
        gracilis—slow growing, tips of branchlets slightly pendulous
        microphylla—leaves very small, ¼″ long or less
        pendula—probably the most popular form at this time because it has
           been available for nearly seventy-five years. This is a particularly
           graceful plant, two or three times as broad as it is tall, round and
           moundlike in habit of growth with slightly pendulous branches.
           Four plants were originally found in the woods near Beacon, New
           York, before 1870 and were named after Mr. Henry W. Sargent,
           the neighbor of General Joseph Howland who originally found
           them. At least two of these specimens are alive today, the one
           given to C. S. Sargent of Brookline is not over 10 feet tall but is
           several times that in width.—Sargent Hemlock

    Many other varieties are named and available, but since it takes years and
years of growth in order that the respective merits of the clons will be evaluated,
this will not be attempted here but left to the Hemlock Arboretum of Philadelphia
where so many of these forms are growing side by side. The Canada Hemlock
is without question one of our best ornamental evergreens either as a specimen
or grouped as a serviceable screen or background. It should always be one of the
first evergreen trees to consider for planting within its hardiness limitations.

    Charles Sprague Sargent, who knew all the trees of North America thor-
oughly, used to say that no other conifer surpassed the hemlocks in grace and
beauty. This is true fifty years later, although many exotic trees have been introduced in the meantime. Particularly is this true of *T. canadensis* and *T. caroliniana*. There is little to choose between them.

    The Canada Hemlock grows over a wide area of the northeastern United
States, while the Carolina Hemlock is confined to comparatively small area of
the mountains of southwestern Virginia and Georgia but at the same time being
perfectly hardy over the same range as *T. canadensis*. The foliage of the Canada
Hemlock tends to be flatter than that of its southern relative.

    The Indians made a paste from the bark by first boiling and then pounding
it, using this for poultices with antiseptic properties. It is definitely not poisonous.
(The poisonous "hemlock" of ancient times, a potion of which was drunk by

Canada Hemlock makes one of the best evergreen hedges. This one is in the
National Cemetery at Arlington, Virginia.

Socrates, was a species of herb (*Conium*) somewhat similar and related to our
common Wild Carrot.)

At least nine trees have been reported in the Philadelphia area that are estimated to have been alive when William Penn first came up the Delaware River
over two hundred fifty years ago. An old stump was reported in New York State
a few years ago which had eight hundred annual growth rings, but no trees of
this great age are known to be alive today.

Because of its wide habitat, over fifty variants of this species have been
noted and described. Some vary only slightly from others, but they vary in habit,
size and foliage. Not all are readily available in the trade by any means, but at
least eighteen of them are. They range in height from one dwarf variety
(*minuta*), which only grows about ½ inch a year (a twenty-year-old plant being
only 6 inches tall), to the standard trees of the forest.

A graceful tree in its own right, the Canada Hemlock can be maintained at
only three to four feet indefinitely by judicial pruning. Pruning or clipping in this
way, it makes one of the best possible hedges. The advantages of using either the
Canada or the Carolina Hemlock in the hedges are that these plants can be
pruned in a stiffly rigid shape if desired, or the hedge can be allowed to grow
in a delightfully informal fashion. This is done by clipping in a general mounded
form, and the long graceful shoots allowed to grow for a year, or even two, without additional clipping. Then they must be pruned back hard in the early spring
or the plant soon grows out of shape. Thus the planting serves the dual purpose
of formal hedge one year and informal hedge the next. It may be of interest to
note that some fifty variants have been generally grouped into the following

classes by John C. Swartley, in a very intensive study he made of these in graduate work at Cornell University about 1938.

Broadleaf	Largeleaf	Sparseleaf
Bushy globe	Littleleaf	Spreading
Cinnamon	Prostrate	Twiggy
Dense	Pygmy	Weeping
Fastigiate	Pyramidal	Whitetip
Globe	Dwarf Pyramidal	Yewlike
Golden	Slender	

These groups might still be further reduced by the home owner who is interested in only a few of the most striking forms to: upright, dense slow-growers; dwarf; weeping; leaf variants (form) and leaf variants (color). Mr. Charles F. Jenkins, owner of the Hemlock Arboretum of Mount Airy, Philadelphia, has done a great deal to promote interest in hemlocks in general and in the variants of the Canada Hemlock in particular. He has collected about fifty different kinds of hemlocks and is growing them about his home on the Wissahickon Creek. Because of his interest and meticulous collecting, many forms are growing now that might otherwise have been lost.

Tsuga caroliniana   75′   Zone 4   Carolina Hemlock

*HABIT: compact, pyramidal tree, often somewhat pendulous branches
*FOLIAGE: evergreen, needlelike, dense
HABITAT: mountains of southwestern Virginia to Georgia

This Carolina Hemlock can also be considered one of the best all-purpose evergreen trees. It grows naturally into a standard tree, yet it can be sheared and clipped and forced to grow in any shape. Everything said above in favor of the Canada Hemlock applies to this Carolina Hemlock as well. (See under *T. canadensis*.) The needles are slightly whorled about the twigs, one of the reasons enabling the tree apparently to withstand the smoke and dust in city gardens better than does its northern relative, *T. canadensis*. It can be used to make splendid hedges. A very dense, compact, pyramidal form was found recently growing in the Arnold Arboretum and has been named "Arnold Pyramid."

Tsuga diversifolia   90′   Zone 5   Japanese Hemlock

*HABIT: horizontal branches, pyramidal
*FOLIAGE: evergreen, needlelike, very dense
HABITAT: Japan
INTRODUCED: 1861

Like most hemlocks, this tree also has a pyramidal outline. It usually grows with several trunks, sometimes almost as a shrub, and because it is rather slow-growing, it makes a neater, smaller tree than some of the other hemlocks. It is the first of the hemlocks to produce new leaves in the spring, and is apparently the only one producing (or holding) needles on eight- to ten-year-old twigs.

Tsuga heterophylla   200′   Zone 6   Western Hemlock

*HABIT: short pendulous branches making a narrow pyramidal head
*FOLIAGE: evergreen, needlelike
HABITAT: northwest Pacific coast

A humid climate and moist soil are needed for this tree. In these conditions it grows rapidly. It does not do at all well in the eastern United States, probably because the atmosphere is not sufficiently moist. It seems to do best on the western slopes off the Cascade Mountains at altitudes between 1500 and 3500 feet and has the ability of growing very well in shaded situations. This very stately tree is the tallest of some eight species of hemlocks.

ULMUS

With six elm species native in the United States, five species native in Europe (and many varieties), and several more species native in Asia, the identification of these shade trees is rather difficult. The elm is, and always has been, a standard shade tree in America and even though it is threatened with partial or complete destruction by various diseases, it is doubtful whether the gardening public will stop planting them.

The American Elm is the most prized of all, growing naturally over the eastern half of North America. Many are the stately specimens recorded in history, and the largest one alive today (on record of the American Forestry Association) stands 99 feet high with a trunk circumference of 28 feet, 7 inches and a branch spread of 140 feet. All the elms are shade trees, some taller than others. None of them has flowers or fruits of ornamental significance, and most of them have leaves that turn yellow in the fall. The Chinese Elm (*U. parvifolia*) is one exception since certain clons of this species have leaves turning a glossy red color in the fall. As a result of these characteristics, they are considered only for their habit of growth and foliage.

Unfortunately, over the period of time they have increased in popularity in this country, disease and insect infestations have plagued them. Although many an arborist will not admit it, these trees require more spraying (and pruning) than most other groups of trees. The Ginkgo, as an example, requires practically no spraying and pruning. This does not mean that the Ginkgo is a "superior" ornamental by any means, but the necessity of spraying elms to keep them in good condition is something that should be kept in mind.

This is not the time nor the place to enter into lengthy discussion of the two serious pests that are now doing tremendous damage to elms, namely the so-called Dutch Elm disease and the phloem necrosis of elms. Much has been written recently about the inroads of these two serious diseases in the eastern part of the country, and, in fact, the Dutch Elm disease is now reported from Denver, Colorado. Much research work is being done with possible control methods for these two diseases, and anything that might be said on this score here might well be antedated in a year or so.

Suffice it to say, first that most elms are susceptible to both diseases, and that at this time each one is prevalent only in certain sections of the country and not in others. This means that at this moment of writing, a glance at a map showing the distribution of these two diseases would indicate the current chances of trees escaping it merely because of their location. Vigorous, well-grown trees, well pruned and sprayed and fertilized, seem to have a better chance of escaping these diseases in infested areas than do sickly trees that are greatly in need of attention.

The "Christine Buisman" Elm (a variety of *U. carpinifolia*) is the only elm being recommended at the moment for trial as resistant to the Dutch Elm disease. We certainly hope that as investigations are carried on and new methods of control can be made the picture will change.

It seems to me that no one should plant elms without a thorough knowledge of the situation. Especially is this true of those responsible for planting streets and highways. Admittedly, there is no shade tree superior to the American Elm for street and highway planting, but those responsible for using large amounts of public funds have a responsibility to the future population as well as the present. If a long line of elms is planted now, with trees dying out intermittently fifteen or twenty years from now because of the ravages of the disease, this would certainly be poor planning. There are enough other trees from which to choose for street or highway planting so that elms can be omitted from planting plans.

The policy should be, especially in disease areas or those adjacent to them, to use other trees where at all possible. Latest developments on control methods should be thoroughly known and understood when planting large numbers of elms, and as I have said, present information would indicate that this can be considered gambling with the future life of the trees. A thorough study of other somewhat similar types should be made (see page 73) and selections made from these. Present indications are that neither disease will be as ravaging as was the chestnut blight for chestnuts, but the emphasis should be placed on the selection of other kinds of trees where at all possible, for the present at least.

Elms should be planted only in situations where it is a foregone conclusion that they will receive the best of *annual* care. Intelligent pruning, spraying and fertilizing should be counted on as insurance against these diseases, and only partial insurance at that, since even some of the best-kept trees eventually succumb.

All elms are easily transplanted, having fibrous roots, and grow vigorously. Their feeding roots are near the surface so that it is difficult to make other plants grow well underneath them. They respond well to surface applications of fertilizers.

Several species and many varieties of native and exotic elms are relegated to the secondary or discard list merely because they do not possess qualities superior to those recommended here. Many of these discards are in use as ornamentals, but with nearly fifty different species and varieties growing side by side in the Arnold Arboretum the division into two groups is made merely to emphasize the better qualities of those mentioned here.

Simple Key to the Elms

The following key is offered as an aid to the identification of elm species on the basis of foliage characters. More exact keys have been made, in which the flowers and fruits are used, but many an amateur is confronted with the perplexing problem of identification when flowers and fruits are not available. Every one of the elm species varies greatly, and to make a key using only one or two characters is not very satisfactory. Therefore, this key is not infallible, but it may serve its purpose to many who are perplexed concerning the identification of these elms.

In using the key, merely go to the first number. If the statement there applies to the specimen, go to the next **higher** number until the tree is identified. If the statement there does not apply, proceed to the following group headed by the **same** number and proceed as above.

It should be noted that this key does not take into consideration the varieties of these species, many of which can be identified by their form alone. Also, and this is very important, it should be noted that *U. japonica, laevis* and *ploti*, are not common in America except in botanical collections, and that other species, like *U. thomasi* and *serotina*, are used very little in landscape work. A knowledge of these facts should make this key much more usable.

The elms are so variable that it is likely they will continue to be difficult to identify for many years to come. These notes and suggestions are offered merely as aids to those interested in this group of trees.

1. Corky ridges or wings on younger branches
    2. Leaves simply serrate...............................*Ulmus crassifolia*
    2. Leaves doubly serrate
        3. Young twigs glabrous or nearly so
            4. Wings usually two and opposite...............*Ulmus alata*
            4. Wings several, not necessarily opposite, flowers in spring, not native........................*Ulmus carpinifolia suberosa*
            4. Wings several, not necessarily opposite, flowers in fall, native...................................*Ulmus serotina*
        3. Young twigs pubescent
            4. Tree irregularly columnar....................*Ulmus thomasi*
            4. Tree not irregularly columnar, oval or rounded in outline
                5. Leaves 2–3″ long, wings occasionally.....*Ulmus procera*
                5. Leaves 3–4¾″ long, wings occasionally..*Ulmus japonica*
1. Leaves three pointed at tip or occasionally so, branches not corky
    2. Mature branches reddish brown, hairy while young; leaves occasionally with one or two extra points at apex....................*Ulmus glabra*
    2. Mature branches pale yellowish or grayish brown, glabrous or nearly so when young; most of the leaves three pointed at apex..*Ulmus laciniata*
1. Leaves simply or almost simply serrate, ¾–2¾″ long
    2. Leaves often nearly equal at base, many leaves showing indications of double serration, young branches pubescent or glabrous, stipules broad, flowers in spring..*Ulmus pumila*

Elm leaves are somewhat similar but they do vary in size and slightly in shape as well. Here are ten leaves of the more important species:
Top row—Ulmus carpinifolia, serotina, glabra
Middle row—U. americana, laciniata, hollandica
Bottom row—U. pumila, procera, laevis, parvifolia

2. Leaves usually unequally rounded at base, young branches pubescent, stipules linear, flowers in fall........................*Ulmus parvifolia*
1. Leaves doubly serrate
  2. Young branches glabrous
    3. Leaves 2¾–6″ long
      4. Leaves usually twice as long as wide, no conspicuous axillary tufts of hair............................*Ulmus americana*
      4. Leaves less than 1½ times as long as wide, usually with conspicuous tufts of hair in axils of veins on under surface of leaves, considerably variable......................*Ulmus hollandica*
    3. Leaves 1¼–3¼″ long
      4. Petioles ¼–½″, leaves 2–3″, smooth above. .*Ulmus carpinfolia*
      4. Petioles less than ¼″, leaves 1¼–2¼″, slightly scabrous above
                                      Ulmus ploti
  2. Young branches pubescent
    3. Leaves often glabrous beneath.................*Ulmus americana*
    3. Leaves pubescent beneath
      4. Leaves 2–3″ long............................*Ulmus procera*
      4. Leaves longer
        5. Leaves often widest at middle, 4–8″ long

6. Branchlets grey to light brown, buds covered with rusty brown hairs..................*Ulmus fulva*
6. Branchlets dark brown, buds without rusty brown hairs, leaves sometimes showing a tendency to be three pointed at tip...............*Ulmus glabra*
5. Leaves usually widest above middle, 2½–4¾" long
6. Leaves scabrous and pubescent above, corky wings on branches occasionally..........*Ulmus japonica*
6. Leaves usually glabrous above, very unequal at base..............................*Ulmus laevis*

Ulmus alata 45′ Zone 6 Winged Elm and Wahoo Elm

HABIT: spreading branches, round-topped
FOLIAGE: rather dense, leaves 1½–2½" long
HABITAT: southeastern United States

One of the interesting things about this elm is that it frequently has large corky "wings" on either side of its branchlets. It makes a vigorous-growing small tree and need be used only as a substitute for the American Elm in places where a smaller-sized tree seems desirable. It has gracefully arching branches and is vigorous in growth.

Ulmus americana 120′ Zone 2 American Elm

*HABIT: vase shaped, widely arching branches
FOLIAGE: open
HABITAT: central and eastern North America
VARIETIES: *ascendens*—narrower, more distinctly columnar than var. *columnaris*
columnaris—upright branches with wide columnar form—Column American Elm
"Lake City"—narrow in general but not as columnar as other varieties
"Moline"—narrow columnar clon, but with a bad reputation of splitting in ice storms after it is 15 inches in diameter. Over five hundred of these were planted along streets in Lansing, Michigan, and eventually all had to be bolted and cabled
pendula—with long pendulous branchlets, a most graceful tree—Weeping American Elm
"Princeton"—narrow and pyramidal
"Augustine"—narrow columnar clon originating at Normal, Illinois, about 1920, and when 80 feet tall it was only 27 inches in diameter at the base. Another tree, fifteen years old, was 35 feet tall with a trunk diameter of 10 inches.

The American Elm is without question the most popular shade tree in North America. Its unique vase-shaped form is not to be found in any other tree growing in this country native or exotic. It is closely associated with the earliest gardens in America, and many a century-old monarch is pointed out by local citizens as being rich in local history. One such tree was the famous "Washington Elm" in Cambridge, Massachusetts, recorded as 60 feet high at the time General George Washington took command of the Continental Armies on July 3, 1775. It was blown down in a storm on October 26, 1923, when its age was between 204 and

210 years. There are many other old specimens revered by all who see them in various localities throughout the central and eastern United States.

Because of its wide distribution and its universal use in this country, several varieties have been noted, especially narrow, columnar types. The typical form is arching, but some trees have more pendulous branches than others, and some are "feathered" down the trunks with numerous small side shoots.

There is no ornamental tree just like the American Elm. It is an excellent lawn specimen, for its lofty branches allow much air circulation underneath, and although they supply excellent shade, the widely arching branches do not obstruct views from houses. This wide-arching habit is not evident in young specimens and varies materially when the trees are grown from seed. Sometimes the variety "urni" is listed in catalogues but this actually is the true species. Propagating elms asexually may be more tedious but certainly results in more uniform specimens.

The elms in general, and *Ulmus americana* in particular, are susceptible to more disease and insect troubles than any other tree. Those whose responsibility it is to care for ornamental trees have long realized this fact, yet because of its unique habit of growth it has been the most popular shade tree, particularly for street and avenue planting.

Now that the Dutch Elm disease and phloem necrosis disease seriously threaten most elms, it seems at last advisable (at the time this is written) to limit the planning of the American Elm. It may be that at some time in the future some good control may be found for these tree-killing diseases, but until that time comes the planting of the American Elm should be done with discretion, and certainly only after thoroughly considering the selection of all other possible tree types.

| Ulmus carpinifolia | 90' | Zone 4 | Smooth-leaved Elm |

*HABIT: variable, many forms
FOLIAGE: bright green
HABITAT: Europe and Western Asia
INTRODUCED: before 1850
VARIETIES: "Christine Buisman"—resistant to both phloem necrosis and Dutch Elm disease. It is interesting to note that this can be readily grafted on roots of *Zelkova serrata*.

cornubiensis—narrowly pyramidal, ascending branches, grows to 80 feet tall but not columnar—Cornish Elm

dampieri—narrow, pyramidal, leaves crowded together along twigs. A tree in the Arnold Arboretum is about 25 feet tall and 15 feet in diameter of branch-spread at the base—Dampier Elm

koopmanni—oval in shape, very dense, with branches to the ground—Koopmann Elm

sarniensis—very compact and densely pyramidal. A splendid small tree. This is excellent for planting along small streets—Jersey Elm

umbraculifera—densely branched, upright in growth, flat topped—Globe Smooth-leaved Elm

A variable species with several very interesting varieties. Usually it has a single trunk with slender branches forming a pyramidal head. Some of these varieties offer excellent material for small-scale planting, especially for use along narrow streets.

Ulmus carpinifolia umbraculifera or the Globe Smooth Leaved Elm is a dense growing small tree, of possible merit for planting along narrow streets.

Ulmus glabra   120′   Zone 4   Scotch or Wych Elm

HABIT: wide spreading, rather open
FOLIAGE: coarse
HABITAT: Europe and western Asia
INTRODUCED: colonial times
VARIETIES: *atropurpurea*—leaves dark purple—Purple-leaved Elm
    camperdowni—round-headed, usually grafted about 6 to 7 feet high on the understock, with pendulous branches. A formal specimen—Camperdown Elm
    exoniensis—upright, columnar—Exeter Elm
    pendula—sometimes confused with the Camperdown Elm since both are grafted high on the understock. This, however, forms a very flat-topped small tree, with branches definitely horizontal and branchlets pendulous, making an excellent arbor effect under which benches can be put—Table Top Elm

    A rather popular tree, especially the varieties, but it should be pointed out that the elm leaf miner will riddle this tree before it will touch most of the other elms. Consequently, preventive sprays should be put on these trees in sufficient time to forestall the inroads of this very destructive insect. The species itself is certainly no better ornamental than *U. americana*.

x Ulmus hollandica major   120′   Zone 4   Dutch Elm

*HABIT: short trunk, wide-spreading branches
FOLIAGE: coarse, lustrous
HYBRID ORIGIN: *U. glabra x U. carpinifolia*
OTHER VARIETIES of *U. hollandica:*

belgica—loosely pyramidal in form, dense and cylindrical while young, an excellent small tree. Our tree is 70 feet tall and 40 feet through—Belgian Elm

"Klemmer"—narrowly pyramidal, tall, dense

superba—narrowly pyramidal—Blandford Elm

These hybrids are usually grouped together and have been generally planted in western Europe as street trees although they have not been used extensively in America as yet.

Ulmus parvifolia   50′   Zone 5   Chinese Elm

*HABIT: round-topped
*FOLIAGE: dense, leaves small, 1–2″ long
AUTUMN COLOR: reddish to purplish
*BARK: mottled and often exfoliating in irregular spots, exposing a much lighter colored bark underneath
HABITAT: China, Korea, Japan
INTRODUCED: 1794
VARIETY: *sempervirens*—leaves evergreen, at least in southern California where it is used a great deal—Evergreen Elm

Some individual trees of the Chinese Elm (Ulmus parvifolia) have very beautiful bark. Such trees should be propagated asexually to keep this desirable quality.

Frequently confused with the Siberian Elm (*U. pumila*), the true Chinese Elm is a better ornamental. The leaves are dark green remaining on the tree long in the fall, the flowers appear in the fall and not in the spring as do those of *U. pumila,* and the beautiful bark of older trees makes them of considerable ornamental interest throughout the entire year. In the warmer temperate regions of China and Japan the leaves are evergreen, but in southern California a special clon has been widely used for this reason and given the varietal name *sempervirens.* It is remarkable for its wide-spreading branches which frequently are pendulous and touch the ground. This variety, easily reproduced by cuttings, is surviving as a small tree in the Arnold Arboretum but has not been tried sufficiently long to prove its hardiness in the North. It has been noted in the Japanese-beetle area around Philadelphia, that where the Siberian and Chinese Elms were growing side by side, the beetles would practically defoliate the former and hardly touch the latter until other food became scarce. The true Chinese Elm is fast growing, is an excellent ornamental and well worth more use in American gardens. It might be used as a temporary or permanent screen or to provide quick growth, and as a permanent tree in the landscape it has considerably more merit, in the East and South at least, than does *U. pumila.*

Ulmus procera (*campestris*)   120′   Zone 5   English Elm

HABIT: oval or oblong head, often wide spreading
FOLIAGE: dense
HABITAT: England and western Europe
INTRODUCED: colonial times
VARIETIES: *myrtifolia*—leaves small, under 2″ in length, the smallest leaves of any elm
  purpurascens—leaves less than 2″ in length and tinged purple—Purple English Elm
  viminalis—rather narrow, dense, branchlets slightly pendulous and slow growing, an elm for the small garden—Willow English Elm

The English Elm, formerly called *U. campestris,* has been widely planted in America since colonial times. It withstands city conditions better than most other elms, but of course lacks the desirable vase-shaped habit of *U. americana.* The foliage remains on the tree about two weeks longer in the fall than does that of the American Elm. The varieties are its chief claim to importance.

Ulmus pumila   75′   Zone 4   Siberian Elm

HABIT: rounded head, rather open
*FOLIAGE: leaves small, ¾–2¾″ long, fine texture
HABITAT: eastern Siberia, northern China
INTRODUCED: 1860
VARIETY: "Coolshade"—more compact and dense and dark green than the species—originated before 1948 in the nurseries of Wild Brothers, Sarcoxie, Missouri

Widely publicized during the past few years and offered as the "Chinese" Elm, this native of Siberia has been much overplanted. It is not a tree to plant indiscriminately in any garden. In the very dry areas of the Great Plains, or on dry banks where other trees will not grow, it has merit. Because of its rapid, vigorous growth it will make a quick screen, but may not grow old gracefully. Seedlings do vary and some have much better form than others. One type, recently named "Coolshade" has proved much stronger wooded in Missouri ice storms and because of this is being propagated asexually. It is slower in growth and much more dense than the species in habit. The foliage is darker green, and all in all this clon appears to be superior to the species in many ways. There are undoubtedly other clons as well. In the eastern United States at least, the Siberian Elm should not be considered as an ornamental tree but as a service tree for certain specific purposes. There are many other trees which will better serve as ornamentals than this. In the drought areas of the Midwest, however, it can be considered one of the most serviceable trees available.

Umbellularia californica   75'   Zone 7   California-laurel

*HABIT: dense rounded head
*FOLIAGE: evergreen, leaves 2–5" long, lustrous, green, aromatic when crushed
HABITAT: California to Oregon

A handsome evergreen tree used on the West coast as a street, park and garden specimen tree of considerable merit. One of the largest of the species is known as "The Laurel of San Marcos" near Santa Barbara, California, being 82 feet in height and with a spread of 104 feet (according to Maunsell Van Rensselaer formerly of the Santa Barbara Botanic Garden) with an estimated age of between two hundred and three hundred years. The wood is very hard and has been used for making house rollers, and the aromatic leaves have been used in flavoring soups. A truly ornamental specimen, this native American tree is worthy of considerable planting where it is hardy.

Vaccinium arboreum   27'   Zone 7   Farkleberry

FLOWERS: white, small, waxy
    TIME: summer
FRUIT: blue berries
    EFFECTIVE: early fall
*FOLIAGE: evergreen, leaves to 2" long
HABITAT: southeastern United States

The Farkleberry is grown as an evergreen in the South where its lustrous green leaves and diminutive, waxy white flowers promote its value as a garden ornamental.

Viburnum lentago   30'   Zone 2   Nannyberry

*FLOWERS: white, in flat clusters
    TIME: late May
*FRUIT: black berries, in flat clusters
    EFFECTIVE: fall and winter
*AUTUMN COLOR: purplish red
HABITAT: eastern United States

A native, vigorous viburnum, which makes a dense mass, and if allowed, the branches of old plants will arch over and rest on the ground, often taking root. It is useful as a background and screen, mostly used as a shrub although it can be trained to grow in tree form and is very effective on the edges of woodlands. The fruit is also valued by the birds as a winter food. Shiny green leaves with a splendid fall color, add to its usefulness.

Viburnum prunifolium   15'   Zone 3   Blackhaw

*FLOWERS: white, in flat clusters
    TIME: mid-May
*FRUIT: blue-black berries, in flat clusters
    EFFECTIVE: fall

*AUTUMN COLOR: shining red
HABITAT: eastern United States

Often this plant has been recommended as a substitute (in form) for some of the hawthorns. Sometimes it is grown as a small tree with a single trunk. The fruits have been used for making preserves since colonial times, and in certain areas strains have been selected particularly because the fruits are large and palatable. Sometimes these fruits are ½ inch long, about the largest on any viburnum and they are produced in great profusion. An excellent plant as a specimen or for massing.

Viburnum rufidulum   30′   Zone 5   Southern Blackhaw

*FLOWERS: creamy white, in flat clusters
    TIME: late May
*FRUIT: dark blue berries, in clusters
    EFFECTIVE: fall
FOLIAGE: lustrous green leaves
*AUTUMN COLOR: red
HABITAT: southeastern United States

The southern counterpart of *V. prunifolium*, it need only be grown in the South where its northern relative is unavailable.

Viburnum sieboldi   30′   Zone 4   Siebold Viburnum

*FLOWERS: creamy white, in flat clusters
    TIME: late May
*FRUIT: red to black berries on red fruit stalks, in flat to rounded clusters
    EFFECTIVE: summer
HABIT: rounded, often rather open
*FOLIAGE: rugose, dark green, lustrous foliage
AUTUMN COLOR: red
HABITAT: Japan
INTRODUCED: 1880

If I were to choose only one viburnum for my garden, I think it would be this because of the splendid long (6″) leaves, its very desirable branching habit which results in rounded masses of foliage interspersed with open areas where lights and shadows add much interest, and also because of its colorful fruits. Although these are black at maturity, they remain unripe and bright red for several weeks in the summer and even after they turn black and fall off or are eaten by the birds, their red fruit stalks remain another three or four weeks to give color to the plant at a time when the fruits of other shrubs are not sufficiently ripened to be colorful. As a specimen plant it is the best of the viburnums, for the northern United States at least.

Washingtonia robusta   90′   Zone 10   Mexican Washington Palm

*HABIT: fan-shaped, foliage only at top of trunk
FOLIAGE: coarse
HABITAT: Mexico

A slender palm with long trunk, leaves fan shaped and dropping off the stem at maturity. It is used a great deal in plantings on the southern California Coast.

Xanthoceras sorbifolium   20′   Zone 5   Shinyleaf Yellowhorn

FLOWERS: small, white, in racemes 10″ long
    TIME: late May
FRUIT: green burrs similar to horse chestnuts
    EFFECTIVE: fall
FOLIAGE: lustrous, dark green
HABITAT: North China
INTRODUCED: 1866

This little-known plant has shiny, pinnately compound leaves with small racemes of white flowers somewhat similar to small wisteria clusters. A rather unusual specimen, good as large shrub or small tree, it is, unfortunately, difficult to transplant.

Zelkova serrata   90′   Zone 5   Japanese Zelkova

*HABIT: round topped, short trunk, many ascending branches
FOLIAGE: medium to fine texture
AUTUMN COLOR: yellow to russet
HABITAT: Japan
INTRODUCED: about 1860

Somewhat similar to a small-leaved elm, it has wide-spreading branches and it is quite graceful in habit. Its primary use is, of course, as a shade tree. It is closely akin to the elm, in fact is often used as an understock on which to graft certain types of elm, and has been recommended for the root understock on which the Dutch-Elm-disease-resistant clon "Christine Buisman" is root grafted.

This tree might be accepted as one of the best substitutes for the American Elm since it is closer in shape to the elm than is any other tree, and it grows very fast. Also it is resistant to the Dutch Elm disease. The rare Chinese species Z. *sinica* does not have this elm habit. The Zelkova yields the highest priced lumber of Japan where it is used for lacquerware, trays, and high grade furniture. This species has proved very satisfactory in the British Isles, where some excellent, very tall specimens have been grown, often with many small trunks instead of one short trunk.

Zizyphus jujuba   30′   Zone 7   Common Jujube or Chinese Date

FRUITS: datelike, up to 1″ long, edible, dark red to black
    EFFECTIVE: September and October
HABIT: spiny, open
FOLIAGE: open
HABITAT: southern Europe and Asia

The Common Jujube is not particularly ornamental but it has been found to withstand heat, drought, and alkaline soils in the southwestern United States, and these would be the excuses for growing it in areas where other trees prove difficult. It is cultivated for its edible fruits in the Mediterranean area and is available from commercial concerns in America.

SECONDARY TREE LIST

THE following trees are among the host of plants grown in this country which should not be grown until the better types recommended have first been tried. They should not be considered "discards" entirely, since it may well be that under certain circumstances, or under certain growing conditions they may possibly do as well as the recommended types. However, the majority of these species and varieties differ only slightly from the recommended plants and so can be omitted from consideration, especially where space is a limiting factor. Persons responsible for planting large numbers of trees along streets or highways would do well to consider only the recommended trees for such plantings.

There have been several reasons for placing these trees in a secondary list. Many plantsmen will not agree with the following lists nor the reasons for placing certain trees in a secondary list. The time for the research necessary in making this list will have been worth while if it merely impresses gardeners with the fact that some trees are more useful in our gardens than others, and time and space should not be given to trees with inferior qualities. The gardener will undoubtedly want to make his own list, and he can well start by critically examining this one:

Numbers after the trees represent the reasons for placing them in this group. They are as follows:

1. The tree is not superior to the varieties given in the recommended list. Many trees are practically identical, from a landscape viewpoint, differing merely in more pubescence on the leaf, a slightly different type of leaf margin, fruit which may be only slightly different in shape, size or pubescence—many factors, but in the garden such plants look alike and serve identical purposes. Such minor differences do not seem sufficient to clutter up our nurseries and gardens with plants of many different names.
2. The tree has inferior flowers to those in the recommended list.
3. The tree has inferior fruits to those in the recommended list.
4. The tree has poor foliage. Included are many variegated-leaved trees and those with so-called "golden" leaves, but actually many of these prove very difficult to grow and may look well for only a very short period. The "Golden"-leaved evergreens are outstanding examples (most of them at least) of trees which look disreputable throughout the winter months. It would seem that such trees should be avoided or used only after serious consideration has been given to better trees.

5. Evergreens with poor winter foliage. If an evergreen does not appear at its best in the winter, it should be given up in preference to one that does.
6. The tree has a poor habit of growth.
7. The tree is usually troubled with an insect or disease pest.
8. The tree cannot be located in the nurseries and arboretums of this country. So many times we run across interesting varieties described in botanical texts, but impossible to locate in nurseries. Upon investigation it is shown that many such interesting varieties are only represented by herbarium specimens, in some cases only the original ones from which they were first named. No such plants have been included in the recommended list.
9. The tree or one of its parts is poisonous.

Abies alba 1
  amabilis, 1, 6
  balsamea 1, 6, 7
    macrocarpa 1, 6, 7
  cephalonica apollinis 1
  cilicica 1
  concolor aurea 1, 4
    lowiana 1, 6
    wattezi 1, 4
  fabri 1, 8
  fargesi 8
  faxoniana 1, 8
  fraseri 1, 6
  grandis 1
  holophylla 1
  homolepis tomomi 1, 6
    umbellata 1
  lasiocarpa 1
  magnifica shastensis 1
  mariesi 1, 8
  nobilis 1
  nordmanniana 1
  numidica 1, 8
  recurvata 1, 8
  sachalinensis 1, 6, 8
    mayriana 1, 6, 8
    nemorensis 1, 6, 8
  sibirica 1, 6, 8
  veitchi nikkoensis 1
  veitchi olivacea 1
  venusta 1, 8
Acer buergerianum 1, 2, 3
  campestre albo-variegatum 2, 3, 4
    hebecarpum 1, 2, 3

  leiocarpum 1, 2, 3
  postelense 2, 3, 4
  schwerini 2, 3, 4
  tauricum 1, 2, 3
  capillipes 1, 2, 3
  cappadocicum 1
  cissifolium 1
  davidi 1, 2, 3
  diabolicum 1, 4
  distylum 1, 2, 3
  francheti 1, 2, 3
  ginnala semenovi 1, 2, 3
  glabrum 1, 2, 3
  grandidentatum 1, 2, 3
  heldreichi 1
  henryi 1, 2, 3
  hyrcanum 1, 2, 3
  japonicum and most vars. 1, 2, 3
  leucoderme 1, 2, 3
  miyabei 1, 2, 3
  mono 1, 2, 3
  monspessulanum 1
  negundo pseudo-californicum 1
    interius 1
    violaceum 1
  nigrum 1, 4
  oblongum 1, 2, 3
  oliverianum 1, 2, 3
  opalus 1, 2, 3
  palmatum "Aoba-no-fuye" 4, 6
    "Aocha-nishiki" 4, 6
    "Akikaje-nishiki" 4, 6
    aureum 4, 6
    dissectum 4, 6

globispica 1, 3, 8
grossa 1, 3
lenta laciniata 3, 8
luminifera 1, 3, 8
lutea 1, 3, 7
mandshurica 1, 3
  japonica 1, 3
  kamtschatica 1, 3
maximowicziana 1, 3
medwediewi 1, 3, 8
microphylla 1, 3, 8
papyrifera cordifolia 1, 3
  p. kenaica 1, 3
    laciniata 1, 3, 4
    minor 1, 3
    neoalaskana 1, 3
    occidentalis 1, 3
    subcordata 1, 3
    variegata 1, 3, 4
  pendula dalecarlica 1, 3
  oycoviensis 1, 3
  purpurea 1, 4
  viscosa 1, 3
  pubescens 1, 3, 6, 8
    urticifolia 1, 3, 6, 8
  raddeana 1, 3, 8
  schmidti 1, 3
  turkestanica 1, 3, 8
  utilis 1, 3, 8
Broussonetia papyrifera laciniata 1, 4
  p. variegata 1, 4
Bumelia lanuginosa 1, 2, 3
Carpinus betulus carpinizza 1
  b. purpurea 1
  exima 1
  fargesiana 1
  laxiflora 1
    macrostachya 1
  orientalis 1
  turczaniovi 1, 4
    ovalifolia 1, 4
Carya aquatica 1, 2, 3
  carolinae-septentrionalis 1, 2, 3
  glabra megacarpa 1, 2, 3
  laciniosa 1, 2, 3
  laneyi 1, 2, 3
  myristicaeformis 1, 2, 3
  ovata halesi 1, 2, 3
    fraxinifolia 1, 2, 3

  nuttalli 1, 2, 3
  ovalis 1, 2, 3
    borealis 1, 2, 3
    hirsuta 1, 2, 3
    obcordata 1, 2, 3
    obovalis 1, 2, 3
    odorata 1, 2, 3
  pallida 1, 2, 3
Castanea—most species 1, 2, 7
Catalpa bignonioides aurea 1, 4
  b. koehnei 1, 4
    nana 1, 4, 6
  bungei 1, 2, 4
    heterophylla 1, 2, 4
  fargesi 1, 4
    duclouxi 1, 4
  hybrida 1, 4
    japonica 1, 4
    purpurea 1, 4
  ovata 1, 2, 4
    flavescens 1, 2, 4
Cedrus atlantica argentea 1
Celtis biondi 1, 8
  caucasica 1, 8
  cerasifera 1, 8
  douglasi 1
  glabrata 1, 8
  julianae 1, 8
  koraiensis 1, 7
  labilis 1, 6, 8
  occidentalis 1, 7
    canina 1, 7
    crassifolia 1, 7
  pumila 1
  reticulata 1, 8
  sinensis 1
  tourneforti 1
Cephalotaxus drupacea 1, 2, 4
  fortuni 1, 2, 4
Cercidiphyllum japonicum sinense 1
Cercis canadensis plena 2
Chaenomeles sinensis 2, 3, 7
Chamaecyparis lawsoniana darleyensis 1, 6
  l. fraseri 1
    krameri 1, 4
    lycopodoides 1, 4, 6
    "Silver Queen" 1, 5
    smithi 1

Chamaecyparis (Continued)
  "Triomphe de Boskoop" 1, 5
  wisseli 1, 4, 6
  nootkatensis lutea 5
  obtusa keteleeri 1
    aurea 5
    crippsi 4
    gracilis aurea 4, 5
    mariesi 4
  pisifera filifera aurea 1, 4, 5
    f. aureo-variegata 1, 4, 5
    plumosa argentea 1, 4, 5
      flavescens 1, 4, 5
    sulphurea 1, 4, 5
    thyoides 1, 4, 6
Chionanthus retusus 1
  virginicus maritimus 1
Cladrastis platycarpa 1
  sinensis 1
  wilsoni 1
Clerodendron trichotomum fargesi 1
Cornus alternifolia 1, 2, 3, 7
  florida welchi 1, 4
  walteri 1
Corylus chinensis 1, 6
  colurna glandulifera 1
  tibetica 1
Crateagus—most species other than recommended on pages 164–171. Over 500 species and varieties have been tested at the Arnold Arboretum.
Crataegomespilus species 1, 6
Cryptomeria japonica lobbi 1
  j. sinense 1, 6
Cupressus arizonica 1
  sempervirens indica 1
    lutea 1, 4
    variegata 1, 4
Cydonia oblonga 1, 2, 6, 7
Davidia involucrata vilmoriniana 1
Diospyros lotus 1, 3
Euonymus bungeana 1, 2, 3
  europaea 2, 3
    angustifolia 2, 3, 4
    atropurpurea 2, 3
    atrorubens 1, 2
    aucubaefolia 1, 4
    chrysophylla 1, 2
    coccinea 1, 2

japonica argenteo-variegata 2, 4
  aureo-variegata 2, 4
  pyramidata 2, 8
  viridi-variegata 2, 4
maaki 1, 2, 3
lanceifolia 1, 2
oxyphylla 2, 8
sanguinea brevipedunculata 1, 2
camptoneura 1, 2
Euptelea polyandra 1, 2, 3
Fagus engleriana 1
  grandifolia caroliniana 1
    pubescens 1
  japonica 1
  longipetiolata 1
  lucida 1
  orientalis 1
  sieboldi 1
  sylvatica albo-variegata 1, 4
    cristata 1, 4
    latifolia 1, 4
    luteo-variegata 1, 4
    quercifolia 1
    rohani 1
    roseo-marginata 1, 4
    tortuosa 1, 6
    zlatia 1, 4
Fontanesia species 1, 2, 3, 4
Forestiera species 1, 2, 3, 4
Fraxinus biltmoreana 1
  cuspidata 1
  mandshurica 1
  nigra 1
  quadrangulata 1
Ginkgo biloba aurea 1, 4
  b. variegata 1, 4
Gleditsia japonica 1, 7
Halesia carolina dialypetala 1
  c. mollis 1
  diptera 1, 2
  monticola vestita 1
Hippophae salicifolia 1, 2
Ilex montana beadlei 1
  m. macropoda 1
    mollis 1
Idesia polycarpa 1, 2, 3
Juglans cathayensis 1, 2
  cinerea 1, 2, 4, 6
  mandshurica, 1, 2

regia heterophylla 1, 2, 4
  monophylla 1, 2, 4
  pendula 1, 2, 6
rupestris 1, 2, 4
sieboldiana 1, 2
Juniperus formosana 1
monosperma 1, 4, 6
occidentalis 1
recurva 8
thurifera 8
virginiana albo-spica 4, 5
  aurea 4, 5
  elegantissima 4, 5
  variegata 4, 5
utahensis 1
Kalopanax pictus maximowiczi 1
Keteleeria davidiana 8
Laburnum alpinum 1
a. autumnale 1
  pendulum 1
anagyroides 1, 2
  aureum 1, 2, 4
  alschingeri 1
  autumnale 1
  bullatum 1, 2, 4
  carlieri 1
  pendulum 1
  quercifolium 1, 2
  sessilifolium 1, 2
Larix eurolepis 1, 6
gmelini 1, 6
  principis rupprechti 1, 6
lyalli 1, 6
marschlinsi 1
mastersiana 1
occidentalis 1
pendula 1
potanini 1
sibirica 1, 6
Liquidambar formosana 1
Liriodendron chinense 1
tulipifera aureo-marginatum 4
  fastigiatum 1, 6
  integrifolium 1
  obtusilobum 1
Maackia amurensis 1
Macludrania hybrida 1, 2, 3
Maddenia hypoleuca 1
Magnolia cylindrica 1

kobus 1, 2
mollicomata 8
proctoriana 1, 2
sargentiana 8
soulangeana candolleana 1
  norbertiana 1, 2
  verbanica 1, 2
sprengeri 8
tripetala 1, 2
Malus "Alaska" 8
"Alexis" 1
"Amisk" 1, 2, 3
angustifolia 1, 3
"Arrow" 1, 2, 3
astracanica 1
"Athabasca" 1, 2, 3
"Babini" 1, 2, 3
baccata columnaris 6
  himalaica 1
  oblonga 1
bracteata 1, 3
"Brier" 1
"Cheal's Crimson" 1
"Chilko" 1, 2, 3
coronaria 1, 3
  dasycalyx 1, 3
  elongata 1, 3
"Dauphin" 1, 2, 3
"Elise Rathke" 1, 3, 6
"Elk River" 1
"Erie" 1, 2, 3
"Exzellenz Theil" 1, 3
"Fairy" 1
florentina 1, 2, 3
fusca 1, 2, 3
  levipes 1, 2, 3
"Geneva" 1, 2, 3
"Gertrude" 8
glabrata 1, 2, 3
glaucescens 1, 3
gloriosa 1
halliana 1
hartwigi 1, 3
heterophylla 1, 3
honanensis 1, 2, 3
"Huron" 1, 2, 3
ioensis 1, 3
  bushi 1, 3
  creniserrata 1, 3

ponderosa 1
bicolor 1
  acicularis 1, 8
  brachytyla 1, 8
  complanata 1, 8
  reflexa 1, 8
  rhombisquamea 1, 8
glauca 1, 4, 6
  aurea 1, 4, 6
glehni 1
jezoensis 1
  hondoensis 1
koyamai 1
likiangensis 1
  balfouriana 1, 8
mariana 1, 6
maximowiczi 1, 4, 6
montigena 1
pungens aurea 1, 4
  glauca 1
purpurea 1, 6
rubens 1, 6
  virgata 1, 6
schrenkiana 1
spinulosa 1, 6, 8
wilsoni 1, 8
Pinus albicaulis 1
armandi 1
attenuata 1
ayacahuite 8
balfouriana 1
caribaea 1, 6
cembroides 1
contorta 1
densiflora albo-terminata 1, 4
  aurea 1, 4
echinata 1, 6
edulis 1
holfordiana 1
massoniana 1
montezumae 8
monticola 1
nigra caramanica 1
  cebennensis 6
  pendula 6
  poiretiana 1
palustris 1, 6
peuce 1
ponderosa 1, 6

pungens 1, 6
sabiniana 1, 6
schwerini 1
serotina 8
tabulaeformis 1
taeda 1
thunbergi oculus-draconis 1, 4
Planera aquatica 1
Platanus acerfolia kelseyana 1, 4
  a. hispanica 1
    suttneri 1, 4
  occidentalis 7
    glabrata 7
  orientalis cuneata 1
    digitata 1
Populus acuminata 1, 3
adenopoda 1, 3
angulata 1, 3
  cordata 1, 3
angustifolia 1, 3
arizonica 1, 3
canadensis 1, 3
  aurea 1, 3, 8
  erecta 1, 3, 8
  eugenei 1, 3, 6
  marilandica 1, 3
  regenerata 1, 3
  serotina 1, 3, 8
canescens 1, 3
cathayana 1, 3
grandidentata 1, 3, 6
heterophylla 1, 3
koreana 1, 3
macdougali 1, 3
nigra 1, 7
  betulaefolia 1, 3, 6
  plantierensis 1, 3, 6
  thevestina 1, 3, 6
sargenti 1, 3
sieboldi 1, 3
suaveolens 1, 3
szechuanica 1, 3
tacamahaca michauxi 1, 3
texana 1, 3
tomentosa 1, 3
tremula 1, 3
  davidiana 1, 3
  villosa 1, 3
tremuloides vancouveriana 1, 3

Populus (*Continued*)
  tristis 1, 3
  wilsoni 1, 3
  yunnanensis 1, 3
Prunus alleghaniensis 1, 2
  americana 1, 2
  angustifolia 1
  apetala 1
  avium 1
  blireiana "Othello" 1
    moseri 1, 2
  buergeriana 1
  cerasifera 1, 4
    divaricata 1, 2
    elegans 1, 4
    purpusi 1, 4
    "Vesuvius" 1, 2
  dasycarpa 1
  davidiana 1, 3, 6
  domestica 1
  fruticans 1, 2
  gracilis 1, 2
  hortulana 1
  incisa 1, 3
    serrata 1, 3
  insititia 1
  lanata 1, 3
  laucheana 1, 3
  mahaleb 1
  mandshurica 1, 3
  mira 1
  munsoniana 1
  orthosepala 1
  padus aucubaefolia 1, 4
    leucocarpos 1
    parviflora 1, 2
    pubescens 1
    sibirica 1
  pensylvanica saximontana 1, 2
  persica 1
    alba 1
    "Aurora" 1
    "Blushing Bride" 1
    caryophylliflora 1
    "Clara Meyer" 1
    coccinea plena 1
    dianthiflora 1
    "Double Crimson" 1

"Double Maroon" 1
"Duplex" 1
"Early Red" 1
"General Bei" 1
"Iceberg" 1
magnifica 1
"Mandarin" 6
pyramidalis 1
rubro-plena 1
sanguinea 1
"San José Pink" 1
versicolor 1
"Woodside" 6
reverchoni 1
salicina 1
serotina asplenifolia 1
  cartilaginea 1
  montana 1
  phelloides 1
  salicifolia 1
serrulata albida 1, 2
  "Asano" 1
  "Ariake" 1, 2
  "Banriko" 1, 2
  "Daikoku" 1
  "Fukurokuju" 1
  "Gijo-zakura" 1
  "Gosho-zakura" 1
  "Habutai" 1, 2
  "Higurashi" 1, 8
  "Hitoye-zakura" 1, 2
  "Hokusai" 1, 8
  "Horinji" 1, 8
  "Hosokawa" 1, 2
  "Ichiyo" 1
  "Ise-zakura" 1, 2
  "Kiku-shidare" 1, 6
  "Kirigaya" 1, 2
  "Kunrinjo-shirotae" 1, 2
  "Kurama-yama" 1
  "Mikuruma-gaeshi" 1
  "Mina-kami" 1, 2
  "Miyako" 1
  "Oh-naden" 1, 8
  "Ojochin" 1
  "Oshima-zakura" 1
  "Senriko" 1
  "Shibori" 1
  "Shirayuki" 1, 2

"Shiro-fugen" 1, 2
"Shogetsu" 1
"Suragadsi-nioi" 1, 2
"Taizan-Fukum" 1
"Tai-haku-zakura" 1
"Tanko-Shinju" 1
"Temari" 1
"Torano-o" 1
"Yae-akebono" 1
"Yae-zakura" 1, 2
"Yedo-zakura" 1
sibirica 1
simoni 1
slavini 1
spinosa 1
subcordata 1
subhirtella ascendens 1, 2
umbellata 1
virginiana 1, 7
Ptelea trifoliata 1, 2, 3, 7
Pterocarya hupehensis 1, 2, 3
Pterostyrax corymbosa 1
Pteroceltis tatarinowi 1, 2, 3
Pyrus betulaefolia 1, 3, 7
bretschneideri 1, 3, 7
calleryana dimorphophylla 1, 3
graciliflora 1, 3, 7
tometella 1, 3
communis 1, 3, 7
cordata 1, 3, 7
pyraster 1, 3, 7
sabauda 1, 3, 7
sativa 1, 3, 7
elaeagrifolia 1, 3, 7
nivalis 1, 3, 7
pashia 1, 3, 7
phaeocarpa 1, 3, 7
pyrifolia 1, 3, 7
regeli 1, 3, 7
salicifolia 1, 3, 7
serrulata 1, 3, 7
ussuriensis honodensis 1, 3, 7
ovoidea 1, 3, 7
Quercus alba latiloba 1, 2, 3
a. repanda 1, 2, 3
aliena 1, 2, 3
acuteserrata 1, 2, 3
castanaefolia 1, 2, 3
dentata 1, 4, 6

durandi 1, 2, 3
ellipsoidalis 1, 2, 3
exacta 1, 2, 3
frainetto 1, 6
glandulifera 1, 4
grosseserrata 1, 2, 3
hartwissiana 1, 2, 3
ilicifolia 1, 4, 6
leana 1, 2, 3
libani 1, 6
liaotungensis 1, 6
lobata 1, 2, 3
lyrata 1, 4, 6
macranthera 1, 2, 3
macrocarpa 1, 4, 6
olivaeformis 1, 2, 3
mongolica 1, 2, 3
muhlenbergi 1, 2, 3
petraea 1, 2, 3
pontica 1, 2, 3
prinoides 1, 6
pubescens 1, 2, 3
pyrenaica 1, 2, 3
robur heterophylla 1, 2, 3
holophylla 1, 2, 3
filicifolia 1, 2, 3
pectinata 1, 2, 3
purpurascens 1, 2, 3
variegata 1, 4
runcinata 1, 6
shumardi 1, 2, 3
acerifolia 1, 2, 3
schnecki 1, 2, 3
stellata 1, 2, 3
suber occidentalis 1, 2, 3
utahensis 1, 2, 3
velutina missouriensis 1, 2, 3
virgiliana 1, 2, 3
Rhamnus caroliniana 1, 2
Rhus glabra cismontana 1, 2
potanini 1, 6, 8
punjabensis sinica 1, 6, 8
sylvestris 1, 6, 8
trichocarpa 1, 6, 8
verniciflua 1, 9
vernix 1, 9
Robinia holdti 1, 7
luxurians 1, 7
pseudoacacia amorphifolia 1, 7

mandshurica 1
maximowicziana 1, 4
miqueliana 1
moltkei 1
mongolica 1
monticola 1
neglecta 1, 4
oliveri 1
paucicostata 1
platyphyllos vitifolia 1
tuan 1
  chinensis 1
Tsuga mertensiana 1
  sieboldi 1
Ulmus carpinifolia italica 1, 2, 3, 7
  c. pendula 1, 2, 3, 7
    propendens 1, 2, 3, 7
    variegata 1, 2, 3, 4, 7
    webbiana 1, 2, 3, 4, 7
    wredei 1, 2, 3, 4, 7
  crassifolia 1, 2, 3, 7
  fulva 1, 2, 3, 4, 6, 7
  glabra cornuta 1, 2, 3, 7
    crispa 1, 2, 3, 4, 7

lutescens 1, 2, 3, 4, 7
  nitida 1, 2, 3, 4, 8
  purpurea 1, 2, 3, 4, 7
hollandica dumonti 1, 2, 3, **7, 8**
  dauvessei 1, 2, 3, 7, 8
  major 1, 2, 3, 7
  pendula 1, 2, 3, **7**
  vegeta 1, 2, 3, **7**
japonica 1, 2, 3, **7**
laciniata 1, 2, 3, **6, 7**
laevis 1, 2, 3, 7
plotti 1, 2, 3, 7
procera australis 1, 2, 3, **7**
  aurea 1, 2, 3, 4, 7
  argenteo-variegata 1, 2, 3, 4, **7**
  berardi 1, 2, 3, 7, 8
  marginata 1, 2, 3, 4, 7
  vanhouttei 1, 2, 3, 4, **7**
  serotina 1, 2, 3, 7
  thomasi 1, 2, 3, 6, 7
Viburnum cylindricum 2, 3
Zanthoxylum americanum 1, 2, 3
  schinifolium 1, 2
  simulans 1, 2
Zelkova carpinifolia 1

INDEX

Only those trees in the General List of Recommended Trees are included in this index. All scientific names are included and most of the common names. All horticultural variety names are not included for they would make this index too cumbersome. They can be easily found by turning to the genus and species in the text, pages 103–355. If a tree is not listed here it may be found in the Secondary Tree list, pages 356–367.

369